QUESTIONS & ANSWERS:
COPYRIGHT LAW

QUESTIONS & ANSWERS: COPYRIGHT LAW

Multiple-Choice, Short-Answer, and Essay Questions and Answers

David Fagundes
Associate Professor of Law
Southwestern Law School

Robert C. Lind
Professor of Law
Director Emeritus, Biederman Entertainment and Media Law Institute
Southwestern Law School

 LexisNexis·

> **NOTE TO USERS**
>
> To ensure that you are using the latest materials available in this area, please be sure to periodically check the LexisNexis Law School web site for downloadable updates and supplements at www.lexisnexis.com/lawschool.

Editorial Offices
121 Chanlon Rd., New Providence, NJ 07974 (908) 464-6800
201 Mission St., San Francisco, CA 94105-1831 (415) 908-3200
www.lexisnexis.com

MATTHEW◆BENDER

Dedications

To Larry Sullivan, a professor who enjoyed copyright law, and those who study it.
And to Joseph De Marco, my best copyright student.—R.C.L.

Table of Contents

QUESTIONS

I-1. Musician has recently created a musical jingle she hopes to license to a greeting card company for its television advertising campaign. Musician has memorized the lyrics and music that make up the musical composition and has often performed the jingle from memory for a large number of friends at parties. Musician has not written down the lyrics or music, nor has she recorded the musical composition. Is the jingle protected by a federal copyright?

(A) No, because the jingle has not been fixed in a tangible medium by Musician.

(B) No, because the jingle was publicly performed prior to its registration with the Copyright Office.

(C) Yes, because a work is protected by copyright law at its creation.

(D) Yes, because the musical composition clearly constitutes expression.

I-2. Musician has recently composed an original musical composition she has recorded on her personal digital audio recorder. She has not performed the composition for anyone, nor has she shared the recording with anyone. She has not placed a copyright notice on the digital recording. Is the musical composition protected by a federal copyright?

(A) Yes, because the musical composition is sufficiently fixed in a copy.

(B) Yes, because the musical composition is sufficiently fixed in a phonorecord.

(C) No, because the recording is not accompanied by a proper copyright notice.

(D) No, because no one can see the musical composition in the digital recording.

I-3. Poet wrote a poem honoring the first butterfly of the season. After writing the poem by hand in a notebook, Poet placed it in a desk drawer where it languished. A month later, Poet recited the poem to members of his local literary society who unanimously commented that the poem was poorly crafted. That evening, in a fit of embarrassment, Poet ripped the page containing the poem from the notebook and burned the page in his fireplace. Does federal copyright protection exist for the poem?

(A) No, because the poem was poorly crafted.

(B) No, because the poem is no longer fixed in a tangible medium of expression.

(C) Yes, because the poem had been fixed in a tangible medium of expression.

(D) Yes, because Poet believed the poem had literary merit at the time he wrote it.

I-4.   Songwriter is performing a live concert in an auditorium. During the concert, she sings a new musical composition she has composed, but not yet recorded or written down. Unbeknownst to Songwriter, Audience Member is sitting in the back of the auditorium recording the performance. Is Songwriter protected by federal law?

ANSWER:

I-5.   One recent evening in Los Angeles, Comedian included in her act at a comedy club a ten-minute extemporaneous original comedy routine concerning the recent firing of a government official. The content of the routine was created on the spur of the moment. Comedian had not written out the material nor did she record the routine when she presented the material at the comedy club. Is Comedian's extemporaneous comedy routine protected?

(A) The routine is protected by federal copyright because a ten minute comedy routine undoubtedly includes expression as well as ideas.

(B) The routine is protected by federal copyright because it is a literary work.

(C) The routine is protected by state common law copyright because it was merely a performance.

(D) The routine is protected by state common law copyright because a ten-minute comedy routine undoubtedly includes original expression as well as ideas.

I-6.   Currently, Novelist A lives in San Francisco where he wrote *The Great West Coast Novel*. One year later, Novelist B wrote and published *The Great East Coast Novel* in New York. Novelist A subsequently registered the copyright in *The Great West Coast Novel*, which remains in manuscript form, with the Copyright Office. The contents of both novels are creative and are identical. Neither Novelist knows the other and neither has seen the other's work. Who owns the copyright in the expression of the novels?

(A) Both Novelist A and Novelist B own the copyrights in their respective literary works.

(B) Novelist A because *The Great West Coast Novel* was created first.

(C) Novelist B because *The Great East Coast Novel* was published first.

(D) Novelist A because *The Great West Coast Novel* was registered first.

I-7.   Artist has created a five-pointed star out of cardboard. A square has been cut out of the middle of the star, permitting the insertion of a small photograph. Is Artist's creation protected by copyright?

(A) No, because the square cut out makes the star an unprotected useful article.

(B) No, because the star is a common shape.

(C)   Yes, because the material used to create a work does not affect its copyrightability.

(D)   Yes, because it is a sculptural work.

I-8.   Videographer came upon a car crash involving a well-known television star who was obviously inebriated. Videographer filmed the scene with the video function of her cell phone. The video was two minutes in length. The quality of the video's audio and images was poor. Videographer uploaded the video onto a viral video website that permits the public to view submitted videos. The best argument for denying copyright protection for the video is:

(A)   The audiovisual work was of poor quality.

(B)   The length of the audiovisual work is too short for copyright protection.

(C)   The audiovisual work lacks sufficient originality.

(D)   Uploading the video onto such a public website constitutes an abandonment of copyright.

I-9.   A motion picture was recently released for general exhibition that depicted a used guitar store on the moon after the moon was colonized by the people of Earth. Two years later, a dramatic television series that depicted a small alien civilization engaged in intergalactic space travel included a stop on the moon where one of the aliens purchased a guitar from a used guitar store. The signage, size, and contents of the stores differed substantially, as did the store's proprietor and customers. Has the television series infringed on the copyright of the motion picture?

(A)   Yes, because it is the similarities between the two works that are at issue, not the dissimilarities.

(B)   Yes, because the idea of a used guitar store on the moon is novel.

(C)   No, because television is a different medium from motion pictures.

(D)   No, because once the motion picture was released to the public, anyone has the right to use ideas found in the motion picture.

I-10.   Museum Services Corporation markets and services the Atmospheric Recordation Device [ARD]. The device provides a continuous daily measurement of room temperature and humidity needed by museums to conserve their collections. ARD provides continuous markings on a specially designed roll of graph paper on which is printed time measurements, as well as temperature and humidity levels. A competitor, Collections Management, Inc., markets rolls of paper suitable for use with the ARD, which provides identical measurements and levels to that found on the paper marketed by Museum Services Corporation. Will Museum Services Corporation be able to enforce its claim of copyright to its graph paper?

ANSWER:

I-11.   In 1975, Artist created a painting of Elvis Presley on velvet. After receiving numerous compliments on her artistic achievement, Artist offered it for sale at a local arts and craft show. What actions could Artist have taken to vest federal copyright protection in the painting?

ANSWER:

I-12.   A work has been fixed in a DVD. Has it been fixed in a copy or a phonorecord?

    (A) Copy.

    (B) Phonorecord.

    (C) Neither a copy nor a phonorecord.

    (D) It depends.

I-13.   Sarah, a professional poker player, dreamed of writing a book about her life in the high stakes world of professional gambling. She often told Fred, her boyfriend of two years, the details of how she would structure the book and the anecdotes she would include. After Sarah's recent unexpected death, Fred wrote the book from memory. Sarah's mother, her only surviving relative, is now suing Fred for copyright infringement. What is the mother's likelihood of success?

ANSWER:

I-14.   Artist has created a digital artwork that appears on a large high-definition plasma screen installed in a local public museum. The screen contains a random combination of images sent to it by ten computers, each with a different bank of images contained on the computer's hard drive. Photographer has taken unauthorized photographs of the images appearing on the plasma screen and sells them in his art gallery. Artist sues Photographer for copyright infringement. Artist's lawsuit will be:

    (A) Unsuccessful, because the images comprising the digital artwork are not fixed in a single object or device.

    (B) Unsuccessful, because the work has been dedicated to the public.

    (C) Successful, because each image is capable of being reproduced.

    (D) Successful, because the photographs taken by Photographer have fixed the images in a tangible medium.

I-15.   Pursuant to an exclusive license, Television Station broadcasts a day baseball game live from the local ballpark. The live broadcast is comprised of images from several television cameras located in the ballpark from which the director of the television program selects the images to be included in the broadcast signal, and is not simultaneously recorded. Bar Owner makes a digital video recording of the game and plays it at night for his customers. Has Bar Owner infringed the federal copyright in Television Station's audiovisual work?

    (A) Yes, because the director's camera location and selection is sufficiently original.

(B) No, because the Television Station did not record the broadcast at the same time it transmitted the game to its viewers.

(C) Yes, but only if the broadcast contains a sufficient amount of commentary by an announcer.

(D) Yes, but only if the bar is larger than 3,700 square feet.

I-16. Law Student is enrolled in a copyright law course and sends numerous emails to her professor asking substantive questions about the course. Professor responded to each email, but did not print a copy of his answers. The following year, Law Student compiled Professor's answers and sold printed copies of them without Professor's permission. Are Professor's email responses sufficiently fixed for federal copyright protection?

ANSWER:

I-17. Arranger has been hired to provide piano accompaniment to Singer on her upcoming concert tour. Singer has had difficulty reaching the high notes of the opening musical composition. Arranger made the musical composition easier to sing by transposing it from the key of C into the key of A. The transposition of the composition from the key of C to the key of A is easily accomplished with mathematical certainty. Does the transposition of the musical composition into the key of A create a derivative work that is protected by copyright?

(A) No, because transposing a musical composition from one key to another is a mechanical exercise that is not protected by copyright.

(B) No, because the lyrics remain the same.

(C) Yes, the notes of the resulting musical work are different from the original musical work.

(D) Yes, because only a person knowledgeable in music would have the ability to transpose a musical composition from one key to another.

I-18. In 1980, Verso conceives and writes the haiku *Leaves of Autumn* on rice paper in ink. Verso deems the work inadequate and puts it in his desk drawer. One day, Verso's friend Poetaster snoops around in Verso's office and runs across *Leaves of Autumn*. Poetaster copies the work verbatim onto a piece of note paper, and later publishes it under his own name in *Poetry* magazine. Verso is incensed that Poetaster has copied his haiku, and sues Poetaster for copyright infringement. Poetaster responds by showing that in 1979, a poet named Quarto wrote a haiku titled *Rainbow Leaves* that is identical to the haiku Verso wrote in 1980. Verso admits that the 1979 and 1980 haikus are identical, but truthfully avers that when he wrote *Leaves of Autumn* in 1980, he had never seen or heard of Quarto's *Rainbow Leaves*. Who will prevail in the infringement suit, Verso or Poetaster?

(A) Verso will prevail because *Leaves of Autumn* possesses the necessary degree of creativity sufficient to meet the standard of originality.

(B) Verso will prevail because *Leaves of Autumn* possessed the necessary degree of creativity sufficient to meet the standard of originality, and that creativity originated with Verso.

(C) Poetaster will prevail because Verso's haiku was identical to a previously created haiku.

(D) Poetaster will prevail because Verso will not be able to prove that Poetaster copied Verso's *Leaves of Autumn*, as opposed to Quarto's *Rainbow Leaves*.

I-19.   A basic rule of copyright law is that ideas cannot be protected, only the expression of ideas may be protected. Are no legal protections available for ideas or the use of ideas?

ANSWER:

I-20.   French Novelist has written a lengthy murder mystery novel in French. French Novelist has assigned the English translation rights to Translator, who has yet to translate the novel. All other rights were retained by French Novelist. Without authorization, Publisher, an American, has translated the French novel into English and has published the English version of the novel. Publisher has entered into a settlement with French Novelist, but has refused to settle with Translator. Publisher claims that its translation was a merely mechanical process and does not constitute an actionable adaptation of the French novel. If Translator sues Publisher for copyright infringement, in the majority of jurisdictions, the law suit will be:

(A) Successful, because there is necessarily sufficient originality in Publisher's translation of the French novel into English to constitute an unauthorized derivative work.

(B) Successful, because Publisher's translation and publication of its English translation of the French novel necessarily constitutes an unauthorized reproduction of the French novel.

(C) Unsuccessful, because the selection of an English word or phrase necessarily follows from the French word or phrase being translated.

(D) Unsuccessful, because Translator has yet to create an English translation and, therefore, does not have standing to sue Publisher for copyright infringement.

I-21.   Police Detective was interviewed by Writer who was writing an article dealing with the discrimination suffered by female police officers within the police department. Writer asked Police Detective questions regarding his activities as a police officer and his attitude towards female officers in the police department. Police Detective's comments included racial epithets and derogatory remarks regarding women. The interview was openly tape recorded by Writer with a cassette recorder that she had purchased for interviewing purposes. The recorder had a built-in microphone. Writer supplied the cassette tapes used to tape the interviews, positioned the recorder in front of Police Detective, turned the recorder on and off, and operated its recording volume. Writer has assigned the print publishing rights to the interview to Publisher. Writer's tape recording of the interview was subsequently stolen and copies are being sold by Audio Company without permission. Can Writer successfully sue Audio Company for infringing her copyright in the sound recording of the interview?

ANSWER:

I-22. An analog sound recording of a musical composition titled Megaron was created in 1965 by Record Company. Recently, Record Company released a digital version of the Megaron sound recording. The digital sound recording was created with the aid of a computerized mastering machine that converted the 1965 analog recording into a digital recording. This process was conducted by an employee of Record Company who "equalized" the digital recording by listening to it and adjusting the volume, tones, and acoustics of the sounds captured in the digital recording. The employee raised the level of the bass guitar and reduced the level of the snare drum. No other adjustments were made to the digital recording. Once the digital recording had been equalized, it was saved to a separate computer file, then pressed onto digital audio compact discs and distributed to retail stores. Website has begun to offer this digital version of the Megaron recording as a download without the authorization of Record Company. If Record Company sues Website for federal copyright infringement of the Digital Sound Recording, will it be successful?

ANSWER:

I-23. Composer is the author of a musical play titled *Flash, Trash & Cash*. The musical play is based on the true story of an aspiring singer who tragically dies in an avalanche. Composer is concerned that *Flash, Trash & Cash* is also the title of an earlier published book, protected by copyright, that discusses the exotic dance clubs that populate the east coast of the United States. Should Composer be concerned about a possible claim of copyright infringement resulting from her choice of title for her musical play?

(A) No, the subject matter of the two works are not substantially similar.

(B) No, titles of books are not protected by copyright.

(C) Yes, the titles are identical.

(D) Yes, because the book's title was used prior to the title's use in the musical play.

I-24. Book Publisher has published a cookbook that contains fifty recipes featuring the use of beets. Each recipe lists the necessary ingredients for each dish, directions for preparation, and nutritional information, without any creative narrative. Newspaper has included in its food section recipes for three of the dishes found in the cookbook. Although there are slight differences in the listing of ingredients, the recipes published by Newspaper will produce substantially the same final products as those described in the cookbook. Does Book Publisher have a valid basis for bringing a copyright infringement action against Newspaper?

(A) No, because the recipes are not protected by copyright.

(B) No, because the recipes constitute useful articles.

(C) Yes, because the final products are substantially the same.

(D) Yes, because the recipes are substantially similar.

I-25. *Space Station* is a video game in which a spaceship maneuvers through obstacles such as alien space vehicles, space creatures, black holes, gravitational fields, and meteors to return to its space station. *Hangar* is a video game in which a World War I biplane maneuvers through obstacles such as anti-aircraft shells, dirigibles, telegraph lines, tall trees, and flocks of birds to return to its hangar. For each and every game element in the *Space Station* game there is a corresponding game element in *Hangar*. The relationship of the game elements in *Hangar* is identical to the relationship of game elements in *Space Station*. The rules for *Space Station* printed on the screen are: "Use joystick to move spaceship up, down, forwards and backwards. The game will end after the destruction of the third spaceship. An additional spaceship is acquired after 30,000 points are accumulated." The rules for *Hangar* are: "Use the joystick to move the biplane up, down, forwards and backwards. The game will end after the third biplane is lost. An additional biplane is won after 25,000 points." The manufacturer of *Hangar* has admitted to playing *Space Station*, but has had no access to the game's computer program. What is the likely outcome if the copyright owner of *Space Station* sues the manufacturer of *Hangar* for copyright infringement?

ANSWER:

I-26.   Hunter creates realistic turkey decoys for a living. He has recently noticed that the turkey decoys sold by Competitor are substantially similar, although not exactly identical, to his decoys. Will Hunter be successful if he brings a copyright infringement action against Competitor and can show that Competitor had access to Hunter's decoys?

(A) Yes, because sculptural works are copyrightable subject matter.

(B) Yes, because the reproduction right protects against copies that are substantially similar.

(C) No, because anyone can copy items found in nature.

(D) No, because depictions of natural objects have limited copyright protection.

I-27.   *All Fall Down* is a best selling novel recently written by Novelist. The novel tells the story of the discovery of an experimental plastic material that is used by a leading architectural firm to construct the world's tallest building in Los Angeles. Shortly after its completion, on the hottest day of the year, the building suddenly melts, smothering thousands of people and shutting down the city for months. Studio has recently released *The Collapsible Tower*, a motion picture that tells the story of the discovery of an experimental plastic material that is used to construct a Presidential Library in Washington, D.C. One of the team of scientists who made the discovery is a member of a spy network. The spy has also discovered a solvent that causes the plastic material to immediately liquefy. During the dedication of the Library, the spy applies the solvent to its structural supports, causing the building to melt, smothering the President and her cabinet. Does Novelist have a viable claim that *The Collapsible Tower* film has infringed the copyright in the *All Fall Down* novel?

(A) No, because only unprotected elements were used in the film.

(B) No, because the defendant's work is in a different medium.

(C) Yes, because the idea of a melting plastic building was taken from the novel.

(D) Yes, because Studio is presumed to have had access to the plaintiff's novel.

I-28. Young Attorney has been asked by a client to draft a copyright mortgage agreement, something Young Attorney had never encountered in her short legal career. Young Attorney went to the nearest law library to look for a form book that contained such an agreement. She found a copy of the *Entertainment Law Form Book* that was published by Publisher. Young Attorney photocopied the pages containing the copyright mortgage agreement, brought them back to her office, inputted the language of the form agreement into her computer verbatim and filled in her client's information. The *Entertainment Law Form Book* has been recently registered with the Copyright Office by Publisher. Is Young Attorney liable for infringing the copyright in the *Entertainment Law Form Book*?

(A) Yes, because Young Attorney reproduced protected material without the permission of the copyright owner.

(B) No, because under the "use doctrine" enunciated by the Supreme Court in *Baker v. Selden*, the use of such a work in the manner intended by the copyright owner does not constitute a copyright infringement.

(C) Yes, because Young Attorney did not own the copy of the *Entertainment Law Form Book* that was used to make the copies of the form agreement.

(D) No, because such form contracts are not protected by copyright.

I-29. Author wrote *Shadow Land*, a biographical literary work about the life of Frances Farmer, an independent, free-spirited actress who fought against the conventions of her time. In *Shadow Land*, Author described how Farmer was institutionalized by her mother, underwent a lobotomy and emerged from the psychiatric facility with her spirit broken. *Shadow Land* was marketed as the "true story" of Frances Farmer. After *Shadow Land* was published, Producer produced *The Farmer Story*, a motion picture based on the life of Francis Farmer. The motion picture presented a dramatization of Farmer's lobotomy and its aftermath that closely resembled the description of those events in the literary work. Author has now sued for copyright infringement. Producer is defending the lawsuit on the basis that she only used the relevant facts that were published in the literary work. Author has argued against the defense, stating that the lobotomy and its aftermath were not facts, but fictional elements that Author had created. Will Author be successful with his copyright infringement claim?

(A) No, because facts are not protectable by copyright.

(B) Yes, because fictional elements are protectable by copyright.

(C) No, because fictional elements that are presented by the copyright owner as fact, will be treated as though it were fact.

(D) Yes, because the elements at issue were important plot points in the literary work.

I-30. Telecom sells various ringtones to its customers that are downloaded to the customer's cell phone at the time of purchase. One of the ringtones offered by Telecom is one line of recorded dialog from the motion picture *Scarface* spoken by actor Al Pacino who portrayed the character Tony Montana: "Say hello to my little friend." Telecom recorded the dialog, converted it into a ringtone and offered it for sale, without the permission of Universal Pictures, the owner of the copyright in the motion picture. If Universal Pictures sues Telecom for copyright infringement, Universal Pictures will likely be:

(A) Unsuccessful, because motion pictures have no public performance rights.

(B) Successful, because the recorded dialog is the most memorable line of dialog from *Scarface*.

(C) Successful, because the motion picture *Scarface* is protected by copyright.

(D) Unsuccessful, because the line of dialog is not protected by copyright law.

I-31. Uncle Unique lives in Pleasant Valley, Wisconsin, and is the town's unofficial greeter. He spend his days walking in the tourist section of town, talking to visitors and providing directions while offering advice and opinions. Every day the bearded Uncle Unique wears his long hair in a braid and wears the same clothes: a floppy weathered hat, a poncho, large boots, and paisley pants. He always carries a copy of *In Watermelon Sugar*, a novel written by Richard Brautigan, and quotes from it throughout the day. Network now airs a new cable series titled *Pleasant Valley* that depicts a fictional town in Oregon with an ensemble of interesting characters. One of the main characters, Uncle Natural, looks exactly like Uncle Unique and carries a copy of *Trout Fishing in America*, another novel written by Richard Brautigan. It turns out that one of Network's producers of the cable series had earlier vacationed in the real Pleasant Valley, had met Uncle Unique, and had taken a photograph of Uncle Unique with his permission. Later, when the *Pleasant Valley* project was in development, the producer shared his photograph of Uncle Unique with the series' writers and instructed them to make the lovable character Uncle Natural look like the person in the photograph. Does Uncle Unique have a copyright infringement claim against Network?

ANSWER:

I-32. Two years ago, Millennium Studios released its motion picture *FangTastic!*. The film deals with a modern-day vampire who lives in a trailer park and details her efforts to have a romantic relationship with a human. Her life style is chronicled throughout the motion picture: sleeping in a coffin during the day, inability to withstand sunlight, living off the blood drained from the necks of humans with her long fangs, superior physical strength, aversion to silver, garlic, and crosses, and the threat of death via stake through the heart. Recently, De Marco Studios has produced *Casket Capers*, a motion picture that deals with a successful married mortician who is a modern day vampire and uses his fangs to drain the blood from the bodies entrusted to his care. The extremely strong mortician must sleep in his coffin during the day, cannot attend funerals during the day due to his inability to withstand sunlight. He has an aversion to silver, garlic, and crosses. It is made clear that the only way the mortician can die is if someone drives a stake through his heart. Millennium Studios has filed a lawsuit against De Marco Studios for copyright infringement. Will the lawsuit be successful?

(A) No, because De Marco Studios has only taken ideas from the plaintiff's motion picture.

(B) Yes, because the elements at issue are nearly identical.

(C)   No, because both motion pictures are in the vampire genre.

(D)   Yes, because the plaintiff's *FangTastic!* used the elements at issue before they were used by defendant's *Casket Capers*.

I-33.   Programmer has created a device she has named Picabrandt that creates drawings on its own. Picabrandt was built by Programmer to use ink and paper to make drawings. Picabrandt was programmed to follow certain basic protocols, such as "no more than two eyes" and "mouth must be below nose." Apart from the protocols, Picabrandt has no limitations on what or how it draws. Some of Picabrandt's drawings have sold for $15,000. Are the drawings by Picabrandt protected by copyright?

ANSWER:

I-34.   *Style Over Substance* is a black and white motion picture, produced by Studio, that is no longer protected by copyright. Network has invested the necessary funds to colorize the motion picture without Studio's permission. Each pixel of each frame of the motion picture was colored from a palette of sixteen million colors. Network has issued a press release stating that no other broadcast or cable television channel or station may transmit *Style Over Substance* without Network's permission. Is Network's claim accurate?

(A)   Yes, because the colorized version of *Style Over Substance* contains all of the elements of the original motion picture.

(B)   Yes, because Network has a copyright in the colorized version of *Style Over Substance*.

(C)   No, because *Style Over Substance* is in the public domain.

(D)   No, because the original version of *Style Over Substance* may be used without Network's permission.

I-35.   Novelist has published a romantic novel concerning the detailed planning and operation of a dinosaur zoo. The novel begins with the selection of a remote island on which to build the zoo, the creation of a dinosaur nursery, the use of uniformed guards and tall electric fences for security, and the design of automated tours for those attending the zoo. Subsequently, Publisher has released a children's book about a visit to an adventure park that contains dinosaurs. The adventure park in the children's book is set on a prehistoric island far from the mainland where the dinosaurs are hatched in a nursery. The children ride on automated vehicles along side tall electric fences that corral the dinosaurs. Throughout the story, the children are accompanied by uniformed guards. Novelist claims that the children's story infringes the copyright in her novel. Will Novelist's infringement action be successful?

(A)   Yes, because strikingly similar elements appear in both works.

(B)   No, because the elements that have been identified by Novelist constitute scene a faire.

(C) Yes, because the children's story will be found to be infringing even if the details of the elements in question differ between the two works.

(D) No, because the two works are directed at different audiences.

II-1. Historian has written a short history of the City of San Angeles. The facts contained in the short history were obtained by Historian from public records and newspaper articles published by the San Angeles Bee, as well as from Historian's personal knowledge. Historian has not received the permission of the San Angeles Bee to use any of its articles. The short history of the City of San Angeles is:

(A) Not copyrightable because it is a factual work.

(B) Not copyrightable because it is an unauthorized derivative work.

(C) Copyrightable, only if the short history was written prior to 1978.

(D) Copyrightable subject matter, though the copyright protection it receives may be more limited than the copyright protection given to a work of fiction.

II-2. Musical Group recently performed six musical works in a nightclub, pursuant to a public performance license obtained by Club Owner. The performance was filmed with a digital camera by Club Owner with the permission of Musical Group, which also agreed to its release on DVD. Musical Group has entered into a contract with Record Company, under which Record Company is assigned the copyright in all sound recordings created by Musical Group. After the release of Musical Group's performance on DVD, Record Company seeks compensation for the unauthorized distribution of its sound recordings on the DVD. Record Company's claim will be:

(A) Successful, because Record Company owns the copyrights in the sound recordings contained in the DVD release.

(B) Successful, because Club Owner's public performance license only addresses the performance of musical compositions, not the creation of sound recordings.

(C) Unsuccessful, because there is no privity of contract between Club Owner and Record Company.

(D) Unsuccessful, because the DVD release contains an audiovisual work, not a sound recording.

II-3. Compare the rights enjoyed by the owner of a copyright in a sound recording to the rights enjoyed by the owner of a copyright in a musical composition.

ANSWER:

15

II-4.   After submitting her latest manuscript for publication, Author decides that she wants to change the ending. She writes a letter to Publisher outlining the ending and asking that Publisher not send the book to press until she revises the manuscript. Under pressure to get the book out, Publisher releases the manuscript in its original form, but includes Author's letter verbatim as an epilogue. Author, who never gave permission for Publisher to publish anything but the manuscript, is angry and sues Publisher for infringing her exclusive rights in the letter. Will she prevail?

   A.   No, because letters are expository, and thus do not count as "literary works" as defined by the Copyright Act.

   B.   No, because by sending the letter to Publisher, Author granted an implied license to publish its contents.

   C.   Yes, the publication of the letter amounts to a violation of her exclusive rights in a copyrightable work of authorship.

   D.   Yes, because the final chapter included in the letter is literature, and this makes the letter sufficient to meet the definition of "literary works" in the Copyright Act.

II-5.   Consider question II-4. Assume that Author demanded that Publisher send her back the letter that she sent. Author refuses, saying that the letter is his property to keep. Who is right, and why?

ANSWER:

II-6.   Author, a noted writer of mysteries who has worked with Agent for years, trusts Agent implicitly. One day, Author sends Agent an email that reads "I want to stop writing mysteries, and instead write an historical romance set in the Middle Ages, where an earnest commoner seeks to woo a princess. The twist is that the royal family wants the princess to wed a prince, and stands in the way of their union. The princess and commoner truly love each other, so they run away, but misfortune befalls them and they die tragically. What do you think?" Agent tells Author that he should stick to mysteries, but the email inspires Agent to pen her own novel following the rough outline and plot points that Author sent her. When Agent's novel is published, Author sues Agent for copyright infringement. Will he prevail?

   A.   Yes, because Agent copied the plot points that Author included in the email.

   B.   Yes, because the material in the email was the sweat of Author's brow, and Agent's conduct amounted to wrongful misappropriation.

   C.   No, because Agent's copying of the material in the email was not verbatim.

   D.   No, because what Agent copied, the general outline of a plot in Author's email, amounted only to unprotected ideas.

II-7.   Employee was recently fired from Company, and is none to happy about it. Late one night, he sneaks into Company's headquarters with revenge on his mind. He rifles through

Company's files and finds several documents: a brochure containing information about Company's secret new product line that it planned to release two months hence; internal memos discussing Company's strategy to bilk employees out of health care; and a video from a Christmas party, produced by a professional videographer as a work made for hire, that shows Company executives sloppily drunk. Employee posts all this material up on his website, and a scandal ensues. Company sues Employee for, among other things, copyright infringement, and seeks an injunction ordering Employee to take the offending material offline. Will Company succeed, and if so, with respect to which documents?

A. Company will succeed, but only with respect to the brochure and the video, because the memo is not copyrightable subject matter.

B. Company will succeed, but only with respect to the brochure and the memo, because the video is not copyrightable subject matter.

C. Company will succeed with respect to the brochure, the memo, and the video, because all of them are copyrightable subject matter.

D. Company will not succeed with respect to any of the documents because none of them amount to copyrightable subject matter.

II-8. Student is a sophomore at the University of Spoiled Children, where he is a member of the biggest fraternity on campus. One night, as a gag, Student takes the University's campus directory (that includes names, phone numbers, and campus addresses of all 2,500 of the students currently enrolled at the University, arranged by year and address) and publishes "Student's Guide to the Most Popular People on Campus" in a printed leaflet. The guide takes fifty of the listings from the campus directory verbatim, those individuals who Student deems to be the most popular on campus, and lists them in alphabetical order. The University claims to own the copyright in the campus directory, and, not amused by the gag, sues Student for infringing its copyright in the directory. Will the University succeed?

A. Yes, the University will succeed because Student copied its protectable expression verbatim.

B. Yes, the University will succeed because its copyright covers the idea of all student directories for their enrollees, regardless of how they are arranged.

C. No, the University will not succeed because directories are in no way copyrightable.

D. No, the University will not succeed because Student copied only unprotectable elements of the directory (information) and nothing that could be copyrighted (such as selection or arrangement).

II-9. Consider question II-8. Assume instead that the University loved the gag and did not sue Student, and further assume that Student's friend Compatriot also loved the Guide and put a PDF copy of it on his personal website without asking Student's permission. Under such circumstances, if Student sued Compatriot for copyright infringement, would he prevail, and why or why not?

ANSWER:

II-10. Professor has been chosen to give the keynote address at his university's Commencement. He crafts various written drafts of the address for weeks before the event. When he is finally satisfied with it, Professor spends days committing it to memory. By the time Commencement rolls around, Professor knows the address word for word, and he delivers the address at Commencement entirely from memory, reciting every word precisely as he had written it down. Student is a big fan of Professor, and digitally records, without permission, the address as Professor gives it, then transcribes the MP3 file into a MicroSoft Word file and posts the text on his personal website. Professor learns of this and sues Student for copyright infringement. Will Professor prevail?

  A. Yes, Professor will prevail because non-extemporaneous speeches that are composed in a written form prior to their delivery are generally considered copyrightable.

  B. Yes, Professor will prevail because his memorization of the text amounts to fixation in a tangible medium of expression.

  C. No, Professor will not prevail because spoken word performances do not amount to copyrightable fixations.

  D. No, Professor will not prevail because speeches are a form of conversation, which is never copyrightable.

II-11. Consider question II-10. Assume that after Commencement, Student met Professor at a cocktail party, where they struck up a conversation, and Student surreptitiously recorded Professor's conversation as he riffed casually about the state of the weather that day. Assume further that Student transcribed this recording and put it online as well, and that Professor sued Student for infringing the copyright in Professor's cocktail party banter. Could Student be held liable for recording, transcribing, and posting this material on the Internet, and why or why not?

ANSWER:

II-12. Archaeologist publishes a blockbuster article in which he reveals that he has discovered a new store of Mayan artifacts deep in the Yucatan, and argues persuasively that this discovery supports the theory that Mayan civilization began several centuries earlier than previously believed. The article draws a lot of reaction. For example, Amateur runs a website devoted to archaeology as a hobby, in which he publishes a brief news item entitled *Big Discovery in the Yucatan*. Amateur's feature recounts the details of Archaeologist's discovery, listing where it happened, what techniques were used in the excavation, and what was uncovered. Subsequently, Archaeologist's longtime academic rival, Nemesis, publishes an article in which he describes Archaeologist's theory about the dawn of Mayan civilization, in Nemesis' own words, and explains why he thinks the theory is bunk. Archaeologist is incensed at both Amateur and Nemesis, and sues each of them for infringing the copyright in his original article. Will Archaeologist prevail?

  A. Yes, Archaeologist will prevail, but only against Amateur, because Nemesis did not copy any protectable subject matter.

    B.   Yes, Archaeologist will prevail, but only against Nemesis, because Amateur did not copy any protectable subject matter.

    C.   Yes, Archaeologist will prevail against both Amateur and Nemesis, because both of them copied protectable subject matter.

    D.   No, Archaeologist will not prevail against either Amateur or Nemesis, because neither of them copied protectable subject matter.

II-13. Cartoonist creates a series of comic books based on a character he calls "SuperCop," who is a bumbling, feckless policeman by day, but morphs into a crime fighter with super powers by night. SuperCop lives in present-day Urbania, a city modeled on Detroit, and typically fights familiar, realistic enemies such as drug kingpins and serial murderers. After the series has become very successful, Cartoonist discovers a comic book series titled *SuperCop in Outer Space*, in which SuperCop lives on a futuristic space station and fights strange creatures from outer space. Cartoonist contacts Publisher, the company that publishes *SuperCop in Outer Space*, and complains about its unauthorized use of his character. Publisher responds, "Sure, it's the same character, but it's not infringement because we didn't copy any of your stories, and in our series SuperCop is in a completely different setting." Unconvinced, Cartoonist sues Publisher for copyright infringement. Will he prevail?

    A.   Yes, Cartoonist will prevail because his original creation of the SuperCop character gives him the right to control all subsequent literary or pictorial representations of police performing extraordinary feats.

    B.   Yes, Cartoonist will prevail because Publisher's use of SuperCop is a verbatim copy of the attributes of Cartoonist's character that comprises an original work of authorship.

    C.   No, Cartoonist will not prevail because Publisher's use of SuperCop sufficiently decontextualized the character from its original setting to such a degree that the taking does not appropriate any protected expression.

    D.   No, Cartoonist will not prevail because graphic characters are not copyrightable.

II-14. Consider question II-13. Assume that another comic book comes along featuring a main character called "PooperCop." This comic is about a bumbling policeman, albeit not one that has any super powers. "PooperCop" is an antic, not a heroic, tale and its main character gets laughs by continually screwing up, rather than earning admiration for saving the day. Still, Cartoonist notices several similarities between PooperCop and SuperCop, such as the fact that each are policeman, each of them are bumbling at least some of the time and that they have similar sounding names. Republisher, the company that publishes the PooperCop series, admits to Cartoonist that it got the idea for PooperCop after reading material that included, but was not limited to, SuperCop. Cartoonist decides to sue Republisher for infringement of copyright in his SuperCop character. Will Cartoonist succeed? Why or why not?

ANSWER:

II-15. Author pens a best-selling series of mystery novels that feature a central character named Judy McGee. Judy McGee is a lovable amateur sleuth who always manages to stumble onto a big case — and solve it. Her demeanor is distinctively understated: she wears blue checked gingham dresses, carries an absurdly oversized, pink-handled magnifying glass to look for clues, and whenever praised, utters the phrase "Aw, jeez Louise." Author's novels become famous and the Judy McGee character becomes an admired and well-recognized cult figure. One day, Studio, which is based in Manhattan, announces that it is going to develop and release a film version of a new Judy McGee story that is based on a plot written by a Studio employee, not by Author. The movie will, though, feature a Judy McGee character that faithfully includes all of her distinctive dress, magnifying glass, speech and characteristics as described in all of Author's novels. Author, who has not licensed the rights to the Judy McGee character to Studio, is incensed and files for an injunction to prevent Studio from developing the movie, arguing that the use of her character amounts to copyright infringement. Assuming that the case is brought in the Southern District of New York, will Author prevail?

    (A) Yes, Author will prevail, because literary characters are always copyrightable as subsets of the literary works in which they appear.

    (B) Yes, Author will prevail because Judy McGee is sufficiently fleshed out with distinctive physical and personality traits to merit copyright protection.

    (C) No, Author will not prevail, because Judy McGee is merely a plot device and does not constitute the story being told.

    (D) No, Author will not prevail, because literary characters, unlike characters depicted in graphic form, are not copyrightable.

II-16. Consider question II-15. Assume that NoveltyCo releases an oversized, pink-handled magnifying glass just like the one that Judy McGee carries throughout her adventures in Author's novels. In fact, NoveltyCo concedes that it designed the magnifying glass based on the description of McGee's magnifying glass in several of Author's novels. Author contacts NoveltyCo, which did not request permission to create and market the novelty, and demands that it pay her royalties for its use of her creation. NoveltyCo refuses, and Author sues for copyright infringement. Who will prevail?

    (A) Author will prevail. Her copyright in the distinctive Judy McGee character extends also to identifying features of the character's persona, such as here, the oversized, pink-handled magnifying glass that Judy McGee uses all the time.

    (B) Author will prevail. Her copyright in the distinctive Judy McGee character extends also to anything associated with that character in any context.

    (C) NoveltyCo will prevail. Extending copyright protection to the idea of magnifying glasses would grant Author control over uncopyrightable ideas.

    (D) NoveltyCo will prevail. The magnifying glass is a useful article that cannot be protected by copyright.

II-17. Consider question II-15. Explain how a court within the Ninth Circuit would approach this issue differently.

ANSWER:

II-18. Animator created the *Mice-a-Roni* comic strip in the mid-twentieth century. *Mice-a-Roni* featured Mikey the Mouse, a lovable anthropomorphic mouse, as its main character. Assume for the purposes of this question that the Mikey character is clearly copyrightable. Animator's *Mice-a-Roni* comic strip enjoyed some success and ran in newspapers for about twenty years, when it fell out of popularity and Animator ceased to produce it. Animator was not careful to include a copyright notice on his comic strip during the first few years that he produced *Mice-a-Roni*, but as the series began to enjoy some popularity, he did a better job of protecting his copyrights by performing the necessary formalities. As a result, the earliest five years of the *Mice-a-Roni* comics have fallen into the public domain. The subsequent fifteen years of the comic strip have contained a copyright notice. One day, Animator learns that Publisher has released a book titled *Classic Comix of the 50s Re-imagined* in which he portrays various old comic characters, including Mikey the Mouse, in a modern setting. Publisher did not seek permission to use the Mikey character. Animator sues Publisher for copyright infringement. What result?

(A) Animator will prevail. As long as a single episode of *Mice-a-Roni* is protected by copyright, the Mikey character is protected by copyright as well.

(B) Animator will prevail. The copyright protection period for graphic characters is limitless.

(C) Animator will not prevail. Characters fall into the public domain when the work of authorship in which they initially appeared falls into the public domain.

(D) Animator will not prevail. A court would regard Animator's failure to comply with copyright formalities during the early years of *Mice-a-Roni* as a form of laches, which means Animator forfeits any right to enforce his copyright in Mikey the Mouse later on.

II-19. Programmer writes and registers the source code for *MacroSoft Bird*, a program that allows birdwatchers to catalog their avian sightings. The program is a big success, and soon after it turns out that Pirate has released a similar program. Pirate's program, titled *Birds in Flight*, not only allows birdwatchers to catalog their avian sightings, but also provides information that enables birdwatchers to identify different species as well as connect with birdwatchers around the globe. Programmer learns that Pirate created *Birds in Flight* by cutting and pasting the entirety of the source code for *MacroSoft Bird* into a file, and then appending additional portions of original source code that enable the other features of the program. Programmer wants to sue Pirate for infringement of the *MacroSoft Bird* source code as well as the program's bird-cataloging component. What will the result be?

A. Programmer will prevail with respect to both the source code and the cataloging component.

B. Programmer will prevail with respect to the source code only.

C. Programmer will prevail with respect to the cataloging component only.

D. Programmer will fail with respect to both aspects of his infringement suit.

II-20. Techie created a new computer chip in 1990, and died in 1995. When will the period of federally enforceable exclusive rights in the structure of the computer chip expire?

A. 2000.

B. 2010.

C. 2065.

D. Computer chips are not considered copyrightable subject matter, so no federal protection is available.

II-21. User is the owner of an authorized copy of *DethKlok 2000*, a popular new video game, and proceeds to play it on his home computer. Any time User activates the game, his computer automatically copies several of the files, written in object code (machine language), that comprise *DethKlok 2000* into its Random Access Memory (RAM). Does this duplication of the object code that comprises *DethKlok 2000* amount to copyright infringement?

A. Yes. The unauthorized duplication of any literary work, including a computer program written in object code, amounts to an infringement of the copyright in that work.

B. No. While computer source code may be copyrightable, a computer program written in object code is not, so this copying is not actionable.

C. No. This kind of copying appears to be prima facie infringement, but the Copyright Act includes an exception to permit it.

D. No. Because User did not intend for any copying to take place, there can be no infringement.

II-22. Consider the facts of question II-21. User buys a new SourBook computer and is disappointed to discover that the version of *DethKlok 2000* he purchased is no longer compatible with the operating system on his new computer. User searches the Internet and finds that by making a few modifications to the source code of the *DethKlok 2000* program he can render the application compatible with his SourBook. User modifies the source code and the alteration successfully renders *DethKlok 2000* compatible with his new computer. Does User's alteration of the *DethKlok 2000* program amount to copyright infringement?

(A) Yes. User's alteration of the source code that comprises *DethKlok 2000* amounts to an unauthorized derivative work, violating the copyright owner's exclusive right of adaptation.

(B) Yes. User's creation of what is essentially a new version of *DethKlok 2000* violates the copyright owner's exclusive right of reproduction.

(C) No. User's ownership of the *DethKlok 2000* program entitles him to alter the source code that comprises that program in any way he sees fit.

(D) No. While User's alteration of the source code that comprises the *DethKlok 2000* program is an unauthorized adaptation of a copyrighted work of authorship, owners of computer programs are entitled to make such alterations in order to make applications compatible with new hardware.

II-23. Printer owns a printing shop. One day, he invents a new typeface script called Scurrier-Book that allows for more characters to appear on a page without sacrificing readability. Printer does a brisk business formatting documents with his new typeface, and refuses to license ScurrierBook to other printers or to makers of word processing software so he can capture all the value associated with the font. Printer discovers that an exact copy of ScurrierBook has been added to the latest edition of the word processing program, Blurb, produced and marketed by MacroSoft. Printer wants to sue MacroSoft for its unauthorized appropriation of his lucrative original font. Will he succeed?

(A) Yes. Fonts are protectable as pictorial or graphical works.

(B) Yes. Fonts are protectable as literary works.

(C) No. Fonts cannot possess the requisite degree of originality to merit copyright protection.

(D) No. Regardless of their originality, fonts or typefaces cannot be protected by federal copyright.

II-24. Polly Math is a multi-talented artist who writes the melody and lyrics to a tune titled *Only Me* and then records a cappella version of the tune using her home recording studio. What copyrights does she own, and in what categories of works of authorship are they included?

(A) Polly owns copyrights in the melody and lyrics of *Only Me* as a musical work.

(B) Polly owns the copyright in the melody and lyrics of *Only Me* as a musical work and the copyright in the recording of her performance of *Only Me* as a sound recording.

(C) Polly owns the copyrights in the lyrics of *Only Me* as a musical work, and the copyright in the melody and her performance of *Only Me* as sound recordings.

(D) Polly owns the copyrights in the melody, lyrics, and performance of *Only Me* as musical works.

II-25. Dancer is known for her powerful live dance performances, during which she performs impromptu ecstatic free form modern dance routines to public domain classical music. Every one of her performances is unique, and none is planned or scripted in any way. Last year, Dancer performed her greatest work to date at Carnegie Hall. The performance was recorded with Dancer's authorization, and copies of the video were released as a DVD titled *Dancer at Carnegie Hall — Live!*. The DVD sold well for a few months, then sales fell off because a much cheaper DVD began to circulate. Titled *Carnegie Hall Hosts Dancer, Live!*, the second DVD was based on an unauthorized recording of the same event. Dancer sues the makers of the second DVD for infringing her federal copyright in the choreographic work she performed at Carnegie Hall. Will she prevail?

(A) Yes. Dancer will prevail because the second DVD infringes her federal copyright in the dance she performed at Carnegie Hall.

(B) Yes, Dancer will prevail because the content of the second DVD infringes the audiovisual work fixed in the original DVD authorized by Dancer.

(C) No. Dancer will not prevail because her dance was not fixed in a tangible medium of expression.

(D) No. Dancer will not prevail because choreographic works that do not communicate a story are not copyrightable.

II-26.   Photog takes a photograph of a wet kitten in a sink and prints it on shirts that he sells via the Internet. The sales of the shirts are a great success. Soon, Knockoff starts a website from where he sells an identical shirt, including its unique button holes and an exact copy of Photog's kitten photograph, for a fraction of the price charged by Photog. Photog sues Knockoff for copyright infringement. Will he succeed?

(A) Yes. Photog will succeed because by appending an original photograph to a functional object like a shirt, he acquires exclusive rights over the entire shirt as well as what is depicted on it.

(B) Yes. Photog will succeed, but only with respect to Knockoff's reproduction and distribution of the photograph contained on the shirt.

(C) No. Photog will not succeed because clothing is not copyrightable.

(D) No. Photog will not succeed because by appending a copyrightable image to a noncopyrightable useful object, he forfeits copyright protection in the former.

II-27.   GamerCo designs, creates, and distributes a video game called *A-Maze-ment*. The game features a two-dimensional display in which players navigate a maze while fighting off monsters. *A-Maze-ment* consists of twenty distinct levels, each with its own distinctively designed maze accompanied by music that has been composed and recorded for the video game. GamerCo seeks to register the video game with the Copyright Office. How will the Copyright Office categorize the video game?

(A) The game screens are pictorial works, and the accompanying music is a sound recording.

(B) The game screens are pictorial works, and the accompanying music is a musical work.

(C) The video game and its components constitute an audiovisual work.

(D) The music may be registered as both a musical work and a sound recording, but the video game screens depicting the distinct levels are not copyrightable because they are not fixed in a tangible medium of expression.

II-28.   Studio releases its big summer blockbuster, *Frantic Man*, that includes a music soundtrack created by the popular rap artist Poppa Bigg as a work made for hire. Studio registers *Frantic Man* with the Copyright Office as an audiovisual work, but does not separately apply for registration of the motion picture's accompanying music soundtrack. Soon after, up and coming rapper Sonny Smallz releases a recording that incorporates wholesale a full minute from the *Frantic Man* music soundtrack. Studio, which owns all rights in the music soundtrack, sues Sonny Smallz for infringement. Among Sonny Smallz' responses to Studio's complaint is that the music soundtrack was never validly registered with the Copyright Office. Is this argument valid?

(A) Yes. Studio's failure to separately register its copyright in the music soundtrack when it registered its copyright in the motion picture means Studio forfeited any opportunity to register the former.

(B) Yes. Studio failed to separately register the copyright in the music soundtrack, but this does not prevent it from registering it at a later time.

(C) No. Studio did not separately register the music soundtrack, but this was not necessary because a motion picture's music soundtrack is protected under the motion picture copyright.

(D) No. Although Studio did not separately register the music soundtrack, this is irrelevant because the Copyright Act's registration provisions do not apply to sound recordings.

II-29. Musician composes a concerto for piano, then performs the concerto himself and records the performance using his own recording equipment. Musician releases the recording as *Musician's Concerto Live* and it becomes a hit in the classical music world. Pianoman is a devoted amateur pianist. He buys a copy of *Musician's Concerto Live* and listens to it so often that he memorizes the whole composition and, without ever having seen the sheet music, can play it by heart. In fact, as an homage to Musician, Pianoman videotapes himself performing Musician's concerto and posts it on the Internet. Musician does not appreciate Pianoman's doing this and sues him for infringing both the musical work that comprises the concerto as well as the sound recording *Musician's Concerto Live*. Will Musician prevail?

(A) Yes. Musician will prevail because Pianoman infringed both the musical work and the sound recording.

(B) Yes. Musician will prevail because Pianoman infringed the sound recording.

(C) Yes. Musician will prevail because Pianoman infringed the musical work.

(D) No. Musician will not prevail because Pianoman did not infringe either the musical work or the sound recording.

II-30. In 1967, Donny Dank penned the melody and lyrics to *Sir Surfs-a-Lot*. Two years later, the band Big Waves, with Dank's permission, records *Sir Surfs-a-Lot* in its own studio and releases it that same year to great success. Assuming that the creators of each work of authorship have retained the rights to them, what are the various federal copyright ownership interests in *Sir Surfs-a-Lot*?

(A) Dank owns the copyright in the musical work that comprises *Sir Surfs-a-Lot*, but the Big Waves recording is not protected by federal copyright.

(B) Dank owns the copyright in the musical work that comprises *Sir Surfs-a-Lot*, and Big Waves owns the federal copyright in the sound recording.

(C)   Dank owns the copyright in the musical work that comprises *Sir Surfs-a-Lot* and in the sound recording that resulted from Big Waves' recording of it.

(D)   Dank owns the copyright in the musical work that comprises *Sir Surfs-a-Lot*. Dank and Big Waves are joint owners of the sound recording.

II-31.   Architect drafts the blueprints for Jones Manor, which is then built to his specifications. Architect's design for Jones Manor consists not only of the original exterior structure of the house, but also of a distinctive interior spiral staircase. Architect has reserved the rights in any and all works of authorship generated by his efforts with respect to Jones Manor. Which of the following statements most accurately characterizes Architect's copyright ownership interests?

(A)   Architect owns copyrights in the blueprints as both pictorial and architectural works; as well as the exterior structure of the house and the interior staircase as an architectural work.

(B)   Architect owns the copyright in the exterior structure of the house as well as the interior staircase as an architectural work.

(C)   Architect owns copyrights in the blueprints as a pictorial work, and in the exterior structure and interior staircase as an architectural work.

(D)   Architect owns copyrights in the blueprints as a pictorial work, and in the exterior structure as an architectural work.

II-32.   Fed and Statie are artists who were recently employed by the federal government and the state of Grace, respectively. They are working on a joint federal-state project to commemorate Grace's bicentennial. Fed's contribution is an original painting depicting the first meeting between explorers and Grace's native inhabitants. Statie produces an original poem that gives narrative context for the events portrayed in the painting. These works of authorship hang in the Grace statehouse next to each other. One day, Copyist releases a pamphlet giving his own version of the history of Grace's founding, and includes in it a photo reproduction of Fed's painting and Statie's poem, without having obtained permission to do so. Accused of copyright infringement, Copyist argues that as works created by government employees, neither the painting nor the poem is copyrightable. Is Copyist correct?

(A)   Yes, Copyist is correct. Neither work of authorship is copyrightable.

(B)   Yes and no. Statie's poem is not copyrightable, but Fed's painting is.

(C)   Yes and no. Fed's painting is not copyrightable, but Statie's poem is.

(D)   No, Copyist is wrong. Both works of authorship are copyrightable.

II-33.   Novelist's book *Nonesuch* is rumored to be his finest work yet, but few can confirm that rumor because Novelist wrote *Nonesuch* in Cornish, a Celtic language spoken by less than a thousand people. Novelist refuses to license translations of *Nonesuch*, and takes care to register his copyright in nations around the world, including the United States. Critic has spent his career studying Novelist's work, and is so anxious to read *Nonesuch* that he learns Cornish and creates his own translation of the novel, which he then posts on his password-protected website to limit access to the translation. However, Publisher breaks the code, makes a copy of the translation, releases an English-language version of *Nonesuch*, and sells many copies. Both Novelist and Critic are incensed, and each sues Publisher for copyright infringement in federal district court. Who will likely prevail?

(A) Novelist will prevail, but Critic will not.

(B) Critic will prevail, but Novelist will not.

(C) Novelist and Critic will both prevail.

(D) Neither Novelist nor Critic will prevail.

II-34. *PoundSigne* is a popular French comic strip featuring an original and distinctive main character, Le Mec. *PoundSigne*'s creator has registered all of his comics with the United States Copyright Office, and has licensed Publisher to create an English translation of the comic strip. Publisher does so with his work consisting only of translating the French-language text in the *PoundSigne* comics into English, while leaving the graphics untouched. Publisher's translated versions of *PoundSigne* become very popular in the United States. Eventually, Fan, an overly enthusiastic reader of Publisher's translations, creates a website on which *Le Mec's New Adventures*, a comic featuring an exact copy of the Le Mec character in new contexts, is presented. *PoundSigne*'s creator and Publisher each sue Fan for copyright infringement. Who will prevail?

(A) Neither *PoundSigne*'s creator nor Publisher will prevail.

(B) *PoundSigne*'s creator will prevail, but Publisher will not.

(C) Publisher will prevail, but *PoundSigne*'s creator will not.

(D) *PoundSigne*'s creator and Publisher will both prevail.

II-35. In 1995, Photog took a picture of a lion during an African safari. He then licensed Adventure magazine to use the photograph on the front cover of the January 1996 issue, but retained all other rights in the photograph. Recently, Adventure released a DVD titled *50 Years of Adventure* that is a digital archive containing an exact copy of each issue of the magazine. The back issues are presented just as they appeared on the newsstand, allowing users to scroll through them page-by-page and see all the material as it was presented in the original print versions. Adventure did not seek Photog's permission to re-use his photo in the context of the DVD. Photog now sues Adventure magazine for infringing his copyright in the lion photograph. Will Photog prevail?

(A) Yes. Photog will prevail because this is a violation of his right to reproduce and distribute his copyrighted work, and Adventure cannot argue that it falls within the section 201(c) privilege for collective works.

(B) Yes. Photog will prevail because the Copyright Act requires users to seek express written permission for any use of a previously licensed analog work in a digital context.

(C)   No. Photog will not prevail, because even though Adventure reproduced and distributed his copyrighted photograph in the DVD, that use is protected by the section 201(c) privilege for collective works.

(D)   No. Photog will not prevail, because a license to use a work of authorship in one context necessarily implies a license to use that same work in any reasonably related context.

II-36.   Webcaster streams recordings of music over its website. Webcaster has obtained no licenses. Music Publisher owns the copyrights in several musical compositions that have been streamed by Webcaster. If Music Publisher sues Webcaster for copyright infringement, the claimed primary infringement will be:

(A)   The adaptation right of section 106(2).

(B)   The public performance right of section 106(4).

(C)   The public display right of section 106(5).

(D)   The digital transmission right of section 106(6).

II-37.   Webcaster streams recordings of music over its website. Webcaster has obtained no licenses. Record Company owns the copyrights in several sound recordings that have been streamed by Webcaster. If Record Company sues Webcaster for copyright infringement, the claimed primary infringement will be:

(A)   The adaptation right of section 106(2).

(B)   The public performance right of section 106(4).

(C)   The public display right of section 106(5).

(D)   The digital transmission right of section 106(6).

III-1. Recently, Florist hired Programmer, an independent contractor, to create a computer program to assist in the operation of Florist's flower shop. Florist described the operation of his business to Programmer, who subsequently delivered a completed computer program to Florist. Who is the owner of the copyright in the computer program?

    (A) Florist.

    (B) Florist, only if Florist and Programmer signed a written work made for hire agreement.

    (C) Programmer.

    (D) Programmer, only if Florist and Programmer had not signed a written work made for hire agreement.

III-2. Author's new novel *Mysterious Friendship* is due to come out on Friday, and Frontera Bookstore is planning a big event to celebrate the book's release. Author's sworn enemy, Envy, breaks into Frontera Bookstore on Thursday night, absconds with all the copies of Author's novel that the bookstore was planning to sell at the event, and then publishes the last chapter of the book on the Internet to ruin the novel's surprise ending. Frontera and Author both sue Envy for copyright infringement. Will they prevail?

    (A) Yes, both will prevail.

    (B) Frontera Bookstore will prevail, but Author will not.

    (C) Author will prevail, but Frontera Bookstore will not.

    (D) No, neither Frontera Bookstore nor Author will prevail.

III-3. Painter recently finished his latest masterwork, a series of oil on canvas paintings, that he painted by himself. Based only on this information, which of the following statements accurately describes Painter's copyright ownership status with respect to the work?

    (A) Painter is the creator, owner, and author of the work.

    (B) Painter is the creator and author of the work, but may not be its owner.

    (C) Painter is the creator and owner of the work, but may not be its author.

    (D) Painter is the creator of the work, but may not be its owner or author.

III-4. Recently Sculptor, as an employee of Left Coast Studios, made a crystal sculpture of a large bird for Left Coast's classic motion picture, *The Maltese Condor*. Upon the completion of the motion picture, in which the sculpture was used, Museum purchased the sculpture. What status, that is, creator, author, and owner, do the parties have with respect to the sculpture on this set of facts?

ANSWER:

III-5.   In 1950, Poet was hired as an independent contractor by a tycoon named Fritzlinger to compose an ode to Fritzlinger's vast fortune. Fritzlinger told Poet that he wanted the poem to comment on Fritzlinger's rise from poverty to wealth, and to compare Fritzlinger's fortune favorably to that of other tycoons. Poet worked on it for a month, then showed it to Fritzlinger, who made substantial suggestions for changes, which Poet dutifully incorporated. At the completion of the work, Fritzlinger paid Poet for his time and the two parted ways, never to see each other again. Assuming that no written agreement memorialized the relationship between Fritzlinger and Poet, who is considered the author of the copyright in the poem?

(A) Fritzlinger, because Poet was an independent contractor.

(B) Fritzlinger, because he initiated Poet's work and paid him for it.

(C) Poet, because he exercised more creative control over the final version than did Fritzlinger.

(D) Poet, because he was an independent contractor.

III-6.   Consider question III-5. Assume that Poet was not an independent contractor, but a regular employee of Fritzlinger. How, if at all, does this affect the authorship of the poem?

ANSWER:

III-7.   Worker has served as a product safety inspector for Manufacturer during the past twenty years. During that time, she has taken very little vacation, and last year her boss agreed to let her take all her six months of accumulated vacation time at once. Worker spent those months fulfilling her lifetime dream of writing a novel about a boy and his dog in Albania. Recently, Worker's novel was published to great critical and commercial success. Manufacturer wants to cash in on Worker's windfall, and claims that it is the novel's author because the novel is a work made for hire. Worker, of course, claims that she is in fact the novel's true author. In the absence of any written agreement addressing the issue, which assertion about authorship is correct?

(A) Worker is the novel's author because her creation of the novel occurred outside the scope of her employment.

(B) Worker is the novel's author because she was effectively functioning as an independent contractor for Manufacturer while she was on her six months' paid vacation.

(C) Manufacturer is the novel's author because Worker was an employee of Manufacturer at the time she wrote the novel.

(D)   Manufacturer is the novel's author because in the absence of a written agreement, any work of authorship created by an individual in the employ of a corporation is assumed to belong to the corporation.

III-8.   Big Press hires Polly Glot to translate a successful Spanish-language novel into English. Polly works on the translation from her home office, refuses to accept any comments from Big Press's editorial staff, and is paid a one-time lump sum fee for her work, without benefits or tax withholdings. She has signed a contract with Big Press, also signed by the President of Big Press, containing a provision that Big Press, not Polly Glot, will be the author of the work. A few months after completing the English translation, Polly noticed that Big Press has used large segments of her translation in promoting itself. This upsets Polly, and she sues for infringement, but Big Press responds that the work belongs to them. Who will prevail?

(A)   Polly will prevail because she clearly worked as an independent contractor when creating the English translation, and any agreements to the contrary are void under federal law.

(B)   Polly will prevail because she, not Big Press, authored the translation.

(C)   Big Press will prevail because, although Polly worked as an independent contractor, her claim of copyright in the English translation was overcome by the agreement defining Big Press as the author of one of the nine categories of works for which such agreements are enforceable.

(D)   Big Press will prevail because Polly created the translation as an employee acting within the scope of her employment.

III-9.   CEO works for DynaCorp. After a poor earnings report came out, the DynaCorp board of directors demanded that CEO produce a memorandum identifying the parties responsible for the corporation's declining profits. CEO went home and penned a long detailed memo in which she placed blame on the board for DynaCorp's poor recent earnings. Shortly thereafter, CEO was fired as the head of DynaCorp. To get revenge, CEO posted the memo on her personal web page. The DynaCorp board was embarrassed by CEO's revelations and filed for an injunction to have CEO take the memo off her web page. DynaCorp's counsel argues that CEO's conduct amounts to copyright infringement because DynaCorp is the author of the memo and did not authorize its reproduction or display. Will DynaCorp prevail?

(A)   Yes, DynaCorp will prevail because anything CEO writes during her employ by DynaCorp is considered a work made for hire.

(B)   Yes, DynaCorp will prevail because the work product of corporate officers is considered a work made for hire of which the corporation is the author.

(C)   No, DynaCorp will not prevail because CEOs are effectively independent contractors and their work product is not work made for hire.

(D)   No, DynaCorp will not prevail because business-related memos are insufficiently creative to merit copyright protection.

III-10. Consider question III-9. The DynaCorp board hires an outside consulting firm, ConsultCo, to investigate the problems associated with a bad earnings report and provide an impartial report. The consulting agreement includes no mention of copyright or ownership of the report. ConsultCo does just this, receives a one-time payment for its work, and later posts its report about DynaCorp on the ConsultCo company website to show an example of its work. DynaCorp is displeased that ConsultCo posted the sensitive material without its permission and sues for an injunction to remove the material from the ConsultCo web page because it infringes DynaCorp's copyright. ConsultCo argues that it is the author of the report and is thus entitled to post it. Who will prevail, and why?

ANSWER:

III-11. GiantCo hires Fuchsia, a well-known muralist, to paint a mural on the interior of its corporate headquarters' lobby, pursuant to an oral agreement. Fuchsia paints the mural using her own design, though she uses materials provided by GiantCo. Fuchsia sticks to her artistic vision, frequently rejecting editorial suggestions from GiantCo as to how the mural should look. When Fuchsia finishes the mural, GiantCo is pleased with the final product and pays her a one-time lump sum, without any tax withholdings. This project is the only time Fuchsia does any work for GiantCo. Who is the author of the mural?

(A) Fuchsia is the author. More of the relevant factors that determine her employment status weigh in favor of Fuchsia being an independent contractor rather than an employee.

(B) Fuchsia is the author. She used her own design, which is dispositive of her status as an independent contractor.

(C) GiantCo is the author. At least one of the relevant factors, whose materials were used in making the mural, weighs against Fuchsia, and this is enough to negate her status as an independent contractor.

(D) It is not possible to say unless we know whether GiantCo provided Fuchsia with health insurance benefits.

III-12. Writer recently created two collaborative projects. One project was called *Spring*, and was a series of meditations on the eponymous season that he co-wrote with Author. To create *Spring*, Writer came up with an outline, then sent it to Author, who fleshed out the text a bit more. Through successive iterations of this process, including a few meetings at which they discussed particular details of the project, Writer and Author eventually arrived at a final version of *Spring* with which they were both pleased. Writer also worked with Musician to create lyrics for Musician's composition, *Autumn*. Musician is a bit of a recluse, and he simply sent Writer the sheet music and a sound recording of *Autumn* when he had finished it. Writer then listened to the composition and penned lyrics that he sent to Musician without any comments, suggestions, or input from Musician. Musician did not even look at the lyrics, instead simply sending the final product on to their publisher. According to the definition of the Copyright Act, which of these compositions are joint works?

(A) *Spring.*

(B) *Autumn.*

(C) *Spring* and *Autumn.*

(D) Neither *Spring* nor *Autumn.*

III-13. Producer wants to produce a CD that will merge East Coast and West Coast hip-hop styles. His only problem is that there is currently an East Coast-West Coast conflict afoot, and all the rappers from the respective camps hate each other and refuse to work together. So Producer approaches West Coast DJ W.C. and asks him to provide the music track for a hip-hop recording. Producer tells W.C. that a big name rapper is attached to provide the lyrics, but that he cannot tell W.C. who it is. W.C. produces the track, and Producer promptly invites East Coast rapper E.C. to create and perform lyrics for it, but does not tell E.C. who created the music track. The resulting musical work is a huge hit, but to Producer's chagrin, he failed to secure the rights to the work. Who does own it?

(A) W.C. owns it, because he began the project.

(B) E.C. owns it, because he completed the project.

(C) Producer still owns it in the absence of a written agreement that secures him the rights, because he was the creative force behind the creation of the work.

(D) W.C. and E.C. own the work as joint authors.

III-14. Screenwriter pens a script about two star-crossed lovers that is set in the Australian outback. In order to make the motion picture as authentic as possible, Screenwriter hires his Aussie friend Haul Pogen to advise him on the details of life in the outback. After Screenwriter finishes a nearly final draft of the script, he sends it to Haul, who returns extensive comments about how to make the settings, scene details, and characters' dialogue consistent with life in the Australian outback. Screenwriter looks at the revisions and says, "Haul, this is great, but I'm swamped. Tell you what: I'll double your fee if you just put these in yourself." Haul does as requested, and makes substantial revisions to the script, even including a new two-page scene. Screenwriter approves the changes, pays Haul double his one-time lump sum fee, and says, "Thanks, buddy, I'll make sure you're listed as a consultant in the credits." Haul responds, "That sounds great. It was my pleasure to chip in a bit." Screenwriter sells the completed script to Studio which produces a successful motion picture based on the script. Haul soon after decides that he is entitled to half of the fee Screenwriter received for the script, claiming that he is joint author of the script. Is Haul correct?

(A) No. Haul is not a joint author because there is no written agreement with Screenwriter identifying him as one.

(B) No. Haul is not a joint author because at the time of his collaboration with Screenwriter, neither he nor Screenwriter intended that he would be a joint author.

(C) Yes. Haul is a joint author because he contributed substantial creative material to the final version of the screenplay.

(D)   Yes. Haul is a joint author because at the time he created material for the script, both he and Screenwriter intended the material to be added to the script.

III-15.   Consider question III-14. Assume instead that when Screenwriter asked Haul for help on the screenplay, he said "the outback scenes in this thing don't ring true. Fix it and I'll give you a piece of the action." Assume further that Screenwriter gave Haul complete control over the revisions, and that Haul's revisions included revising the title page to read "Screenplay by Screenwriter and Haul Pogen," that remained part of the script when it was sold to Studio. How would these facts affect Haul's claim to joint authorship, and why?

ANSWER:

III-16.   Author works on a novel for six months and then comes down with a case of writer's block. He gives his half-done manuscript to his friend Advisor and says "I need some fresh ideas to get going. Can you help me out?" Author tells his agent that he has recently given the manuscript to Advisor for comments, and that if Advisor comes up with any good thoughts, he will include Advisor in the acknowledgments page of the final draft. Advisor, however, tells other friends that he is now "collaborating as a co-author" with Author on the novel. Eventually, Advisor reads the manuscript, meets with Author, and shares some fruitful suggestions that spur Author to finish the novel, which he then publishes with great success. However, when the novel is released, Advisor is shocked to see that he is not credited as a co-author, but merely received an acknowledgment from Author. As a result, Advisor now sues Author for fifty percent of the royalties resulting from the exploitation of the novel. Advisor believes he is entitled to the royalties as a joint author. Is he correct?

(A)   Yes. Advisor is a joint author because his creative contribution was critical to completion of the project.

(B)   Yes. Advisor is a joint author because his conversation with a friend reveals his subjective expectation that he was in a co-authorial relationship at the time of the contribution.

(C)   No. Advisor is not a joint author because his contribution to the novel was objectively less significant than Author's.

(D)   No. Advisor is not a joint author because Author clearly did not regard him as a co-author at any point during their collaboration.

III-17.   Worker and Slacker decide to co-author a screenplay. They sign a contract beforehand stating that the product of their collective labor will be regarded as a joint work of authorship for the purposes of copyright analysis. The agreement does not specify how any proceeds from the potential sale of the script will be divided. Worker slaves away on the screenplay for six months, and during that time produces forty-four scenes. By contrast, Slacker works hardly at all and ends up contributing only a single original three-page scene to the final product, a screenplay consisting of forty-five scenes. Producer reads the script, loves it, and offers to buy it from Worker and Slacker for $1 million. Worker and Slacker then dispute the appropriate split of the fee in court. Worker claims that he should get almost all of the money because he did almost all of the work. Slacker responds that the contract requires that as joint authors, Worker must split the proceeds equally. How will a court rule in this dispute?

(A) Slacker will prevail. Judges regard any contribution by a co-author as deserving an equal distribution of profits realized from the use or licensing of the screenplay as a matter of law.

(B) Slacker will prevail. As a contractually defined joint author of the work of authorship, he owns the work as a tenant in common with Worker, and this entitles him to an equal share.

(C) Worker will prevail because he did significantly more work than Slacker.

(D) Worker will prevail because Slacker's contribution to the final work is not copyrightable.

III-18. Composer has been working on a musical composition for the past several weeks. She has completed the music and most of the lyrics, but has been stuck on a rhyme for the last verse. Composer is visited by Neighbor, who notices that Composer is toiling at her piano and is in a frustrated state of mind. Composer tells Neighbor that she has been "pulling her hair out" because she cannot find a work to rhyme with "orange." Neighbor suggests that she try "door hinge," a suggestion that fits the composition nicely and is used by Composer to complete the composition. Is Neighbor entitled to joint authorship status in light of this contribution?

ANSWER:

III-19. Author loves his spouse, Wife, very much, and wants her to be a co-owner of his forthcoming nonfiction literary work on the history of copyright law. Which of the following statements most completely describes means by which Author can extend co-owner status to Wife?

(A) Author can assign a fifty percent interest in the copyright of the literary work to Wife while reserving a fifty percent interest for himself.

(B) Author can create a partnership with Wife and make the copyright of the literary work one of the assets of the partnership.

(C) Author can write an introductory note stating, "while she may not have written a line of this work, Wife is an author in spirit because she has always been my biggest supporter."

(D) (A) and (B) are both valid means of making Wife a co-owner of the copyright in the literary work.

III-20. Biggie and Smalls co-write a musical work titled *Young and High-Strung*. Smalls then performs and records the musical work on his own, and the resulting track becomes a big success in physical CD and digital download sales. Which of the following statements accurately reflect the copyright ownership rights of Biggie and Smalls in the musical work and the sound recording of *Young and High-Strung*?

(A) Biggie and Smalls each own an undivided interest in the copyrights in both the musical work and sound recording.

(B) Biggie and Smalls each own an undivided interest in the whole of the copyright in the musical work, while Smalls owns the copyright in the sound recording.

(C) Biggie owns 100% of the copyright in the musical work, while Smalls owns 100% of the copyright in the sound recording.

(D) Biggie and Smalls each own an undivided interest in the copyright in *Young and High-Strung* and share equally in profits from its exploitation.

III-21. The Midnights are a three-piece rock band consisting of Vocalist, Guitarist, and Drummer. The three members of Midnights co-author the melody, harmony, and lyrics for a musical work entitled *Fighty Aphrodite*. They then record the musical work and the resulting track becomes a big hit. A year later, Pianist approaches Guitarist and says she wants to record a version of *Fighty Aphrodite* on piano, and offers a licensing fee of $1,000 for the nonexclusive right to re-arrange the musical work, and to perform, record, and release a piano version of the new arrangement. Guitarist agrees, but the other members of Midnights are incensed about the deal because they know and despise Pianist's work. Vocalist and Drummer file suit to enjoin Pianist from going forward with her project. Will they prevail?

(A) No. Co-owners of a work can nonexclusively license derivative works, but they owe their co-owners accounting for any profits generated by the license.

(B) No. Co-owners of a work can nonexclusively license derivative works, and the licensor is entitled to keep all the profits generated by the license.

(C) Yes. Nonexclusive licensing of a co-owned work requires the assent of more than fifty percent of the owners; one co-owner of three is insufficient.

(D) Yes. Nonexclusive licensing of a co-owned work requires the assent of all owners; one co-owner out of three is insufficient.

III-22. Consider question III-21. Assume that Guitarist granted Pianist an exclusive rather than a nonexclusive license. How would this change the analysis, and why?

ANSWER:

III-23. Composer and Lyricist co-write the musical work *Temptations*, and then they each agree to exclusively license Singer to record her own version of the musical work, and to publicly perform *Temptations* as well. The resulting sound recording of *Temptations* becomes a big hit, but while Composer likes it, Lyricist thinks it is awful and wants to rescind the license. Over Composer's strong objection, Lyricist's lawyer sends Singer a letter saying that the license is rescinded, and that Singer is no longer permitted to publicly perform *Temptations*. Singer, on advice of counsel, continues to publicly perform the musical work, and Lyricist sues to enjoin Singer from doing so. Will Lyricist prevail?

(A) No. Lyricist will not prevail, because once an exclusive license to perform or otherwise use a copyrighted work of authorship has been granted, it can never be rescinded.

(B) No. Lyricist will not prevail, because an exclusive license to perform or otherwise use a copyrighted work of authorship can be rescinded only by unanimous consent of all its owners.

(C) Yes. Lyricist will prevail, because an exclusive license to perform or otherwise use a copyrighted work of authorship can be rescinded by any one of its owners.

(D) Yes. Lyricist will prevail because one co-owner's desire to rescind an exclusive license is sufficient evidence from which the desire for rescission by all owners may be inferred.

III-24. Consider question III-23. Once Singer's licensed recording of *Temptations* was released to the public as a digital download, Record Company decided to have one of its recording artists record *Temptations* without any authorization by Composer and Lyricist. Record Company has now released its recording on physical CDs and as a digital download. Composer and Lyricist now sue Record Company for copyright infringement. This lawsuit will likely be:

(A) Successful, because Record Company is making unauthorized reproductions of the *Temptations* musical composition.

(B) Successful, because Record Company has no privity of contract with Composer and Lyricist's exclusive license with Singer.

(C) Unsuccessful, because the compulsory mechanical license provided by section 115 of the Copyright Act becomes applicable only when the musical composition has been released to the public on phonorecords, not digital downloads.

(D) Unsuccessful, because Record Company can take advantage of the compulsory mechanical license provided by section 115 of the Copyright Act.

III-25. Clark and Michael recently co-wrote a novel that remains unpublished. Clark, a frustrated screenwriter, thinks the novel could be the basis for a great movie, but Michael does not trust the "Hollywood Machine" that would ruin the story and characters developed in the novel. Clark decides to write a screenplay based on the novel. Clark then enters into an agreement with Studio pursuant to which Clark assigns to Studio his copyright interest in the novel for $100,000, as well as all right, title, and interest in the copyright of the screenplay for $250,000. In addition, Clark is hired by Studio to write two sets of revisions of the script for $50,000. Studio ultimately makes a motion picture based on Clark's revised script that makes a profit of $10 million. Nothing has been paid to Michael, who now sues Studio and Clark for copyright infringement and, in the alternative, an accounting. Analyze the possibility of Michael's success with this lawsuit.

ANSWER:

III-26. Studio owns the copyright in *Tiger Woman*, a recently produced motion picture. Studio licenses Distributor, a film distribution company, to release the film, but under very limited circumstances. Studio grants to Distributor the exclusive right to exhibit *Tiger Woman* only in theaters that seat fifty or more patrons, only in states bordering the Atlantic Ocean, and only for two months. Distributor agrees to the terms of the license, but one day its in-house counsel advises that the agreement is unenforceable. Is Distributor's lawyer correct, and if so, why?

(A) Distributor's lawyer is correct because a copyright owner cannot limit via license the venues in which their work is shown, and this license limited showings of *Tiger Woman* to larger theaters.

(B) Distributor's lawyer is correct because a copyright owner cannot limit via license the geographical area in which a work is exploited, and this license limited the exhibition of *Tiger Woman* to states bordering the Atlantic Ocean.

(C) Distributor's lawyer is correct because a copyright owner cannot limit via license the time during which a licensee may exploit a work, and this license limits the time of Distributor's exploitation of *Tiger Woman* to two months.

(D) Distributor's lawyer is wrong, the license is valid.

III-27. Writer pens a novel that Speculator thinks is excellent and wants to acquire its copyright. Writer and Speculator orally agree that Writer will sell Speculator the copyright in the novel for $500. After Speculator has paid the $500 to Writer, he learns that Writer subsequently licensed the rights to make a screenplay based on the novel to Studio. Speculator contacts Writer and says, "You can't do that, I own the copyright now." Is Speculator correct?

(A) No. Speculator is wrong because when a creator sells a copyrighted work of authorship, he reserves the right to nonexclusively license uses of that work.

(B) No. Speculator is wrong because his agreement with Writer was invalid since it was not memorialized in writing.

(C) Yes. Speculator is correct because the transfer of copyright ownership from Writer means that Writer retains no enforceable rights in the novel.

(D) Yes. Speculator is correct because Writer's conduct was in bad faith.

III-28. Consider question III-27. Assume that instead of an oral agreement, the parties had executed a written agreement that said, "Writer hereby agrees to transfer the copyright in his novel to Speculator in exchange for a fee of $500" and was signed by Speculator. How would this change the outcome, and why?

ANSWER:

III-29. Publisher admires Artist's most recent sculpture, *ClownTown*, and offers to purchase the copyright in the sculpture. Publisher and Artist orally agree that Artist will transfer the copyright in the sculpture for $1000. Publisher makes out a check to Artist in the amount of $1000. In the memorandum area of the check, Publisher writes, "Fee for purchase of copyright in Artist's *ClownTown* sculpture." Artist receives the check signed by Publisher, endorses the back of it, and writes her initials next to Publisher's note in the memorandum area of the check. Is this transfer enforceable?

(A) Yes. The transfer is enforceable because it is in writing and signed by the transferee, Publisher.

(B) Yes. The transfer is enforceable because it is in writing and signed by the transferor, Artist.

(C) No. The transfer is not enforceable because a check is too informal to count as the kind of written memorandum required by the Copyright Act.

(D) No. The transfer is not enforceable because the memorandum was written by the transferee, Publisher, rather than the transferor, Artist.

III-30. In 1958, Screenwriter completes a script. Screenwriter does not publish the script or register it with the Copyright Office, but does begin talking the script up around Hollywood, and gets some significant buzz going. In 1959, Executive calls Screenwriter and tells him that Executive's company, Studio, wants to purchase all the rights to Screenwriter's script. Screenwriter is thrilled with the offer. He drives over to Studio, enters Executive's office with a copy of the screenplay, places it on Executive's desk, and says "Here you go. I can't wait to see this baby on the silver screen!" Executive shakes Screenwriter's hand and gives him a check for the full amount of the agreed-upon fee. At no point during the exchange is any written agreement executed. Is the agreement enforceable?

(A) Yes. The agreement is enforceable because prior to 1978, transfers of unpublished and unregistered works of authorship could be effected by oral agreements and implied by courses of conduct.

(B) Yes. The agreement is enforceable because under the 1909 Act, no writing was required to transfer ownership of a copyright.

(C) No. The agreement is not enforceable because it was never memorialized in a writing signed by the transferor copyright owner, Screenwriter.

(D) No. The agreement is not enforceable because the parties never discussed the copyright in the work.

III-31. ShoeCo recently hired Designer to create a logo for its new line of running shoes. Designer created a creative logo design that met the approval of ShoeCo. Thereafter, the two parties executed a valid written agreement assigning all of Designer's rights in the logo to ShoeCo, including all copyrights, in exchange for valuable consideration. Soon, BigCorp decided it wanted the logo for use in connection with its multinational enterprise. BigCorp offered ShoeCo a substantial fee in exchange for an assignment of all rights in the logo. ShoeCo accepted the offer and the two parties signed a written agreement assigning the copyright in the logo to BigCorp. BigCorp started to use the logo in connection with its products. This new use came to the attention of Designer who is a staunch opponent of multinational companies such as BigCorp. Designer became incensed and now seeks an injunction preventing BigCorp from using the logo. Will Designer prevail?

(A) Yes. Designer will prevail because an assignment of copyright does not include the right to assign the copyright to other parties.

(B) Yes. Designer will prevail because, although copyright assignees can assign those copyrights to other parties, they retain a right of first refusal with respect to those third-party assignments.

(C) No. Designer will not prevail because ShoeCo, as the assignee of all rights in the logo, is free to assign its copyright to whoever it chooses.

(D) No. Designer will not prevail because the assignment from ShoeCo to BigCorp was invalid.

III-32. Consider question III-31. Assume that rather than an assignment of copyright ownership, Designer granted to ShoeCo an exclusive license to use the logo in connection with any product, and that ShoeCo subsequently granted BigCorp an exclusive license to use the logo on its products. Would this variation change the outcome of the case and, if so, why?

ANSWER:

III-33. AdAgency recently requested Musician to deliver a dozen short musical compositions to be used in television commercials for a storage company. AdAgency agreed, in a hand-shake deal, to pay Musician $600 for his services and an additional $500 for each musical composition used for a commercial on a buy-out basis, under which AdAgency would be given all of the rights, including copyright, in the composition. Musician delivered twelve musical compositions that she had created a year earlier and was paid $600 by AdAgency. After reviewing the compositions, AdAgency selected one for use in the storage company commercial. Musician was paid an additional $500 for that musical composition. Six months later, AdAgency has used the same musical composition in a radio commercial for a local bank. Musician has demanded an additional $500 payment from AdAgency for the use of the musical composition in the bank commercial. AdAgency has refused payment on the ground that it "owns the rights to the composition."

If AdAgency claims that its rights to the musical composition are based on the fact that the composition was a work made for hire, AdAgency will likely be:

(A) Successful, because it obtained the musical composition via an agreement entered into by both parties and the composition was used for a television commercial that falls within the statutory category of audiovisual work.

(B) Unsuccessful, because the musical composition was not created pursuant to the agreement.

(C) Successful, because Musician was paid for creating and delivering the musical compositions.

(D) Unsuccessful, because the composition was used for a radio commercial that does not fall within any of the work made for hire statutory categories.

III-34. Consider question III-33. Musician decides not to sue AdAgency for breach of contract and opts to sue for copyright infringement of the musical composition. Musician will likely be:

(A) Unsuccessful, because AdAgency acquired the copyright to the musical composition through a valid assignment.

(B) Successful, because AdAgency never acquired a lawful right to use the composition.

(C) Unsuccessful, because Musician's course of conduct with AdAgency evidences the grant of a nonexclusive license from Musician to AdAgency to use the musical composition.

(D) Successful, because, even if an implied nonexclusive license was created, it encompassed only the use of the musical composition in a television commercial for a storage company, not a radio commercial for a bank.

III-35. Crafty McGee owns the copyright in the poem *FireBash*. Crafty executes a written agreement to transfer ownership of the copyright in *FireBash* to Publisher for $500. Publisher does not record the transfer with the Copyright Office. Crafty then offers to execute another written agreement transferring ownership of the copyright in *FireBash* to Collector. Collector is aware of the original agreement between Crafty and Publisher, but enters into the agreement anyway, paying $700 to Crafty in exchange for the transfer of copyright ownership. Six months later, Publisher releases an anthology of poems that includes *FireBash*, and Collector sues Publisher for infringement. Will Collector prevail?

(A) Yes. The initial transfer of ownership to Publisher was invalid because Publisher failed to record it.

(B) Yes. As the first party to record a transfer of ownership of the copyright in *FireBash* from Crafty, Collector has rights superior to all other purported transferees, including Publisher.

(C) No. Because Crafty transferred the copyright in *FireBash* to Publisher before he transferred it to Collector, Publisher's rights are superior to Collector's.

(D) No. Because Collector was not a good faith transferee, her recordation of the transfer cannot create superior rights, and the initial transfer to Publisher remains valid.

III-36. In 1950, Novelist signed a publishing agreement with Publisher. The agreement stated that Novelist licensed the copyright in his novel, *Holidaze*, for the purpose of publishing it "in hardcover, paperback, or other printed form" for the life of the copyright. The agreement contained a clause explicitly reserving in Novelist the right to license the rights in *Holidaze* for "any other uses." Recently, Publisher partnered with CompuCo, the maker of BitBook, a technology that allows books to be read in digital form on a palm-held device. Publisher provided CompuCo with the text of its most profitable 500 works, including *Holidaze*, so that CompuCo could reduce them to digital form, readable on the BitBook. Novelist was incensed that Publisher did so without seeking a license, and sued Publisher for copyright infringement. Publisher responded that the 1950 agreement allowed it to publish, or facilitate the publication of *Holidaze* in any book form possible, including digital media like the BitBook. Who will prevail?

(A) Novelist. The grant of a license to publish a work in analog format never implies a right to publish that same work in digital format.

(B) Novelist. This particular grant was narrowly worded to apply only to "printed form," which excludes digital media.

(C) Publisher. The grant of a license to publish a work in analog format always implies a right to publish that same work in digital format.

(D) Publisher. This particular grant did not exclude digital media, so it should be construed in favor of the licensee.

III-37. It is 1970 and the artist Avant has a studio from which he sells his artwork and accepts commissions to create paintings. Collector visits the studio, finds a painting, *Sunrise Over Shatto*, to her liking, and pays the asking price of $5,000. Avant takes the canvass down from the wall and hands it to Collector who walks out of the studio to her apartment where she hangs the painting in her living room. Which of the following is correct?

(A) Avant is the creator and author, and Collector is the owner of the copyright in *Sunrise Over Shatto*.

(B) Avant is the creator, and Collector is the author and owner of the copyright in *Sunrise Over Shatto*.

(C) Avant is the creator, author, and owner of the copyright in *Sunrise Over Shatto*.

(D) Collector is the creator, author, and owner of the copyright in *Sunrise Over Shatto*.

III-38. It is 1970 and the artist Avant has a studio from which he sells his artwork and accepts commissions to create paintings. Collector visits the studio, but does not find a painting to her liking. Collector pays Avant $5,000 to paint *Sunset Over Palms*, a painting that depicts the setting sun through the leaves of several palm trees. Collector arrives at the studio a month later to pick up the painting. Avant takes the canvass down from the wall and hands it to Collector who walks out of the studio to her apartment where she hangs the painting in her living room. Which of the following is correct?

(A) Avant is the creator and author, and Collector is the owner of the copyright in *Sunset Over Palms*.

(B) Avant is the creator, and Collector is the author and owner of the copyright in *Sunset Over Palms*.

(C) Avant is the creator, author, and owner of the copyright in *Sunset Over Palms*.

(D) Collector is the creator, author, and owner of the copyright in *Sunset Over Palms*.

III-39. It is one month ago and the artist Avant, Jr. has a studio from which he sells his artwork and accepts commissions to create paintings. Collector visits the studio, finds a painting,

Sunrise Over Moon Bay, to her liking and pays the asking price of $5,000. Avant, Jr. takes the canvass down from the wall and hands it to Collector who walks out of the studio to her apartment where she hangs the painting in her living room. Which of the following is correct?

(A) Avant, Jr. is the creator and author, and Collector is the owner of the copyright in *Sunrise Over Moon Bay*.

(B) Avant, Jr. is the creator, and Collector is the author and owner of the copyright in *Sunrise Over Moon Bay*.

(C) Avant, Jr. is the creator, author, and owner of the copyright in *Sunrise Over Moon Bay*.

(D) Collector is the creator, author, and owner of the copyright in *Sunrise Over Moon Bay*.

III-40. It is one month ago and the artist Avant, Jr. has a studio from which he sells his artwork and accepts commissions to create paintings. Collector visits the studio, but does not find a painting to her liking. Collector pays Avant, Jr. $5,000 to paint *Sunset Over Calm*, a painting that depicts the setting sun through the leaves of several palm trees. Collector arrives at the studio a month later to pick up the painting. Avant, Jr. takes the canvass down from the wall and hands it to Collector who walks out of the studio to her apartment where she hangs the painting in her living room. Which of the following is correct?

(A) Avant, Jr. is the creator and author, and Collector is the owner of the copyright in *Sunset Over Calm*.

(B) Avant, Jr. is the creator, and Collector is the author and owner of the copyright in *Sunset Over Calm*.

(C) Avant, Jr. is the creator, author, and owner of the copyright in *Sunset Over Calm*.

(D) Collector is the creator, author, and owner of the copyright in *Sunset Over Calm*.

IV-1. Animator currently works on the creation of an animated feature film for Studio. He creates several animation cels, all of which are owned by his employer, Studio, as works made for hire. The cels feature fanciful anthropomorphic animals in a medieval setting with castles and quaint villages. None of Animator's cels are ultimately used in the final version of Studio's film, though, and Animator takes them home. Animator subsequently creates his own project, an animated short film featuring cartoon human characters that is also set in the Middle Ages. Almost all of Animator's short film consists of his own work, but in a few scenes, he copies and uses background images of a castle and segments of the cels he created for the feature film to fill out the background of some of the cels for his short film. While Animator never screens his short film publicly, an executive of Studio hears that some features of Animator's short film are the same as the ones Animator created for Studio. Studio sues Animator for copyright infringement. Will Studio prevail?

(A) Yes. Studio will prevail because by copying some features of the animated cels owned by Studio, Animator violated Studio's right of reproduction in those works of authorship.

(B) Yes. Studio will prevail because, by copying some features of the animated cels owned by Studio, Animator violated Studio's right of public display in those works of authorship.

(C) No. Studio will not prevail because the animation cels that Animator created for Studio never appeared in the ultimate work of authorship for which they were originally intended.

(D) No. Studio will not prevail because Animator used only segments of the original cels in his short film.

IV-2. Joe buys a copy of the popular video game Bonestorm to play on his personal computer. Joe's roommate, Bo, also enjoys video games, and notices Joe's copy of Bonestorm lying around their shared apartment. One day when Joe is out, Bo takes the Bonestorm CD-ROM, places it on his own personal computer, and plays a few games. Although Bo does not install the application onto his computer hard drive, during his game play, a copy of the object code of the Bonestorm program is made in the RAM of his computer. Joe later finds out what Bo did, and reports him to SoftCo, owner of the copyright in the Bonestorm object code. SoftCo then brings a copyright infringement suit against Bo. Will SoftCo prevail?

(A) No. SoftCo will not prevail because the object code placed in RAM are temporary and evanescent, and thus do not count as copies.

(B) No. SoftCo will not prevail because the Digital Millennium Copyright Act held that RAM copies of object code can never violate a copyright owner's exclusive right of reproduction.

(C) Yes. SoftCo will prevail because Bo's reproduction of the object code in the RAM of his computer amounts to a violation of SoftCo's reproduction right in that object code.

(D) Yes. SoftCo will prevail because Bo's reproduction of the object code in the RAM of his computer amounts to a violation of SoftCo's adaptation right in that object code.

IV-3.   Consider question IV-2. Assume that rather than surreptitiously taking and using Joe's Bonestorm CD-ROM for the purpose of playing the game, Bo took and used the CD-ROM only because his personal computer was malfunctioning, and he needed to use a CD-ROM in order to diagnose and fix the problem. Would this change the result, and if so, why?

ANSWER:

IV-4.   Synchro is creating the music soundtrack for the new motion picture to be released by his employer, Studio. Synchro finds a great track titled *Speed Demon* that he uses as the background music for a chase scene, and does not secure rights because he understands that the musical work that comprises *Speed Demon* is in the public domain. However, when the motion picture is released, the owner of the copyright in the sound recording that comprises *Speed Demon* sues Studio for infringement. What exclusive right does Synchro's unauthorized use of the *Speed Demon* track violate prior to the exhibition of the motion picture in theaters?

(A) Public distribution.

(B) Public display.

(C) Reproduction.

(D) Public performance.

IV-5.   Groupie is a big fan of Band, and goes to one of its concerts with a hidden recording device. Groupie records Band's live performance of public domain musical compositions and later listens to the recording on his portable music player. Does Groupie's conduct subject him to any liability?

(A) Yes. Groupie is liable for infringing Band's exclusive right of reproduction.

(B) Yes. Groupie is liable for violating federal anti-bootlegging provisions.

(C) No. Groupie cannot be held liable because Band's live performance was unfixed and thus uncopyrightable.

(D) No. Groupie cannot be held liable because he never sold or distributed the copy he made of Band's performance.

IV-6.   San Begonio Public Library (SBPL) is a municipal institution that is open to the population of the small town of San Begonio. One day, local resident Adam comes to SBPL and asks for a copy of a recent article from the *San Begonio Times* about the town's early history, which Adam wants solely for his personal edification. Librarian makes one copy of the requested piece, writes "© 2008 San Begonio Times" at the top of the article, and gives it to Adam. While Librarian is occupied with this project, Bob sneaks into SBPL and, using the library's photocopy machine that is situated under a sign that informs those using the machine that the making of a copy may be subject to the copyright law, makes a photocopy of *Novel*, a popular book that Bob intends to scan and put online for the public to read free of charge. Later that day, Archivist, an employee of the Santa Garganta Public Library calls SBPL and asks Librarian if she could send a CD-ROM containing a rare and discontinued spoken word version of *Dated Tome*, a difficult to find novel via inter-library loan. Archivist explains that SBPL's copy of the spoken word version of *Dated Tome* has been stolen and SBPL needs to replace it so it can make the recording available to its borrowing public. Librarian burns a copy of SBPL's spoken word recording of *Dated Tome* onto a CD-ROM, writes "Dated Tome, © 2008" on the disc, and sends it to Archivist, along with SBPL's printed warning concerning copyright restrictions contained on its order form. Which, if any, of these acts of reproduction will subject SBPL to infringement liability?

(A) Librarian's making a photocopy of the news article for Adam, and Bob's use of SBPL's photocopier to make an unauthorized copy of *Novel*.

(B) Bob's use of SBPL's photocopier to make an unauthorized copy of *Novel*, and Librarian's creation of a duplicate CD-ROM of *Dated Tome* for Archivist.

(C) Only Bob's use of SBPL's photocopier to make an unauthorized copy of *Novel*.

(D) None of these uses will expose SBPL to infringement liability.

IV-7.   Journalist, who is based in New York, pens an investigative essay that he markets to various news outlets. Finally, *Bi-Coastal Magazine* makes Journalist a lucrative publication offer of $10,000 in exchange for the exclusive right to publish the piece in its next issue. Journalist accepts. *Bi-Coastal Magazine* is a national publication that publishes separate East Coast and West Coast editions each month. Each edition contains eighty-five percent of the same material, including artwork and advertisements. Journalist's article appears in both editions without Journalist's consent. Journalist sues *Bi-Coastal Magazine* for reproducing the article in the West Coast edition without permission. Will Journalist prevail?

(A) Yes. Journalist will prevail because his agreement with *Bi-Coastal Magazine* included only the right to publish the article in one edition of the magazine.

(B) Yes. Journalist will prevail because *Bi-Coastal Magazine*'s use of his article in the West Coast edition amounts to an unauthorized public distribution of that work.

(C) No. Journalist will not prevail because *Bi-Coastal Magazine*'s use of the article in its West Coast edition falls within the federal privilege for publishers of collective works to republish individual contributions in new editions.

(D) No. Journalist will not prevail because by authorizing *Bi-Coastal Magazine* to use his article in one edition of its magazine, he also granted an implied license to *Bi-Coastal Magazine* to use the article in any other print medium.

IV-8.   Consider question IV-7. Assume that *Bi-Coastal Magazine* licensed the content of its issues, including the article written by Journalist, to an online database. The online database allows users to search and retrieve articles that then appear in a text-only version, as opposed to being featured in the context of their original publication. How, if at all, would this affect Journalist's likelihood of success in a copyright infringement suit against *Bi-Coastal Magazine*?

ANSWER:

IV-9.   Composer writes a concerto for piano titled *Winter* that he performs and records on his own, and releases as a CD titled *Composer Performs Winter*. Dilettante purchases Composer's CD and, based only on hearing the CD, performs and records the concerto herself. Without payment to or authorization from Composer, Dilettante releases the CD under the title *Dilettante Performs Winter*. Composer sues Dilettante for copyright infringement. Will Composer succeed?

   (A)   Yes. Composer will succeed in showing that Dilettante infringed his copyright in both the musical work and sound recording of *Winter*.

   (B)   Yes. Composer will succeed in showing that Dilettante infringed his copyright in the *Winter* musical work.

   (C)   No. Dilettante is free to make a new sound recording of the *Winter* musical work, so long as she does not duplicate the original; and she is free to reproduce the *Winter* musical work because it is subject to a compulsory mechanical license by statute.

   (D)   No. Dilettante must obtain a "master use" license to use the sound recording that comprises *Winter*, even if the musical work is subject to a compulsory mechanical license by statute.

IV-10. Consider question IV-9. Assume that instead of recording her own version of *Winter* without Composer's permission, Dilettante visited Attorney first and asked whether she needed to obtain Composer's permission in order to record *Dilettante Performs Winter*. Under these circumstances, what advice should Attorney give Dilettante?

ANSWER:

IV-11. Composer has composed and recorded a musical work titled *Songbird*. Her recording of *Songbird* has only been available on Composer's personal website for a small fee. Techie runs a website called "indiecheap.com" that allows users to stream and download MP3 versions of their favorite independent music tracks at a significant discount. Techie paid to download a copy of *Songbird* from Composer's website. He then included it among the tracks that are available on "indiecheap.com" without the permission of Composer.

   Which of the following statements most accurately describes Techie's liability under the Copyright Act for his use of the *Songbird* musical work?

   (A)   Techie will be liable for copyright infringement under the Copyright Act only if he fails to obtain a mechanical license.

(B) Techie will be liable for copyright infringement under the Copyright Act only if he fails to obtain a public performance license.

(C) Techie will be liable for copyright infringement under the Copyright Act if he fails to obtain both a mechanical license and a public performance license.

(D) Techie will not be liable for copyright infringement under the Copyright Act because the recording of *Songbird* was not released in a physical copy, therefore no license is necessary.

IV-12. Consider question IV-11. Which of the following statements most accurately describes Techie's liability under the Copyright Act for his use of the *Songbird* sound recording?

(A) Techie will be liable for copyright infringement under the Copyright Act only if he fails to obtain a master use license.

(B) Techie will be liable for copyright infringement under the Copyright Act only if he fails to obtain a public performance license.

(C) Techie will be liable for copyright infringement under the Copyright Act if he fails to obtain both a master use license and a public performance license.

(D) Techie will be liable for copyright infringement under the Copyright Act if he fails to obtain both a master use license and a license to digitally transmit the sound recording to the public.

IV-13. Pal decides to make a mix tape to give to Friend as a gift. Pal does this by selecting several recordings of music that he has legally downloaded from the Internet to his home computer, with which he then burned those recordings onto a CD. How, if at all, does Pal's conduct violate the exclusive rights of the copyright owners in the musical works and sound recordings that comprise the tracks on the mix tape he burned for Friend?

(A) Pal's conduct violates the reproduction rights of the copyright owners of both the musical works and sound recordings.

(B) Pal's conduct violates the reproduction rights of the copyright in the musical works only.

(C) Pal's conduct violates the reproduction rights of the copyright in the sound recordings only.

(D) Pal's conduct does not violate the exclusive rights of any copyright owner.

IV-14. Pomo is a contemporary "appropriation" artist whose work alters the creations of other artists in an effort to comment on those creations. Pomo acquires a copy of *Idyll*, the latest work by Artist, who is a popular contemporary painter of oil landscapes. Pomo then composes an original paragraph decrying the mundane character of landscape painting, and writes the text all over an authorized copy of *Idyll*, purchased by Pomo, which he then displays in his art gallery for all to see, but not to purchase. When Artist learns about this, he becomes incensed and files a suit against Pomo for infringing his copyright in *Idyll*. Fair use issues aside, did Pomo's conduct violate any of Artist's exclusive rights in *Idyll*?

(A) Yes. Pomo's conduct violates Artist's exclusive right of public display.

(B) Yes. Pomo's conduct violates Artist's exclusive right of adaptation.

(C) No. Pomo's alteration of a copy of *Idyll* rather than the original means that none of Artist's exclusive rights are at issue.

(D) No. Pomo's conduct did not violate any of Artist's exclusive rights in *Idyll* because the work altered by Pomo was not offered for sale.

IV-15. Consider question IV-14. Assume that rather than composing an original text and altering *Idyll* using that text, Pomo had made a pleasing frame for the Artist's work, and then sold the framed copy of *Idyll* at an auction for a substantial sum. On these facts, would Pomo be subject to any copyright liability?

ANSWER:

IV-16. Linguo is a language buff and avid reader. He buys a copy of Author's latest book, *Novel*, which is written in English. Linguo wants to impress his language-buff friends and translates his copy of *Novel* into the Esperanto language. Linguo does this by photocopying his purchased copy of *Novel* on his employer's photocopier, and then making notes on the photocopy, which he then uses to type up the Esperanto version of *Novel*. He then gives the translation to three of his close friends in order to show off his accomplishment. What exclusive rights in *Novel* did Linguo violate?

(A) Reproduction.

(B) Reproduction and public distribution.

(C) Reproduction and adaptation.

(D) Reproduction, adaptation, and public distribution.

IV-17. Biglaw, LLC declines to promote Associate to partner, and Associate leaves the firm in anger. Associate surreptitiously takes several copies of Biglaw's employee handbook with him on his last day of employment and leaves them around town with a note attached to the front reading, "Biglaw treats their employees like dirt — read all about it inside!" Biglaw discovers this, and sues Associate for copyright infringement, alleging that Associate's conduct violated its exclusive right of public distribution. Is Biglaw's public distribution argument valid?

(A) Yes. Associate's making Biglaw's copies of the handbook available to the public without authorization amounts to a violation of Biglaw's public distribution right.

(B) Yes. As the owner of the copyright in its employee handbook, Biglaw has the right to control any dissemination of copies of the work,

(C) No. Associate's conduct is protected under the first sale doctrine.

(D) No. Associate cannot be held liable for violating Biglaw's right of public distribution in the handbook because he did not select a particular audience for his distribution, but rather made it generally available.

IV-18. Consider question IV-17. Assume that instead of making copies available at public places around town, Associate made three copies, gave each to close friends who are specialized in employment law, and asked them to consider whether, in light of Biglaw's employment policies, it may create the basis for a wrongful termination lawsuit. On these facts, would Biglaw be able to successfully argue that Associate's conduct violated its exclusive right of public distribution in the employee handbook?

ANSWER:

IV-19. Techie writes the original code for the Tech-Neeks computer program. Techie gives a copy of the program on CD-ROM to his friend, Computo, saying "I want you to have this program — I think you'll really like it!" Later, Techie is dismayed to learn that Computo was not impressed with the program, and that Computo gave the CD-ROM to the local public library in case any members of the public might have more interest in it. Techie sues Computo, arguing that Computo violated Techie's right of public distribution in the code of the Tech-Neeks computer program. Is Techie's argument correct?

(A) Yes. The first sale doctrine does not apply in this case because Techie did not sell the CD-ROM to Computo, but gave it to him as a gift.

(B) Yes. By facilitating the public library's distribution to the public of the CD-ROM containing Techie's protected code, Computo himself can be held liable for violating Techie's exclusive right of public distribution.

(C) No. Computo's conduct does not amount to public distribution of the source code that comprises the Tech-Neeks computer program.

(D) No. Computo's conduct amounts to public distribution of the source code that comprises the Tech-Neeks computer program, but it is permitted under the first sale doctrine.

IV-20. Entrepreneur has a great idea for a new business venture. He opens a business that purchases CD copies of all new major music releases and rents them to the public at a price much lower than it would cost to purchase the CD outright. This way, Entrepreneur theorizes, he can capture the market consisting of people who do not want to buy a CD outright, but still have enough interest in the music that they might pay a lower price to listen to it for a week or so. Entrepreneur's business presents no risk of music piracy. All of the rented CDs are heavily protected so that the tracks contained on them cannot be ripped. Soon, Entrepreneur finds himself sued by record companies who argue that his business violates their right of public distribution in the sound recordings embodied in the CDs that Entrepreneur rents. Will the record companies' argument succeed?

(A) Yes. The first sale doctrine does not apply in this case because the Copyright Act was amended to exclude the rental of musical works embodied in phonorecords.

(B) Yes. A purchaser of a CD cannot sell, lease, or give it to another person without running afoul of the copyright owner's exclusive right of public distribution.

(C) No. The first sale doctrine immunizes Entrepreneur from liability because it entitles him to sell, lease, or give away the physical CDs in which he rightfully acquires ownership.

(D) No. Because Entrepreneur has carefully crafted his business model to eliminate any risk of piracy, record companies cannot argue that they are harmed by his conduct.

IV-21. Orchestra puts on a concert in New York City where it plays a piece of modern classical music and authorizes Radio Station to broadcast the concert live. Fan, a big classical music aficionado in Hartford, Connecticut, tunes in to Radio Station's broadcast of the concert and plays it on his home stereo system for an assembled group of fifteen other music lovers. Which of these amounts to a "performance" within the meaning of the Copyright Act?

(A) Orchestra's concert.

(B) Orchestra's concert and Radio Station's transmission of the concert.

(C) Radio station's transmission of the concert and Fan's retransmission of the concert.

(D) Orchestra's concert, Radio Station's transmission of the concert, and Fan's retransmission of the concert.

IV-22. Which of the following performances are "public" within the meaning of the Copyright Act?

I. An outdoor classical music concert at a municipal park.

II. A poetry reading at a café that is attended by twenty people.

III. A comedy routine at a private club that is by invitation only.

IV. A weekly presentation, that includes the performance of recorded music, by an employee of a private firm to a group of fifteen fellow employees.

(A) I only.

(B) I and II.

(C) I, II, and III.

(D) I, II, and IV.

IV-23. Hoteles Grandes (HG) offers its numerous guests a distinctive in-room, on-demand movie service. Each HG location has an off-site server with hundreds of legally acquired digital versions of major motion pictures, including several for which Studio owns the copyrights. HG guests can use their in-room televisions to request any of these films, at which time the film is transmitted from the hotel's server to the guest's in-room television. Studio hears about HG's service and sues HG for copyright infringement, arguing that each transmission to a guest's room amounts to an unauthorized public performance of the copyrighted work. Will Studio prevail on this claim?

(A) Yes. Every time a user plays a digital version of a motion picture, it is a public performance of that work of authorship.

(B) Yes. HG's transmission of motion pictures from its central server to guest rooms amounts to an unauthorized public performance of those works of authorship.

(C) No. While HG's transmission of motion pictures from its central server to guest rooms amounts to an unauthorized performance of those works of authorship, it is not a public performance because the guest rooms are all private.

(D) No. Merely transmitting a work of authorship from one point to another does not amount to a performance of that work.

IV-24. Consider question IV-23. Assume that instead of offering an in-room on-demand movie service, HG offers its guests in-room Internet service. The Internet service is also routed through an off-site server to each HG site, so that whenever a guest requests a URL offering motion pictures on the guest's in-room Internet terminal, the HG server negotiates the request and passes it along to HG's Internet Service Provider that sends the resulting information to the requesting guest's terminal. Under these facts, if owners of copyrighted information that HG guests requested sued HG for publicly performing that material, would HG suffer liability?

ANSWER:

IV-25. Restaurateur owns a restaurant that is 4,000 gross square feet in size. The restaurant has no stage or dance floor. Restaurateur has purchased a receiver, tuned it to a local radio station that broadcasts music and has attached the receiver to a sophisticated ten-speaker sound system installed by a high-fidelity sound engineering company at considerable expense. Which of the following would make it more likely that Restaurateur will not be able to take advantage of the section 110(5)(B) small business exception, requiring her to pay public performance fees?

(A) The size of the restaurant is 4,000 gross square feet.

(B) The restaurant has an expensive sophisticated sound system.

(C) The restaurant is a food service and not a drinking establishment.

(D) The restaurant is not a venue for live music.

IV-26. The Children's Play Center has installed a CD player, a low power amplifier, two home-style speakers and a compact disc library to play recordings of musical compositions protected by copyright in response to requests by children. Such performances would:

(A) Infringe the copyrights in the musical compositions, but only if the musical compositions were distributed compositions that had been distributed on phonorecords to members of the public for their private use.

(B) Infringe the copyrights in the musical compositions because the *Aiken* exception codified in section 110(5)(A) would not apply.

(C) Not infringe the copyrights in the musical compositions because sound recordings do not have a public performance right.

(D) Not infringe the copyrights in the musical compositions because the performances would be at the direction of the children.

IV-27. Karma runs a store in the town of New Hayvensburg that sells tie-dyed prints and clothes made entirely from hemp. One day, officers of the New Hayvensburg Police Department (NHPD), acting on an anonymous tip, raid Karma's store looking for illegal drugs. The NHPD confiscate a substantial amount of material, including some of Karma's original pencil sketches, but ultimately find nothing illegal. The NHPD delays in returning the confiscated items to Karma, and she ultimately files a series of legal actions against the NHPD based on its failure to return these items. Among these actions is a copyright infringement suit in which Karma argues that the NHPD's failure to return her pencil sketches amounts to a violation of her exclusive rights as the owner of the copyright on those protected works of authorship. Will Karma prevail on this copyright-based claim?

(A) Yes. The NHPD's failure to return the sketches violates Karma's exclusive right to control her work.

(B) Yes. The NHPD's failure to return the sketches violates Karma's exclusive rights to earn a profit from her copyrighted works by preventing her from selling them.

(C) No. The creator of an original pictorial or graphical work owns the copyright in the work of authorship contained in the work, but retains no rights in the physical object, so Karma has no right to have the drawings returned.

(D) No. Karma's ownership of the copyright in the drawings does not give rise to any copyright-based claim to have them returned.

IV-28. Superfan is a schoolteacher and is also a big enthusiast of Novelist's famed science fiction. Novelist releases a new literary work, *Ultraworld*, that Superfan is very excited about. She uses *Ultraworld* as a teaching tool for her sixth graders, reading them a chapter of the novel every day and engaging them in a discussion of how Novelist uses style to create his distinctive tone and mood. Superfan also invites the fifteen members of the local Novelist fan club to her home, where she regales them with a dramatic reading of her favorite passages from *Ultraworld*. One member of the fan club admires Superfan's readings and invites her to give a dramatic reading of *Ultraworld* at the open-mic night at the local coffeehouse. Superfan does a reading at the open-mic night, which is attended by a crowd of about twenty people, each of whom pay a nominal fee of $5 to hear the various performers. Novelist hears about Superfan's conduct and sues her for violating Novelist's exclusive right of public performance of *Ultraworld*. Which of Superfan's readings violate Novelist's exclusive right of public performance in *Ultraworld*?

(A) Superfan's reading at the open-mic night only.

(B) Superfan's reading to the fan club and her reading at the open-mic night.

(C) Superfan's reading to her students and her reading at the open-mic night.

(D)   Superfan's reading to her students; her reading to the fan club; and her reading at the open-mic night.

IV-29.   Musician performs and records an original version of *Delight*, a musical work that is in the public domain, which she then makes available on her website for download in MP3 format for ninety-nine cents. Not wanting to pay anything for the recording, Pirate hacks into Musician's website, makes an unauthorized copy of the MP3 file containing the recording of *Delight*, and places it onto his computer hard drive. Pirate then streams the recording of *Delight* over his own website so that any visitor can listen to Musician's recording of *Delight* free of charge. Musician learns about Pirate's website and sues him for copyright infringement, arguing that Pirate has violated her exclusive rights to reproduce and publicly transmitting a digital audio of her sound recording. Will Musician's claim succeed?

(A)   Yes. Both of Musician's bases for arguing that Pirate violated her exclusive rights are valid.

(B)   Musician can successfully argue that Pirate violated her right of reproduction in her sound recording, but not her right of digital transmission.

(C)   Musician can successfully argue that Pirate violated her right of digital transmission, but not her right of reproduction.

(D)   No. Neither of Musician's bases for arguing that Pirate violated her exclusive rights is valid.

IV-30.   Consider question IV-29. Assume that instead of streaming Musician's *Delight* sound recording over his personal website, Pirate broadcast the sound recording over analog radio waves during his night shift at a local college radio station. In light of this variation, would Musician be able to successfully sue Pirate for violating her exclusive rights to reproduce and digitally transmit her sound recording?

ANSWER:

IV-31.   The final installment in Novelist's popular graphic novel fantasy series, *Finality*, just came out, and Bookseller has stocked numerous copies of the volume. To encourage sales, he places a copy of *Finality* in his store window with the book open to a random page in order to show passers-by a sample of the book's color illustrations and to give a brief taste of the plot. Bookseller also scans a copy of the same page he has shown to the public in his store window and puts it on his website to tempt readers to purchase copies of *Finality* through his online store. Novelist hears about Bookseller's conduct and sues him for copyright infringement on the theory that he has violated her exclusive right of public display in her graphic novel. Leaving the issue of fair use aside, will Novelist's claim succeed?

(A)   No. There is no right of public display in literary works such as those embodied in Novelist's fantasy series.

(B)   No. There is no violation of the right of public display unless the entire work of authorship, as opposed to just a small portion of that book, is displayed online.

(C)   Yes. While both Bookseller's physical and online showing of parts of *Finality* amount to unauthorized public displays, the physical display is permissible while the online display is not.

(D)   Yes. Both of Novelist's unauthorized displays of parts of Novelist's book amount to violations of her exclusive right of public display in the book.

IV-32.   BigMedia wants to enter the digital music business. It has various projects in the works. First, BigMedia plans to purchase a broadcast FM radio station and convert its operations from analog to digital form. Second, BigMedia plans to set up a website called BigMedia.com where ten different digital radio stations will stream various genres of music online. Users will be able to go to the site and select which station's stream they want to tune in to, though BigMedia will choose which sound recordings it will stream. BigMusic's streaming music service is free, but it also plans to offer an on-demand music service on BigMusic.com called "BigMusic Plus" that will allow listeners, in exchange for a $10/month fee, to request particular sound recordings to be played at any time. What kind of licenses does BigMedia need to have with the owners of the copyrights in the sound recordings it plans to transmit via these three means?

(A)   None. There is no public performance right in sound recordings, so BigMedia needs no licenses from the owners of the copyrights in the sound recordings it plans to transmit.

(B)   BigMedia needs no license to broadcast the sound recordings from its digital radio station or to stream the sound recordings from BigMedia.com, but it must negotiate a license with the owners of the sound recordings it plans to make available via its on-demand service.

(C)   BigMedia owns a statutory (compulsory) license to broadcast the sound recordings from its digital radio station and to stream the sound recordings from BigMedia.com, but must negotiate a license with the owners of the sound recordings it plans to make available via its on-demand service.

(D)   BigMedia needs no license to broadcast the sound recordings from its digital radio station, needs a statutory (compulsory) or consensual license to stream the sound recordings from BigMedia.com, and must negotiate a consensual license with the owners of the sound recordings it plans to make available via its on-demand service.

IV-33.   Writer pens a manuscript of a novel and then signs an agreement with Publisher. The agreement states that Publisher will publish the novel and pay a percentage of its revenues obtained from book sales to Writer, but that Writer retains the copyright in the work of authorship. After signing the agreement, Publisher decides that the book will sell more copies if it has the name of a more famous person attached to it, so the version of the book that is released wrongly lists Author, a well-known popular novelist, rather than Writer, on the front cover. Writer is incensed and sues Publisher for, among other things, copyright infringement. Will Writer succeed?

(A)   Yes. Writer will succeed because Publisher created a derivative work by placing Author's name on the cover of Writer's book, thereby violating Writer's exclusive right of adaptation.

    (B)   Yes. Writer will succeed because Publisher failed to accurately attribute the book's origin to him, robbing Writer of his due recognition.

    (C)   No. Writer will fail because this is a moral-rights claim, and federal law recognizes no moral rights-based claims.

    (D)   No. Writer will fail because copyright law does not recognize a cause of action for copyright infringement based solely on failure to correctly attribute authorship.

IV-34.   Painter paints a picture of the Grand Canyon, which she then sells to Buyer. Buyer then delivers the painting to the local public art gallery for it to sell. However, before he presents the painting to the gallery, Buyer puts it in a frame that covers Painter's signature, and which labels the work "Panorama of the Grand Canyon by Buyer." When the owner of the gallery asks if Buyer painted the picture himself, Buyer replies "I sure did!" Painter then visits the gallery, tells the owner of the gallery that the work is actually hers, and the gallery owner asks Buyer to take back the painting. Buyer does so, and for a time hangs the painting in his living room. Eventually, though, Buyer feels so ashamed of his attempted subterfuge that he gives the painting back to Painter. When Painter takes it back, she notices that the work has faded because sunlight entered Buyer's living room through a skylight and the oil paints Painter used were particularly sensitive to degradation under those conditions. Painter sues Buyer for violating her moral rights of attribution and integrity in the painting. Will she succeed?

    (A)   Yes. Painter will succeed on both claims.

    (B)   Painter will succeed on the right of attribution claim, but will fail on the right of integrity claim.

    (C)   Painter will succeed on the right of integrity claim, but will fail on the right of attribution claim.

    (D)   No. Painter will fail on both claims.

IV-35.   Consider question IV-34. Assume that instead of purchasing a painting of the Grand Canyon from Painter, Buyer acquired a photograph of the Grand Canyon that was one in a limited series of 250 prints, all numbered and signed by Painter. If all other facts were the same, would Painter be able to successfully sue Buyer on a moral rights theory under VARA?

ANSWER:

IV-36.   In 1992, Artist paints a canvas entitled *DarkSyde* that depicts brutal police beating up innocent citizens. Artist sells the work to Collector, who loans it to the local museum of contemporary art. Artist dies in 2008. In his will, Artist states that he no longer agrees with the message expressed by *DarkSyde* and wants the work destroyed as an expression of his repudiation of what the canvas depicted. The executor of Artist's estate files an action under VARA to have the painting returned to the estate's possession and destroyed as per its creator's wishes. Will Artist's executor's action succeed?

(A)   Yes. To allow a picture to hang in a museum after an artist has repudiated it is considered a misrepresentation of the artist's views that violates the right of attribution.

(B)   Yes. To allow a picture to hang in a museum after an artist has repudiated it is considered a mutilation of the artist's work that violates the right of integrity.

(C)   No. Artist's VARA rights expired upon his death in 2008.

(D)   No. While Artist's VARA rights are still enforceable, a right to have the painting removed from existence is not among them.

V-1. Which of the following factors is determinative of whether notice is a prerequisite for copyright protection?

(A) The type of work of authorship.

(B) The date the work was published.

(C) The citizenship status of the author.

(D) Whether the work is co-authored.

V-2. Author of a novel recently assigned its registered copyright to Publisher A who did not record the assignment with the Copyright Office. Three months later, Author assigned the copyright in the same novel to Publisher B, a good faith purchaser, for a large advance against royalties. Publisher B recorded the assignment immediately with the Copyright Office. While Publisher A continued to edit the manuscript of the novel in preparation for its release to bookstores, Publisher B printed and distributed the novel, that contained a copyright notice, to bookstores for sale to the public. Can Publisher A successfully sue Publisher B for copyright infringement?

(A) Yes, because Publisher A was preparing the novel for publication.

(B) Yes, because Publisher A was assigned the copyright first and thereafter Author had nothing left to assign.

(C) No, because Publisher B, not Publisher A, is the owner of the copyright in the novel.

(D) No, because Publisher B, not Publisher A, was the first to release the novel to the public with a copyright notice.

V-3. In 1910, Graphic Designer, employed by the Anderson Print Shop, was asked to create a drawing of the building occupied by the print shop. This task was within the scope of Designer's employment. Designer worked for the company until he died in 1934. The original drawing was kept by Gary Anderson, the owner of the Anderson Print Shop, in his personal safe. In 1954, Gary gave the original copy of the drawing, which did not contain a copyright notice, to his Grandson. Gary died that same year. In 1960, Grandson gave a copy of the drawing to each of his three fraternity brothers, with instructions not to copy the work. These copies did not contain a copyright notice. One of the fraternity brothers, Henry Historian, obtained proper authorization to publish the drawing in 2004 as part of a collection of turn of the century buildings. The collection contained a proper copyright notice. In what year was the drawing invested with federal copyright protection?

(A) 1910.

(B) 1960.

(C) 1978.

(D) 2004.

V-4. MelodyCo owns all the rights in the musical work *Executive Sweet*. In 1949, MelodyCo permitted a band to perform the musical work in a session closed to the public, but broadcast live over the radio. This performance created a demand for the work and, in 1950, MelodyCo created the first phonorecord of *Executive Sweet*, which it released to record stores for sale in a limited edition of one thousand copies. In 1951, MelodyCo re-released the recording of *Executive Sweet*, this time on a larger scale, distributing tens of thousands of copies of the phonorecord to retail music establishments. Each released phonorecord was accompanied by a proper copyright notice. By 1975, the entire inventory of *Executive Sweet* recordings had been sold by MelodyCo. When, if at all, was *Executive Sweet* generally published?

(A) 1949. The live performance of the musical work was sufficient to effect general publication.

(B) 1950. The limited-edition release effected general publication.

(C) 1951. The large-scale release effected general publication.

(D) Never. Musical works distributed in phonorecords before January 1, 1978, are deemed not to have been published.

V-5. Consider question V-4. Assume that all the acts described in that question took place in the 1990s, rather than in the 1940s and 50s. In light of this change, at what stage, if at all, would publication have occurred?

ANSWER:

V-6. In 1960, Writer penned an original manuscript for a novel titled *Clouded Sunset*, but told no one about it and placed the manuscript in his desk drawer. In 1961, Writer handed the manuscript over to Literary Agent, who sent a copy of the manuscript containing a proper copyright notice to each of five studio executives, seeking bids for motion picture rights to the novel. Literary Agent told each of the five executives, "You can keep this copy to see if you want to bid on the novel, but keep it all very hush-hush." Shortly thereafter, the head of FilmCorp, one of the executives that reviewed the manuscript, called Literary Agent with a generous offer to buy the motion picture rights to the novel. Writer happily accepted. In 1962, the *Clouded Sunset* novel was published by Robust Reader Publications exclusively for the Bi-Monthly Book Club, which offered it for sale to its members. Following a year of production, FilmCorp released a motion picture in 1963 that contained the main character of *Clouded Sunset* involved in a different story line. When, if at all, was the novel first generally published under the 1909 Copyright Act?

(A) 1960. The act of embodying the expression of a fictional idea in a tangible medium of expression effected general publication.

(B) 1961. The distribution of the manuscript to potential buyers effected general publication.

(C) 1962. The offering of copies of the novel exclusively to Bi-Monthly Book Club members effected general publication.

(D) 1963. The release of a motion picture resulting from the purchase of the motion picture rights to *Clouded Sunset* effected general publication.

V-7. In 1970, Zealot becomes convinced that he has found the one true path to enlightenment. That same year, he writes and self-publishes a pamphlet proclaiming this fact, and leaves a thousand copies of the pamphlet at bus stops, libraries, and other public places throughout Zealot's local area. Soon thereafter, Zealot learns that he inadvertently failed to attach a copyright notice to nine hundred copies of the pamphlet. Zealot has never registered the copyright in the contents of the pamphlet. Are the contents of the pamphlet forfeited to the public domain?

(A) Yes. By releasing physical copies of the pamphlet to the general public, the vast majority of which lacked notice, Zealot has forfeited the contents of the pamphlet to the public domain.

(B) Yes. Zealot's failure to register the copyright in his literary work prevented the curing of the omission of copyright notice.

(C) No. By including notice on even a single copy, Zealot preserved his copyright in the pamphlet's contents.

(D) No. Because Zealot's failure to include copyright notice was inadvertent, it cannot result in forfeiture of his copyright.

V-8. Consider question V-7. Assume that instead of including notice on only 100 out of a thousand pamphlets, Zealot left notice off of only ten of the thousand pamphlets. In light of this change, would the contents of Zealot's pamphlet still be forfeited to the public domain?

ANSWER:

V-9. In 1982, Writer wrote a short story using her personal computer. In 1998, Thief stole her computer, discovered the file on the hard drive containing Writer's short story, and posted the file on the Internet, all without Writer's knowledge. Did this act amount to a publication of Writer's literary work?

(A) Yes, because it was a general release of a physical instantiation of the work.

(B) Yes, because the dissemination of a work on the Internet always constitutes a general publication.

(C) No, because posting material on the Internet does not count as publication since it was not explicitly contemplated by the 1976 Copyright Act.

(D) No, because the dissemination of the short story was not with Writer's consent.

V-10. In 1980, Novelist released her self-published literary work, *American She*. Novelist failed to place copyright notice on any of the thousands of copies of her work sold to the public in California, the state of her birth. The work has not been registered. Which of the following statements most accurately describes the status of Novelist's copyright in *American She*?

(A) *American She* is irrevocably part of the public domain.

(B) *American She* is in the public domain now, but Novelist can reclaim it if she takes steps sufficient to cure her original omission of copyright notice.

(C) The copyright in *American She* was restored to Novelist pursuant to section 104A of the 1976 Copyright Act on January 1, 1996.

(D) *American She* is protected by copyright and will remain so regardless of whether Novelist adds any copyright notice.

V-11. Consider question V-10. Assume that all the facts remain the same, except that Novelist publishes *American She* in 1995 rather than 1980. How would this change in the facts affect the copyright status of the novel?

ANSWER:

V-12. Under the 1976 Copyright Act, which of the following most accurately describes a copyright owner's obligations upon publication of a work of authorship?

(A) The copyright owner must register the work with the Copyright Office and deposit two copies of the work with the Library of Congress.

(B) The copyright owner must register the work with the Copyright Office.

(C) The copyright owner must deposit one copy of the work with the Library of Congress.

(D) The copyright owner is under no affirmative obligations pursuant to the 1976 Copyright Act.

V-13. Author outlines the detailed plot for his next novel and unsuccessfully attempts to register the outline with the Copyright Office as a literary work. A few months later, Author discovers that Poseur has been claiming as his own a very similar plot outline. Author wants to sue Poseur for copyright infringement. Will Author be able to file suit?

(A) Yes. Author will be able to file suit because the act of registration is unrelated to Author's ability to file an infringement suit.

(B) Yes. Author will be able to file suit, but only if he notifies the Copyright Office of the lawsuit and provides it with a copy of the complaint.

(C) No. The Copyright Office's rejection of Author's application for registration means copyright has not vested in the work.

(D) No. Registration is a jurisdictional prerequisite for copyright enforcement, so Author's failure to attain registration means that he will not be able to file an infringement action in federal court.

V-14. Your client, Author, comes to you and says, "I've read a bit about copyright law, and it appears that I have a copyright without having to go through all the rigmarole of registration. I'm going to save myself the registration fee and a whole lot of hassle, and not register my latest novel." How should you advise Author? In particular, of which particular advantages of copyright registration should you advise your client?

ANSWER:

V-15. Owner sues Pirate for infringing the copyright in Owner's musical work. At trial, Owner places into evidence a copyright registration certificate, which she obtained two years after creation of the musical work in suit. What, if any, evidentiary advantage does Owner gain by doing this?

(A) The registration certificate is irrebuttable evidence of the copyright's validity.

(B) The registration certificate creates a rebuttable presumption of the copyright's validity.

(C) The registration certificate shifts the burden of proof to Pirate to show that he has not infringed Owner's copyright.

(D) The trial judge has the discretion to determine whether the registration certificate creates a rebuttable presumption of copyright validity.

V-16. Screenwriter spent several years polishing a screenplay, titled *Fast Track*, that she eventually licensed to De Marco Studios in 1961. Pursuant to its exclusive motion picture license, which encompassed the initial term of copyright protection, renewals, and all extensions, De Marco Studios produced a motion picture, *Clashing Clouds*, that it released for exhibition in 1962. The motion picture included all of the copyrightable elements contained in *Fast Track* and was accompanied by a copyright notice that read: Copyright 1962, De Marco Studios. Screenwriter has never filed a document regarding her *Fast Track* screenplay with the Copyright Office. Screenwriter has never authorized any additional uses of *Fast Track*. De Marco Studios filed a proper application for renewal of registration for the copyright in *Clashing Clouds* in 1989.

Recently, Cinemasters Publishing has published a compilation of highly regarded motion picture scripts from the 1960s, including *Fast Track*. Cinemasters Publishing has not obtained permission from Screenwriter to use *Fast Track*. Should Screenwriter decide to sue Cinemasters Publishing for copyright infringement, would her action be successful?

ANSWER:

VI-1. Architect created an original architectural drawing in 2001. Architect died in 2006 leaving in her will the copyright to the architectural school from which she received her Bachelor of Architecture degree. Architect had no children. Architect's husband, Widower, has filed an action in United States District Court requesting that the court declare Widower the owner of the copyright in the architectural drawing. Will Widower be successful?

(A) No, because any legal issue regarding the interpretation of a bequest via will must be determined by a state court.

(B) No, because ownership of the copyright in the architectural drawing was vested in Architect at the time the work was created in 2001.

(C) Yes, because Widower has priority of ownership as a statutory successor.

(D) Yes, because any bequest of a copyright via will must be made to a person, not an institution.

VI-2. A novel was both registered with the Copyright Office and published in 1922. The copyright in the novel was properly renewed. The author of the novel died in 1940. When did or will the copyright protection for the novel end?

(A) At the end of 2010.

(B) At the end of 2017.

(C) At the end of 1997.

(D) At the end of 1978.

VI-3. Poet wrote a poem in 1950. The poem was never published and its copyright was never registered. No renewal of copyright was ever filed with the Copyright Office. Poet died in 1970. The copyright in the poem did/will expire:

(A) At the end of 2047.

(B) At the end of 2002.

(C) At the end of 1978.

(D) At the end of 2040.

VI-4. Novelist published her novel with proper copyright notice in 1958, but never registered the copyright in the novel with the Copyright Office. Novelist died in 1984, survived only by her Son. In her will, Novelist left the copyright in the novel, including the remainder of the initial term of copyright, as well as all renewals and extensions, to her Neighbor. In 1986, the twenty-eighth year of the initial term of copyright, Son and Neighbor each file a copyright renewal application with the Copyright Office. Who owns the copyright in the novel until the copyright expires?

ANSWER:

VI-5. A work was published with proper copyright notice in 1908 and properly renewed. The copyright in the work did/will expire at the end of what year?

(A) 1983.

(B) 1964.

(C) 2003.

(D) 1997.

VI-6. A novel was written by Author in 1863. The manuscript was left in a desk drawer until it was discovered by Author's nephew in 1991. Author died in 1905. The novel was first published in 1994. Copyright protection for the novel:

(A) Never existed.

(B) Will expire at the end of 2047.

(C) Ended on January 1, 1978.

(D) Expired at the end of 2002.

VI-7. Composer entered into a work for hire agreement in 1955 to compose a music score for a motion picture produced and released by Film Studio that same year. Five years later, Film Studio assigned the copyright in the music score to Composer, who immediately assigned the copyright in the music score to Music Publisher. Can Composer terminate the grant of rights to Music Publisher?

(A) Yes, because the agreement Composer seeks to terminate is not a work made for hire agreement.

(B) Yes, because Composer regained the status of author through the 1960 assignment from Film Studio.

(C) No, because grants of copyright in works made for hire are not eligible for termination.

(D) No, because only the first transfer of copyright after a work is created can be terminated.

VI-8. In 1905, Photographer took a photograph of a group of his fellow employees at the Artistic Studio, owned by Employer. The photograph was a work for hire. Photographer died in

1934. The photograph was hung on the wall of Employer's private office until his death in 1954. The photograph was first published in 2004 as part of a collection of turn of the century photographs. At the end of what year did/will the photograph's copyright protection cease?

(A) 1961.

(B) 2004.

(C) 2025.

(D) 2099.

VI-9. In 1980, Author and Collaborator write a screenplay together, explicitly taking on the status of joint authors. In 1985, Author and Collaborator are in an accident. Author dies immediately, while Collaborator lingers on for another five years, ultimately dying in 1990. Author and Collaborator have each left their estates, including all of their copyrights, to CharityCo, their favorite nonprofit organization. When does the copyright in the screenplay expire?

(A) 2050.

(B) 2055.

(C) 2060.

(D) It does not expire because it is now owned by a corporation that lacks a natural life to create an expiration date.

VI-10. The literary work, *Stubbed Life* was written by Author in 1995. In 2000, *Stubbed Life* was released, but under the name "Pseudonym," which is also the name under which the work is registered with the Copyright Office. No one ever found out that Author actually wrote *Stubbed Life*, and the secret died with Author in 2005. At the end of what year does the copyright in *Stubbed Life* expire?

(A) 2070.

(B) 2075.

(C) 2095.

(D) 2115.

VI-11. Consider question VI-10. Assume that in 2004, Author changed the name in which the work was registered from "Pseudonym" to his own, and then died the next year. Author's identity did not become widespread public knowledge until 2015, when a scholar researching Author's life discovers the revised copyright registration. In light of these revised facts, when would the term of copyright in *Stubbed Life* expire?

ANSWER:

VI-12.   Artist created a painting titled *Nocturne in Blue* on January 1, 1980, but kept the work in his private studio without showing it to the public until May 1, 1985, when he included the work in a public showing and registered it with the Copyright Office. Artist died on June 1, 1990, bequeathing all of his copyrights to his heirs. Fast forward to September 1, 2060, when Joe Public makes unauthorized reproductions of *Nocturne in Blue* and starts selling them to the public. The heirs of Artist's estate claim that Joe Public has infringed their copyright in the work. Assuming that United States copyright law regarding the length of copyright protection has not changed in the intervening years, will Artist's heirs prevail?

  (A)   No, the work has been in the public domain since June 1, 2060.

  (B)   No, the work has been in the public domain since 2055.

  (C)   Yes, the unpublished work has perpetual copyright protection.

  (D)   Yes, the work is protected until December 31, 2060.

VI-13.   Writer composes a poem in 1930. He never shows it to anyone, instead keeping it in his desk drawer. Writer then dies in 1935. At the end of what year does federal copyright in the poem expire?

  (A)   1958.

  (B)   1986.

  (C)   2002.

  (D)   2005.

VI-14.   Writer composes a play in 1910, but is not convinced of its quality, and puts it aside without ever showing it to anyone. It remains in his desk drawer through his death in 1920, and now exists only as a part of his personal effects. In 2005, one of Writer's heirs discovers the play and wonders whether it is still protected by copyright. Is it?

  (A)   No, copyright in the play expired at the end of 1938.

  (B)   No, copyright in the play expired at the end of 1990.

  (C)   No, copyright in the play expired at the end of 2002.

  (D)   Yes, the play is still protected by copyright.

VI-15.   Consider question VI-14. Assume instead that Writer's heir found his ancestor's play in 2000 and published it the next year. How, if at all, would this change the duration of copyright protection?

ANSWER:

VI-16.   Musician composes the musical work *Summer Rapture* in 1910 and registers the work the same year. He renews the copyright in 1938, then dies in 1950. At the end of what year does the copyright in *Summer Rapture* expire?

(A) 1966.

(B) 1985.

(C) 2002.

(D) 2020.

VI-17. Artist creates an original painting titled *House in the Woods* in 1960, and secures a valid federal copyright in the work that same year. Artist then dies intestate in 1985, survived only by his ex-wife, their son, and a single grandchild. In 1987, the twenty-eighth year of copyright protection, a dispute erupts as to which of Artist's heirs are entitled to renew the copyright in *House in the Woods* and possess the rights to its renewal term. Which of the following individuals will prevail?

(A) Artist's son.

(B) Artist's ex-wife.

(C) The executor of Artist's estate.

(D) Artist's grandson.

VI-18. Consider question VI-17. Assume instead that Artist has an ex-wife, a widow, a son, a daughter, and two grandchildren. In light of this change, who owns the renewal rights to *House in the Woods*?

ANSWER:

VI-19. In 1955, BizCorp ordered one of its employees, Writer, to write a book chronicling the history of the company. BizCorp then assigned the rights in the literary work to Magazine Publisher. Magazine Publisher died in 1970, leaving all of his estate to Heir. Assuming that the literary work was a work for hire, who owns the rights in the renewal term?

(A) BizCorp.

(B) Writer.

(C) Magazine Publisher.

(D) Heir.

VI-20. Consider question VI-19. Assume that the proprietor of the copyright in the literary work at issue failed to renew the copyright in its twenty-eighth year of protection (1983). What are the implications of this failure?

ANSWER:

VI-21. Sculptor created a sculptural work titled *Elk at Rest* in 1970, and obtained a valid federal copyright in the work that same year. In the twenty-eighth year of the work's copyright (1997), Sculptor did not file a renewal application with the Copyright Office. At the end of which year did or will *Elk at Rest* enter the public domain?

    (A) 1998.

    (B) 2026.

    (C) 2045.

    (D) 2065.

VI-22. Writer penned a screenplay in 1942, and registered it with the Copyright Office that same year. Writer subsequently fell on hard times and assigned to Shyster the remainder of the initial term, the renewal term, and the right of renewal in the copyright for $10,000. Writer's downward spiral continued and ended with his death in 1958. During the twenty-eighth year of copyright in the screenplay (1960), a dispute arises between Shyster and Writer's statutory successor about which of them is the true owner of the copyright. Which of the following statements most accurately reflects the relative interests in the copyright?

    (A) Writer's statutory successor owns the right of renewal; Shyster owns the initial term.

    (B) Writer's statutory successor owns the right of renewal and the initial term; Shyster owns nothing.

    (C) Writer's statutory successor owns the renewal term; Shyster owns the right of renewal and the initial term.

    (D) Writer's statutory successor owns nothing; Shyster owns the right of renewal and the initial term.

VI-23. Consider question VI-22. Assume that Writer died in 1961 rather than 1958. How, if at all, would this change the analysis regarding ownership of the copyright?

ANSWER:

VI-24. In 1966, Author published a novel entitled, *Empire*, with valid copyright notice. The novel becomes a bestseller and, in 1970, De Marco Studios entered into a licensing agreement with Author. The agreement stated that, in exchange for a substantial fee, De Marco Studios was given the exclusive right to adapt *Empire* into a screenplay and to make a motion picture based on that screenplay. The resulting motion picture, titled *The Simmering Sun*, was released in 1973 and became a critical and commercial success. In 1992, Author died without known heirs or will. Then, in 1999, Daughter announced that she has just learned through a DNA test that she is the daughter of Author, born out of wedlock. Daughter sues De Marco Studios for copyright infringement based on its continued exploitation of the film version of *Empire*. Will Daughter prevail on this argument?

(A)   Yes. Author's death before the end of the initial term of protection means that his statutory successor owns the copyright to *Empire*, which in turn means that Daughter controls the rights to *Empire*, even to the exploitation of preexisting derivative works.

(B)   Yes. Author's death before the end of the initial term of protection automatically terminated all licensing agreements he had with the makers of derivative works based on *Empire*, so that new licenses must be negotiated with his statutory successor.

(C)   No. Author's death before the end of the initial term of protection gave his statutory successor control over preexisting derivative works only if the successor affirmatively filed for renewal of the copyright in *Empire* during the twenty-eighth year of copyright protection.

(D)   No. Author's death before the end of the initial term of protection allows his statutory successor to exercise control only over future, not preexisting, derivative works based on *Empire*.

VI-25.   Consider question VI-24. Assume that Daughter appeared in 1996, and that she affirmatively filed for renewal of the copyright in *Empire* in the twenty-eighth year of protection (1997). How, if at all, would this change the analysis of her ability to force De Marco Studios to negotiate new licenses for its continued exploitation of preexisting derivative works based on *Empire*?

ANSWER:

VI-26.   Musician composed the musical work *Blue Betty* in 1980. In 1985, Musician granted to Production Company the exclusive right to use *Blue Betty* as theme music for the *Beautiful Betty* television series. In 1990, Musician died, leaving a widow and two sons. What is the earliest year in which the assignment can, if at all, be terminated?

(A)   2015.

(B)   2020.

(C)   2041.

(D)   It cannot be terminated because termination can be effected only by a work's author, and here the author is deceased.

VI-27.   Consider question VI-26. In light of Musician's death, which of the following individuals can effect termination of the assignment to Studio?

(A)   The assignment can be terminated by Musician's widow alone.

(B)   The assignment can be terminated by Musician's widow acting alone or by both of Musician's sons acting together.

(C)   The assignment can be terminated by Musician's widow acting together with one or both of Musician's sons.

(D)   Termination is not possible via any of these combinations.

VI-28.   Consider question VI-26. Assume that Musician composed *Blue Betty* not in 1980, but in 1970, and that federal statutory copyright in the musical work vested that same year. How would this change effect the termination date of the grant?

ANSWER:

VI-29.   Author penned a novel titled *Molto Maria* in 1990. In 1995, Author died, and his copyright in *Molto Maria* was left to his sole heir, Son. On December 5, 2000, Son granted to Producer an exclusive license to create a screenplay based on *Molto Maria*. When is the earliest date on which Son can terminate this license?

(A)   December 5, 2025.

(B)   December 5, 2030.

(C)   December 5, 2035.

(D)   The license is not terminable.

VI-30.   Consider question VI-29. Assume instead that Author's copyright in *Molto Maria* vested in 1960, that Author died in 1965, again leaving Son as his sole heir, and that Son executed an exclusive perpetual license to create a screenplay based on *Molto Maria* with Screenwriter on July 10, 1970. Assume further that Son exercised his right to renew the copyright in *Molto Maria* during its twenty-eighth year of copyright protection (1987). In light of these changes, what would be the earliest date on which the exclusive license could be terminated, if at all?

ANSWER:

VI-31.   Federal copyright in Poet's epic verse saga *Great Plains* vested in 1940. In 1950, Poet transferred all rights in the initial and renewal term, as well as the right of renewal, to Publisher. Publisher proceeded to commission, as a work for hire, a prose version of *Great Plains* titled *Greater Plains*. Federal copyright in the derivative work *Greater Plains*, over which Publisher retains full ownership, vested in 1960. Publisher validly renewed the copyrights in both *Great Plains* and *Greater Plains*. Poet died in 1990. Six years later his sole statutory successor, Heir, successfully terminated Poet's 1950 assignment of the copyright in *Great Plains* to Publisher. Heir seeks from Publisher all profits from any post-termination exploitation of *Greater Plains*. Will this argument succeed?

(A)   Yes. The termination of the transfer in the underlying work, *Great Plains*, gives Heir full rights to any profits from the exploitation of derivative works, such as *Greater Plains*, post-termination.

(B) Yes. The termination of the transfer in the underlying work, *Great Plains*, automatically causes copyright in any derivative works created pursuant to the 1950 agreement to revert to Heir.

(C) No. While termination of the transfer causes ownership of the copyright in the underlying work, *Great Plains*, to revert to Heir, this does not affect derivative works such as *Greater Plains*, which Publisher remains free to continue to exploit as it did pre-termination.

(D) No. Termination of transfer in underlying works like *Great Plains* do not prevent transferees from exploiting derivative works created pre-termination or creating new derivative works based on those pre-termination derivative works.

VI-32. Musician composed the musical work *Andalucia* in 1934 and then registered the work with the Copyright Office the same year. Five years later, Musician assigned all rights in the initial and renewal term of copyright to Music Publisher, which was also given a power of attorney to renew the copyright in *Andalucia* in Musician's name. Subsequently, Music Publisher permitted RecordCo to record *Andalucia*, in 1940, which proved to be commercially successful. Music Publisher properly renewed the copyright in the musical work's twenty-eighth year of protection (1961). Musician died in 1970, and his lone statutory successor, Heir, successfully terminated the transfer of *Andalucia* to Music Publisher in 1991. After the termination, Heir assigned all right, title, and interest to the copyright in *Andalucia* to Music Town Publishing for a large advance against royalties. RecordCo has continued to sell its 1940 recording of *Andalucia*. Music Town Publishing now claims that it should receive the mechanical license fees generated by the post-termination sales of RecordCo's recording of *Andalucia*. Will Music Town Publishing prevail?

(A) Yes. Due to Heir's termination of the 1939 transfer to Music Publisher and post-termination assignment to Music Town Publishing, Music Town Publishing is entitled to all post-termination mechanical license fees generated by the exploitation of the copyright in the *Andalucia* musical work.

(B) No. Heir's termination of the 1939 transfer to Music Publisher and post-termination assignment to Music Town Publishing entitles Music Town Publishing to all mechanical license fees generated by any new use or new recording of the *Andalucia* musical work, but not recordings of the work exploited in the same manner that took place pre-termination.

(C) Yes. Heir's termination of the 1939 transfer to Music Publisher requires it to disgorge to Heir or his assigns all past and future mechanical license fees derived from the sales of recordings of *Andalucia*.

(D) No. Termination of the 1939 transfer to Music Publisher does not entitle Heir or his assigns to any of the mechanical license fees generated by any past or future exploitation of recordings of *Andalucia* permitted by Music Publisher, though it does entitle Heir or his assigns to license other record companies to use the work.

VI-33. Composer created the musical work *Dancing Shoes*, for which federal copyright vested in 1933. Composer then assigned all rights in *Dancing Shoes* to MusicCo in 1935. In 1990, Composer sought to terminate the assignment of *Dancing Shoes* to MusicCo pursuant to section 304(c) of the Copyright Act. MusicCo claimed the attempted termination was invalid. To support this argument, it pointed to language in the 1935 assignment agreement stating that in addition to assigning the copyright in *Dancing Shoes*, Composer also assigned "any future rights of termination" to MusicCo. Because Composer no longer possesses any termination rights, MusicCo's lawyers reasoned, he cannot exercise them to terminate the assignment. Will this argument prevail?

(A) Yes. Termination rights, like all the statutory privileges granted to authors pursuant to the Copyright Act, can be freely sold, devised, or assigned.

(B) Yes. Termination rights can be alienated as long as the party alienating them is the original author.

(C) No. Termination rights can be assigned, but only to individuals, not to corporate entities.

(D) No. Termination rights are inalienable and cannot be assigned by contract.

VI-34. Consider question VI-33. In attempting to effect termination, Composer served on MusicCo a written, signed notification on July 31, 1986, stating "I hereby give notice of my intent to terminate the 1935 transfer of all copyright interest in the musical work 'Dancing Shoes,' effective January 1, 1990." On January 2, 1990, Composer recorded the notice with the Copyright Office. Later in 1990, MusicCo argued that the termination was unenforceable because the notice was procedurally invalid. Will it prevail?

(A) Yes. The notice was invalid because it was recorded after, not before, the effective date of the termination.

(B) No. The intent of Composer to terminate the 1935 grant was sufficiently evidenced by the July 31, 1986 notice.

(C) Yes. The notice was invalid because it was served too far in advance of the date of termination.

(D) No. The notice was entirely valid.

VI-35. Consider question VI-33. If, for whatever reason, a court were to find that Composer's attempt to terminate the transfer of copyright in *Dancing Shoes* to MusicCo was invalid, would this mean that MusicCo would then be the owner of the copyright for the rest of its term?

ANSWER:

VII-1. Motion Picture Studio has entered into an agreement with Distributor that grants Distributor an exclusive license to distribute DVD copies of a motion picture in the United States for five years. Five years have recently passed and the Distributor has continued to sell DVD copies of the motion picture in the United States without the authorization of Motion Picture Studio. Can Motion Picture Studio successfully sue Distributor for copyright infringement?

    (A)   No, because Motion Picture Studio no longer owns the distribution right to the motion picture.

    (B)   No, because the termination right may be exercised by Motion Picture Studio only after thirty-five years from the date of the grant.

    (C)   Yes, because copyright infringement is the only remedy available to Motion Picture Studio.

    (D)   Yes, because Distributor has continued to distribute the motion picture after the license has terminated.

VII-2. Author pens a popular novel, then grants to Production Company an exclusive license to develop the novel into a screenplay for a flat fee. Later, Whanna Bee sells to Studio a screenplay that is based directly on Author's novel, which was created without permission. Who has standing to sue Whanna Bee for infringing the copyright in the novel?

    (A)   Author.

    (B)   Production Company.

    (C)   Author and Production Company.

    (D)   Neither Author nor Production Company.

VII-3. Consider question VII-2. Subsequent to granting the exclusive license to Production Company, Author has been approached by Book Publisher which seeks an exclusive license to translate and publish the novel in Spanish. Does Author have the right to grant such a license to Book Publisher?

ANSWER:

VII-4. Consider question VII-2. Assume that instead of assigning an exclusive license to Production Company to develop a screenplay based on his novel, Author granted to Production Company a nonexclusive license to develop a screenplay based on his novel. In light of this variation, who would have standing to sue Whanna Bee?

ANSWER:

VII-5. Composer created the musical work *Red Rhapsody* in 2000. Two years later, in 2002, he assigned the copyright in the musical work in its entirety to Lyrical Publishing, a music publisher. The agreement stated that in exchange for the assignment, Composer will receive fifty percent of the proceeds from any exploitation of the *Red Rhapsody* musical work. *Red Rhapsody* has not generated much revenue. Recently, it has come to the attention of Composer that a musical work written and recorded by Lil Flasher, *Blue Thug Lullaby*, includes melody and lyrics that are substantially similar to those in *Red Rhapsody*. When Composer brought his concerns to the attention of Lyrical Publishing, the company responded that it did not believe the two compositions were similar and that it would not file a copyright infringement action. Composer, noting that Lil Flasher is signed to a recording contract with a record company affiliated with Lyrical Publishing, has decided to bring a copyright infringement action against Lil Flasher and her music publishing company, Flasher Music. Will Composer be successful?

(A) No, because Lyrical Publishing has determined that the two music compositions were not substantially similar.

(B) No, because Composer has assigned the entirety of the copyright in *Red Rhapsody* to Lyrical Publishing and has no standing to bring a copyright infringement action.

(C) Yes, because Lyrical Publishing is merely administering Composer's music catalog and is not able to bring an action for copyright infringement.

(D) Yes, because Composer is a beneficial owner who has standing to sue Lil Flasher and Flasher Music for copyright infringement.

VII-6. Big Biz is a rap artist whose recent single, *In tha Biz* has enjoyed enormous popularity. Recently, Big Biz was sued in federal district court by his longtime collaborator, Pen E. Wise, who claims that she is entitled to a share of the royalties generated by *In tha Biz*. Wise claims that Biz assigned half the royalties in the musical work to her. Biz claims that the assignment agreement produced by Wise is invalid. Biz further argues that, even if the assignment agreement were valid, it cannot be construed to grant Wise more than twenty percent of the royalties generated by *In tha Biz*. Wise also argues in the alternative that she should receive half of the royalties generated by *In tha Biz* because she is a joint author of the musical work as defined by the Copyright Act. Biz has moved to have the case dismissed for lack of federal jurisdiction. How should the judge rule on Biz's motion?

(A) All of Wise's claims can be heard in federal court.

(B) A federal court can hear the claim based on a construction of the Copyright Act, but not the claims based on the validity of the assignment or the construction of the assignment.

(C)   A federal court can hear the claim based on a construction of the Copyright Act, and the claim based on the validity of the assignment, but not the claim based on the construction of the assignment.

(D)   None of Wise's claims can be heard in federal court.

VII-7.   Author has sued User for copyright infringement in federal district court. Author seeks both statutory damages from User and a permanent injunction ordering User to cease his allegedly infringing conduct. As the matter proceeds to trial, User moves to have the case heard by a jury rather than the judge. What will be the result of User's motion?

(A)   The judge will deny the motion and conduct a bench trial on both issues.

(B)   The judge will grant the motion for a jury trial as to statutory damages, but will rule on the issue of injunctive relief from the bench.

(C)   The judge will grant the motion for a jury trial as to injunctive relief, but will rule on the issue of statutory damages from the bench.

(D)   The judge will grant the motion and conduct a jury trial on both issues.

VII-8.   DistroCo is a film distribution company, based in the United States, with both domestic and international operations. DistroCo's subsidiary, EuroDistro, has begun to distribute Studio's hit film, *Action Man*, on DVD to retail stores, though without obtaining permission from Studio to do so. EuroDistro obtained a copy of *Action Man* in France and manufactures its DVDs in Germany. EuroDistro's range of distribution extends only to Western Europe, and none of its conduct takes place in the United States. Studio sues DistroCo and EuroDistro in United States federal district court for violating its exclusive right of public distribution. Will Studio prevail?

(A)   Yes. This is a clear violation of Studio's exclusive right of public distribution.

(B)   Yes. Although normally extraterritorial conduct is not actionable under United States copyright law, there is an exception where, as here, the conduct is that of a subsidiary whose parent is domestically based.

(C)   No. United States copyright law has no application to acts that take place entirely outside its borders.

(D)   No. EuroDistro's conduct does not amount to a "public distribution" within the meaning of the Copyright Act.

VII-9.   Consider question VII-8. Assume that Studio discovers that DistroCo, acting out of its main office in New York, explicitly authorized EuroDistro to engage in the unlicensed reproduction and distribution of *Action Man* throughout Western Europe. How, if at all, does this affect Studio's ability to bring a copyright infringement suit, based on United States copyright law, against DistroCo in United States federal district court?

ANSWER:

VII-10. *Le Courant* is a French-language newspaper produced in Quebec City, Canada, and distributed almost exclusively within the Canadian province of Quebec. Yves Anglais, a freelance reporter, researched and wrote a devastating story about overfishing in the Great Lakes that was published in *Le Courant*. The next week, an English translation of the article appeared in the St. Louis *Post-Journal*, under the byline of *Post-Journal* reporter John Smith. Smith did not seek permission or a license from *Le Courant* or Anglais before publishing the piece, instead assuming that no one would find out about his plagiarism, allowing him to take credit for the story. However, both *Le Courant* and Anglais discovered Smith's conduct, and each filed suit against Smith in United States federal court. The suits were joined by the district court judge in order to address the related question whether *Le Courant* or Anglais owns the copyright in the original article. Which country's law applies to each of the critical issues in this case: ownership of the copyright and copyright infringement?

(A) Canadian copyright law governs the ownership issue; American copyright law governs the infringement issue.

(B) Canadian copyright law governs both the ownership and the infringement issue.

(C) American copyright law governs the ownership issue; Canadian copyright law governs the infringement issue.

(D) American copyright law governs both the ownership and the infringement issue.

VII-11. Hot Ten is a website that hosts photos of models in swimsuits. Hot Ten earns profits based on charging users a monthly fee to access its site. Payment of the fee provides users with access to view pictures only and does not extend to users the right to download or distribute Hot Ten's copyrighted photos. Hot Ten has discovered that one authorized user, Alex Brown, has been downloading Hot Ten's photos and storing them on his personal computer. Brown has not carefully read his user agreement with Hot Ten and knows nothing about copyright law, and believes in good faith that he is free to download the images to his own computer. Brown does not have any intention of distributing the photographs to the public. Hot Ten sues Brown, alleging that his unauthorized reproduction of its copyrighted photos amounts to infringement. Who will prevail?

(A) Brown. Personal use of copyrighted works is a full defense to infringement.

(B) Brown. Brown's intent not to distribute means that his downloading of the photos could cause Hot Ten no harm, therefore, his conduct does not amount to infringement.

(C) Hot Ten. While Brown's conduct would not normally amount to infringement, the fact that he violated the user agreement makes it a copyright issue.

(D) Hot Ten. Copyright infringement is a strict liability offense, so Brown's good faith is not a defense to what is otherwise a prima facie case of infringement.

VII-12. Consider question VII-11. Assume that in addition to suing user Alex Brown for copyright infringement, Hot Ten also sues NationOnLine (NOL), the Internet service provider that Alex uses to connect to the Internet. If all of Alex's allegedly infringing conduct related to his downloading of Hot Ten's copyrighted photographs occurred while accessing the internet over NOL, and if Alex's conduct amounts to infringement, would NOL also be liable to Hot Ten on a direct infringement theory?

ANSWER:

VII-13. Musician creates the melody and harmony for an original musical work. At Musician's request, Lyricist writes lyrics to accompany Musician's music. The resulting work is a musical composition for piano and vocalist titled *View From My Window*. Musician wastes no time in booking shows around the city where she performs both the musical and lyrical components of *View From My Window*, all without asking Lyricist's permission. When Lyricist confronts Musician about the issue, Musician tells him, "Too bad. It's my work too and I can do what I want with it. And the proceeds from the performances are all mine because I did the shows. If you want to make money performing our work, you're free to go out and do it." Incensed, Lyricist sues Musician. Will Lyricist prevail, and if so, on what theories?

(A) Lyricist can show that Musician violated his exclusive right of public performance.

(B) Lyricist can show that Musician is obligated to give him half of the profits derived from the use of *View From My Window* in her public performances because of the common-law duties of co-owners.

(C) Lyricist can show both that Musician violated his exclusive right of public performance, and also that Musician is obligated to give him half of the profits derived from the use of *View From My Window* in her public performances because of the common-law duties of co-owners.

(D) Lyricist has no valid cause of action against Musician.

VII-14. Author discovers that his literary work, *Big Fun in Little Siam*, has been infringed. The CEO of major movie studio G-M-G purchased one copy of Author's published novel, photocopied it several times, and distributed the copies to a team of five screenwriters G-M-G has hired, telling them to collaborate on a screenplay version of the literary work, all unbeknownst to Author. G-M-G has now produced a screenplay version of *Big Fun in Little Siam*, though it has yet to start production of the motion picture that will be based on it. Author files a copyright infringement suit against G-M-G's CEO, but not against G-M-G itself. Will he prevail?

(A) Yes. CEO violated Author's right both to reproduce *Big Fun in Little Siam*, and to authorize adaptations of it.

(B) Yes. Although CEO was entitled to make copies of Author's novel pursuant to the first sale doctrine, he violated Author's exclusive right to authorize adaptations of the literary work.

(C) No. Where infringement by a corporation is at issue, only the corporate entity itself can be held liable, not any of the corporate officers who engage in the infringement.

(D) No. Where infringement by multiple parties, such as, here, a corporation and one of its officers, is at issue, all parties must be joined or the suit lacks standing to proceed in federal court.

VII-15. Author creates the original musical work *Blue Skies* in 1990, first publishing it that same year. He obtains registration for the work from the Copyright Office in 1993. In 1996, Author sues User for sampling part of *Blue Skies* in User's sound recording *Red Seas*. At the onset of litigation, Author produced his copyright registration certificate as evidence of his ownership of the work. Later, User moved for summary judgment, producing a valid agreement, dated 1995, transferring ownership of *Blue Skies* from Author to User. Author argues that his infringement suit should survive summary judgment on the strength of the registration certificate alone. Will he prevail?

(A) Yes. The presumption of valid ownership created by a copyright registration certificate can be overcome only at trial.

(B) Yes. Timely filing a registration certificate amounts to incontrovertible proof of copyright ownership.

(C) No. In order for a registration certificate to provide prima facie proof of validity, it must be filed within a year of first publication.

(D) No. Although a registration certificate filed within five years of first publication amounts to prima facie proof of copyright validity, this rebuttable presumption may be overcome by the submission of sufficient evidence to the contrary.

VII-16. Writer has filed an infringement suit against Pirate. Writer argues that Pirate's literary work *Bells for Lou* infringes Writer's literary work, *Lulubelle*. Among the various arguments Pirate advances at trial to resist infringement liability is that Pirate had no access to *Lulubelle* prior to creating *Bells for Lou*. In opposition to this claim, Writer produces evidence indicating that Pirate had a reasonable opportunity to read *Lulubelle* prior to creating *Bells for Lou*, though Writer cannot show with certainty that Pirate actually did read *Lulubelle*. Who will prevail on the access issue?

(A) Pirate. In the absence of any evidence that Pirate actually read *Lulubelle* before creating *Bells for Lou*, an independent creation defense will succeed.

(B) Pirate. Because Writer bears a particularly high burden of proof on the access issue, which is clearly not met here.

(C) Writer. Writer need only produce evidence that Pirate had a reasonable opportunity to read *Lulubelle* before creating *Bells for Lou*, and he has met this burden.

(D) Writer. While Writer cannot successfully show access, this is irrelevant because access is a relatively minor consideration in copyright infringement suits.

VII-17. Consider question VII-16. Assume instead that the only evidence of access that Writer produces is that when Writer first published *Lulubelle*, he sent a copy of the novel to Sid Bishop, a literary agent at the Creative House Publishing, during the time Pirate worked part-time as a manuscript reviewer in Sid's department. Writer produces no direct evidence that Pirate actually saw or read

Lulubelle. On these facts, and only these facts, could Writer successfully show that Pirate had a sufficient degree of access to *Lulubelle* to support a finding of infringement?

ANSWER:

VII-18. Consider question VII-16. Assume instead that the only evidence of access that Writer produces is that *Lulubelle* enjoyed commercial success, climbing into the top ten of many nationally prominent bestseller lists and earning its author both literary and popular acclaim. Writer produces no direct evidence that Pirate actually saw or read *Lulubelle*. On these facts, and only these facts, could Writer successfully prove that Pirate had a sufficient degree of access to *Lulubelle* to support a finding of infringement?

ANSWER:

VII-19. Artist created an original painting titled *Man Overboard* that depicts a view of Niagara Falls. The background and major setting for the picture is the standard view of Niagara Falls that one sees when one stands on the main observation deck. However, Artist added to his picture a distinctive original element: a horrified-looking, black-haired man in a brown rowboat plunging to his demise, halfway down the waterfall. Artist has accused Painter of copying *Man Overboard*. Painter has created a painting, *Overboard Man*, that is also set in Niagara Falls from the perspective of the main observation deck. Painter's work also depicts a horrified-looking man in a rowboat plunging to his demise, halfway down the waterfall. Painter's work depicts the man identically, except that in Painter's work the man has brown (not black) hair, and is in a black (not brown) rowboat. Will Artist be able to successfully argue that Painter's *Overboard Man* is substantially similar to his *Man Overboard*?

    (A)   Yes, because the setting Painter has chosen is identical to the one Artist has chosen.

    (B)   Yes, because the falling man is an original element of Artist's work, and Painter's depiction of that element is substantially similar.

    (C)   No, because the two works are not completely identical.

    (D)   No, because the similarity of the two works consists largely of a public domain element.

VII-20. Boney Eagle is an old-school skateboarder and filmmaker who created some of the original skateboarding movies back in the late 1970s. These films featured Boney and his cronies, nicknamed the "Goons Brigadiers," performing advanced skateboard maneuvers on half-pipes. He later learned that some rogue skaters had gotten a hold of unauthorized copies of these movies, and had conducted a local screening of the old "Goons Brigadiers" films for the general public without Boney's consent. Boney confronted Owner, the proprietor of the theater where the screening took place about this event, and Owner replied: "Sure, I knew this was an illegal showing, and okay, I made a few bucks on it, but hey — I just rented the place to these guys and sold and collected some tickets. I didn't make the movie and I didn't own it, and I didn't even operate the projector, so I'm not on the hook. Go find the guys who rented the theater that night — if you can!"

Assume that Boney owns a valid copyright in the "Goons Brigadiers" motion pictures. Boney cannot find the person who showed the movie and wants to bring a copyright infringement lawsuit against Owner, the proprietor of the theater where the unauthorized screening took place. On what, if any, theory of secondary infringement is he likely to prevail against Owner?

(A) Owner is liable on both contributory and vicarious infringement theories.

(B) Owner is liable for contributory, but not vicarious infringement.

(C) Owner is liable for vicarious, but not contributory infringement.

(D) Owner is not liable on any secondary infringement theories.

VII-21. Stealio Co. is a technology company that developed a hot new computer software application called VidCap. VidCap allows Internet users to easily select and download screenshot images from streaming videos. If a user is watching a streaming video on a site such as YouTube, and the user has installed VidCap, the user need only click on the computer screen as the desired image appears, and VidCap automatically downloads a high-quality JPEG image file to the desktop of the user's computer. The primary use of VidCap is to create bootleg movie posters. Stealio promotes the VidCap application to users, running advertisements that state: "Why pay for pricey movie posters when you can create your own — for free — using VidCap?" G-M-G, a major motion picture studio, has filed a copyright infringement suit against Stealio. G-M-G argues that Stealio is liable on a theory of inducement. Will G-M-G prevail?

(A) Yes, because there is clear evidence that Stealio had knowledge of VidCap's infringing uses and that Stealio actively encouraged the application's infringing uses.

(B) No, because VidCap is capable of substantial noninfringing uses.

(C) Yes, because the Supreme Court's decision in *Metro-Goldwyn-Mayer Studios, Inc. v. Grokster* overruled its earlier decision in *Sony Corp. v. Universal City Studios, Inc.*

(D) No, because there is no evidence that Stealio profited financially from its creation of VidCap.

VII-22. Matt is an experimental musician who specializes in electronic remixes of modern classical music. He contacted ten of his favorite modern classical musicians and paid for nonexclusive licenses from each of them that gave Matt the right to use a fifteen-second sample of their most recent musical works. Matt then created a sound recording in which he compiled the music samples, calling the selection *Three-Bar Loop*. He did so by juxtaposing the ten samples in different sequential orders in order to bring out new insights about the similarities and differences between the ten works. Tiffany, a producer, heard *Three-Bar Loop* and wanted to include Matt's sound recording in a forthcoming CD collection of experimental music, but Matt refused outright. Tiffany then purchased all of the copyrights in the ten musical works that Matt included in *Three-Bar Loop*. She then included her recording of *Three-Bar Loop* on her CD without Matt's permission. Matt sues Tiffany for infringement. Will he prevail?

(A) Yes. Matt's purchase of a nonexclusive license to use the samples gives him standing to sue for infringement of the works of authorship embodied in those samples.

(B) Yes. *Three-Bar Loop* is an original compilation based on the ten licensed samples, and Tiffany's unauthorized use of that work violates Matt's copyright in the compilation.

(C) No. Because Matt's work is only a compilation of other authors' material, it does not possess any separate, copyrightable originality.

(D) No. Matt acquired only a limited use right to the samples that comprise *Three-Bar Loop*, which does not give him any rights in the underlying musical works from which those samples were taken.

VII-23. Consider question VII-22. Assume that instead of creating *Three-Bar Loop* by compiling copyrighted works of authorship, Matt used samples of classical music that belonged to the public domain and were wholly unprotected by copyright. Would this change the outcome of Matt's infringement suit against Tiffany for her unauthorized use of *Three-Bar Loop*?

ANSWER:

VII-24. Studio owns the copyright in the motion picture *Her Ben*. MovieCo releases a film entitled *Sure, Gwen* that Studio believes infringes its copyright in *Her Ben*. At trial, Studio and MovieCo jointly place only two facts in the record. A scientific survey of average people found that the survey participants regarded the works as possessing largely the same aesthetic appeal; and that the same survey participants were each able to identify an average of five points of difference in the theme, plot, or mood of the two films. In terms of substantial similarity, which party has adduced more persuasive evidence to support a finding in its favor?

(A) MovieCo. Survey data is inadmissible to prove the presence of substantial similarity.

(B) MovieCo. Any points of difference between two films are enough to overcome a showing of substantial similarity.

(C) Studio. Because the two works possess the same essential aesthetic appeal, they are substantially similar.

(D) Studio. A copyright defendant must be able to show at least ten points of salient difference between the two works in suit in order to overcome a finding of substantial similarity.

VII-25. Author penned a successful mystery novel in which he named the main female villain "Eva Destruction." Writer later wrote a romance novel, and named one of her characters "Eva Destruction." Writer's "Eva Destruction" character is otherwise entirely unlike Author's "Eva Destruction," and her romance novel bears no other similarities to Author's mystery novel. Author accosted Writer and said, "You're a thief! I know you took the name of your 'Eva Destruction' character directly from my book." Writer responded, "You're right, I did.

Sue me." Author does. Will he prevail?

(A) Yes. Because Writer intentionally copied the name of Author's character, she is liable for copyright infringement.

(B) Yes. Because literary characters are copyrightable, their names are too.

(C) No. This is at most a de minimis taking that does not rise to a level sufficient to trigger copyright infringement.

(D) No. Literary characters are not copyrightable, so their names are not copyrightable either.

VII-26. Ray is a singer-songwriter, and the author of the musical work and the sound recording that comprise the minimalist vocal track *Only Just*. In 2004, two years after releasing the track to moderate critical and commercial success, Ray hears a recording of a musical work that is entirely identical to his. Titled *Number Three*, it is the work of Zao, a Buddhist monk in rural Laos who had no contact with western society until 2005, when he was discovered by explorers who recorded Zao's singing to bring it to a worldwide audience. All of Zao's musical works on the CD were composed by him prior to his contact with the explorers. Incensed, Ray sues Zao for copyright infringement of *Only Just* in United States federal court. Will Ray prevail?

(A) Yes, because the author of a work that possesses verbatim similarity to preexisting works is per se liable for infringement of the preexisting work.

(B) Yes, because Zao's work will cut into the profitability and market share of Ray's work.

(C) No, because any copying by Zao would have lacked conscious intent to infringe.

(D) No, because Zao has independently created *Number Three* and thus has a complete defense to the claim that he infringed the copyright in *Only Just*.

VII-27. Consider question VII-26. Assume that Zao was not a monk in rural Laos cut off from western society, but an American who was part of mainstream society. In response to Ray's allegations of copyright infringement, Zao produces proof that despite the moderate popular success of Ray's *Only Just*, Zao had no conscious awareness of that work when he composed and recorded *Number Three*. Assuming that Zao's assertions are truthful, are they sufficient to escape copyright liability?

ANSWER:

VII-28. Ben sells printing equipment to publishing companies such as book publishers, newspapers, and magazines. One day, Joe contacts Ben, seeking to purchase a large printing press. Ben recognizes Joe from a news item a year ago in which Ben was nabbed by federal authorities for a scheme in which Joe printed unauthorized copies of novels, which he then sold cheaply to booksellers. Joe says to Ben, "I got out of that other infringement suit, and now I've got a great idea for a quick score," but Ben interrupts and says "What you do with this printing press is your business; I don't want to know a thing about it." Joe buys the printing press, and several weeks later he runs into Ben and says "Thanks for that press, man — I'm making a killing selling bootleg copies of popular novels!" Soon after, Joe was again caught using the press to make unauthorized copies of novels. This time, Ben is joined in the infringement suit against Joe on a theory of contributory infringement. Will Ben be held liable on a contributory infringement theory for the infringement of the copyrights in the novels?

(A) No. Ben's knowledge of the illegality of Joe's conduct arose only after Ben sold Joe the printing press that was used to engage in copyright infringement.

(B) No. Ben was conscious only of the fact that Joe was making copies of novels, not that this conduct was unlawful.

(C) Yes. Ben can be constructively charged with knowledge of the illegality of Joe's conduct.

(D) Yes. As long as the primary infringer was aware of the illegality of his conduct, that knowledge can be imputed to the secondary infringer.

VII-29. Barry operates a website that provides visitors with information regarding other sites around the Internet where infringing digital music files can be downloaded for free. Barry's site has a disclaimer at the top that says, "Many of these sites are engaging in copyright infringement. Visit these sites at your own risk, and don't hold me responsible for your own actions!" Barry does not directly link visitors to the sites where the infringing music files are found. Rather, he refers to each with text that, when cut and pasted into a search engine, will return the site as the first result. Barry supports himself from the revenue he makes from selling advertising on his website. Can Barry be held liable on a secondary infringement theory?

(A) Yes, because Barry has a financial interest in directing visitors to infringing websites.

(B) Yes, because Barry's website materially contributes to copyright infringement with full knowledge of the illegality of the conduct.

(C) No, because Barry is not directly linking to the infringing websites, but merely providing information that allows users to locate them.

(D) No, because Barry notifies site visitors that the listed sites are infringing, and provides a full disclaimer of liability.

VII-30. The Clean Channel Network is a radio network that has fifty independently owned affiliate AM radio stations throughout the United States. Each independently owned station has agreed to Clean Channel's affiliate agreement pursuant to which the network agrees to provide programming in exchange for which the station agrees to broadcast network programming, give Clean Channel five minutes of advertising time each hour that Clean Channel can sell to national advertisers, and give Clean Channel approval rights to any programming created by the affiliate. One of those affiliate radio stations, WXTM, is best known for its controversial local talk show host, Birch Barlow. Numerous listeners have complained to Clean Channel that they are offended by Barlow's show, but Clean Channel always responded by saying that local content is best determined by local affiliates. Barlow has introduced a new feature in which he reads whole chapters of books that express political views with which he disagrees, and then derides the opinions of the authors, none of whom have provided Barlow with permission to read from their works on air. Barlow's new feature both has made his show draw even more listeners than usual and has caused several of the authors to complain to Clean Channel about the unauthorized use of their literary works. Getting no response, the authors have sued both Barlow for direct infringement and Clean Channel on a vicarious infringement theory. Assuming that Barlow is indeed directly liable for infringement, can Clean Channel also be held liable on a vicarious infringement theory?

(A) Yes. Clean Channel had knowledge of Barlow's infringing conduct, and provided him with the material means to engage in that infringement.

(B) Yes. Clean Channel both directly profited from Barlow's direct infringement and had the ability to control Barlow's public performance of the literary works.

(C) No. Clean Channel had no ability to control the conduct of its affiliate radio stations.

(D) No. Clean Channel may have profited from Barlow's performances, but only indirectly.

VII-31. James owns a vacant lot in Maine, though he lives in Oregon and has no family and friends anywhere in New England. James has owned the lot for years, refusing to develop or sell it, in the hope that someday the lot will increase in value and he can sell it for a profit. One day, James gets a call from Dan, who says, "Listen, if you want to make some cash on that old lot you've got, I'll pay you $1,000 to rent it for a month. I promise at the end of the time I'll be gone and the lot will be just as good as it was before. Just don't ask any questions, all right?" James replies, "Well, I've never done anything like this before, but sure — as long as you agree not to mess up the property, you've got a deal." A week later, James receives a check in the mail from Dan for $1,000, which he cashes, and then never thinks about it again. Six months later, James is joined in a copyright infringement suit against Dan. It turns out that throughout the month, during which James never set foot in Maine, Dan was using the lot to run an informal market where he sold bootleg copies of DVDs and CDs, all of which infringed their owners' copyright, to the public at a big discount. Assuming that Dan is liable on a direct infringement theory, will James be liable on a secondary infringement theory as well?

(A) Yes. James had constructive knowledge of Dan's infringing conduct, and provided him with the material means to engage in that infringement.

(B) Yes. James profited directly from Dan's infringing conduct, and had supervisory control over the infringing conduct as well.

(C) No. While James directly profited from Dan's infringement, he did not have control over or the ability to supervise Dan's infringing conduct on the lot.

(D) No. While James had supervisory control over Dan's infringing conduct, he did not profit directly from that infringement.

VII-32. Bill lost his job and was desperate to make ends meet. For a couple of months, he made unauthorized copies of popular DVDs, knowing full well that he is engaging in copyright infringement, and operated an illicit door-to-door business in bootleg DVDs. Unfortunately for Bill, one day he sold to an undercover FBI agent, who placed him under arrest for criminal copyright infringement. Over the course of his enterprise, Bill made only $750 in sales. What criminal penalties might Bill face?

(A) Bill will not face criminal liability because his net sales did not exceed $1000.

(B) Bill will not face criminal liability because his conduct was not willful.

(C) Bill may face fines, but will not face imprisonment.

(D) Bill may face imprisonment and fines.

VII-33. LOA is a typical major provider of Internet access. Users pay LOA a monthly fee, and LOA provides those users with access to email and to the World Wide Web through its own network. For an added fee, LOA also allows users to store up to one gigabyte of information on LOA's servers. LOA has adopted and publicized its policy of terminating any users who repeatedly use its service to engage in copyright infringement, and has an agent designated to receive and review takedown notices. LOA does not interfere with content owners' attempts to use standard technology protection measures.

Alice is an LOA user who frequently engages in illegal music filesharing, but has never been accused of copyright infringement. Alice transmits infringing music files back and forth to other users via email, all the while using LOA as her Internet service provider. Also, pursuant to automated LOA procedures that apply to all its users, Alice's email transmissions, including attachments consisting of infringing music files, are typically archived on LOA's servers, sometimes for as many as five days. At no time do any of the owners of the material whose copyright Alice has infringed learn about or notify LOA of Alice's infringing conduct. Nor does any of Alice's conduct give rise to a reasonable suspicion that she is engaging in repeat infringement. Which of Alice's actions can render LOA liable for damages for copyright infringement on a secondary infringement theory?

(A) Both Alice's email transmissions with infringing attachments and LOA's archiving of those emails subject LOA to liability on a secondary infringement theory.

(B) Neither Alice's email transmissions with infringing attachments nor LOA's archiving of those emails subject LOA to liability on a secondary infringement theory.

(C) Alice's email transmissions with infringing attachments subject LOA to liability on a secondary infringement theory, but LOA's archiving of those emails does not.

(D) LOA's archiving Alice's email communications with infringing attachments does not subject LOA to liability on a secondary infringement theory, but Alice's emails do.

VII-34. Consider question VII-33. Further assume that Alice has also paid for LOA's enhanced storage service, and takes advantage of it to store approximately ten to twenty infringing music files on LOA's servers. Nothing about this storage reasonably gives rise to suspicion that Alice's conduct amounts to copyright infringement. Nor do any of the owners whose copyrights Alice infringes know of or notify LOA about her infringing conduct. In light of these facts, can LOA be held liable on a secondary infringement theory for Alice's storage of infringing files on its servers?

ANSWER:

VII-35. Consider questions VII-33 and VII-34. Now assume that one of the copyright owners discovers Alice's infringing conduct, and sends a letter to LOA asking that it remove the infringing files from the LOA servers. The letter, composed by the copyright owner's attorney, specifically identifies Alice as the individual responsible for the infringement; provides Alice's full legal name, email address, and phone number; identifies the infringed works and their particular location on LOA's servers; includes the signature of the owner's attorney as well as an attestation by the attorney, under penalty of perjury, that the information in the letter is accurate, and that she is legally authorized to act on the owner's behalf. Is this document sufficient to give rise to a duty on behalf of LOA to remove Alice's infringing files from its server?

(A) No. This notice is insufficient because it does not include a sworn attestation that Alice's use is unauthorized.

(B) No. This notice is insufficient because it does not include the owner's signature.

(C) No. This notice is insufficient because it does not include copyright registration certificates for all works that the owner seeks to have removed.

(D) Yes. This document meets all applicable statutory requirements and gives rise to a duty on behalf of LOA to remove Alice's infringing files from its server.

VII-36. Consider questions VII-33, VII-34, and VII-35. Now assume that LOA receives a takedown notice relating to Alice's storage of infringing material on its servers that is legally sufficient in all respects. Which, if any, of the following statements *incorrectly* describes LOA's obligations upon receipt of the takedown notice?

(A) Take reasonable steps to promptly notify the subscriber that it has removed or disabled access to the allegedly infringing material.

(B) Remove or disable access to the infringing material within a reasonable time.

(C) Cease to act as Alice's Internet service provider.

(D) Inform the copyright owner of LOA's receipt of a written communication from Alice contesting the denial of access.

VIII-1. Tanya owns both the musical work and the sound recording that comprise the musical track *Fast Dog*. Don owns and operates the website "Feel the Beat" on which he discusses new releases of music. Don posts an unauthorized, 20-second audio stream of each release he critiques, including *Fast Dog*. Tanya sues Don for copyright infringement, and Don counters by raising a fair use defense. Part of Don's argument is that his streaming of *Fast Dog* amounts to fair use because providing such streams on music review websites without licensing or compensation is customary practice in the music industry. Don further argues that courts should consider unauthorized uses that are also customary industry practices as more likely to be fair uses. May a court consider Don's argument in its consideration of his fair use claim?

(A) Yes. Customary use is one of the four statutory fair use factors that courts must consider.

(B) Yes. Although customary use is not one of the four statutory fair use factors that courts must consider, the factors are not exclusive, so a court is permitted to take additional factors into account.

(C) No. Customary use is not one of the four statutory fair use factors, so it may not enter into a court's analysis of the issue.

(D) No. Fair use relates exclusively to the market effects the defendant's work has on the plaintiff's work, so the notion of custom cannot factor into a fair use analysis.

VIII-2. A company called FreeBooks.com has recently started operating. FreeBooks.com is accessible only to subscribers, who pay a membership fee, and its paying members then receive a new chapter of a copyrighted book every month for a year that can only be read online. Accessing books through FreeBooks.com allows readers to read them for a fraction of the price they would pay for a hard copy of the novel in a bookstore. At no time has FreeBooks.com obtained a license for the use of any of the works it makes available online. FreeBooks.com is sued for infringement by the owner of the copyright in the *Grave Runner* novel that it has made available on its site. FreeBooks.com responds by conceding infringement and raising a fair use defense. Will this defense succeed?

(A) Yes. FreeBooks.com's use is transformative because it translates the physical novel *Grave Runner* into an online medium.

(B) Yes. FreeBooks.com's use would not harm any current or potential markets for sales of the physical novel *Grave Runner*.

(C) No. FreeBooks.com's use does not transform the purpose of *Grave Runner*, and it would likely trade off with current or future markets for the novel.

(D) No. Courts have held that the fair use defense categorically does not apply to Internet uses of copyrighted works.

VIII-3. John is a writer who loathes President Bill Clinton. John composed a humorous, fictional work titled *The Trial of Slick Willie* in which he repeatedly mocks Clinton. John's literary work is an adaptation of the plot of a successful novel published several years earlier called *The Trial of Sick Billy*, which has nothing to do with Bill Clinton. Betty, the author of *The Trial of Sick Billy*, is a fan of Bill Clinton and does not appreciate John's mocking the President by reference to her literary work, especially because John never asked her for permission to use that work. Betty contacts John and voices her distaste. John responds, "Don't take it personally, Betty. I'm not saying anything about you or your novel. I'm just using it to make fun of that jerk Clinton." Betty is not satisfied by this, and sues John for copyright infringement. John responds by conceding infringement, but then arguing that he can take advantage of a fair use defense. Assuming that a court agreed with John's descriptive assessment of his work, would John's fair use claim likely succeed?

(A) Yes. John's work is a parody, not a satire, and the Supreme Court has held that parodies are always fair uses.

(B) Yes. John's work is political commentary, and political commentary is always fair use.

(C) No. John's work is a satire, not a parody, and the Supreme Court has held that satire is never fair use.

(D) No. John's work is a satire, not a parody, and the Supreme Court has held that satire is less likely to merit a fair use defense.

VIII-4. Consider question VIII-3. Assume instead that when Betty contacted John, he told her, "I know why you're upset. It's not really that I made fun of Bill Clinton, but that I made fun of your dumb book. Well, that was my point — I think your book is awful and I wanted to show everyone just why." Assuming that a court agreed with John's descriptive assessment of his work, would he be likely to succeed on a fair use defense?

ANSWER:

VIII-5. Which of the following statements most accurately describes the source of fair use law in the United States?

(A) Fair use is an affirmative defense to copyright infringement that was first articulated in the 1976 Copyright Act.

(B) Fair use is an affirmative defense to copyright infringement that is located explicitly in the United States Constitution and has also been passed as a federal statute.

(C) Fair use is an affirmative defense to copyright infringement that has longstanding common-law roots, but was first codified in statutory form in the 1976 Copyright Act.

(D) Fair use is an affirmative defense to copyright infringement that consists exclusively of judicial interpretations of explicit constitutional language.

VIII-6. *Eat at Joe's* is a very popular television situation comedy set at a greasy-spoon diner. In the seventh year of the show's run, two books are published about it. The first is *The Definitive Guide to "Eat at Joe's,"* which purports to be a complete compendium of all facts about the show. The guide consists of a list of the actors who have appeared in the show; a list of the characters played by each of the actors who appeared in the show; a list of all the episodes that ran in each season; and a summary of each episode taken (with permission) from the official publicity material distributed by the producers of *Eat at Joe's.* The second publication is titled *Deconstructing "Eat at Joe's,"* and it consists of seven essays written by academic literary critics about *Eat at Joe's.* The essays each make different points about the social meaning of the show. Several of the essays include images or paragraph-long blocks of dialogue from *Eat at Joe's,* none of which were used with permission, in order to illustrate their points. The owner of the copyright in *Eat at Joe's* sues the publishers of each of the two books for copyright infringement. Each of the publishers responds by raising a fair use defense. With respect to the question whether the books' use of material from *Eat at Joe's* is transformative, how would a court rule?

(A) *The Definitive Guide to "Eat at Joe's"* is transformative, but *Deconstructing "Eat at Joe's"* is not.

(B) *Deconstructing "Eat at Joe's"* is transformative, but *The Definitive Guide to "Eat at Joe's"* is not.

(C) *Deconstructing "Eat at Joe's"* and *The Definitive Guide to "Eat at Joe's"* are both transformative.

(D) Neither *Deconstructing "Eat at Joe's"* nor *The Definitive Guide to "Eat at Joe's"* are transformative.

VIII-7. Kara is a commercial photographer who works in Africa, where she accompanies hunters on safaris and takes colorful pictures of the hunters with the game the hunters have killed. Jody is a visual artist and an environmentalist. She finds hunting odious and strongly dislikes that her fellow artist Kara capitalizes on the killing of wild animals to make a living. Jody lawfully acquires several prints of Kara's photographs, and makes paintings based on each of them. Jody's paintings depict exactly the same content as Kara's photographs — hunters and their recently killed prey — but in Jody's paintings she has given the hunters vicious expressions rather than smiles, and Jody has also written words like "murder" and "cruelty" in blood-red paint over each of the scenes. Kara is horrified when she learns about Jody's work, and she sues Jody for copyright infringement. Jody concedes that she created unauthorized adaptations of Kara's work, but argues that her infringement is defensible because it is a fair use. In considering Jody's fair use defense, how would a court rule on the issue whether her adaptations are transformative of the originals?

(A) Jody's work is not transformative because she depicted exactly the same content in her paintings as Kara did in her photographs.

    (B) Jody's work is transformative because she created paintings, while Kara created photographs.

    (C) Jody's work is not transformative because she could have expressed her criticism of Kara's work via other means that did not entail unauthorized appropriation of Kara's work.

    (D) Jody's work is transformative because it recasts Kara's work in a menacing rather than positive light, and does so in order to make a political point.

VIII-8. SoundSearch.com is an online search engine that allows users to search for and locate sound files on the web. Users enter a search string in the form of text on SoundSearch-.com's home page, and the site returns matches in the form of links. Clicking on one of these links then produces an automated, low-fidelity five-second version of the sound file. SoundSearch.com broadly combs the Internet for sound files to produce in response to user searches. It does not seek permission from the relevant copyright owners to use the sound files that embody their musical works or sound recordings. Several of those copyright owners now sue SoundSearch.com for its unauthorized copying and performance of these protected works of authorship. SoundSearch.com responds by conceding the fact of copying, but raising a fair use defense. Would a court considering this fair use defense regard SoundSearch.com's use as transformative?

    (A) Yes. Any use of copyrighted material by a search engine amounts to fair use.

    (B) Yes. By using only partial versions of the sound files, and by producing them for information and search, rather than entertainment, purposes, SoundSearch.com engaged in transformative use.

    (C) No. Because SoundSearch.com did not offer any commentary on the sound files, their use cannot be transformative.

    (D) No. Because SoundSearch.com did not alter the sounds in the five-second versions, their use cannot be transformative.

VIII-9. The Sludge Retort is a libertarian website that aggregates news and information from around the web and provides acerbic commentary about it. Its founder, Cat Sludge, does not charge viewers a fee to access his site. He does sell ad space, though the nominal revenues go almost entirely toward the costs of website maintenance. Rather, Cat's primary source of income is his day job as an information technology professional. Between his job and the modest profits generated by the Sludge Retort, Cat has amassed a reasonably significant savings account. Although the Sludge Retort typically posts only links to news items, some of Cat's editorials include large block quotes from other news outlets' articles, about which Cat comments. Cat has never asked permission from any of these news outlets to copy substantial portions of their articles. Several of the news outlets sue Cat for infringing the copyrights in their articles, and Cat responds by conceding unauthorized copying, but raising a fair use defense. On the particular issue of whether Cat's unauthorized use of the selections from the news outlets' articles is commercial, how would a court be likely to rule?

    (A) The use is commercial because Cat Sludge intends for it to increase his profit.

   (B)   The use is not commercial because Cat Sludge makes only a nominal amount on the Sludge Retort's advertising.

   (C)   The use is commercial because it helps enable the Sludge Retort to generate advertising revenue.

   (D)   The use is not commercial because users are not charged a fee for accessing the Sludge Retort.

VIII-10. Consider question VIII-9. Assume **for the sake of this question only** that a court were to find that Cat Sludge's use was commercial. Would this finding have a dispositive effect on the outcome of the overall fair use analysis?

ANSWER:

VIII-11. Janie is a nurse by day and an aspiring romance novelist by night. She has recently completed a manuscript of an original literary work entitled *Tempest at Sea*, that she hopes will be a great success. *Tempest at Sea* consists of a fictional story line, with fictional characters, set in a realistic historical milieu, the Massachusetts whaling communities of the late nineteenth century, about which Janie has done much original historical research. Because she has never published anything, Janie arranges a meeting with her friend Alice, an established romance novelist, to ask about the ins and outs of the business. During their dinner, Janie gives Alice a copy of *Tempest at Sea*, saying "I'd really appreciate your thoughts on this, but please don't show it to anyone else. You're the only person I've let see the manuscript." Alice reads and loves the manuscript, and a week or so later, without Janie's permission, Alice posts several paragraph-long excerpts from Janie's manuscript on her web log, praising them as "tantalizing bits from the work of America's next new romance novel star." Janie is not pleased, despite Alice's praise, and sues Alice for copyright infringement. Alice concedes that posting the excerpts online amounted to unauthorized reproduction, but advances a fair use defense. When analyzing the second fair use factor, the nature of the protected work, the court is likely to find in favor of which party?

   (A)   Alice, because the historical character of Janie's work makes it factual, and because Janie published the manuscript by giving Alice a copy.

   (B)   Janie, because her manuscript is fictional, although she published it by releasing it to Alice.

   (C)   Janie, because her manuscript was unpublished and is fictional.

   (D)   Janie, because her manuscript was unpublished, although its historical character makes it factual.

VIII-12. Consider question VIII-11. Assume **for the purposes of this question only** that a court found that Janie's manuscript was unpublished. Would a court find this fact dispositive of Alice's fair use defense, and if so, which party would prevail?

ANSWER:

VIII-13. Jayne Martel is a mystery writer with a large following. Her novels are distinctive in that they never reveal the solution to the mystery until the final page. Max is a huge Jayne Martel fan, and runs a website devoted to her work. Recently, Max has created a section of his website called "Solving the puzzle" in which he publishes, without permission, the last page of each Jayne Martel novel, verbatim, for readers who can't wait to figure out the solution to the mystery. Jayne Martel discovers the website and sues Max for copyright infringement. Max counters with a fair use defense. In terms of the third factor, the amount and substantiality of the taking, in favor of which party would a court likely rule?

    (A)   Max. His takings represented only a single page from each of Jayne Martel's books, and so represent only a small fraction of each literary work.

    (B)   Jayne. Max's takings took the critical portion of each of her works, the ending, and are qualitatively, if not quantitatively, substantial.

    (C)   Max. His takings were in good faith and would not undermine the market for Jayne Martel's novels.

    (D)   Jayne. Max's takings were verbatim, so the amount they appropriated is irrelevant.

VIII-14. Lloyd is a professor of film studies who specializes in horror movies. At an academic conference, Lloyd gives a lecture called "Text and Subtext in American Slasher Films." In his hour-long lecture, Lloyd plays three two-minute clips from his favorite horror movie, *Bloody Mary*, the running time of which is ninety minutes. During each of these clips, none of which were performed with permission, Lloyd continues to lecture as he illustrates in detail how each of the excerpts illustrates the three points that comprise the thesis of his academic paper. Shortly after the lecture, Gory Studios, the owner of the *Bloody Mary* audiovisual work, sues Lloyd for copyright infringement. Lloyd concedes that his conduct amounted to an unauthorized public performance of the audiovisual work, but counters with a fair use defense. In terms of the third element of a fair use defense — the amount and substantiality of the taking — in favor of which party would a court likely rule?

    (A)   Gory Studios. By taking six minutes of a ninety-minute film, Lloyd has appropriated the heart of Gory Studio's work.

    (B)   Gory Studios. Taking more than five percent of an audiovisual work categorically results in the third fair use factor weighing against the defendant.

    (C)   Lloyd. Because his taking was for the purpose of academic commentary, factor three weighs in his favor.

    (D)   Lloyd. Because his taking took no more than was necessary to support his thesis, factor three weighs in his favor.

VIII-15. Mark is a businessman specializing in emerging markets. He discovers a demand for independent films in China, and sets up businesses selling DVDs of independent films throughout the country, without ever seeking the permission of the copyright owners. Mark ships the motion pictures from the United States. One of the movie studios that owns the copyright in several of these motion pictures, Crawling Id Films, complains to Mark about his practices, and Mark responds, "This is fair use. You don't have any distribution in Asian markets, and you haven't announced any plans to expand here. No harm, no foul." Would a court considering Mark's argument on the fourth fair use factor find his argument convincing?

(A) Yes. Because Crawling Id Films is not currently exploiting the market that Mark has moved into, there is no harm to that market.

(B) Yes. Because Crawling Id Films has no current plans to exploit the market that Mark has moved into, there is no harm to that market.

(C) No. Because Mark did not at least attempt to negotiate a license with Crawling Id Films, the fourth factor necessarily weighs against him.

(D) No. Because Crawling Id Films might reasonably choose to exploit Asian markets in the future, Mark's use harms its potential markets.

VIII-16. Consider question VIII-15. Assume **for the purposes of this question only** that a court found that the fourth factor of the fair use analysis weighed in favor of Crawling Id. Would this conclusion be dispositive of Mark's fair use defense?

ANSWER:

VIII-17. *Very Ben* is a popular situation comedy on the television network CBA. Gina loves the show and invents a board game called *The Very Ben Game* that is structured around names, likenesses, and facts about the show. The producers of *Very Ben* contact Gina and tell her that they love the game and want to use it as part of their marketing. For about a year, Gina sells CBA copies of *The Very Ben Game* at a large discount. Then, without warning, CBA decides that it wants to produce its own version of a board game based on *Very Ben*, and sues for an injunction to stop Gina from producing *The Very Ben Game*. CBA argues that *The Very Ben Game* is an unauthorized derivative work, and thus amounts to infringement. Gina argues, among other things, that *The Very Ben Game* is defensible as a form of fair use. When analyzing the fourth factor of this fair use claim, for which party is a court likely to favor?

(A) CBA, because fair use is not a valid defense when injunctive relief is at issue.

(B) CBA, because the market for *The Very Ben Game* is also a reasonably foreseeable potential future market for *Very Ben*.

(C) Gina, because at the time she first created *The Very Ben Game*, CBA had no pending plans to create a game based on *Very Ben*.

(D) Gina, because by allowing Gina to produce *The Very Ben Game* for a year without complaint, CBA implicitly conceded that the game did not harm its ability to exploit *Very Ben*.

VIII-18. Consider question VIII-17. Assume **for the purposes of this question only** that Gina adduces evidence that *The Very Ben Game* has increased the show's popularity, and, correlatively, its profitability, enough that any possible losses CBA suffered from the revenues it might have gained from a license were dwarfed by the revenue it gained by the game's existence. In other words, Gina can show that her unauthorized creation of *The Very Ben Game* helped rather than hurt the market for the show, on-balance. Would this fact convince a court that the fourth factor of a fair use analysis should weigh in Gina's favor?

ANSWER:

VIII-19. Dolly Billionaire is a famous socialite who writes a mawkish self-help book titled *Yours for the Asking.* Wendy Wanamaker is a newspaper columnist who considers Dolly to be a loathsome dilettante and writes a book-length parody of Dolly's book titled *Yours for the Trashing.* Dolly is incensed and sues Wendy for copyright infringement, and Wendy responds by raising a fair use defense. In addressing the fourth fair use factor, Dolly argues that Wendy harmed a potential market by shortchanging Dolly's ability to license parodies and criticisms of her work. Will a court find this argument sufficient to conclude that the fourth fair use factor weighs in favor of Dolly?

(A) Yes. Because the work at issue is one of nonfiction, the fourth factor must weigh in favor of Dolly.

(B) No. There is no present or reasonably foreseeable market in parody or criticism, so Wendy's parody could not have supplanted any possible licensing deals for Dolly.

(C) Yes. The fourth factor considers possible future markets as well as present ones, so the possibility that Wendy's parody may have supplanted these licensing deals means that the fourth factor weighs in favor of Dolly.

(D) No. In the absence of evidence that Dolly was negotiating licensing deals, Dolly cannot plausibly argue that Wendy's parody supplanted a future market for derivative works.

VIII-20. Jack loves the television program *Crime Dogs*, and he records every episode on his old-style VCR and keeps the videotapes in a locked cabinet. Jack never actually watches these taped programs, but just keeps them because he is an obsessive collector and is reassured by their mere presence. Jack's conduct is clearly verbatim copying, but would it be defensible to charges of infringement via the fair use defense?

(A) Yes. The Supreme Court held in *Sony Corp. of America v. Universal City Studios, Inc.* that videotaping television programs in order to create a library of tapes is fair use.

(B) Yes. Because Jack's use is solely for personal purposes, it counts as a fair use.

(C) No. The Supreme Court ruling in *Sony Corp. of America v. Universal City Studios, Inc.* concerning personal copying held only that videotaping television programs for purposes of time-shifting is a fair use.

(D)   No. While the Supreme Court held in *Sony Corp. of America v. Universal City Studios, Inc.* that videotaping television programs is fair use, this holding was overturned by *Metro-Goldwyn-Mayer Studios Inc. v. Grokster, Ltd.*

VIII-21. Kendra is a biochemist who works for a major pharmaceutical company. During the course of her latest project, she has to make a presentation to a group of potential investors about the nature of the company's research. In preparing for this presentation, Kendra visits the company's library (which does not lend out physical copies of its holdings) and photocopies an article from a scientific journal. She then takes the article back to her office, where she uses the information contained in it to construct her presentation. Kendra's photocopying of the article clearly amounts to verbatim copying, but is it defensible as fair use?

(A)   Yes. Kendra's use is not transformative, but because it would have no effect on the copyright owner's market for exploiting their work, it is a fair use.

(B)   Yes. Kendra's use is transformative and would have no negative effect on the copyright owner's market for exploiting its work, so it is a fair use.

(C)   Yes. Kendra's use would have a negative effect on the copyright owner's market for exploiting its work, but because it is transformative, it is a fair use.

(D)   No. This conduct is not transformative, and allowing the practice has a negative effect on the copyright owner's market for exploiting its work, so it is not a fair use.

VIII-22. Greco is a rock musician. In 2000, he composed and recorded the musical work *Only Me*. The track became a huge international success, and Greco, who retained ownership of both the musical work and sound recording that comprise the track, made tons of cash. "Strange Mel" Petrovic is a musician who is famous for his parodic send-ups of popular music. In 2001, "Strange Mel" released the track *Golly Gee*, which parodized Greco's *Only Me*. That same year, Greco's agent told him about "Strange Mel's" unlicensed take-off of *Only Me*. Greco replied, "Whatever. I don't give a toss what that little twerp does." Greco never heard *Golly Gee*, and for years, he forgot about the issue. "Strange Mel" assumed that Greco had no objection to his parody, and relied on this assumption to create an expensive music video to promote *Golly Gee* in 2003. Then, in 2004, Greco happened to see the music video for *Golly Gee* and became incensed at what he felt was a disrespectful use of his works of authorship. Greco sued "Strange Mel" for copyright infringement in late 2008. Aside from fair use, what affirmative defenses might "Strange Mel" plausibly raise to Greco's lawsuit?

(A)   Abandonment and statute of limitations.

(B)   Abandonment and laches.

(C)   Statute of limitations and laches.

(D)   Abandonment, statute of limitations and laches.

VIII-23. Chuck writes a poem titled *Well Hey*, and shows a copy of it to his friend Jeff, who is also a poet, to elicit Jeff's comments. Jeff thinks *Well Hey* is brilliant, but tells Chuck that it is awful because he wants to claim credit for the poem himself. Jeff then registers *Well Hey* with the Copyright Office, listing himself as the work's author. Soon after, Mike releases an anthology of poetry that includes *Well Hey*, though he has not secured anyone's permission to do so. Jeff sues Mike for copyright infringement. Will Jeff prevail?

(A) Yes. Because he is the registered owner of the copyright in *Well Hey*, he has the right to sue for infringement, though Chuck may be able to join the action and recover any judgment.

(B) Yes. Because Chuck has failed to file a competing copyright registration, he has abandoned the copyright in *Well Hey* to Jeff, making Jeff the valid owner.

(C) No. Only the original author of a copyrighted work of authorship is entitled to sue for infringement.

(D) No. Jeff's conduct amounts to fraud on the copyright office, and Mike can raise that point as a full defense to the infringement suit.

VIII-24. Seeking to broaden protection for the entertainment industry, California passes a law stating that its state laws will extend exclusive rights of reproduction, adaptation, public distribution, and public performance to creators of ideas, in addition to the protection of expression already afforded by federal law. Would a court regard this California law as enforceable?

(A) No, a court would invalidate the California law because it is explicitly preempted by federal statute.

(B) No, a court would invalidate the California law because it creates a conflict whereby it is impossible to comply with state and federal law at the same time.

(C) Yes, states are permitted to provide authors with more, though not less, protection than prescribed by federal law, so the law is valid.

(D) Yes, a court would find the California law enforceable because Congress has decided it will not provide ideas with copyright protection.

VIII-25. In 1980, Harold Hermit, an architectural artist, created a detailed painting titled *Promises of Tomorrow*. The painting depicted a theme park in which various versions of the future were displayed and populated by actors. Later that year, Hermit met with executives of Amusement Development, a large corporation involved in the building of amusement parks around the world. At that meeting, Hermit attempted to persuade Amusement Development to use his design for a new amusement park in the United States. Hermit provided the executives with a copy of *Promises of Tomorrow* as a prototype for such an amusement park. A few weeks later, Hermit was informed that the corporation was not interested in his design.

Shortly thereafter, Hermit moved to a small town in East Dakota with his wife who became ill. Hermit spent most of his time caring for his wife who was in a near-vegetative state. They became isolated and disengaged from society. They never left their town, had no children, and did not own a television. Hermit was hospitalized for open heart surgery in the fall of 1990. After his release from the hospital, he remained a recluse, caring for his sick wife and tending to his own poor health.

In September 1990, Amusement Development opened a new theme park, "Futureland" in the state of South Virginia. Futureland, a park that specifically targets children as its patrons, is strikingly similar to the images contained in Hermit's *Promises of Tomorrow* painting. The opening of Futureland was accompanied by massive media attention and has been widely advertised since its opening. Hermit has recently filed suit in United States District Court against Amusement Development for infringement of the copyright in *Promises of Tomorrow*. Hermit claims that he had not known of Futureland until he saw photos of it in a magazine article while visiting his local barbershop two months before filing his lawsuit. Amusement Development has moved for a dismissal of Hermit's lawsuit on the basis that the statute of limitations has run. Will Amusement Development's defense succeed?

ANSWER:

VIII-26. Five years ago, Ripp-Off, Inc. manufactured and distributed 200,000 CDs featuring unauthorized copies of a copyrighted MusicCo compilation of sound recordings, earning a net profit of $1 million. MusicCo now has evidence that Ripp-Off is once again engaging in the unauthorized copying of the record company's copyrighted sound recordings, manufacturing and distributing 35,000 phonorecords of the same compilation for a net profit of $175,000. All of the copyrights owned by MusicCo had been registered prior to Ripp-Off's infringement. MusicCo has filed a copyright infringement action against Ripp-Off and has successfully proven willful infringement. What is the likeliest measure of MusicCo's damages?

(A) MusicCo will be awarded all of Ripp-Off's net profits: $1,175,000.

(B) MusicCo will be awarded all of Ripp-Off's net profits and the maximum statutory damages amount: $1,325,000.

(C) MusicCo will be awarded the maximum statutory damages amount: $150,000.

(D) MusicCo will be awarded the net profits from Ripp-Off's most recent infringing activity: $175,000.

VIII-27. The East Dakota state legislature has recently enacted legislation that creates a compulsory master use license for pre-1972 sound recordings made available for download by any website that transmits from a server located in the state of East Dakota. The legislation requires the website to pay 16 cents for each sound recording downloaded by users of the website to the owners of the master recordings. The legislation also mandates that pre-1972 sound recordings may be streamed by such websites without payment. Relying on this legislation, DeadVinyl.com has been streaming pre-1972 sound recordings without obtaining a license to do so. In addition, DeadVinyl.com sells downloads of pre-1972 sound recordings for 50 cents. The website pays all necessary license fees to the owners of the musical compositions fixed in the recordings, as well as the state compulsory license fees for the downloads of the pre-1972 sound recordings. Bleeding Ears Records has brought an action against DeadVinyl.com for copyright infringement for its use of the record company's pre-1972 sound recordings, claiming that the East Dakota legislation is preempted by federal copyright law. Will Bleeding Ears Records be successful with its preemption argument?

ANSWER:

IX-1. Publisher owns the copyright in the musical work titled *Sand Generation*. Pirate is a rogue online webcaster who streams unlicensed music on his website. Publisher has issued numerous cease and desist letters to Pirate, but Pirate has ignored them all. Finally, Publisher sues Pirate in a United States district court in New York, where Pirate is domiciled, for infringing its exclusive right to public performance. Soon after being served with Publisher's complaint for copyright infringement, Pirate goes bankrupt and ceases operations of his website. Publisher learns that Pirate has decided to cease his online operations and change the course of his life. Pirate joins a monastery in a remote area of Alaska for at least five years. Undaunted, Publisher presses its suit, seeking damages for Pirate's past infringements as well as an injunction in the event that Pirate ever decides to re-start his unlawful online operations. Will a court grant Publisher's request for an injunction?

(A) Yes. Injunctions are appropriate to make sure that infringement will not recur, even if it has substantially ceased.

(B) Yes. Injunctive relief follows automatically upon a showing of copyright infringement.

(C) No. Because Pirate has ceased his unlawful operations and has given no indication that he will begin them again, a court will not enter an injunction.

(D) No. A United States district court does not have national jurisdiction to enjoin a party that moves to another state.

IX-2. Consider question IX-1. Assume **for the purposes of this question only** that an injunction did issue, and Pirate argued that it was unconstitutional because it constituted a prior restraint and burdened his First Amendment speech rights. Would a court agree with Pirate's First Amendment argument?

ANSWER:

IX-3. Author wrote the popular novel *Jezebel* and also owns the copyright in that literary work. Author has recently discovered that Seller has produced thousands of unauthorized copies of *Jezebel* that Seller then vends online at cut-rate prices. Author sues Seller for copyright infringement, and in so doing immediately moves for a preliminary injunction. Seller responds to the motion in part by arguing that Author has not shown irreparable harm, because Seller can make Author whole by providing money damages. Would a court accept Seller's argument about irreparable harm?

(A) Yes. Because Author's damages are exclusively financial and can be made whole with money damages, they are not irreparable.

(B) Yes. Unless Author can show that he experienced emotional or reputational harm, he cannot successfully argue that the harm is irreparable.

(C) No. A showing that money damages are available for ongoing harm does not disprove that those harms are irreparable.

(D) No. Any injury that happened in the past is automatically considered irreparable.

IX-4. Consider question IX-3. Assume **for the purposes of this question only** that upon learning of Seller's infringement, Author waited six months to file suit, and that during those six months, Seller continued to sell unauthorized copies of *Jezebel*. Assuming that all other facts are as they were in question IX-3, would a court regard the harm inflicted on Author by Seller as irreparable?

ANSWER:

IX-5. Painter is a famed conceptual artist whose original canvases fetch millions in high-end art markets around the world. Mimic is a talented forger who produces nearly perfect knock-offs of famous paintings and sells them, with the buyer's full knowledge of their provenance, relatively cheaply. Painter learns that Mimic has painted a fake version of Painter's work *Opus One*, and sues Mimic for copyright infringement. Painter has a strong case against Mimic, but Mimic has decent representation and has a slim but not negligible chance of prevailing, based on one of several affirmative defenses to infringement. At the onset of litigation, Painter moves for a preliminary injunction, arguing, among other things, that he can show a reasonable likelihood of success on the merits. Is the trial court likely to find that Painter has met the likelihood of success element required for a preliminary injunction?

(A) Yes. All a movant need show on this element is a reasonable likelihood of success on the merits of its infringement claim, and Painter has done so.

(B) Yes. All a movant need show on this element is some plausible chance of success on the merits of its infringement claim, and Painter has done so.

(C) Yes. All a movant need show on this element is any conceivable chance of success on the merits of its infringement claim, and Painter has done so.

(D) No. Painter has failed to make a successful showing on this element of the test for a preliminary injunction because he has not shown a certainty of success on the merits of his claim.

IX-6. Consider question IX-5. Assume **for the purposes of this question only** that a court were to find that Painter showed a reasonable probability of eventual success in his forthcoming litigation against Mimic. If a court were to come to such a conclusion, what if any impact would it have on that court's analysis of the irreparable harm element of the preliminary injunction test?

ANSWER:

IX-7.   Author pens an historical novel titled *Five Days in August*. A year later, Satirist writes an unauthorized parody of Author's novel called *Jive Ways in August*. Several weeks before it is due to be released, Satirist writes to Author to seek an approving quote about *Jive Ways in August* for the book's dust jacket. It turns out that Author did not know that Satirist was parodying *Five Days in August*, and Author is incensed by the situation. Author sues Satirist for infringement, and immediately seeks preliminary injunctive relief in order to bar *Jive Ways in August* from ever being released to the public. In analyzing the public interest factor of the test for preliminary injunctive relief, in favor of which party would a court be likely to rule?

ANSWER:

IX-8.   Al runs a bootleg DVD operation out of a warehouse where he uses a computer to download unauthorized digital copies of popular films from the Internet, and then creates hundreds of DVD copies of each film using a mass-producing device that he constructed. Al also keeps copies of his business records on the computer's hard drive, as well as hard-copy printouts of those files in a cabinet in the warehouse. Several of the studios who own the copyrights in the audiovisual works that Al is copying discover his activities and sue him for copyright infringement. At the outset of litigation, in addition to filing a motion seeking a preliminary injunction preventing Al from continuing his bootleg DVD business, the studios move for an ex parte order impounding the contents of Al's warehouse. Assuming that no showing has yet been made on the merits of the infringement suit, would a court be likely to order the requested impoundment?

(A)   Yes. Pursuant to the Copyright Act, ex parte impoundment orders must issue upon a plaintiff's requesting them.

(B)   Yes. Pursuant to rules issued by the United States Supreme Court, ex parte impoundment orders must issue upon a plaintiff's requesting them.

(C)   No. Impoundment is not a remedy available to plaintiffs until a judgment of infringement has been entered.

(D)   No. Impoundment lies in the discretion of the court, and courts tend not to order ex parte impoundment in light of reservations about the constitutional validity of such orders.

IX-9.   Consider question IX-8. Assume **for the purposes of this question only** that a court granted the studios' motion for impoundment. Which of the following materials in Al's warehouse could be validly included in the impoundment order?

(A)   Al's bootleg DVDs.

(B)   Al's computer and DVD-making device.

(C)   The records contained in Al's file cabinet.

(D)   All of the above.

IX-10.   Composer is generally well-known among Christians for his wholesome, religiously themed musical works. One of these works, in which Composer owns the copyright, is titled *Happy Springtime*. Recently, Composer learned that *Happy Springtime* was used ironically, and without authorization, as the background music in an adult film produced by Xplicit Entertainment. Composer is upset both that he lost the licensing fees that Xplicit should have paid him, and also that his work has been associated with material that is inconsistent with his religious beliefs. Indeed, since the release of Xplicit's adult film, many of Composer's fans have boycotted his records, and Composer's sales have dropped precipitously. Composer sues Xplicit for copyright infringement, wins a default judgment, and seeks nonstatutory damages. Which answer best describes the appropriate measure of those damages?

    (A) Composer is entitled to the profits that Xplicit earned through use of *Happy Springtime*.

    (B) Composer is entitled to the profits that Xplicit earned through use of *Happy Springtime*, and to the lost revenues that Xplicit's unauthorized use caused by inflicting reputational harm.

    (C) Composer is entitled to the lost revenues that Xplicit's unauthorized use caused by inflicting reputational harm.

    (D) Composer is not entitled to nonstatutory damages.

IX-11.   Consider question IX-10. Assume **for the purposes of this question only** that Composer discovers that Xplicit used *Happy Springtime* in its adult film knowing that it was protected by copyright, and knowing that the composer and owner of the musical work was a devout Christian who would be particularly upset by the film's subject matter. Under these circumstances, if Composer requested punitive damages in his prayer for relief, would a court be likely to award them?

ANSWER:

IX-12.   Alice is a famed nature photographer. Betty self-published a very successful wildlife guide that featured her own writing as well as Alice's photographs, which Betty did not receive permission to use. Alice sued Betty for copyright infringement and won a judgment in her favor. During trial, Alice sought nonstatutory damages, and produced evidence showing that Betty's gross revenues for her wildlife guide were $50,000, of which half was attributable to Alice's photographs. Betty responded by producing evidence that it cost her $10,000 in direct expenses to create the book. What is the most accurate measure of Alice's damages?

    (A) $50,000.

    (B) $20,000.

    (C) $12,500.

    (D) $10,000.

IX-13.   Consider question IX-12. Assume **for the purposes of this question only** that at trial,

Alice adduced evidence of Betty's gross profits of $50,000, but that Betty did not produce evidence about the costs associated with producing the wildlife guide. Neither Alice nor Betty produced evidence about how much of Betty's gross profits were attributable to Betty's infringement. In light of this variation, what would the court order in nonstatutory damages?

(A) $50,000.

(B) $25,000.

(C) $20,000.

(D) $0.

IX-14. Consider questions IX-12. Assume **for the purposes of this question only** that Alice adduces evidence that Betty knew Alice's photographs were protected by copyright, but used them in her book anyway, without ever seeking permission. In addition to the $10,000 in direct expenses, Betty produced evidence of $5,000 in overhead costs associated with the production of the wildlife guide. In light of this variation, would the measure of damages be any different?

ANSWER:

IX-15. Ed created a computer program called *Genius* and retains copyright ownership in both the object and source code that comprise the program. Ed sells *Genius* online, and as a condition of sale, requires sellers to enter into a contract stating that they will not copy Ed's program without his permission. Vic purchases a copy of *Genius* and proceeds to make hundreds of copies of it and sell them online at cut-rate prices. Ed sues Vic for copyright infringement and breach of contract, winning on each claim. Based on undisputed evidence offered at trial, Ed seeks actual damages of $50,000 for lost profits related to the copyright infringement and $50,000 for lost profits related to the breach of contract. What amount of damages will a court award?

(A) $100,000.

(B) $75,000.

(C) $50,000.

(D) $0.

IX-16. Hy completed his screenplay titled *Queen Harriet* in January of last year. Hy's agent shopped the screenplay broadly around town in an effort to persuade a studio to acquire it for development. To assist with those efforts, Hy placed the screenplay on his personal website when he delivered it to his agent. In February of last year, Guy (a studio executive to whom Hy's agent pitched the screenplay) took a legitimately acquired copy of Hy's screenplay, made several unauthorized copies of it, and showed it to his colleagues, representing it as his own work. Hy discovered Guy's subterfuge in March of last year, after which he immediately registered his work that same month and then sued Guy for infringing his exclusive right of reproduction. Hy seeks statutory rather than actual damages as a remedy. Will statutory damages be available to him?

(A) Yes. Registration is not a prerequisite for seeking statutory damages.

(B) Yes. By registering the screenplay within three months of its publication, Hy preserved the opportunity to seek statutory damages.

(C) No. Because he failed to register the screenplay before Guy infringed his copyright, Hy forfeited the opportunity to seek statutory damages.

(D) No. Hy cannot seek statutory damages because statutory damages are not available for unpublished works.

IX-17.   Consider question IX-16. Assuming **for the purposes of this question only** that Hy has registered in time to seek statutory damages, which of the following statements best describes Hy's options for seeking money damages?

(A) Hy can seek only statutory damages.

(B) Hy can seek both statutory and actual damages.

(C) Hy can seek either statutory or actual damages, but must elect one or the other when he files his initial complaint against Guy.

(D) Hy can seek either statutory or actual damages, but must elect one or the other prior to the entry of final judgment.

IX-18.   Zed is a composer and musician who owns the rights to several original zydeco compositions, including the undistributed musical work *King Cake*. Yancey includes a version of Zed's *King Cake*, without authorization and fully aware that it was protected by copyright, on a CD compilation of zydeco music. The CD sells hardly any copies, but Zed still sues Yancey for infringing his exclusive rights of reproduction and public distribution, and wins a judgment in his favor. Zed has validly elected to seek statutory damages, and following the judgment, moves that the court enter a damage award of $1.5 million — $150,000 for each of the ten copies of the zydeco CD Yancey sold. The judge orders Yancey to pay a total of $150,000, and Zed appeals. Will he prevail?

(A) Yes. The judge's award failed to allocate damages for each of the ten separate acts of infringement.

(B) No. The judge's award is within the appropriate range for willful infringement.

(C) Yes. Statutory damages are capped at $30,000 per work infringed.

(D) No. Awards of statutory damages are subject to judicial discretion, so they cannot be upset on appeal.

IX-19.   Consider question IX-18. Assume **for the purposes of this question only** that when Yancey included Zed's *King Cake* on the compilation CD, Yancey was acting under the sincere, but mistaken, impression that Zed had executed a valid license permitting Yancey to include *King Cake* in the compilation. In light of this variation, what would be an appropriate measure of damages?

ANSWER:

IX-20. Wall of Reality is a television production company that has produced a dramatic series, titled *Insurgents*, that focuses on the fictional lives of those involved in insurgent conflicts throughout the world. The series consists of twelve episodes, each of which has been registered with the Copyright Office. Wall of Reality licensed the broadcast rights to *Insurgents* to three independent television stations for a single use of the series. The three stations violated the license by rerunning the series once during the summer without permission. Wall of Reality now sues each of the three stations for violating its exclusive right of public performance, and validly seeks statutory damages as a remedy. How many different acts of infringement are at issue?

(A) One.

(B) Three.

(C) Twelve.

(D) Thirty-six.

IX-21. Consider question IX-20. What is the maximum amount of statutory damages Wall of Reality could recover against the three independent television stations?

ANSWER:

IX-22. Tasty Cola, Inc., produces a popular carbonated soft drink. The company commissions as a work for hire an original intricate detailed artistic design called the "Tasty Swoop" that it uses as the distinctive symbol associated with Tasty Cola. The company federally registered the "Tasty Swoop" as both a trademark and a copyrighted work of authorship. Mitch and Fred want to cash in on Tasty Cola's commercial success, and they seek to do so by purchasing a generic competitor soda that costs much less, repackaging it and selling it as "Tasty Cola." Mitch and Fred's repackaging extensively incorporates the Tasty Swoop, which they use, of course, without permission. Tasty Cola eventually discovers Mitch and Fred's subterfuge and sues them for both copyright and trademark infringement. Tasty Cola wins on both the copyright and trademark theories. Can a court order Mitch and Fred to pay damages on both theories?

(A) Yes. Because the interests protected by copyright and trademark are different, Tasty Cola can recover damages on each theory.

(B) Yes. Plaintiffs are entitled to recover damages on as many different theories as they can plausibly articulate.

(C) No. Because the interests protected by copyright and trademark are largely identical, Tasty Cola can recover damages on only one theory.

(D) No. Plaintiffs may recover on only one theory in intellectual property cases, though they are entitled to elect whichever theory of recovery will produce the highest award.

IX-23. Consider question IX-22. Assume **for the purposes of this question only** that Tasty Cola wins a $1 million judgment in statutory damages against Mitch and Fred for copyright infringement, and that shortly after the judgment is entered, but before any of the damages are recovered, Fred flees the country, leaving behind no assets and making him entirely judgment-proof. In light of this variation, what amount of damages can Tasty Cola recover from Mitch alone?

ANSWER:

IX-24. Norm is suspected of running an online file-sharing operation in which he copies and distributes hundreds of copyrighted motion pictures without permission. De Marco Studios brings a civil copyright infringement action against Norm. The Department of Justice also brings a criminal copyright infringement action against Norm. The two cases are assigned to the same judge and are consolidated for trial. At trial, it becomes clear that the charges against Norm were based on a complete misunderstanding and that Norm is innocent of any wrongdoing. The court dismisses both the civil action filed by De Marco Productions and the criminal action filed by the Department of Justice. Following the dismissal, Norm moves to have the United States government reimburse him for the court fees and expert witness fees that he expended in defending the litigation. Will he succeed in recovering his costs of suit?

(A) Yes. Norm can recover his costs of suit, but that includes only court fees, not expert witness fees.

(B) Yes. Norm can recover the costs associated with the civil action, but not the costs associated with the criminal prosecution.

(C) No. Prevailing parties in copyright actions can typically recover costs of suit, but not against the United States government.

(D) No. Prevailing parties in copyright actions are entitled to expert witness fees, but not costs of suit.

IX-25. Jane finishes writing the novel *Norm's Diner* in January 2010, and the novel is published in March of that same year. In June of 2010, InterPub starts offering for sale MicroSoft word files over the Internet with the text of *Norm's Diner* at a much lower rate than the retail price of the hard-copy book. Jane becomes aware of InterPub's unauthorized use as of July 2010 and files suit that same month. At the same time she files her complaint, Jane also registers *Norm's Diner* with the Copyright Office. Jane fails to win a preliminary injunction, and InterPub continues to sell unauthorized copies of *Norm's Diner* over the Internet throughout the litigation. Ultimately, Jane prevails in her infringement suit against InterPub, and after judgment is entered in her favor, Jane seeks to recover attorney's fees from InterPub. Will she succeed?

(A) Yes, because many of InterPub's acts of infringement took place after *Norm's Diner* was registered.

(B) No, because *Norm's Diner* was not registered at the time of the initial infringement.

(C) Yes, because Jane registered *Norm's Diner* within three months of learning about InterPub's infringement.

(D) No, unless Jane can show that InterPub's infringement was willful or malicious.

IX-26. Jackson is an eminent historian. In 2005, he publishes a 700-page monograph entitled *America in the Age of FDR*, in which he retains copyright ownership. Soon after, Henderson, another historian, publishes a negative review of Jackson's monograph in the scholarly journal *American Historical Review*. Henderson's five-page review contains five excerpts from Jackson's book, each about two sentences long, that Henderson included solely to support his criticisms of Jackson's book. Jackson is enraged at Henderson's negative view of his work and sues Henderson for copyright infringement in the Eastern District of California. In his complaint, Jackson alleges that by including the several sentences verbatim from Jackson's book in his review, Henderson violated Jackson's exclusive right of reproduction. Henderson moves for and wins summary judgment based on a de minimis taking argument and, in the alternative, a fair use defense. In her ruling, the judge describes the outcome of the case as "an unambiguous one, both in terms of law and facts, in favor of the defendant." Following the entry of judgment in his favor, Henderson moves to have Jackson pay Henderson's attorney's fees. How will a court likely rule on this motion?

(A) Jackson will win. Because Jackson filed his lawsuit in good faith, he cannot be liable for Henderson's attorney's fees.

(B) Jackson will win. Because there was some chance, however infinitesimal, that Jackson might have prevailed, he cannot be liable for Henderson's attorney's fees.

(C) Henderson will win. Jackson's lawsuit was without sound factual or legal basis, Henderson's success was total, and an award of attorney's fees would help to discourage future baseless lawsuits.

(D) Henderson will win. Prevailing parties in copyright infringement lawsuits are entitled to attorney's fees as a matter of course.

IX-27. Consider question IX-26. Assume **for the purposes of this question only** that Jackson were to prevail in his infringement suit against Henderson, and were to seek an award of attorney's fees. Would Jackson's status as the plaintiff rather than the defendant affect the availability of an award of attorney's fees?

ANSWER:

IX-28. Following entry of a successful copyright infringement judgment in their client's favor, the attorneys of Bram & Gower, LLC, filed a motion for an award of attorney's fees on behalf of their client. Bram & Gower provided the court with documentation that showed that they expended 1,000 hours on the litigation, and that they normally bill $300 per hour, for a total requested fee award of $300,000. The court agreed that attorney's fees were appropriate. However, after reviewing Bram & Gower's billing records, the court found 100 of the hours frivolous and excessive. The court thus entered an award of attorney's fees in favor of Bram & Gower's client, but only in the amount of $270,000. On appeal, is the court's order likely to stand?

(A) Yes. A court is entitled to deviate from the fee request entered by the prevailing party where it finds that the hours or rates are unreasonable and/or excessive.

(B) Yes. A court has absolute discretion to award whatever attorney's fees it deems appropriate, regardless of the parties' submissions.

(C) No. Once a court finds that an award of attorney's fees is appropriate, it is required to enter the amount determined by applying the lodestar method (hours billed times hourly billing rate).

(D) No. A court can only reduce an attorney's fee award upon motion from the non-prevailing party.

IX-29. The West Company manufactures women's dresses made of original fabric designs for retail stores located on the west coast of the United States. While displaying its new line of dresses at a fashion trade show in St. Louis, West Company discovered that the East Company had infringed its fabric designs from its new line. The East Company, which also displayed its infringing fabric designs at the trade show, limits its sales to retail stores on the East Coast of the United States. After the trade show, the West Company was informed by one of its long-time customers, Phasion Phrenzi, that the retailer believed the West Company had stolen fabric designs from the East Company and refused to place an order for West Company's new line of dresses. As a result of this decision, West Company lost sales in the amount of $25,000. West Company brought an action for copyright infringement against East Company. During trial, it was proven that East Company made a profit of $60,000 from its sales of dresses attributable to its use of the infringing fabric designs. To what amount of damages is West Company entitled?

(A) $25,000.

(B) $35,000.

(C) $60,000.

(D) $85,000.

IX-30. Consider question IX-29. Assume **for the purposes of this question only** that, in addition to the facts stated above, Phasion Phrenzi bought infringing dresses from East Company, for which East Company made a profit of $20,000 attributable to its infringing activities. To what amount of damages is West Company entitled?

ANSWER:

X-1. Which of the following statements best describes the Digital Millennium Copyright Act (DMCA)?

    (A) The DMCA provides increased protection for the digital transmission and licensing of works protected by copyright by prohibiting certain efforts to circumvent protective technologies.

    (B) The DMCA provides increased protection for the digital transmission and licensing of works protected by copyright by prohibiting certain efforts to circumvent protective technologies and protecting the use of copyright management information.

    (C) The DMCA provides increased protection for the digital transmission and licensing of works protected by copyright by protecting the use of copyright management information.

    (D) The DMCA provides increased protection for the digital transmission and licensing of works protected by copyright by prohibiting any efforts to circumvent protective technologies and protecting the use of copyright management information.

X-2. George owns and operates the website funfish.com, a compendium of information and resources for people who love keeping fish as pets, including many of George's original essays about and photographs of exotic fish. George seeks to make funfish.com available only to paying members, and so the site can be accessed only by entering a password. George charges members ten dollars per month to access his site, and in exchange for the monthly fee, George gives each member the password that provides access for the current month.

Jane is a computer programmer whose hobby is keeping fish as pets. She invented a software program that allows users to freely access funfish.com bypassing George's attempts to password-protect the site. Jane uses the program to access funfish.com herself, and she has emailed it to her friend Harriet, so she can access the site for free as well. Harriet has a lifetime membership to funfish.com, so she has not used the program to access the site. However, Harriet has sent the program as an email attachment to fifty of her fish-loving friends, and tells each of them to send it along to anyone else who wants to access funfish.com without paying. Many of the recipients of Harriet's email use the program to do just that.

George sues Jane and Harriet under the DMCA's anti-circumvention and anti-trafficking provisions. Will George succeed?

    (A) Yes, Jane and Harriet are both liable under the DMCA.

    (B) Yes, Jane is liable under the DMCA, but Harriet is not.

(C) Yes, Harriet is liable under the DMCA, but Jane is not.

(D) No, neither Jane nor Harriet is liable under the DMCA.

X-3. Consider question X-2. Assume that when she hears of George's lawsuit, Jane says, "That's absurd, because the password-protection George used didn't provide any real protection at all. George used the most basic password-protection system around to control access to funfish.com. A first-year computer science major could easily write a program to get around that thing." If Jane's observations about the rudimentary nature of George's password-protection efforts are correct, does that absolve her and Harriet of DMCA liability?

ANSWER:

X-4. Greta is a well-known nature photographer who has recently started a website, Gretaspic-s.com, through which digital copies of her works can be purchased. The copies of Greta's photos are all encoded with a security device called Photo Security System (PSS), which assures that purchasers of digital copies of Greta's photos cannot make further copies or digitally manipulate them.

Warren is a fan of Greta's photos and also an amateur computer programmer. He was given a computer program called dePSS, which undoes the copy and use controls that PSS encodes into the digital copies of Greta's photos. Warren uses dePSS only to enable him to alter some of Greta's photos he purchased for use in a birthday card he makes for his wife. Warren's hacker friend Lloyd also obtains the dePSS program and makes the program available on his website which makes available computer programs and information that Lloyd believes the programming community will find of interest. As a result, hundreds of users take advantage of dePSS to make unauthorized copies of Greta's photos. Greta learns of this, and files suit under the DMCA against Warren and Lloyd. Will she prevail?

(A) Yes, both Warren and Lloyd are liable under the DMCA.

(B) Yes, but only Warren is liable under the DMCA.

(C) Yes, but only Lloyd is liable under the DMCA.

(D) No, neither Warren nor Lloyd is liable under the DMCA.

X-5. Consider question X-4. Assume that as part of his response to Greta's DMCA allegations, Lloyd argues that his inclusion of dePSS on his website constituted a fair use, and that this point should shield him from liability. Assuming for purposes of this question that Lloyd's assertion that his use of the dePSS program would be considered a fair one under the Copyright Act's four-part statutory test, would this argument absolve him of any DMCA liability he might have to Greta?

ANSWER:

X-6. Vanna is an amateur computer programmer, and one of her favorite hobbies is seeing if she can write software to circumvent the latest technology protection measures. Vanna relishes this because she strongly dislikes major corporations. One such technology protection measure is ContentKey, a digital lock developed by DynaCorp. ContentKey allows users to encrypt data on their laptops to prevent anyone else from accessing the content of the hard drive. Vanna develops a program that circumvents DynaCorp's ContentKey by decrypting the encrypted material. Pleased with herself, Vanna posts an executable version of her program on her personal website under the title "Stick it to DynaCorp by Unlocking ContentKey." Although Vanna does not tell DynaCorp about this, DynaCorp discovers Vanna's site and brings a DMCA suit against Vanna. Who will prevail?

(A) Vanna, because her work was not for profit.

(B) Vanna, because encryption research is protected under the DMCA.

(C) DynaCorp, because there are no research safe harbors under the DMCA.

(D) DynaCorp, because Vanna's encryption research was not in good faith.

X-7. Sculptor creates a bronze sculpture of a man's foot entitled *Step*, which Sculptor likes and keeps in his studio. Collector sees *Step* and asks if Sculptor will license Collector to show the sculpture in Collector's private gallery for three months. Sculptor agrees, and before handing *Step* over to Collector, affixes a label to the bottom of the statue that reads "Licensed to Collector for limited gallery showing only."

Collector places *Step* in his gallery, where he removes the label that Sculptor had applied, and promptly sells *Step* to a rich art aficionado for a large sum. Sculptor sues Collector under the DMCA. Will Sculptor prevail?

(A) Yes. By intentionally removing Sculptor's copyright management information from *Step*, Collector is liable under the DMCA.

(B) Yes. By violating the clear terms of the licensing agreement with Sculptor, Collector is liable under the DMCA.

(C) No. The DMCA's copyright management information provisions apply only to digital material.

(D) No. Collector is not liable under the DMCA because the information on the label did not identify Sculptor as the author of *Step*.

X-8. Consider question X-7. Assume **for the purposes of this question only** that when Collector receives *Step* from Sculptor, he cleans the sculpture, and in so doing, inadvertently causes the label with the licensing terms to fall off. Never aware of the label or its absence, Collector nevertheless sells *Step* to a rich art aficionado in violation of the licensing agreement with Sculptor, and Sculptor sues Collector under the DMCA. In light of this variation, will Sculptor prevail?

ANSWER:

X-9. Which of the following statements most accurately describes the penalties available to a court when a defendant is found to have violated the anticircumvention or CMI integrity provisions (sections 1201 and 1202) of the DMCA?

    (A) Injunctive relief; actual or statutory damages; court costs; and attorney's fees.

    (B) Injunctive relief; actual, statutory, and punitive damages; court costs; attorney's fees; criminal fines; and imprisonment.

    (C) Injunctive relief; actual or statutory damages; court costs; attorney's fees; criminal fines; and imprisonment.

    (D) Injunctive relief; actual or statutory damages; court costs; attorney's fees; and criminal fines.

X-10.   Steve and Olga are each found separately liable for several violations of the DMCA's anticircumvention provisions. A court initially concludes that both Steve's and Olga's civil liability amounts to $5,000. The court then learns that Olga violated these provisions without knowledge and with no reason to know she had committed the violation, and that Steve has violated the DMCA's anticircumvention provisions several other times in the past two years. How do these additional facts affect how the judge should impose damages on Steve and Olga?

    (A) The judge must increase Steve's damages three times, and may lower Olga's by fifty percent.

    (B) The judge may increase Steve's damages three times, and may lower Olga's by fifty percent.

    (C) The judge must increase Steve's damages three times, and may lower Olga's by whatever amount he sees fit.

    (D) The judge may increase Steve's damages three times, and may lower Olga's by whatever amount he sees fit.

X-11.   Christa Liss is an eccentric filmmaker. She worked for some time on a project for Vista Productions that she and she alone writes, directs, performs in, and edits. Then, a week before she was due to submit the final version of the film to Vista, she decided that it was a failure, and told Vista that she would not submit it. The only copy of the film exists on Christa's computer's hard drive in an MP4 file. Christa's refusal to show the film to Vista, or to the public generally, generates enormous curiosity. The film critic Eber Rogert hacks into Christa's computer, circumventing the technological protection of her content that she put in place, views the film, and considers it a triumph. Eber publishes an article about Christa's film, and includes three images directly taken from the MP4 file to illustrate points made in his article. Christa is incensed and sues Eber for the unlawful circumvention of a technological measure under 17 U.S.C. § 1201(a). Eber counters with a fair use defense, arguing that the film images in his article were simply there in order to illustrate the points he made in his article. Will his defense succeed?

    (A) No. Regardless of the validity of Eber's fair use argument, it is irrelevant here because fair use is not a defense to DMCA liability.

(B)   No. Fair use is categorically unavailable where it occurs in conjunction with wrongful behavior like computer hacking.

(C)   Yes. Fair use is designed to assure broad access to material that authors would otherwise choose not to release publicly.

(D)   Yes. Fair use gives critics a limitless right to access and use material regardless of authorial consent.

X-12.   Kent Con, a long time client has called you. He is distressed about the fact that his daughter, Lexi, has "hacked" the eBooksOnline.com website from which she rents eBook titles to read on her Digital Reader Book. Rented titles are placed in the memory of the Digital Reader Book, but cannot be accessed after thirty days from the date of purchase. Apparently, Lexi has purchased a computer program, *Free Gutenberg*, that allows her to pay the rental fee for eBooks, but upgrade the rented copy to a full-priced copy for free by circumventing the digital rights management installed in each eBook file. A full-priced copy of an eBook typically sells for three times the rental price. By manipulating the digital rights management in the eBook file with the aid of *Free Gutenberg*, Lexi can access each "rented" eBook on her Digital Reader Book at any time. Mr. Con wants to know whether his daughter has violated any laws.

ANSWER:

X-13.   Winsome Maxwell recently has created a website through which he makes rare and obscure films, the copyrights in which have expired, available for viewing on a pay per view or subscription basis. Maxwell has encrypted the works shown on his website to ensure that only those who pay can see them. One of the films available on the website is *The Dark Vegan*, an early science fiction film. Winsome Maxwell recently purchased a pristine copy of *The Dark Vegan* at a swap meet.

Qualitative Cinema, Inc. is a company that specializes in marketing high quality DVDs of artistic films. Qualitative Cinema decided to release a DVD set of the films of Homer Chatsky. The only copy Qualitative Cinema could find of *The Dark Vegan*, one of Chatsky's most important films, was on Maxwell's website. Qualitative approached Maxwell to obtain a reproduction of his copy of *The Dark Vegan*. Maxwell refused to permit access to the motion picture or to license a copy of the film to Qualitative Cinema because Maxwell wanted to have the exclusive copy of the film on his website.

In response, the employees of Qualitative Cinema, acting within the scope of their employment, created a computer program that permitted the circumvention of Maxwell's encryption protection. The program gave Qualitative Cinema access to the films located on Maxwell's website without the payment of a fee and the ability to digitally reproduce those films. Employees of Qualitative Cinema were able to download a copy of *The Dark Vegan*, which was then included in the Chatsky DVD set that contained six of Chatsky's films, a documentary on his life, and a film historian's analysis of Chatsky's film techniques. The DVD set was sold to the public. Maxwell has filed a lawsuit against Qualitative Cinema for the circumvention of his copyright protection system. Maxwell will not be successful because:

(A) Qualitative Cinema had made a good-faith effort to license the use of *The Dark Vegan* before it circumvented its encryption protection.

(B) Reasonable access must be provided to works that are in the public domain.

(C) The purpose of circumventing the encryption protection was to produce a creative work that provided a benefit to the public.

(D) The audiovisual works protected by the encryption are not protected by copyright.

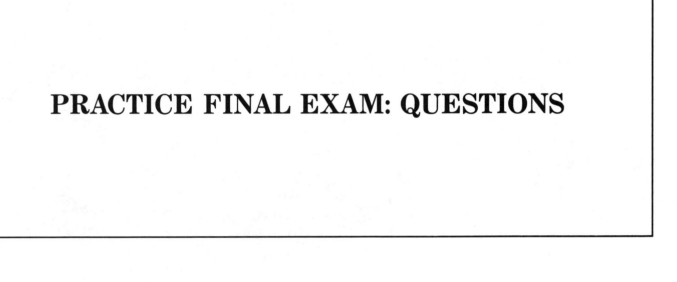

PRACTICE FINAL EXAM: QUESTIONS

XI-1. Bernard is a designer and tattoo artist. For years, he has been conceptualizing a design in his imagination of a dragon eating a motorcycle called *Gorgon's Delight*. *Gorgon's Delight* is very clear and specific in Bernard's head but until this year he has never committed it to canvas or any other medium. Then, earlier this year, Bernard tattooed the design onto his friend Carlos' back. Bernard did not sketch *Gorgon's Delight* before tattooing Carlos, but worked entirely from memory and imagination. Carlos was very pleased with the way the tattoo came out, but unfortunately, just three minutes after Bernard completed the design, Carlos spontaneously combusted and turned into a pile of ash. Bernard was so traumatized by this freak tragedy that he has never tattooed or drawn *Gorgon's Delight* in any other context ever since it happened. Is *Gorgon's Delight* protected by federal copyright?

(A) No, because it was never fixed in a tangible medium of expression.

(B) No, because it was fixed in a tangible medium of expression for too brief a period of time.

(C) Yes, because it was fixed in a tangible medium of expression.

(D) No, because works of authorship fixed on human flesh are uncopyrightable as a matter of public policy.

XI-2. Gene is an aspiring screenwriter who has been thinking about a new project. Gene pens a plot treatment that encapsulates this project, called *Seeing the Light*.

> **" 'Seeing the Light' is about Melissa's journey to love. At the beginning, Melissa is dating Jack, a rich playboy who's lots of fun but doesn't treat Melissa well at all. Jack is always getting drunk and being a jerk to Melissa. Then one day, Melissa meets Alan, a shop worker who's poor and simple, but very sweet and kind to her. One day when Jack is being a drunk jerk, Melissa realizes Alan is the one for her. 'He may be poor but he has a heart of gold,' she says, 'and that's what really matters.' So Melissa dumps Jack and goes off with Alan. Alan and Melissa then get married, have lots of kids, and are happy as clams. The end!!!"**

Gene sends this plot treatment to Bill, a producer he met at a party. Bill reads the treatment, but tells Gene that there's no way any film company will be interested in producing *Seeing the Light*. Gene is so disappointed that he never develops the project further. But the next year Gene is shocked and angry when he learns that Bill wrote the screenplay for and produced a hit movie titled *The Last Runaway*. The main character in *The Last Runaway* is a girl who runs away from home. But her parents are an unhappy couple. The father (who is named Jack) drinks a lot and is often abusive to the mother (who is named Melissa), and by the end of the movie, Melissa gets sick of Jack's bad treatment and leaves him for another man.

Gene sues Bill in the U.S. District Court for the Southern District of New York, alleging that the "Jack" character in *The Last Runaway* infringed the copyright in the character of Jack in *Seeing the Light*. Who will prevail in the infringement suit, Gene or Bill?

(A)   Gene, because in the Second Circuit, literary characters enjoy distinctively broad copyright protection.

(B)   Gene, because the name "Jack" in combination with his other distinctive qualities created an original, and hence copyrightable, literary character.

(C)   Bill, because his use of the "Jack" character in *The Last Runaway*, which is a motion picture, could not infringe the "Jack" character in *Seeing the Light*, which is a literary work.

(D)   Bill, because the "Jack" character in *Seeing the Light* lacked sufficient originality to merit copyright protection.

XI-3.   Cal, a self-employed computer programmer, composes and fixes in digital form the source code for *Iterate*, a computer program that will allow users to prioritize the tasks in their personal and professional lives. Cal does not publish in any analog form the source code for *Iterate*, though he does sell copies of the program's object code embedded in CD-ROMs for use on personal computers. Mal, a notorious hacker, buys a copy of *Iterate*, runs it on his computer, and then acquires the object code that has been compiled by his computer's operating system when executing *Iterate*. Mal studies this object code, eventually figures out how *Iterate* works, and then releases an equivalent of Cal's program, called *ReIterate*. *ReIterate* sells for much less than *Iterate*, and sales of *Iterate* plummet. Cal discovers what Mal has done, and sues him for infringing the copyright Cal owns in *Iterate*. Assuming that Mal's conduct does not amount to fair use, who will prevail?

(A)   Cal will prevail because Mal copied without permission the *Iterate* object code, which is a protected literary work.

(B)   Cal will prevail because Mal violated an implied contract that he would use *Iterate* only in a personal, noncommercial manner.

(C)   Mal will prevail because Cal's copyright in *Iterate* extends only to the source code that Cal composed, not to the object code compiled by Mal's operating system.

(D)   Mal will prevail because it was Mal's computer that read the object code of *Iterate*, not Mal.

XI-4.   Betty creates the lyrics and music that comprise an original musical composition for guitar and voice called *Summer Fugue*. Chris, a singer and guitarist, records his version of *Summer Fugue* in a home recording studio that he owns and operates entirely by himself. Chris' version of *Summer Fugue* hews very closely to Betty's original version, making no major changes in lyrics or arrangement. Chris distributes CDs containing his sound recording of *Summer Fugue* for self-promotion, and one of them becomes popular with the DJs at the local analog radio station KHIT, who play the track many times a day. Which statement best describes the obligations of the various parties under federal copyright law?

(A) Chris must pay a mechanical license fee to Betty for his reproduction of *Summer Fugue*, and KHIT must pay Chris royalties for its public performance of his sound recording of *Summer Fugue*.

(B) Chris must pay a mechanical license fee to Betty for his reproduction of *Summer Fugue*, and KHIT must pay Betty public performance royalties for its playing of Chris' sound recording of *Summer Fugue*.

(C) KHIT must pay Chris and Betty public performance royalties for its playing of Chris' sound recording of *Summer Fugue*.

(D) Chris must pay Betty a mechanical license fee for his reproduction of *Summer Fugue*, but KHIT need not pay public performance royalties to Chris or to Betty each time it plays Chris' sound recording of *Summer Fugue*.

XI-5. MWB makes fine German cars. One day MWB tells its head designer to come up with a fanciful design for a futuristic car. The designer pens a sketch of a design for a hover-car called the "ZoomMeister," and the MWB management is so delighted that they arrange for very small, scale models of the ZoomMeister to be given to the company's top twenty employees as paperweights. The models do not work and do not represent serious or realistic aspirations for future cars, but are still very popular, simply because, in the words of one MWB manager, "They look so cool."

Then, when an executive from toy company FunCo is visiting a colleague at MWB, the executive notices one of the toy ZoomMeister models, commits its details to memory, and a year later FunCo releases an identical scale model of a hover-car it calls "Mr. Zoom." The executives at MWB are incensed and sue FunCo for copyright infringement. Will FunCo prevail?

(A) Yes, FunCo will prevail because the ZoomMeister is not a useful article, and thus not protected by federal copyright.

(B) Yes, FunCo will prevail because while the ZoomMeister is a useful article, its aesthetic features are not separable from its utilitarian ones, and it thus cannot be copyrighted.

(C) No, FunCo will not prevail because the ZoomMeister is not a useful article.

(D) No, FunCo will not prevail, because while the ZoomMeister is a useful article, its aesthetic features are separable from its utilitarian ones and may be copyrighted.

XI-6. Len pens the musical composition *Green Acres* in 1965; federal copyright in the musical work *Green Acres* vested that same year. In 1967, Len's friend Janine performs and records a rendition of *Green Acres* with Len's permission in Janine's own home recording studio. Janine's rendition of *Green Acres* is released to the public on vinyl as a single that same year. As of 1980, who owns federal copyrights in the *Green Acres* musical work and sound recording?

(A) Len owns the federal copyright in the *Green Acres* musical work and sound recording.

(B) Len owns the federal copyright in the *Green Acres* musical work.

(C) Len owns the federal copyright in the *Green Acres* musical work, and Janine owns the federal copyright in the *Green Acres* sound recording.

(D) Len owns the federal copyright in the *Green Acres* musical work, and Len and Janine share the federal copyright in the *Green Acres* sound recording as joint authors.

XI-7. KaraokeCo releases a CD of music tracks for karaoke performers to sing along with. All the sound recordings on the CD are based on arrangements of popular musical works created by KaraokeCo employees, and were performed by session musicians who agreed to cede any rights in the resulting sound recordings to KaraokeCo. Each track of the CD also contained the lyrics of each musical work that could be read by those singing the tune. KaraokeCo did not ask any of the owners of the copyrights in the musical works for permission to make karaoke arrangements of their works.

One day, a viral video circulates on the Internet of a man named Krooner Ken performing hilariously bad karaoke, and using all of the tracks on KaraokeCo's CD. Ken then parlays his Internet stardom into lots of cash by selling DVDs of his awful singing, entitled *Krooner Ken Kills 'Em!*. KaraokeCo wants a bite of Krooner Ken's DVD sale profits, and sues Ken for infringement, accurately pointing out that Ken did not get a license or permission to perform any of KaraokeCo's arrangements. Will KaraokeCo succeed in its infringement suit?

(A) Yes, because copyright is a strict liability offense, and Krooner Ken is liable regardless of whether his initial intent was to profit from his rendition of KaraokeCo's musical works.

(B) No, because Krooner Ken's renditions of KaraokeCo's arrangements were clearly fair use.

(C) No, because Krooner Ken's performances fell within section 115's compulsory mechanical license, which makes it unnecessary for recording artists and record companies to pay for creating renditions of musical works.

(D) No, because KaraokeCo had no copyright in the arrangements, because it unlawfully used the underlying musical works on which the karaoke arrangements were based.

XI-8. Lola loves Los Angeles, and especially its many restaurants. One day she decides to create a guide to her favorite L.A. eateries, called *The Lola Guide: Where to Eat in the City of Angels*. Lola researches restaurants throughout Los Angeles County, chooses her favorites, writes distinctive descriptions of each venue, and lists them in her guide by alphabetical order. Which of the following statements most accurately describes the scope of Lola's copyright in *The Lola Guide*?

(A) Lola's guide has no copyright protection because it consists of uncopyrightable facts and research.

(B) The arrangement of information in Lola's guide, the selection of information in Lola's guide, and her original descriptions of restaurants are copyrighted.

(C) Both the arrangement of information in Lola's guide and her original descriptions of restaurants are copyrighted.

(D)   Both the selection of information in Lola's guide and her original descriptions of restaurants are copyrighted.

XI-9.   Melissa is an artist specializing in painting pictures of naturalistic scenes. She works part-time for the U.S. government, for whom she paints pictures of wild animals that adorn information centers in various national parks. The federal government gives her a monthly check from which it takes out taxes and health insurance costs, and provides her an office (stocked with supplies) where she can create the paintings the government requests. Melissa spends the rest of her work time in her home studio, painting pictures (with materials she supplies for herself) for private clients who request pictures of various nature scenes.

Because Melissa truly loves her work, she often paints portraits of nature in her free time, purely for her own enjoyment. During a recent weekend when Melissa had no obligations for the government or any private client, she created in her home studio a particularly compelling nature scene called *Against the Current*. This painting depicted salmon swimming upstream in Northern California's Klamath River, which she had recently observed while on vacation there.

Melissa's government boss, Albert, came over to Melissa's house one night to visit and was impressed by *Against the Current*. Albert said to Melissa, "Thanks for doing such work for the feds." Melissa insisted that the copyright in the painting was hers, while Albert insisted that the copyright actually belonged to the United States. Who is right?

(A)   Albert, because Melissa is an employee of the federal government.

(B)   Melissa, because she is not an employee of any organization, but an independent contractor.

(C)   Melissa, because she created *Against the Current* while acting outside the scope of her employment.

(D)   Neither, because the U.S. government cannot own copyrights of works created by its employees.

XI-10.   Hilda wrote the literary work *South Atlantic* in 1919, using ink pen and notebook paper. Two years later, in 1921, she published *South Atlantic* with proper copyright notice. Hilda validly renewed the copyright in the 28th year of its initial term. At the end of which year did the copyright in *South Atlantic* enter the public domain?

(A)   1975.

(B)   1977.

(C)   1994.

(D)   1996.

XI-11.   Helen and Greg jointly author the musical composition *Prohibition Blues* in 1925. They never published the work, though they did register with the Copyright Office as an unpublished work in 1928. In 1930, Helen died suddenly. The work was validly renewed in the twenty-eighth year of its initial term. Greg, in contrast to Helen, lived a long life, dying in 1970. At the end of which year did (or will) the copyright in *Prohibition Blues* enter the public domain?

(A) 1984.

(B) 2003.

(C) 2023.

(D) 2040.

XI-12. In 1890, amateur artist Sam painted a self-portrait and hung it in the parlor of his private home, where it was seen only by a small group of family and friends that come to Sam's home. Sam died in 1940, leaving his entire estate to his daughter, Juana. Juana placed the self-portrait in her attic for storage. In 1990, Tracy approached Juana and informed her that many of Sam's other works have recently become discovered and made a splash in the art world. Juana told Tracy about the self-portrait, and Tracy bought the portrait and all copyrights in it from Juana for a handsome price. In 1992, Tracy unveiled Sam's self-portrait to the art world for the first time at a gallery opening in Manhattan to which all were invited, and that night more than a thousand people viewed the portrait. At the end of which year did (or will) the copyright in Sam's self-portrait enter the public domain?

(A) 1946.

(B) 2002.

(C) 2010.

(D) 2047.

XI-13. Sal is a struggling playwright who is currently developing a play titled *August Haze* while waiting tables to make a bare-bones living. One day, Sal strikes up a conversation with Ed, a wealthy dilettante. Ed likes Sal's description of *August Haze*, and gives Sal $15,000 so Sal can quit his waiter job and focus exclusively on developing the play. Sal accepts the offer, and makes enormous strides toward finishing *August Haze* in the next couple of months. During that time, Sal and Ed occasionally meet for coffee, and sometimes chat about the play. Ed constantly gives Sal writing suggestions, and though Sal usually ignores them, he does incorporate a few of Ed's proposed lines of dialogue verbatim. Ed eventually thinks of himself as Sal's collaborator, and Ed tells acquaintances that he's "co-writing a play with an up-and-coming playwright." Sal, by contrast, does not see Ed in this light, and tells friends that he "puts up with this rich guy's lame ideas because he gives me money." *August Haze* eventually makes a huge splash on Broadway, and Sal is surprised to find that Ed expects that he is entitled to half of the playwright royalties earned by the play's performances, claiming that he is a joint author. Is Ed's claim to joint authorship of *August Haze* viable?

(A) No, because Sal did not consider Ed a joint author.

(B) Yes, because Ed's financial contributions were indispensable to Sal's completing *August Haze*.

(C) Yes, because Ed considered himself a joint author.

(D) Yes, because *August Haze* contained several lines of Ed's original, creative expression.

XI-14. Which of the following circumstances give rise to a jointly owned copyright?

I. A lyricist and a musician collaborate with each other to create a musical work.

II. The owner of the copyright in a lucrative literary work dies, leaving a will that devises all his property to his three children.

III. A woman who is married in a community property state solely creates a copyrighted work of authorship.

IV. Three friends create a partnership, and that partnership hires an employee to create a copyrighted work of authorship in the course of his employment.

(A) I only.

(B) I and II.

(C) I, II, and IV.

(D) I, II, III, and IV.

XI-15. Kelly, a poet, composed a villanelle entitled *Good Friends* in 2007 using a word processor. Later that year, Kelly then inscribed the text of *Good Friends* on parchment with ink, signed her name at the bottom of the parchment, framed it, and gave the framed copy of the villanelle to her friend Rosalind as a birthday present. When Kelly presented the gift to Rosalind, she said "This poem is yours!" In 2008, Kelly died, leaving a will devising all her worldly goods — including copyrights in all her poems — to James. In 2009, James published an anthology of Kelly's poetry that included *Good Friends*. Rosalind sues James for infringement of the copyright in *Good Friends*. Will she succeed?

(A) Yes. Kelly's signature on the parchment effected a transfer of the copyright in *Good Friends* as well as transferring ownership of the object.

(B) Yes. Kelly's statement effects verbal transfer of the copyright in the poem.

(C) No. Kelly's gift of the framed copy of *Good Friends* gave Rosalind ownership of that physical copy of the poem, but did not effect transfer of the copyright in the poem.

(D) No. Kelly's devise to James voided the 2007 transfer of copyright in *Good Friends* to Rosalind, and vested ownership in James instead.

XI-16. KLOQ is an analog radio station specializing in popular music. KLOQ broadcasts pursuant to a five-second delay, so that all of the content it broadcasts is saved digitally for five seconds, then immediately taped over. One day, the owner of one of the most popular musical works broadcast by KLOQ, *My Portrait*, sues the radio station for violating her exclusive rights of reproduction and public performance for the unlicensed broadcasts. The owner asserted that KLOQ's five-second tape-delay recordings amounted to unauthorized reproductions of her musical work. KLOQ had a valid license to publicly perform *My Portrait*, but the license did not extend to any other exclusive rights. Will the owner prevail on this argument?

(A) Yes. Copyright is a strict liability offense, so any unauthorized copying — however temporary — violates the owner's reproduction rights.

(B) No. KLOQ, as a transmitting organization entitled to transmit *My Portrait*, may make an ephemeral recording of the work.

(C) No. Courts have held that public performance licenses impliedly extend to reproduction by licensees as well.

(D) No. Because KLOQ did not copy the entirety of *My Portrait*, but rather only five-second snippets of it, they did not violate the owner's reproduction right.

XI-17. Paramecium Records specializes in rare and specialized records, including obscure bootleg versions of live concerts. Paramecium does not create any bootlegs, but often buys bootlegs from sellers, and then re-sells them to the public. One day Paramecium receives a cease-and-desist letter from lawyers for the popular band "Smack," demanding that Paramecium stop selling any more bootlegs of Smack's live musical performances. Paramecium has sold numerous Smack concert bootlegs in the past, and does not want to stop selling them. As a matter of federal law, does Paramecium's continued sale of Smack concert bootlegs expose them to liability?

(A) Yes, sale of the Smack bootlegs exposes Paramecium to both criminal and civil liability.

(B) No, because Paramecium's sale of the Smack bootlegs is excused from liability pursuant to the first sale doctrine.

(C) No, because concerts are not fixed, and thus cannot be the basis for federal copyright liability.

(D) No, because Paramecium did not engage in the initial copying of Smack's live performances, but only sold copies of the bootlegs.

XI-18. Grace is a well-known poet who is down on her luck, and she sells the copyrights in all of her poems to her brother, Deke, in exchange for a substantial amount of cash. Deke then grants a nonexclusive license to B.P. McGee, a publisher, to create an anthology of Grace's poems. B.P. McGee spends a few months culling out the weaker poems, decides to organize the selected works around a seasonal theme, and finally releases the anthology, called *Finding Grace*, which becomes a commercial success. Several years later, B.P. McGee releases a second edition of *Finding Grace*, which includes the same poems, but adds a critical essay along with them and prints the new edition on higher-end paper stock. B.P. McGee did not negotiate a new license with Deke before releasing the second edition. As soon as the new edition comes out, Zed — a rogue publisher — makes thousands of unauthorized copies of it, and floods the market with lower-priced versions of the second edition of *Finding Grace*. Deke is outraged and sues both B.P. McGee and Zed for copyright infringement; B.P. McGee sues Zed as well. To which parties, if any, will Zed and B.P. McGee be liable?

(A)   Zed will be liable to both B.P. McGee and Deke, and B.P. McGee will be liable to Deke.

(B)   Zed will be liable to Deke.

(C)   Zed and B.P. McGee will both be liable to Deke.

(D)   Zed will be liable to both B.P. McGee and Deke.

XI-19.   Ray is a budding media entrepreneur who wants to start a number of radio ventures. Ray seeks to own and operate an analog radio station, KRAY, which will also stream its content online over its website affiliate, www.kray.com. Ray also wants to branch out into two new digital radio services. The first is a satellite radio service, where he will offer digital streams of set playlists to subscribers via satellite. The second is an on-demand digital radio service, where he will offer listeners the opportunity to choose from a wide array of music titles, which will then be streamed instantly to them. Neither option will permit users to download any of the tracks. Ray comes to you and asks about his obligations to sound recording copyright owners for these four ventures. Which of the following answers most accurately describes his obligations under federal copyright law?

(A)   Ray has no obligations to sound recording copyright owners for public performances of the works via his analog radio station, KRAY, but will have to negotiate a license with them for transmitting their works to the public via the other three means.

(B)   Ray has no obligations to sound recording copyright owners for transmitting their works to the public via the analog or online versions of KRAY, but will have to pay them a compulsory license for transmitting their works to the public via the satellite radio and on-demand streaming services.

(C)   Ray has no obligations to sound recording copyright owners for publicly performing their works via the analog version of KRAY, but will have to pay them a compulsory license for transmitting their works to the public via www.kray.com and via satellite radio, and will have to negotiate a license with them for transmitting their works to the public via the on-demand streaming service.

(D)   Ray has no obligations to sound recording copyright owners for transmitting their works to the public via the analog or online versions of KRAY, but will have to pay them a negotiated license for transmitting their works to the public via the satellite radio and on-demand streaming services.

XI-20.   Bill takes an impromptu snapshot of Denise with his cellphone. He later prints out a copy of the photo and shows it to her. Denise hates the picture so much that she takes out a pen and scribbles all over it, ruining the copy. Bill is enraged, and claims that Denise has violated his moral rights by defacing the photograph. As a matter of law, does Bill have a claim under the Visual Artists Rights Act ("VARA")?

(A) Yes, because photographs are a protected work under VARA as long as the author does not print more than 200 copies.

(B) No, because this particular photograph is not a protected work under VARA.

(C) No, because VARA does not extend to authors a right of integrity.

(D) No, because Denise has an affirmative defense to violating VARA, because the photograph violated her right of publicity under state law.

XI-21. Iris composed an original pamphlet about fast food and health problems on her word processor in 1980. In 1981, she printed the pamphlet in her home, made several hundred copies, and distributed them in person to passers-by outside Queen Burger, a local fast-food restaurant. The pamphlet identified Iris as its author, but did not contain a copyright notice. Recently, Queen Burger published a brochure called *Fighting the Lies*, in which it answers critics' objections to the health of its food. Included in the pamphlet is an exact reproduction of Iris' pamphlet. Iris sues Queen Burger for copyright infringement. Assuming Queen Burger's reproduction is not fair use, will Iris prevail?

(A) Yes, because federal copyright in her work vested upon fixation of her literary work in a tangible medium of expression in 1980.

(B) Yes, because federal copyright in her work vested when she distributed the pamphlet to the public in 1981.

(C) No, because while Iris' federal copyright vested when she first fixed the work in a tangible medium of expression in 1980, she ceded it to the public domain through failure to include proper notice, or cure that failure with a reasonable effort after the omission was discovered.

(D) No, because Iris' work was ceded irrevocably and immediately to the public domain in 1981, when it was published without proper copyright notice.

XI-22. In 1950, Jean wrote a politically charged tract about the government. In 1951, Jean posted a copy of the speech on the wall of the break room in her workplace, a small private company with about twenty employees. In 1952, Jean applied for and was permitted to read her speech during the "Citizen Editorial" segment of the local evening news broadcast. The speech became popular enough that in 1953, Jean created one hundred copies of the speech using a makeshift printing press in her own home, handing them out only to close personal acquaintances who expressed an interest in her political beliefs and sought copies of the speech for their personal edification only. Finally, in 1954, Schriver & Co., a publisher, executed a contract with Jean to publish the speech in book form. Schriver & Co. released copies of the hardbound speech to bookstores for sale later that year. Proper copyright notice was affixed to all the aforementioned copies of the speech. Which of the foregoing acts amounted to publication under the then-applicable federal copyright law?

I. Posting the speech in the break room.

II. Reading the speech on the evening news.

III. Printing the speech and giving copies to interested acquaintances.

IV. Publishing the speech in book form.

(A) I and IV.

(B) I, II, and IV.

(C) I, III, and IV.

(D) IV only.

XI-23. Ken writes a screenplay entitled *Blood Feud* in 1953, showing it only to his agent. The agent pitched the screenplay to RCP Films in 1954. The RCP executives loved the screenplay, and paid handsomely for the exclusive right to develop the screenplay into a motion picture. For the next year, RCP developed the motion picture version of *Blood Feud*, showing the script only to the director, actors and actresses, and other employees who needed to see it in order to perform their job duties. Finally, in 1956, the motion picture, based largely on Ken's screenplay, is released to the general public. The screenplay does not include any copyright notice, but the motion picture does. The copyright in the motion picture was properly renewed, though no renewal was filed for the screenplay. What is the copyright status of the screenplay and the motion picture, respectively?

ANSWER:

XI-24. Logan writes a screenplay entitled *Max Furious*, and registers the work with the Copyright Office, listing himself as the copyright owner. Later, Logan assigns all rights in the *Max Furious* screenplay to Royal Studios, a film production company. Royal creates a motion picture largely based on Logan's screenplay, but never registers the copyright in the motion picture. A couple of years later, Royal learns that a bootlegger in Cleveland is making and selling unauthorized DVDs of the *Max Furious* motion picture, selling them for cut-rate prices. Royal sues the bootlegger in the Northern District of Ohio for copyright infringement of the motion picture. The bootlegger moves to dismiss for lack of subject-matter jurisdiction. Who will prevail?

(A) The bootlegger. Royal's failure to separately register the derivative work it created based on Logan's screenplay deprives the district court of jurisdiction.

(B) The bootlegger. Royal's failure to have Logan's initial copyright registration amended to reflect Royal as the new owner of the copyright in the original work deprives the court of jurisdiction.

(C) Royal Studios. Logan's registration of the original work gives the court jurisdiction of infringement suits concerning all derivative works.

(D) Royal Studios. The bootlegger's willful infringement waives the standard jurisdictional requirement of copyright registration.

XI-25. Initech is a Delaware corporation, incorporated in 1970, specializing in the creation of ergonomic computer keyboards. In 1980, one of its employees, Vince Virtual, acting within the scope of his employment, wrote a brochure called *The Ergonomic Advantage*, saving a copy of the brochure to a disk. Virtual died in 1990. In 1995, Initech released the brochure to the general public for the first time by uploading it onto its company website. In 2000, Initech becomes a casualty of the burst Internet bubble, goes out of business, and ceases to exist as a corporate entity. At the end of which year will *The Ergonomic Advantage* enter the public domain?

(A) 2060.

(B) 2070.

(C) 2090.

(D) 2100.

XI-26. Harriet is a screenwriter who wants to sell her script to a movie studio. She has a meeting with several executives at Acme Films, who consider her pitch and then decide to pass on the project. Harriet has no success selling her script at any other studio, and eventually decides to shelve it and work on other projects. A year later, Harriet is surprised to find that Zenith Pictures released a movie that bears substantial similarity to her script. Although Harriet never had a meeting with Zenith, one of the executives in the room during her Acme meeting retired shortly after that meeting, but immediately after began working part-time as an independent consultant in the development division of Zenith Pictures. Harriet sues Zenith for infringement, and Zenith raises an independent creation defense, arguing that there is insufficient evidence that Zenith had access to Harriet's script. Which party will prevail on the access argument?

(A) Harriet, because access is presumed when two works are substantially similar.

(B) Harriet, because there is sufficient evidence here to infer that Zenith had access to her script.

(C) Harriet, because of the corporate receipt doctrine.

(D) Zenith, because a showing of copying must be based on direct, not circumstantial, evidence.

XI-27. Ken is a botanist who writes a copyrighted 125-page treatise on ferns. A year later, Jamie, who is also a botanist, releases her own 150-page treatise on ferns. Jamie's treatise is distinct from Ken's except for page 86, where six paragraphs of text are identical to six original paragraphs that Ken wrote in his treatise. When Ken confronts Jamie about the unauthorized taking, Jamie is surprised, and responds that the taking must have been an unconscious product of her using Ken's treatise in researching her own. Assuming that Jamie's claim that she inadvertently incorporated the six paragraphs of Ken's work into her own treatise is truthful, does her conduct amount to infringement?

(A) No, because copying that is unconscious or inadvertent is not actionable.

(B) No, because Jamie's taking is de minimis.

(C) No, because Jamie's taking was small in relation to the overall size of Ken's treatise.

(D) Yes, Jamie infringed Ken's copyright.

XI-28. New Biz is a profitable vendor that sells only $5 music CDs at the First Waltz flea market which charges an entrance fee, a rental fee for vendor stalls, and sells food and beverages to shoppers. The CDs consist entirely of music that has been unlawfully downloaded. New Biz does not create these CDs, but accepts them from a distributor who sells the CDs to New Biz for $1. The distributor is able to make CDs so cheaply because he downloads MP3 files from a foreign website that enables the unauthorized distribution of sound recordings, and then burns them onto blank CDs that he purchases in massive quantities. The owner of New Biz has said to the First Waltz management on several occasions, "You know how I get these songs I'm selling so cheap, right?" The First Waltz management consistently responds by saying, "I don't know, and I don't want to know, so keep your methods to yourself." First Waltz does not have any direct knowledge of the distributor's illegal activity, but it is aware that equivalent CDs created through legal means typically wholesale for at least $7. On what, if any, theory of secondary liability can First Waltz be held liable for the distributor's or New Biz's infringement?

(A) Contributory infringement and vicarious infringement.

(B) Contributory infringement, but not vicarious infringement.

(C) Vicarious infringement, but not contributory infringement.

(D) Neither contributory nor vicarious infringement.

XI-29. Tina is an amateur photographer. In her apartment hangs a framed copy of a photo she took of a particularly spectacular sunset. Tina's friend Quentin visits her, sees the photo, and tells Tina that he would like a copy of it. Tina declines, saying, "It may not be worth any money, but my pictures are mine and mine alone." Undeterred, Quentin sneaks into Tina's study, finds the JPEG file containing the photograph on her computer, and downloads it to a portable hard drive. While Quentin originally intended to print a copy of the photograph to put in his private home, he eventually forgets all about the issue, and never even prints a copy of Tina's photograph. Does Quentin's conduct render him liable for criminal copyright infringement?

(A) Yes, because Quentin willfully copied Tina's photographic work.

(B) Yes, because Quentin acted in bad faith.

(C) No, because Quentin did not create the infringing copy for private financial gain, nor was the photograph worth more than $1000.

(D) No, because Quentin never actually printed an infringing copy of the photograph.

XI-30. As a college student in 1978, Felice wrote a since-forgotten incendiary thirty-page tract advocating the dissolution of all American government in favor of a completely unregulated market-based state. Now Felice serves as a moderate California state congresswoman. Edgar, a reporter for the San Francisco *Voice*, discovers Felice's old tract, and (without seeking permission) writes a five-page feature about it, using three separate quotes, ranging from ten to thirty words, from the text to illustrate Felice's college-era beliefs. Edgar's boss at the *Voice* is so impressed with the piece that he gives Edgar a big raise.

A few weeks after the article appears in the *Voice*, Felice sues Edgar for copyright infringement, and Edgar counters by raising the fair use defense. Does Edgar have a successful fair use defense to infringement liability?

(A)   Yes. Edgar's article is news reporting, which is per se fair use.

(B)   Yes. Edgar's article was a reportorial piece that did not harm Felice's economic interests (if any) in her tract, and Edgar's takings were not unreasonable in comparison to the initial work or his need to explain the character of the tract.

(C)   No. Because Edgar received a raise after writing the article, it is commercial and thus not fair use.

(D)   No. Because Edgar did not ask Felice for permission to use the tract, he is precluded from raising the fair use defense.

XI-31.   Which of the following statements most accurately describes the fair use defense as embodied in 17 U.S.C. § 107?

(A)   It is a codification of a constitutional right to which all users are entitled that outlines four nonexclusive factors that courts must consider.

(B)   It is a codification of a constitutional right that outlines four exclusive factors that courts may consider.

(C)   It is a codification of a common-law doctrine that outlines four nonexclusive factors that courts must consider.

(D)   It is a codification of a common-law doctrine that outlines four exclusive factors that courts may consider.

XI-32.   Dennis is a fundamentalist Christian, and rejects the biological idea of evolution completely. Genevieve is a schoolteacher who writes a biology text for sixth graders that assumes the veracity of evolution. Dennis is incensed by this, and posts the entirety of Genevieve's text on his personal website without her permission. Dennis urges visitors to his site to download the book rather than purchase it from Genevieve's publisher, and asks that users who do so give him voluntary donations. While several users do give him donations, most are outraged by Dennis' piracy, which creates a wave of positive publicity for Genevieve's book. As a result, in the following school year, thousands of teachers assign her text, increasing book orders and earning Genevieve substantial royalties. Soon after, Genevieve sues Dennis for infringement, and he counters by raising a fair use defense. Will Dennis prevail?

(A)   Yes, because he transformed the text from an analog to digital medium by posting it online.

(B)   Yes, because Dennis did not sell Genevieve's book, but sought only voluntary donations.

(C)   Yes, because his unauthorized use of Genevieve's text helped her sell more books rather than harming the biology text's market share.

    (D)   No, because Dennis' use was essentially commercial, not meaningfully transformative, and aimed to undermine the market for Genevieve's book (even if it failed to do so).

XI-33.   In 1978, Fran wrote a screenplay called *One Man Down*. Fran gave a copy of the screenplay, with Fran's ownership of the copyright clearly indicated, to Zelda for comments, but never hears back from her. Then, in 1980, Lloyd, Fran's friend and an executive at D Films, calls Fran and tells her that Zelda has pitched *One Man Down*, claiming that the work is actually Zelda's. Moreover, Lloyd tells Fran, D Films loves the script and wants to produce it. Fran is angry, but never takes any action. By 1982, D Films assumes that Fran would have brought an infringement suit if she were so inclined, and begins production on *One Man Down*. D Films releases *One Man Down* in 1984, and it earns a healthy sum from box office proceeds and after-market sales over the next five years, after which D Films stops all exploitation of the motion picture. Fran keeps a close tab on all of these developments, but never gets around to retaining counsel to pursue infringement. Then, in 2005, Fran sues D Films for copyright infringement. Which affirmative defenses can D Films invoke to overcome Fran's infringement suit?

ANSWER:

XI-34.   Joe directs and produces an adult motion picture, *Bump in the Night*, and registers it with the Copyright Office as an audiovisual work. Joe does not disclose on the registration form that the film includes explicit sex scenes. The motion picture is released on DVD, and is soon pirated and distributed without authorization and for free over various P2P filesharing websites. Joe makes no effort to become aware of or stop this piracy until a year passes and he notices that the DVD sales of *Bump in the Night* have dropped to nearly zero. He then discovers the piracy and sues several of the parties who have created and distributed unauthorized copies of Joe's motion picture. Shortly before Joe filed his copyright infringement action, a state court found *Bump in the Night* to be obscene. Will Joe succeed in his infringement suit against these parties, assuming that they are primarily responsible for violations of Joe's exclusive rights in his audiovisual work?

    (A)   Yes. The infringers have no valid affirmative defenses to their conduct.

    (B)   No, because Joe's failure to disclose the adult content of his film constitutes a fraud on the Copyright Office.

    (C)   No, because Joe's film is obscene, and copyright is not available for such works.

    (D)   No, because Joe failed to carefully police infringements of his work for a year, he forfeited any right to bring suit against those infringements.

XI-35.   Helen recently painted a self-portrait, and then agreed to let the local Museum of Modern Art (MoMA) display it in its main hall for three weeks. Helen and MoMA agreed that she was granting only a license to permit the museum to display her self-portrait, and she has reserved all other exclusive rights in the work. Later, without Helen's permission, MoMA featured a digital copy of the self-portrait on its website, on a page entitled "New Work at the MoMA" that is designed to generate interest in the museum's collection. Helen sues MoMA in state court, claiming that MoMA's unauthorized reproduction and display of the portrait entitle her to recovery on three theories: right of publicity, conversion, and unfair competition. MoMA rejoins that these causes of action are all preempted by federal copyright law. Which, if any, of Helen's causes of action actually are preempted?

(A) Right of publicity and conversion.

(B) Conversion and unfair competition.

(C) Conversion and right of publicity.

(D) Right of publicity, conversion, and unfair competition.

XI-36. Hank engaged in early-stage discussions with Welter Publishing about an exclusive publication deal for Hank's novel, *Trains and Levees*. Early on in the negotiations, Welter grew so excited about the prospect of a deal that, without Hank's knowledge or approval, it printed ten thousand copies of Hank's novel to prepare for distribution and sale. The deal went bad, though, and Hank eventually took a better publication offer from Welter's competitor in publishing, Gladman Books. Gladman plans to release Hank's book in about a year. Welter is incensed, and tells Hank that it is going to sell the ten thousand copies of Hank's work immediately. Hank then sues Welter for infringement in the U.S. District Court for the Northern District of Georgia, accurately stating that he never authorized Welter to make any of the copies of *Trains and Levees* that now sit in Welter's warehouse. Hank also moves for preliminary injunctive relief pending litigation. Will a court grant Hank's motion for a preliminary injunction?

(A) Yes, because Hank has shown all four elements necessary to warrant preliminary injunctive relief.

(B) Yes, because plaintiffs in infringement suits are presumptively entitled to preliminary relief, and Welter has not overcome this presumption.

(C) No, because the injury Hank would suffer in the absence of a preliminary injunction is solely financial, and therefore is not irreparable.

(D) No, because any injury Hank would suffer in the absence of a preliminary injunction would be offset by the injury that such an injunction would inflict on Welter.

XI-37. Madelyn is a folk musician who writes and performs her own musical compositions, and produces her own CDs as well, using her home recording studio. During 2009, Madelyn learns that her sales have declined precipitously and, after some investigating, she discovers that the cause for this is a P2P filesharing network, owned and operated by the TekCo corporation, that allows users to download unauthorized copies of her sound recordings for free. Madelyn sues TekCo for copyright infringement, and wins a judgment in her favor. Madelyn submits evidence proving that her sales declined by $10,000 in 2009, and that this decline was attributable solely to sales that Madelyn would have made but for TekCo's infringement. Madelyn also submits evidence proving that in 2009, TekCo's gross profits were $1 million. TekCo then submits evidence proving that only $5,000 of its 2009 profits were attributable to its distribution of Madelyn's sound recordings, and that distributing those sound recordings required $1,000 in delivery costs. Assuming that Madelyn seeks actual damages from TekCo, what is the appropriate measure of those damages?

(A) $1 million.

(B) $10,000.

(C) $5,000.

(D) $4,000.

XI-38.   Vic writes *Tales of Horror*, a book containing four separate stories about macabre themes. Vic registers *Tales of Horror* with the Copyright Office as a collective work, listing himself as the author of all four stories. Amy, Mike, and Jane are filmmakers who, without authorization, jointly write a screenplay based on Vic's *Tales of Horror*, and then co-produce and co-direct a motion picture based on that screenplay. Vic sues Amy, Mike, and Jane for copyright infringement, wins a judgment in which the three defendants are named jointly liable, and seeks statutory damages. The amount of statutory damages is set at $1,000 per infringement. What is the total amount of statutory damages for which Amy, Mike, and Jane are jointly liable?

(A) $1,000.

(B) $6,000.

(C) $12,000.

(D) $24,000.

XI-39.   Jane is a nature photographer living in Redwood Town. The Redwood Town Council contacts Jane and tells her they want to feature one of her photographs as the main image on the Redwood Town home page. In a brief, written agreement, Jane agrees to sell one copy of the photo to Redwood Town for $500, and to permit display of the photo on the Redwood Town home page. Jane retains copyright in the work. Pursuant to this agreement, Jane sends the Redwood Town Council a digital copy of her photograph as an email attachment. The photo that Jane sends has a digital watermark reading, "© Jane 2010." Jane receives payment from Redwood Town as per the agreement, but when she visits the town's site, Jane is surprised to find that the photo does not include the digital watermark. She contacts the Redwood Town Council about this issue, and it responds that it was free to remove the watermark, since it is the owner of the authorized copy. Jane sues Redwood Town under the DMCA. Will she prevail?

(A) No, because Redwood Town removed the watermark from a validly acquired copy of Jane's work for which it paid value.

(B) No, because Redwood Town is a state actor.

(C)   No, because Redwood Town did not wrongfully identify itself, instead of Jane, as the author of the photograph.

(D)   Yes. Redwood Town's unauthorized removal of Jane's copyright management information violates the DMCA.

XI-40.   YouFace is a popular social networking program created by software giant MacroHard. Because MacroHard wants YouFace to create demand for its software, MacroHard limits the interactive elements of YouFace by password, so that there is only one account per copy of the program. Moreover, MacroHard has engineered YouFace so that the program cannot run on competing operating systems. Brad is a skilled hacker who dislikes MacroHard's market dominance. Brad develops two clever hacks. One allows him both to access the interactive elements of YouFace without getting a password, and the other allows the YouFace software to run on his non-MacroHard operating system. Even though Brad develops these hacks only for his personal use, MacroHard somehow discovers them and brings suit against Brad under the DMCA for circumventing its copyright protection systems. On which, if any, theory of liability will MacroHard prevail?

(A)   Brad's circumvention of MacroHard's use limitations.

(B)   Brad's circumvention of MacroHard's access control measures.

(C)   Brad's circumvention of MacroHard's use limitations and its access control measures.

(D)   Brad has not engaged in any conduct actionable under the DMCA's provisions regulating circumvention of copyright protection systems.

Instructions: Try to answer each of these questions in no more than 90 minutes.

XI-41.   Harry Hopper [HH] wrote a fictional novel, titled *An Inventor in Paradise*, that was published with proper copyright notice in 1940, the same year it was registered with the United States Copyright Office. The novel depicted the fictional life of an inventor, Whitfield Diffie, who spent most of his life disassembling appliances and using them for experiments. Due to a tragic accident while playing poker, Diffie went into a coma for several months. During his coma, Diffie's soul visited purgatory where the souls of the machines on which he had experimented had their revenge. When Diffie regained consciousness, he changed his ways and became a machine rights activist.

On September 2, 1942, Harry Hopper signed an exclusive motion picture license agreement with Left Coast Pictures [LCP] to make a motion picture based on Hopper's novel. The agreement granted Left Coast Pictures the "exclusive right to make a motion picture based on *An Inventor in Paradise*, as well as remakes, sequels and prequels, in any medium now known or hereinafter devised." Left Coast Pictures was granted the exclusive license for the initial and renewal term of the copyright in *An Inventor in Paradise*. Left Coast Pictures was also given permission to "use the novel or any adaptation or version thereof for the purpose of advertising, publicizing or exploiting the motion picture." The agreement indicated that Harry Hopper, or his heirs and assigns, was to receive five percent of all gross revenues derived from the exploitation of the motion picture.

The motion picture, *Mr. Diffie's Soul*, was released in 1944 with proper copyright notice and was registered that year with the Copyright Office. The motion picture contained the characters and plot of *An Inventor in Paradise*. The copyright in the novel was properly renewed by Harry Hopper in the twenty-eighth year of its initial term of protection. The copyright in the motion picture was also properly renewed.

Harry Hopper died in 1985, leaving his daughter, Grace, as his only heir. On January 10, 1989, Grace Hopper sent a proper termination notice to Left Coast Pictures, notifying it that the September 2, 1942 agreement would be terminated as of January 5, 1999. Left Coast Pictures released *Mr. Diffie's Soul* on videocassette in 1990. Prior to the termination of the September 2, 1942 agreement, Left Coast Pictures had no Internet presence. On March 15, 1999, Left Coast Pictures released *Mr. Diffie's Soul* on DVD. The DVD version of *Mr. Diffie's Soul* resulted from a transfer of the entire original analog version of the motion picture into a digital version utilizing digital compression technology. No portion of the original motion picture was changed during the transfer process. No additional information or features were included in the *Mr. Diffie's Soul* DVD.

In July, 1999, Left Coast Pictures premiered its website on the Internet. In addition to announcing its upcoming releases, Left Coast Pictures uses its website to sell videocassette and DVD copies of its library of motion pictures. As a means of facilitating such sales, Left Coast Pictures created a web page that contains a menu of the titles of its best known motion pictures, including *Mr. Diffie's Soul*. By clicking on a title, visitors are able to access a single scene from that motion picture. At the end of the scene, the visitor sees a screen with the message: "If you liked this film, you would undoubtedly like one of the following films. Click on one of the titles listed below to order a copy." The visitor can then click on the title of one of the suggested titles, including the motion picture that had been viewed in part. After the title is clicked, the visitor is given the opportunity to enter credit card and delivery information to purchase a videocassette or DVD copy of the selected motion picture.

The scene from *Mr. Diffie's Soul* that can be viewed by a visitor to Left Coast Pictures' website is the classic purgatory scene for which both the novel and motion picture are renowned. The motion picture's purgatory scene closely followed the written description of the scene found in the novel. Left Coast Pictures has continued to pay Grace Hopper five percent of the gross revenues derived from the sales of videocassette and DVD copies of *Mr. Diffie's Soul*.

Alan Cadabra [AC] created a musical composition, *Optical Rectosis*, that was used as the theme music for *Mr. Diffie's Soul*. *Optical Rectosis* was written in 1944 pursuant to a standard studio composer agreement that indicated *Optical Rectosis* would be created as a work made for hire. *Optical Rectosis* was not independently registered with the copyright office. The musical composition was listed as a work made for hire in the *Mr. Diffie's Soul* copyright registration.

Five years ago, Left Coast Pictures released *American Outback*, a motion picture that contained the musical composition *Piety and Iron*. The musical composition was created in 1995 by Winston James pursuant to a work made for hire agreement. The only use ever made of *Piety and Iron* was in the soundtrack of *American Outback*, which is now available on DVD. *Piety and Iron* was never released on a soundtrack album and has never been licensed to another party to record or distribute the musical composition.

Three of your clients have contacted you for advice.

1. Grace Hopper wants to bring a copyright infringement lawsuit against Left Coast Pictures. She believes Left Coast Pictures has no post-termination right to continue selling videocassette copies of *Mr. Diffie's Soul* without her consent. She also believes that Left Coast Pictures has no post-termination right to release *Mr. Diffie's Soul* on DVD, nor the post-termination right to use the three minute film clip of the purgatory scene from her father's novel as a means of selling copies of *Mr. Diffie's Soul* or any other films. Since terminating the September 2, 1942 agreement, Grace Hopper has retained all of the rights to *An Inventor in Paradise*.

2. Alan Cadabra wants to terminate his 1944 agreement with Left Coast Pictures and obtain the rights to *Optical Rectosis*.

3. Bert Schreck [BS], a record producer, wants to record a selection of musical compositions from various motion pictures and distribute the recordings on phonorecords. The original recordings of the musical compositions will not be used. He wants to include *Piety and Iron* in this compilation without negotiating directly with Left Coast Pictures.

Discuss and analyze the viability of your clients' requests. Do not address any possible fair use defenses or remedies.

ANSWER:

PRACTICE FINAL EXAM: ESSAY QUESTIONS

XI-42. Rick Rail [RR] was the preeminent surfing music guitarist of the 1960s. Rail had several hits, including *Bail Before They Bite* ["*Bail*"], a musical composition he wrote in 1965 and immediately registered with the Copyright Office. He recorded the musical composition with his band, Rick Rail and the Bailettes, for Flusterated Records in 1966. The recording was distributed to retail stores throughout the country. Flusterated Records, which recorded all of Rail's recordings pursuant to a mechanical license from Rail, owns all rights in the *Bail* sound recording.

At the end of the 1960s, Rail left the music business and became a successful surfboard manufacturer. In 1975, Rail was approached by Anne Droid [AD], a documentary film maker. Droid was interested in doing a documentary on the life of Rick Rail. Droid paid Rail $1,500 for the rights to use his life story, rights to use his musical compositions, and his cooperation in the making of the documentary. The parties entered into a contract, which stated in relevant part:

> **6. Rick Rail hereby grants to Anne Droid a nonexclusive right to use any and all of his musical compositions in connection with a documentary. Anne Droid shall have the right to exhibit, distribute, exploit, market and perform said documentary perpetually throughout the world, including all renewals and extensions, by any means or methods now or hereafter known.**

> * * * * *

> **9. Rick Rail reserves all rights and uses in and to said musical compositions, except those herein granted to Anne Droid.**

Before work on the documentary could begin, Rick Rail died in a freak surfing accident one month after he signed the agreement with Anne Droid.

In 1990, Flusterated Records released a digital audio compact disc titled, *Rick Rail's Greatest Hits*, which included *Bail*. To prepare this release, Flusterated Records made digital recordings of the original analog master recordings of Rick Rail and the Bailettes. The original analog master recordings had been recorded on ¼" reel-to-reel tapes which had been kept in a vault in Flusterated Records' headquarters. A computerized mastering machine, purchased by Flusterated Records from DigiCom, Inc., was used to convert the analog ¼" original master tapes into digital recordings. The mastering machine plays the analog tape on an analog tape deck, during which a computer program created by DigiCom samples the sounds on the analog tape at the rate of 44,100 times a second and records the digital information onto a computer hard drive. This process was conducted by Bobby Banger [BB], a Flusterated Records employee acting within the scope of his employment, in Flusterated's recording studio.

Once the recording was completed, Banger "equalized" the digital recordings by listening to them while sitting at a sound board from which he could adjust the volume, tones, and acoustics of the sounds captured on the digital tape. Banger raised the level of the bass guitar and reduced the level of the snare drum. No other adjustments were made to the digital recordings. Once the digital recordings had been equalized, the digital files were sent to Flusterated Records' mastering plant where the digital recordings were pressed into digital audio compact discs and distributed to retail stores.

Anne Droid now is the sole owner of Seedy Roms, a company which creates and markets multimedia CD-ROM computer programs for use in home computers. In 1993 the company released a CD-ROM program titled: *Before California Fell Into the Ocean*. The program presents a history of California surfing music through the use of biographical textual material, photographs, and sound recordings. One of the individuals featured in the CD-ROM program is Rick Rails.

Anne Droid wrote the biographical material concerning Rails, obtaining the information from public domain sources. She paid a license fee for the use of ten photographs taken of Rails in the 1960s. The section of the CD-ROM dealing with Rick Rails uses the digital recording of *Bail*. While using the CD-ROM, the computer user listens to the sound recording and has the option of reading Rail's biography, looking at the photographs of Rail in any order determined by the user, or reading the lyrics of the musical composition. In producing the CD-ROM program, Droid copied the digital recording of *Bail* from the 1990 *Rick Rail's Greatest Hits* compact disc, without obtaining permission. Droid, relying on her 1975 agreement with Rail, did not seek any additional permission to use the musical composition in the CD-ROM program.

When Rick Rail died in 1975, he had never married, had made no assignments of his copyrights and left no will. Unbeknownst to him, however, he had a daughter out of wedlock, Ambigua Peace [AP], who was two years old at the time of his death. On her eighteenth birthday, Peace was informed that Rail was her birth father. At no time has Peace filed any document with the Copyright Office.

You have recently acquired Anne Droid as a client. She has received two cease-and-desist letters claiming federal copyright infringement. A letter from Flusterated Records threatens to sue for federal copyright infringement due to Droid's unauthorized use of the sound recording of *Bail*. Ambigua Peace has also sent a letter claiming that Droid's unauthorized use of the *Bail* musical composition is an infringement of Peace's copyright. Discuss the federal copyright issues raised by these letters.

ANSWER:

XI-43. Fiona Photog is a well-known photographer. She specializes in photographs of news events that chronicle the event's historical significance and capture its human drama. Fiona has won numerous awards and accolades for her work. Fiona has authorized the appearance of her work in a variety of different newspapers and news magazines over the course of her long career, but during the past five years, she has authorized the publication of her photographs only in the pages of the print news magazine *Tempo*.

Tempo, which is one of several magazines published by the media conglomerate PubliCo, regards itself as the premier news magazine in America. It has won acclaim for its unflinching, original coverage of major news events, and its articles are always accompanied by dramatic photographs, including — but by no means limited to — Fiona's. PubliCo has attempted to distinguish itself from its competitor publications by refusing to create an Internet presence, insisting that its high-quality content cannot be fully appreciated in an online medium.

One day, Fiona Photog visits your law office to seek your advice. She reports:

> Those jerks over at PubliCo really gave me a raw deal. You remember those awful fires up in Blanco Valley last month? Well, I risked my life to be there, and I took a great pic of these cowboys saving some horses from a burning ranch. There were flames and drama and, well, it was some of my best work yet. I titled the photograph *Ranch Heroes*. As usual, *Tempo* loved my work and they ran "Ranch Heroes" on a full page alongside an article they did about animal rescue during the Blanco Valley fires.

Now that was fine with me. We've got a good thing going, me and *Tempo*. I mean, I could work with anyone — goodness knows there are tons of other news mags who'd love me to run my photos in their pages — but PubliCo pays top dollar, and I've got to admit there's a lot of professional cachet in saying I'm a *Tempo* photographer. Plus, I like that they don't publish an online version of their magazine; that makes it harder for people to steal my work. But the agreement I sign every time I let them use one of my photos is very clear: they pay me a one-off fee for the picture, and I authorize them to use it in that issue of *Tempo* — and *only* in that issue.

But get this: I get an email from a friend the other day that says, "I saw your picture of the horse-ranch evacuation on the Internet — great stuff!" So I follow the link and it turns out that PubliCo started a website in order to seek Pulitzer Prizes. You know what the Pulitzer is, right? Well, I'll tell you anyway: it's the highest national honor in journalism. Winners of the award receive $10,000, a certificate, a medal, and an enormous amount of prestige. PubliCo's site is called "The Best of PubliCo", and it has excerpts from all the stories in PubliCo magazines from the past year that they think deserve Pulitzer consideration. Of course they included the *Tempo* piece on the Blanco Valley fires, and lo and behold, there's my photograph on their website.

What's really annoying is that they bastardized my great photo in order to cram the article into an online format. The original version of *Ranch Heroes* in *Tempo* was colorful and took up a whole page. But the one on the website was only a couple inches square, and in black-and-white too. They even cropped the top section off. That was the best part of the picture — it showed how the smoke from the fires made the horizon appear blurry and distorted.

And you know, despite all that, I probably wouldn't even be here if the folks over at PubliCo weren't being such jerks about all this. I called them the other day to give them a piece of my mind, and they said I was overreacting and being a total diva. And then they made a bunch of excuses to try to justify what they did.

First off, they said "Fiona, you know you're a *Tempo* photographer, so that means we can do whatever we want with your work." But I don't know where they get that idea. Sometimes I call myself a "*Tempo* photographer", but that's just to impress people or get media access when there's a tightly controlled scene. I do my own thing on my own schedule, not on *Tempo*'s or anyone's assignment. Sure, sometimes Tempo tips me off that an event is going down, and they've even given me a ride to event sites in their company helicopter. But, whenever I cover an event, I choose whether I'm going to shop my photos to them — or anyone else if I feel like it. Plus, I work out of my own studio, not the *Tempo* offices, and all my equipment is my own. Well, most of it, anyway — actually, for the past three years, *Tempo* has given me a fancy new camera as an annual holiday gift, so about half of my cameras come from them.

Then the PubliCo folks claimed that I gave them the go-ahead to use *Ranch Heroes* on their website. What a crock! There was this one time two weeks ago at a party where one of their executives came up to me, reeking of booze, and mentioned something about doing a website only for Pulitzer publicity purposes. Then he said they thought the animal rescue article with my photo would be good on the site. I told this guy, "Sure, whatever you say" — mainly to get him to go away. I didn't even remember the conversation until they brought it up the other day.

But worst of all, they're telling me that *I* should be thanking *them* for putting *Ranch Heroes* on the publicity site. I told them I don't think that dinky, shrunken version of my great photo is going to impress anyone. And just the other day, I got an angry call from the folks over at Eagle Prints, the company that I work with exclusively to create and sell limited-release prints of my best photographs. They'd seen *Ranch Heroes* on PubliCo's website too, and they said that if I'm going to start publishing my work online where anyone can just download it, they'd have to reconsider their relationship with me.

Look: the way I see it, my photos are mine and mine alone, and no one should be doing anything with them unless I give them the go-ahead. I don't want to stir up trouble, but I'm pretty upset and I'm thinking I should sue PubliCo for misusing my work.

Assess the likelihood of Fiona Photog's success in a copyright infringement lawsuit against PubliCo. In answering this question, you should assume that PubliCo is the appropriate defendant and that *Ranch Heroes* amounts to copyrightable subject matter. Limit your answer to theories of recovery based on the Copyright Act. DO NOT address moral rights theories based on the Visual Artists Rights Act.

ANSWER:

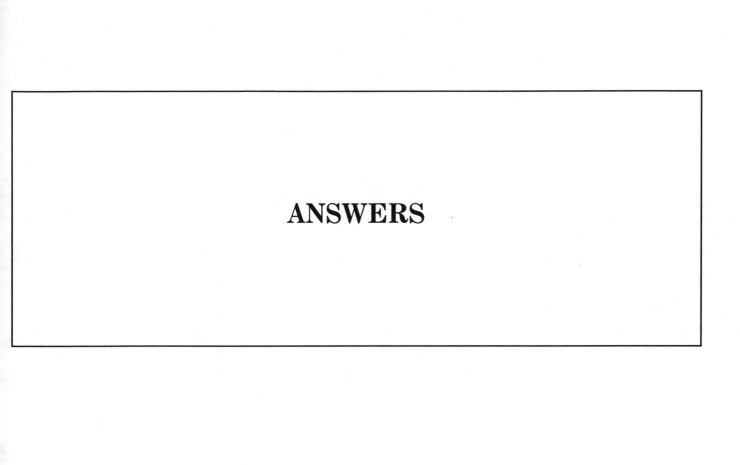

ANSWERS

I-1.   **Answer (A) is correct.** The musical composition is not protected by a federal copyright because it lacks fixation. Federal copyright protection automatically attaches to a work once, and only if, it is " 'fixed' in a tangible medium of expression . . . by or under the authority of the author." 17 U.S.C. § 101; *Community for Creative Non-Violence v. Reid*, 490 U.S. 730, 737 (1989). Since January 1, 1978, when the current federal copyright law came into effect, state law can protect only those original works of authorship that are *not* fixed in any tangible medium of expression. *See, e.g.*, Cal. Civ. Code § 980(a)(1).

The fact that Musician has performed the musical composition often and that a large number of her friends have heard the musical composition does not constitute fixation. A performance is not tangible. Not until Musician permits the composition to be placed in a tangible form will it be sufficiently fixed to meet the prerequisite for federal copyright protection. Until that time, the musical composition may only be protected by state common law copyright.

Answer (B) is incorrect because registration with the Copyright Office is not a prerequisite for federal copyright protection.

Answers (C) and (D) are incorrect for the reasons given above.

I-2.   **Answer (B) is correct.** The musical composition is fixed in the tangible medium of the digital recording Musician has made. The digital recording is a phonorecord because it is an object containing sounds other than those accompanying an audio visual work that can be perceived with the aid or a machine or device. The prerequisites of federal copyright have been met and federal copyright protection attaches immediately.

Answer (A) is incorrect because the digital recording is not a copy for the reason explained above. If the musical composition had been fixed on a video recording depicting Musician as she performed the musical composition, the composition would have been fixed in a copy.

Answer (C) is incorrect because after 1977, a federal copyright is not vested as a result of the existence of a copyright notice. Prior to 1978, a work was invested with federal copyright protected when it was published with proper copyright notice, or when it was registered with the United States Copyright Office. Prior to publication, the work was protected by state common law copyright. *See Goldstein v. California*, 412 U.S. 546, 562 (1973); *Capitol Records, Inc. v. Naxos of America, Inc.*, 372 F.3d 471, 477–78 (2d Cir. 2004).

Answer (D) is incorrect because a work is sufficiently fixed if it can be "perceived, reproduced, or otherwise communicated, either directly or with the aid of a machine." 17 U.S.C. § 101. The human perceptibility doctrine enunciated in *White-Smith Music Pub. Co. v. Apollo Co.*, 209 U.S. 1 (1908), will likely not prohibit copyright protection to a work fixed in a digital medium.

I-3. **Answer (C) is correct.** The poem was fixed on the notebook page, therefore it automatically received federal copyright protection. The destruction of the only copy of the poem creates problems in proving infringement or depositing a copy of the work with the Copyright Office, but these difficulties do not negate the federal copyright protection accorded the work from the date of its creation in a tangible form. *See Peter Pan Fabrics, Inc. v. Rosstex Fabrics, Inc.*, 733 F. Supp. 174, 177 (S.D.N.Y. 1990) (once work is fixed, its subsequent destruction does not vitiate its copyright).

Answer (B) is incorrect for the reason just given.

Answers (A) and (D) are incorrect because the aesthetic quality of a work has no impact on its protection by copyright. *Bleistein v. Donaldson Lithographing Co.*, 188 U.S. 239, 250 (1903); *Campbell v. Acuff-Rose Music, Inc.*, 510 U.S. 569, 582–83 (1994).

I-4. Songwriter does not have a viable copyright infringement action under federal copyright law because the musical composition does not meet the fixation requirements of the Copyright Act. To be fixed, a work may be placed in a tangible medium by someone other than the author, but only with the author's authorization. Here, Songwriter did not give his authorization for Audience Member's recording of the musical composition. Regardless of the lack of fixation, however, Songwriter, as a performer, is protected by 17 U.S.C. § 1101. Section 1101 was enacted by Congress as part of The Uruguay Round Agreements Act that implemented the obligations of the United States under the Uruguay Round Agreement of GATT, the General Agreement on Tariffs and Trade. Section 1101 prohibits the unauthorized fixation of the sounds of a live musical performance, as well as its unauthorized reproduction, transmission, or distribution. This section makes copyright remedies available in a manner never before recognized by federal law. It protects the performance of a work that may not have been fixed within the definition of copyright law. It protects a performance, rather than a work of authorship. And it provides this protection to a person, the performer, who may not be the author or copyright owner of the work being performed. Prior to the enactment of section 1101, performances were not protected by federal law against bootlegging. Only the works being performed, or the sound or the audiovisual recording of the performance, was protected by copyright. The sale of unauthorized recordings of live performances continues to be the subject of state criminal laws. *See Kiss Catalog v. Passport Int'l Prods*, 405 F. Supp. 2d 1169 (C.D. Cal. 2005); *United States v. Martignon*, 492 F.3d 140 (2d Cir. 2007) (federal anti-bootlegging statute was validly enacted under commerce clause).

I-5. **Answer (D) is correct.** The comedy routine is protected by California's state common law copyright because it has not been fixed. A comedy routine that is ten minutes in length will include protectable expression. Cal. Civ. Code § 980(a)(1).

Answers (A) and (B) are incorrect because the comedy routine cannot be protected by federal copyright law due to the lack of fixation.

Answer (C) is incorrect because a performance is not protected by copyright; only the work being performed may be protected.

I-6. **Answer (A) is correct.** Copyright acknowledges the possibility of independent creation; the notion that the same work could be independently created by two separate authors. *See Feist Publications, Inc. v. Rural Telephone Service Company, Inc.*, 499 U.S. 340, 345–46 (1991); *Grubb v. KMS Patriots, L.P.*, 88 F.3d 1, 3 (1st Cir. 1996); *Alfred Bell & Co.*

v. Catalda Fine Arts, Inc., 191 F.2d 99, 103 (2d Cir. 1951). "[I]f by some magic a man who had never known it were to compose anew Keat's Ode on a Grecian Urn, he would be an 'author,' and, if he copyrighted it, others might not copy that poem, though they might of course copy Keat's." *Sheldon v. Metro-Goldwyn Pictures Corp.*, 81 F.2d 49, 54 (2d Cir. 1936); *Bryant v. Gordon*, 483 F. Supp. 2d 605, 616 (N.D. Ill. 2007) (independently produced photograph entitled to copyright protection despite its identical nature to prior work). *But see Susan Wakeen Doll Co., Inc. v. Ashton-Drake Galleries*, 272 F.3d 441, 450 (7th Cir. 2001) ("The more a work is both like an already copyrighted work and . . . unlike anything that is in the public domain, the less likely it is to be an independent creation."); *Acuff-Rose Music, Inc. v. Josten's, Inc.*, 155 F.3d 140, 144 (2d Cir. 1998) (given the widespread usage of the phrase "You've got to stand for something," court held it exceedingly unlikely that composer had independently created the phrase). Because each of the Novelists created fixed original expression, each owns a copyright in her work.

Answer (B) is incorrect because copyright protection is based on the existence of fixed original expression, not on whether the work is new to the world, which is a patent law concept. *See Alfred Bell & Co. v. Catalda Fine Arts, Inc.*, 191 F.2d 99, 102 (2d Cir. 1951).

Answer (C) is incorrect because copyright protection is invested due to the existence of fixed original expression, not on the date of publication, which could invest federal copyright protection in a work prior to 1978.

Answer (D) is incorrect because copyright protection is invested due to the existence of fixed original expression, not on registration with the Copyright Office, which did invest federal copyright protection in a work prior to 1978.

I-7. **Answer (B) is correct.** Copyright does not protect common geometric shapes. *See Bailie v. Fisher*, 258 F.2d 425 (D.C. Cir. 1958); *Atari Games Corp. v. Oman*, 888 F.2d 878 (D.C. Cir. 1989); 37 C.F.R. § 202.1 ("familiar symbols or designs" and "mere variations of typographical ornamentation, lettering or coloring" are not subject to copyright protection).

Answer (A) is incorrect for the reason stated above and because the square was cut out after the star was created, making the usefulness of the square separate from the overall shape of the star under the physical separability test. *See Mazer v. Stein*, 347 U.S. 201, 218 (1954).

Answer (C) is incorrect for the reason stated above and because the material used in creating a work may dictate the level of creativity of the work.

Answer (D) is incorrect for the reason stated above.

I-8. **Answer (C) is correct.** Videographer was not responsible for the situation she was filming, so she did not create any of the elements in front of the lens such as costuming, expression, and lighting, which were the creative elements in a photograph recognized by the United States Supreme Court in *Burrow-Giles Lithographic Co. v. Sarony*, 111 U.S. 53 (1884). She had minimal control of the elements behind the lens such as aperture, selection of film medium, focus, audio, and other automatic operations of the camera, which were the creative elements recognized in *Time, Inc. v. Bernard Geis Associates*, 293 F. Supp. 130 (S.D.N.Y. 1968). Videographer did select the cell phone and decided what to film and where to film it, as well as when to start and end the filming. However, a good argument could be made that these elements of originality are minimally creative in nature.

Answer (A) is incorrect because no matter how artistically lacking a work may be, it is protectable by copyright. *See Bleistein v. Donaldson Lithographing Co.*, 188 U.S. 239, 250 (1903); *Campbell v. Acuff-Rose Music, Inc.*, 510 U.S. 569, 582–83 (1994).

Answer (B) is incorrect because there is no required length for an audiovisual work to be protected by copyright, so long as there is more than one image and the images are related.

Answer (D) is incorrect because making a copyrighted work available to the public does not dedicate the work to the public domain. Such an action by Videographer may be seen as an implied nonexclusive license to download the audiovisual work, but such action does not demonstrate an intent to abandon the copyright in the audiovisual work. *See Micro Star v. Formgen, Inc.*, 154 F.3d 1107, 1114 (9th Cir. 1998).

I-9. **Answer (D) is correct.** Copyright law does not preclude others from using the ideas revealed by the author's work. *See Nash v. CBS, Inc.*, 899 F.2d 1537, 1542 (7th Cir. 1990).

Answer (A) is incorrect. Although it is true that "no plagiarist can excuse the wrong by showing how much of his work he did not pirate," *Sheldon v. Metro-Goldwyn Pictures Corp.*, 81 F.2d 49, 56 (2d Cir. 1936), this rule applies only to expression not ideas.

Answer (B) is incorrect for the reason stated above. The novelty of an idea may be relevant in some jurisdictions to the issue of whether the disclosure of the idea is deemed sufficient consideration for an implied-in-fact contract.

Answer (C) is incorrect because a difference in medium, a questionable proposition in this case, is not a defense to copyright infringement. *See Walt Disney Productions v. Filmation Associates*, 628 F. Supp. 871 (C.D. Cal. 1986) (copying of motion picture character onto storyboards constituted infringement).

I-10. No. The graph paper does not teach, it merely records information. Under the blank form doctrine resulting from the United States Supreme court decision in *Baker v. Selden*, 101 U.S. 99, 107 (1879) (forms that convey no information and serve only to provide blank space for recording information may not be protected by copyright), therefore, the graph paper cannot be protected by copyright. *See Advanz Behavioral Management Resources, Inc. v. Miraflor*, 21 F. Supp. 2d 1179, 1189–91 (C.D. Cal. 1998). Further, as a cooperating part of a machine, the graph paper may not be protected by copyright. *See Brown Instrument Co. v. Warner*, 161 F.2d 910, 911 (D.C. Cir. 1947) (chart acting as a cooperating part of temperature monitoring machine held not copyrightable).

I-11. This scenario takes place prior to January 1, 1978, therefore, the painting was initially protected by state common law copyright at the time of its creation. By offering the painting for sale, it became a published work, causing it to automatically lose its common-law protection immediately. Federal copyright protection attached to the painting if Artist had written a copyright notice on the painting, front or back, that contained the term "copyright," Artist's name and the year of publication. Another alternative was for Artist to apply to register the copyright in the painting with the Copyright Office. Such registration would have divested the common law copyright in the work at the same time it invested the work with federal copyright protection. *See Goldstein v. California*, 412 U.S. 546, 562 (1973); *Capitol Records, Inc. v. Naxos of America, Inc.*, 372 F.3d 471, 477–78

(2d Cir. 2004); *Palmer v. DeWitt*, 47 N.Y. 532, 536–37 (1872).

I-12.   **Answer (D) is correct.** The determination of whether the object in which a work is fixed is a copy or a phonorecord is dependent on what type of work is fixed. Phonorecords are material objects in which sounds, other than those accompanying an audiovisual work, are fixed and from which the sounds can be perceived, reproduced, or otherwise communicated, either directly or with the aid of a machine or device. 17 U.S.C. § 101. *See ABKCO Music, Inc. v. Stellar Records, Inc.*, 96 F.3d 60 (2d Cir. 1996) (karaoke CD-ROM on which sounds and visual representations of lyrics were fixed was a copy, not a phonorecord within the grant of § 115's compulsory mechanical license). Copies are material objects, other than phonorecords, in which a work is fixed and from which the work can be perceived, reproduced, or otherwise communicated, either directly or with the aid of a machine. 17 U.S.C. § 101. *See Midway Manufacturing Co. v. Artic International, Inc.*, 547 F. Supp. 999 (N.D. Ill.), *aff'd*, 704 F.2d 1009 (7th Cir. 1982).

If the work is a sound recording, and it does not accompany an audiovisual work, it is fixed in a phonorecord. For example, a sound recording fixed in an audio CD is fixed in a phonorecord. If a sound recording has been fixed in a DVD as part of the soundtrack of a motion picture that is also fixed on that DVD, the sound recording is fixed in a copy.

Answers (A) and (B) are incorrect because it is not known what work is fixed.

Answer (C) is incorrect because fixation offers only a binary choice. A work must be fixed in either a copy or a phonorecord, there is no other alternative.

I-13.   Sarah's detailed plans for the literary work seems to constitute sufficient original expression for federal copyright. The difficulty here is that Sarah did not fix her proposed literary work in a tangible medium of expression prior to her death. Although Fred has placed Sarah's expression into a tangible medium of expression, it was without Sarah's authorization. Therefore, Sarah's literary work is not fixed and is without federal copyright protection. However, Sarah's mother and sole heir may be able to lay claim to Sarah's unfixed work to the extent that is protected by state common law copyright and can be devised by will. While unfixed works cannot be protected by federal copyright law, 17 U.S.C. § 102(b), such works may be protected by state law, *e.g.*, Cal. Civ. Code § 980(a)(1). *See also* Paul S. Bilker, *The Showdown Continues at the Circle C Ranch: Non-Preemption of State Copyright Protection for Unfixed Improvisational Works*, 18 Sw. U. L. Rev. 415, 436–39 (1989).

I-14.   **Answer (C) is correct.** Every image that can be seen on the plasma screen can be obtained from one of the computers used in the installation. The fact that the images are reproduced from different sources does not mean the individual images or the combination of images appearing on the screen are not fixed. *See Midway Manufacturing Co. v. Artic International, Inc.*, 547 F. Supp. 999 (N.D. Ill.), *aff'd*, 704 F.2d 1009 (7th Cir. 1982) (audio-visual work component of video game properly fixed in several ROM chips).

Answer (A) is incorrect because it is only necessary that the work be capable of being perceived or reproduced. There is no limitation on the number of sources needed to reproduce the work.

Answer (B) is incorrect because the display of an audiovisual or pictorial work to the public does not cause the work to lose its copyright protection.

Answer (D) is incorrect because the mere fact that a work is contained in a tangible medium of expression does not constitute fixation unless the author has placed them in the tangible medium herself, or has authorized that action.

I-15.   **Answer (B) is correct.** A live performance is fixed if it is recorded at the same time it is being transmitted. 17 U.S.C. § 101 (definition of "fixed"). *See National Football League v. McBee & Bruno's, Inc.*, 792 F.2d 726 (8th Cir. 1986) (live broadcast of football game was fixed because it was videotaped at the same time it was transmitted to viewers). Here, because Television Station did not simultaneously record their broadcast, it is unfixed and thus Bar Owner cannot have violated a federal copyright in the broadcast (because one did not vest).

Answer (A) is incorrect. It is very likely that the director's location of the cameras and the selection of which camera feed to include in the broadcast has sufficient originality for federal copyright protection. *See Los Angeles News Service v. Tullo*, 973 F.2d 791, 794 (9th Cir. 1992) (originality of videotape taken from a helicopter was found in "the choices of the heights and directions from which to tape"); *Baltimore Orioles, Inc. v. Major League Baseball Players Ass'n*, 805 F.2d 663 (7th Cir. 1986). However, regardless of the broadcast's originality, it will not be protected by federal copyright if it is not recorded at the time it is being transmitted.

Answer (C) is incorrect because the location of the cameras and the selection of which camera feed to include in the broadcast will be sufficient for federal copyright protection, regardless of whether the broadcast contains statements of an announcer, provided that the broadcast is fixed.

Answer (D) is incorrect. Bar Owner will be liable for unauthorized reproduction if the broadcast is protected by federal copyright. The size of the bar is relevant to the question of whether a public performance license is required, *see* 17 U.S.C. § 110(5)(B), but has nothing to do with the primary infringement here.

I-16.   **Probably.** This situation initially concerns whether Professor's email messages are "sufficiently permanent or stable to permit [them] to be perceived, reproduced, or otherwise communicated for a period of more than transitory duration" to be within the 17 U.S.C. § 101 definition of "fixed." There are at least four mediums in which Professor's email messages may have been fixed: the RAM [Random Access Memory] of Professor's computer, the RAM of Law Student's computer, the computer disk on which Law Student saved her questions and Professor's responses, and the printed copies sold by Law Student. Professor placed his messages in the first two of these mediums. Therefore, the first question is whether placing an email message in RAM is a sufficiently permanent embodiment of the Professor's messages.

The case law in this area indicates that capturing such messages in a computer's RAM satisfies the fixation requirement. These decisions have found that the booting up of a computer program into a computer's RAM creates a fixed copy of that program. The Copyright Act does not define what is meant by the phrase "for a period of more than transitory duration" used in the definition of fixation. These decisions also failed to provide a bright line rule, but found that information loaded into RAM may be contained in the RAM for extended periods of time. *See MAI Systems Corp. v. Peak Computer, Inc.*, 991 F.2d 511 (9th Cir. 1993); *Ticketmaster v. RMG Technologies, Inc.*, 507 F. Supp. 2d 1096 (C.D. Cal. 2007) (RAM capture of website constitutes a copy of the website); *Advanced*

Computer Services of Michigan v. MAI Systems, Corp., 845 F. Supp. 356 (E.D. Va. 1994); Ira Brandriss, *Writing in Frost on a Window Pane: E-Mail and Chatting on Ram and Copyright Fixation*, 43 JOURNAL OF THE COPYRIGHT SOCIETY OF THE USA 237 (1996).

Some have argued that these cases dealt with the question of what constitutes sufficient fixation for a finding of infringement, but that a higher degree of fixation should be required for a work to be invested with federal copyright protection.

As for the third and fourth mediums in which the messages were embodied, Law Student's computer disk and the printed copies of the messages, Professor did not bring about the embodiment of his messages in those forms. Because the embodiments were caused by someone other than the author and without his authorization, there is no fixation for copyright purposes.

I-17. **Answer (A) is correct.** The transposition of a musical composition from one key to another, where it is done with mathematical certainty, is accomplished with no variation or creativity. Under such circumstances there is insufficient originality for copyright protection. *See Jarvis v. A & M Records*, 827 F. Supp. 282, 291 (D.N.J. 1993) (easily arrived at phrases and chord progressions are usually noncopyrightable).

Answer (B) is incorrect because a change in the music of a musical composition may be sufficient for the creation of a derivative work, for example a new arrangement, even though no change has been made in the lyrics of the musical composition.

Answer (C) is incorrect. Even though the notes are different, they are in the same relationship to one another in the key of A as they were in the key of C. There is no creativity where the change in notes is done with mathematical certainty for the purpose of merely changing the key of the musical composition.

Answer (D) is incorrect. Although the statement itself is true, it does not follow that every musical change made by a trained musician is necessarily sufficiently original to be protected by copyright. Mechanical transformations such as derivative works resulting from a simple molding process or obvious translations of a limited nature are not protected by copyright. *See Tempo Music, Inc. v. Famous Music Corp.*, 838 F. Supp. 162 (S.D.N.Y. 1994) (harmony that is a mechanical by-product of melody is not protected by copyright).

I-18. **Answer (B) is correct.** Verso will prevail not only because *Leaves of Autumn* is creative on its own terms, but also because that creativity originated with Verso. The originality requirement is satisfied if two tests are met: independent creation and a modicum of creativity. Proving that the work is the result of independent creation and, therefore, original, is required to meet the burden of proving copyright validity. *See Reader's Digest Ass'n v. Conservative Digest, Inc.*, 821 F.2d 800, 806 (D.C. Cir. 1987) ("Originality" means "only that the work owes its origin to the author — *i.e.*, that the work is independently created rather than copied from other works."). However, the concept of independent creation also recognizes the possibility that the defendant did not copy the plaintiff's work, but created the defendant's work independently. If that can be proven, the defendant will not be held liable for copyright infringement. *See Selle v. Gibb*, 741 F.2d 896 (7th Cir. 1984) (defendants' tape recording of the creative process by which defendants' musical work was composed constituted defense to infringement claim); *Murray Hill Publications, Inc. v. Twentieth Century Fox Film Corp.*, 361 F.3d 312, 326 (6th Cir. 2004) (elements of a defendant's work that were created prior to access to plaintiff's work found not to infringe); *Sturdza v. United Arab Emirates*, 281 F.3d 1287, 1297 (D.C. Cir. 2002) (elements present in submission by other architect before defendant had access to plaintiff's drawings excluded from liability).

Answer (A) is incorrect. As indicated above, the plaintiff in every copyright infringement lawsuit must prove that the work at issue has a valid copyright. As part of that requirement, the plaintiff must prove that its work contains at least a modicum of creativity. However, evidence of creativity is insufficient to prove originality without additional evidence that the haiku was independently created by Verso.

Answer (C) is incorrect. As indicated above, copyright law accepts the possibility that a person can create a work that is identical to a preexisting work, without having copied that preexisting work. The fact that the second work is identical to the first does not preclude copyright protection for the second work. Verso's haiku is not denied copyright protection merely because it is identical to the previously created haiku.

Answer (D) is incorrect. As a practical matter, proof that a defendant copied one source of a work, rather than another source, may be difficult to prove, though proof of access will likely decide that issue. In this case, the facts clearly indicate that Poetaster copied Verso's work. There are no facts that indicate Poetaster had access to Quarto's *Rainbow Leaves* until after the copyright infringement suit was filed.

I-19.   Ideas cannot be protected by copyright. *See* 17 U.S.C. § 102(b); *Baker v. Selden*, 101 U.S. 99 (1879); *Curtin v. Star Editorial Inc.*, 2 F. Supp. 2d 670, 674 (E.D. Pa. 1998) (plaintiff could not claim copyright protection for his "idea" to display photographs of Elvis Presley with celebrities); *Berkic v. Crichton*, 761 F.2d 1289, 1293 (9th Cir. 1985) (basic story ideas are not protectable by copyright, no matter how novel or distinctive). However, other legal theories are available to protect an idea itself or the use of an idea.

Trade secret law can protect an idea that has commercial value if reasonable steps have been taken to keep it secret. Under trade secret law, a formula, such as the formula for Coca Cola®, may be protected. Some ideas, such as the title of a motion picture, novel, or musical work, may be protected as a trademark.

Patent law may protect the application of an idea to an invention, if the invention meets the statutory requirements of utility, novelty, and nonobviousness. The disclosure of ideas may be protected by contract, either express or implied by conduct. When a television writer pitches an idea for a television series to production company executive, an implied-in-fact contract may be created, for which the disclosure of the idea by the writer is deemed the writer's consideration for the contract and the executive's implied agreement to pay a reasonable fee for the use of the disclosed idea by the production company constitutes the consideration by the company.

I-20.   **Answer (A) is correct.** In the majority of jurisdictions, an infringement of the adaptation right can occur only if the defendant has created a work that constitutes an unauthorized derivative work that contains sufficiently original new elements. The translation of a lengthy novel from French into English is a creative endeavor that is protected by copyright as a derivative work, separate from the copyright protecting the underlying French novel. The elements of creativity involved in the translation of the French novel into English by Publisher are not merely mechanical. Such a translation involves numerous choices of words to translate the novel, selecting proper grammar, phrasing, and rendering French slang terms and idioms into understandable English terms. Had the underlying French work been more limited, such as a list of ten words needed to order in a restaurant, the English word choices would be fewer. Such a mechanical translation would not be protected by copyright. *See Grove Press, Inc. v. Greenleaf Publishing Co.*, 247 F. Supp. 518 (E.D.N.Y. 1965).

Answer (B) is incorrect. Although the statement in answer B is correct, it is not relevant to Translator's lawsuit. The exclusive right of reproduction had been retained by French Novelist with whom Publisher has reached a settlement. Translator does not own the reproduction right in Novelist's work, nor has Translator created a derivative work that has its own reproduction right.

Answer (C) is incorrect. See the correct answer above.

Answer (D) is incorrect. Translator owns the exclusive right to create an English translation of the French novel. This right is not dependent of whether Translator has yet to exercise that right.

I-21. Yes. The interview tape is an object in which two copyrighted works are fixed: (1) the words spoken by Police Detective and Writer during the interview may be protected as a literary work; and (2) the recording of the sounds made during the interview. Writer no longer owns the copyright in the literary work fixed in the interview tape because she has assigned that copyright to Publisher. However, the assignment of print publishing rights to Publisher did not include any of the rights to the sound recording, which cannot be reproduced in print. Writer will have to prove that the sound recording at issue meets the originality requirement. The original elements of the sound recording are not the words uttered by Police Detective and Writer, they are the decisions made that allowed the sounds to be recorded. These include the decisions as to what recorder to use, the type of recording tape, the positioning of the microphone, the determination of who and when to record, and the operation of the volume control. The creative decisions made by Writer during the sound recording of the interview with Police Detective will be deemed sufficiently original to be protected by copyright. Although the scope of protection afforded sound recordings under the 1976 Copyright Act is more limited than other categories of works, requiring proof of duplication and not mere substantial similarity, Audio Company has duplicated the Writer's sound recording. Writer has a successful cause of action against Audio Company.

I-22. Because the analog sound recording was first fixed prior to 1972, it is not protected by federal copyright law, but may be protected under state common law copyright or other state law theories, such as unfair competition. *See Capitol Records, Inc. v. Naxos of America, Inc.*, 372 F.3d 471, 477 (2d Cir. 2004) (sound recordings fixed before February 15, 1972, are neither protected nor preempted by federal copyright law, until federal preemption occurs on February 15, 2067); *Daboub v. Gibbons*, 42 F.3d 285, 288 (5th Cir. 1995). The question asked whether Record Company could successfully sue Website for federal copyright infringement. To do so, Record Company would have to prove that it owns a federal copyright in the digital version of the Megaron sound recording, that is, the digital reissue of the original analog recording. The digital reissue has been fixed in a tangible medium by Record Company and undoubtedly contains protected expression.

However, Record Company can successfully sue for federal copyright infringement of its recent digital reissue only if it is sufficiently original. It is clear that if the creation of the digital reissue had simply been a conversion process utilizing the computerized mastering machine without creative human intervention, the digital reissue would lack sufficient originality for copyright protection. If such were the case, the digital recording would be no more original than the duplication of the 1965 analog recording onto an analog cassette tape. It is also clear that if Record Company's employee had digitally "remastered" the original analog recording by changing the volume, tone, and acoustics of each of the instruments on each of the recording tracks, the resulting digital recording would be sufficiently creative for copyright protection.

In most jurisdictions, Record Company will have to prove that the digital reissue of the Megaron sound recording constitutes more than a mere trivial variation of the 1965 analog sound recording. In this case, the employee engaged in more than a mere mechanical transfer of the analog recording to the digital recording. He listened to the recording and made a creative decision to only change the levels of the bass guitar and snare drum. Record Company will argue that such a change is sufficiently creative and that the employee's decision not to change the sound of the other instruments also constituted creative input. Website will argue that such decisions are less than minimal and lack sufficient creativity, resulting in a digitized sound recording that almost identical to the original analog sound recording of *Megaron*. Website will also question the policy of extending copyright protection to unprotected subject matter through digitization. Website has clearly reproduced the digital reissue without authorization and would be found liable for federal copyright infringement if the digital reissue is found to be protected as a derivative work.

I-23.   **Answer (B) is correct.** Titles of books are not protected by copyright, because they are not sufficiently original for copyright protection or are deemed to constitute mere ideas. Although a well-known book title may be protected as a trademark, it cannot be protected by copyright. *See, e.g., Shaw v. Lindheim*, 919 F.2d 1353, 1362 (9th Cir. 1990) (title of "The Equalizer" television series not protected by copyright); *Trenton v. Infinity Broadcasting Corp.*, 865 F. Supp. 1416, 1426 (C.D. Cal. 1994) (title of "Loveline" radio program not protected by copyright); *Morgan Creek Prods Inc. v. Capital Cities/ABC Inc.*, 22 U.S.P.Q.2d 1881, 1883 (C.D. Cal. 1991) (title of film "Young Guns" cannot be protected by copyright); *Perma Greetings, Inc. v. Russ Berrie & Co., Inc.*, 598 F. Supp. 445, 448 (E.D. Mo. 1984) ("Cliched language, phrases and expressions conveying an idea that is typically expressed in a limited number of stereotypic fashions, are not subject to copyright protection."). *But see Universal City Studios, Inc. v. Kamar Industries, Inc.*, 217 U.S.P.Q. 1162, 1166 (S.D. Tex. 1982) ("I Love You, E.T." and "E.T. Phone Home" protected by copyright).

Answer (A) is incorrect. Composer's concern was for the similarity in the titles, not the contents of the works.

Answer (C) is incorrect. The identical nature of the titles is not relevant for the reasons stated above.

Answer (D) is incorrect. The fact that the title was first used in connection with the book has no bearing on a possible copyright infringement action for the reasons stated above.

I-24.   **Answer (A) is correct.** Individual recipes comprising lists of required ingredients and directions for combining them to achieve final products, without expressive elaboration, constitute a "procedure" and are not entitled to copyright protection. There can be no monopoly in the ideas for producing foodstuffs, nor in the method of preparing and combining the necessary ingredients. *See Publications Int'l, Ltd. v. Meredith Corp.*, 88 F.3d 473, 480–81 (7th Cir. 1996).

Answer (B) is incorrect. The useful article exception to copyright protection only applies to pictorial, graphic, or sculptural works, not literary works. In addition, something that merely conveys information is not deemed a useful article. *See* 17 U.S.C. § 101 (definition of "useful article"); *Pivot Point Int'l, Inc. v. Charlene Products, Inc.*, 372 F.3d 913, 919 (7th Cir. 2004).

Answer (C) is incorrect. Copyright infringement is not based on a comparison of final products, but on the similarity of protected expression. Beet dishes are not copyrightable subject matter.

Answer (D) is incorrect. Although the recipes may be substantially similar, they are not protected by copyright for the reasons stated above.

I-25.   Depending on the jurisdiction in which the case is brought, the Owner of *Space Station* may be successful for part of its claim of infringement. Owner will argue that *Space Station* is protected by copyright as an audiovisual work. As such, the sequence of images on the screen is protected. The number and sequence of the game elements presented in the video game, regardless of the exact image used, are protected expression, not merely ideas. The possible variety of game elements in such a game are unlimited, therefore, the merger doctrine would not apply. However, even if the merger doctrine were found to be applicable, the majority rule grants copyright protection to one of a limited number of expressions against the type of identical copying engaged in by Manufacturer. The majority rule, stated in *Herbert Rosenthal Jewelry Corp. v. Kalpakian*, 446 F.2d 738, 742 (9th Cir. 1971) (jeweled bee deemed limited expression, but deserving limited copyright protection), would also protect the expression of the *Space Station* game rules which are almost identical to the rules stated in *Hangar*.

Manufacturer will argue that games cannot be protected by copyright, only images and other independently protected expressions associated with the game are protectable. Therefore, the number and sequence of the game elements presented in the video game are integral to the game itself and constitute an unprotected system or process under section 102(b) of the Copyright Act. It is especially true in this case where the images on the screen are so completely different. In addition, the number and sequence of game elements available for use in such a video game are limited. Therefore, under the minority view of *Morrissey v. Procter & Gamble Co.*, 379 F.2d 675 (1st Cir. 1967) (copyright will not protect any of the limited number of expressions), they merge with the idea of obstacles presented on a video game screen and remain unprotected by copyright.

The same is true for the simple game rules that appear on the screen in *Space Station*. As a general principle, the rules by which games are played are not copyrightable, though their expression may be. Particularly here, where the game rules are so basic, the merger doctrine may limit or bar copyright protection. Even if the game rules are deemed to be expression, the limited number of forms of expressing the rules causes the expression to be merged with the idea of the rules themselves. This is true under the minority view that would deny all copyright protection. It is also true under the majority view that would grant copyright protection only against verbatim or near-verbatim copying. As can be seen from a comparison of the two statements of game rules, the rules for *Hangar* are not identical, nor nearly identical, to the rules for *Space Station*.

I-26.   **Answer (D) is correct.** Where the subject matter of the copyright is a depiction of an object that appears in nature, the scope of copyright protection is limited. To prove copyright infringement, the owner of the copyright must prove that the defendant's work is a verbatim or near-verbatim copy of the plaintiff's work. In this case, Hunter is only able to show that Competitor's decoys are substantially similar. *See Streeter v. Rolfe*, 491 F. Supp. 416 (W.D. La. 1980); *Satava v. Lowry*, 323 F.3d 805, 812–13 (9th Cir. 2003) (realistic depictions of live animals were "first expressed by nature, are the common heritage of humankind, and no artist may use copyright law to prevent others from depicting them"); *Franklin Mint Corp. v. National Wildlife Art Exchange, Inc.*, 575 F.2d 62 (3d Cir.1978) (paintings of cardinals). *But see Mattel, Inc. v. Goldberger Doll Mfging Co.*, 365 F.3d 133, 135–36 (2d Cir. 2004) ("There are innumerable ways of making upturned noses, bow lips, and widely spaced eyes [for dolls]."); *Hamil America, Inc. v. GFI*, 193 F.3d 92, 100–01 (2d Cir. 1999) (where the plaintiff's work is a stylized floral pattern, mere substantial similarity need be shown).

Answer (A) is incorrect. It is true that sculptural works are copyrightable subject matter, but the protection is limited because the accurate depiction of a turkey limits the possible number of means of expression.

Answer (B) is incorrect. Substantial similarity is the traditional infringement test used in connection with the reproduction right. However, the more demanding test of verbatim or near-verbatim copying is employed where natural objects are the subject of the reproduction.

Answer (C) is incorrect. The statement is true, but Hunter is not complaining of Competitor copying a natural turkey. Hunter is claiming that Competitor has copied Hunter's decoy, which is protected by copyright.

I-27.   **Answer (A) is correct.** Copyright law does not preclude others from using the ideas revealed by the author's work. *See Nash v. CBS, Inc.*, 899 F.2d 1537, 1542 (7th Cir. 1990).

Answer (B) is incorrect. So long as the resulting use is substantially similar to the copyrightable elements in the plaintiff's work, the medium used by the defendant is not a bar to liability. In addition, defendant Studio in this case did not reproduce any of the protectable elements contained in plaintiff's novel.

Answer (C) is incorrect. As indicated above, ideas can freely be taken from a work that has been disclosed to the public.

Answer (D) is incorrect. Although it is presumed that Studio had access to the novel, it was free to use any of the ideas contained in the novel.

I-28.   **Answer (B) is correct.** When a person uses a work protected by copyright in a manner commensurate with the manner the copyright owner intended the work to be used, an implied license will be recognized as a complete defense to a claim of copyright infringement. In this case, the intended purpose for a collection of legal forms is to provide templates to assist in the drafting of legal agreements, including the reproduction of the language published in the collection. If a person were to reproduce the entire collection of forms published as the *Entertainment Law Form Book* and market them under a different title, such use would constitute infringement because it was not the intent of the copyright owner to permit the copying of the forms *en masse*.

Answer (A) is incorrect. Although there was no express authorization by Publisher to allow Young Attorney to make reproductions of the copyright mortgage agreement, the publication of the agreement in a form book intended to be used by attorneys when drafting agreements for clients constituted an implied license to reproduce the agreement for that purpose.

Answer (C) is incorrect. The use doctrine is not limited to copies of works owned by the person making the use of the protected work. Form books are intended to be used by practicing attorneys in this manner, whether they are owned by the attorney or are made available by libraries.

Answer (D) is incorrect. A contract is protectable as a literary work. The practice of transactional law often requires attorneys to customize or make changes to pre-existing contracts obtained from various sources. Under such circumstances, an attorney would be unable to claim ownership of the copyright in the underlying contract. However, there is nothing stated in the facts that places the originality of the contract at issue.

I-29. **Answer (C) is correct.** The doctrine of copyright estoppel is an exception to the general rule that fictional elements in a work are protectable under copyright law. Once a plaintiff's work has been held out to the public as factual, the copyright owner cannot then claim that the work is, in actuality, fiction and thus entitled to copyright protection. *See Houts v. Universal City Studios, Inc.*, 603 F. Supp. 26, 28 (C.D. Cal. 1984).

Answer (A) is incorrect. This statement of law is correct, but the material at issue is not factual. It is the fictional product of Author's creativity.

Answer (B) is incorrect. This statement of law is correct as a general rule, but the copyright estoppel exception is applicable in this case.

Answer (D) is incorrect. No matter how important stated facts are to a work, they will not be protected by copyright. The same holds true for fictional elements, presented as fact, which are therefore treated as though they were actual facts.

I-30. **Answer (D) is correct.** An individual line of dialogue from a motion picture is not protected by copyright. It does not contain sufficient originality and in some cases is merely an idea. *See Murray Hill Publications, Inc. v. ABC Communications, Inc.*, 264 F.3d 622, 633 (6th Cir. 2001).

Answer (A) is incorrect. This is an incorrect statement of law. Motion pictures are audiovisual works that do enjoy a public performance right. In addition, the downloading of recording of the dialog is a reproduction.

Answer (B) is incorrect. As indicated above, a single line of dialog is not protected by copyright. The fact that the line of dialog is the most memorable of the motion picture may make it protectable under trademark law, but not copyright law.

Answer (C) is incorrect. A line of dialog is not protected by copyright. In addition, the copying of a single line of dialog would be considered to be a de minimis taking that is not actionable as an infringement. *See Ringgold v. Black Entertainment Television*, 126 F.3d

70, 76 (2d Cir. 1997) (where "the allegedly infringing work makes such a quantitatively insubstantial use of the copyrighted work as to fall below the threshold required for actionable copying, it makes more sense to reject the claim on that basis and find no infringement. . . .").

I-31.   It is unlikely that Uncle Unique will have any legal remedy and certainly no copyright infringement claim. First, he has no copyright interest in the photograph that formed the basis for the Uncle Natural character. The subject of a photograph is not a copyrightable element and is not the author of the work, unless it has been created as a work made for hire, which is not the case here. *See Masterson Marketing, Inc. v. KSL Recreation Corp.*, 495 F. Supp. 2d 1044, 1048 (S.D. Cal. 2007) ("[A] photograph does not and cannot create a copyright in the underlying subject matter. The subject matter is factual material, available for use by all photographers."); *Natkin v. Winfrey*, 111 F. Supp. 2d 1003, 1008–10 (N.D. Ill. 2000) (photographs of Oprah Winfrey); *Gentieu v. John Muller & Co.*, 712 F. Supp. 740, 742 (W.D. Mo. 1989) (photographs of babies).

Secondly, Uncle Unique has no copyright in his personal appearance. Copyright does not protect human beings. *See Downing v. Abercrombie & Fitch*, 265 F.3d 994, 1003–04 (9th Cir. 2001); *Brown v. Ames*, 201 F.3d 654, 658 (5th Cir. 2000). Lastly, Uncle Unique has not presented himself as a fictional character and has not used his distinctive appearance as a fictional character. He has created a persona, not a copyrightable character. *See Columbia Broadcasting System, Inc. v. DeCosta*, 377 F.2d 315 (1st Cir. 1967).

I-32.   **Answer (C) is correct.** The elements that appear in both motion pictures are elements that are necessary for a work dealing with the genre of vampire stories. As such, they constitute scene a faire that is not protected by copyright and may be copied without permission.

Answer (A) is incorrect. The elements at issue are sufficiently detailed to constitute expression. However, these elements are necessary for a motion picture dealing with the genre of vampire stories. As such, they constitute scene a faire and are not protectable. The difference between the unprotectability of ideas and the unprotectability of elements that constitute scene a faire is that ideas were never protectable. The elements at issue in this case were protectable when first used in a story about vampires. It was only after the genre of vampire stories emerged, utilizing these elements, that they lost their copyright protection and were treated similarly to ideas. *See Twentieth Century-Fox v. MCA*, 6 Media L. Rep. 2016 (C.D. Cal. 1980).

Answer (B) is incorrect. The similarity of the elements at issue is not relevant because the elements constitute scene a faire and are not protected by copyright.

Answer (D) is incorrect. Priority of use is generally not relevant in a copyright infringement action and is completely irrelevant where the material at issue is not protected by copyright.

I-33.   To be protected by copyright, the drawings must constitute fixed original expression. The paper on which the drawings are fixed constitutes a tangible medium. They are not copied from another source, therefore the independent creation requirement is met. As for the required minimum level of creativity, the fact that purchasers pay $15,000 per drawing is a strong indication of sufficient creativity. The variety of the created designs and images constitutes more than a mere idea and would be viewed as expression.

The main issue under these facts, however, is the question of authorship. To be protected by copyright, a work must have been created by a human. *Urantia Foundation v. Maaherra*, 114 F.3d 955, 958 (9th Cir. 1997) (to be protected by copyright, a work must be the product of some element of human creativity). Programmer would argue that the computer program she wrote for Picabrandt made the creation of every drawing possible and that the protocols she included in the computer program affected the content of each of the drawings. In addition, the drawings could not exist without the ink and paper loaded into Picabrandt. According to Programmer, these contributions constituted sufficient human creativity to make these drawings protected by copyright.

A contrary argument could be raised that the provision of ink and paper are merely supplying the tools needed for the work to be created, but in no way could be viewed as providing creativity. An art supply store does not have authorship status merely because it sells paints and brushes to an artist. The computer program addresses what cannot be drawn, such as a third eye. It is questionable whether such negative instruction can be the basis for a claim of human creativity. A purchaser who asks a painter to make a landscape without buildings would not be considered an author of the pictorial work.

I-34. **Answer (D) is correct.** Network's claim of copyright protection of the colorized version of *Style Over Substance* is limited to the original new elements that make it a protected derivative work. The portions of the black and white version of the motion picture that entered the public domain remain in the public domain.

Answer (A) is incorrect. Because the original black and white version of *Style Over Substance* is in the public domain, anyone may use it, including all broadcast and cable channels and stations. While it is true that the colorized version of *Style Over Substance* contains all of the elements of the original motion picture, Network can only preclude others from using the new elements created by the colorization. Network's claim of copyright protection is limited to those new elements. Anyone who has a copy of the black and white version of the motion picture remains free to transmit it without authorization from Network.

Answer (B) is incorrect. Although Network does have a copyright in the colorized version of *Style Over Substance* as a derivative work, only the original elements added to the underlying work, the color added to the original images, which is insufficient to preclude the use of the underlying work.

Answer (C) is incorrect. The black and white version of the motion picture is in the public domain, but that does not preclude the protection of the original new elements created by Network. Any reproduction or transmission to the public of the colorized version of *Style Over Substance* requires Network's permission.

I-35. **Answer (B) is correct.** Elements or sequences of events that necessarily result from a chosen concept do not enjoy copyright protection. The setting of a dinosaur zoo or adventure park, with electrified fences, automated tours, dinosaur nurseries, uniformed workers, and placing dinosaurs on a prehistoric island far from the mainland "are classic scenes a faire that flow from the uncopyrightable concept of a dinosaur zoo." *Williams v. Crichton*, 84 F.3d 581, 589 (2d Cir. 1996).

Answer (A) is incorrect. Although the elements are very similar, they are not protected by copyright because they constitute scene a faire for the reasons stated above.

Answer (C) is incorrect. As indicated above, the elements are not protected by copyright.

Answer (D) is incorrect. Although the fact that two works are intended for different audiences may have relevance to a jury in determining whether there is substantial similarity between two works, this is not the case where the elements in question are nearly identical. More important is the question of whether the elements at issue are protected by copyright. In this case, they are not because the elements necessarily flow from the novel's high concept of a dinosaur zoo and, therefore, are deemed unprotected scene a faire.

II-1.   **Answer (D) is correct.** The expression of factual information is protected by copyright. Factual works, however, are more susceptible to a claim of fair use than are works of fiction. Furthermore, there may be more limitations on the protection given to the organization and structure of a nonfiction literary work.

Answer (A) is incorrect. Although facts are not protected by copyright, the original expression of facts is protected. For example, the Encyclopedia Britannica is protected by copyright.

Answer (B) is incorrect. The short history would not be deemed a derivative work of the newspaper articles because only unprotected facts were taken from the articles, therefore, the short history cannot be said to constitute a derivative work as it did not substantially copy protectable expression from the prior work.

Answer (C) is incorrect. The nonprotection of facts and the protection of the expression of facts by copyright have remained constant before, during, and after 1978.

II-2.   **Answer (D) is correct.** The sound contained in the DVD accompanies a series of related images. As such, the work fixed in the DVD is an audiovisual work, not a sound recording.

Answer (A) is incorrect. Sound recordings are not contained in the DVD. See the answer above.

Answer (B) is incorrect. The statement of the law is correct, but not relevant to Record Company's incorrect claim that the filmed performance constituted a sound recording.

Answer (C) is incorrect. If the DVD did contain sound recordings owned by Record Company, the absence of any contractual relationship between Club Owner and Record Company would prohibit Club Owner from distributing the copyright protected sound recordings without the permission of Record Company. However, the DVD contained only six musical works and an audiovisual work, not sound recordings.

II-3.   Federal copyright protection for sound recordings is more limited than that accorded other categories of copyrightable subject matter, including musical works. There is no federal copyright protection for United States sound recordings that were first fixed prior to February 15, 1972. It should be noted that a "pre-1972" sound recording created by a foreign author may be protected under section 104A. The reproduction right of section 106(1) offers protection only against duplication of the sound recording, although a musical composition is generally protected against substantial similarity. This means that simulation of a work may constitute infringement, but not if the protected work is a sound recording. For a violation of the adaptation right, section 106(2), the unauthorized derivative work must contain a portion of the plaintiff's actual sound recording, not an imitation. The public distribution right of sound recordings is not limited by the first sale doctrine of section 109 in the case of rental, lease, or lending of sound recordings, except for nonprofit libraries and educational institutions, whereas musical works not fixed in sound recordings may be rented, leased, or lent. Sound recordings enjoy no public performance right under section 106(4) or public display right under section 106(5), though musical works are protected by both the public performance and public display rights. Sound recordings are the only works protected by section 106(6), the digital transmission right.

II-4.   **Answer (C) is correct.** Letters may not be regarded as literature in a colloquial sense, but this is irrelevant to the question whether they are considered works of authorship for the purpose of copyright analysis. Courts have consistently held that letters are copyrightable. *See, e.g., Salinger v. Random House, Inc.*, 811 F.2d 90, 94–95 (2d Cir. 1987) (author of the letter owns the copyright in its contents). So Publisher's unauthorized publication of Author's copyrighted material amounts to infringement.

          Answer (A) is incorrect because expository materials certainly do count as "literary works" within the meaning of the Copyright Act. The term "literary works" is not given a narrow or colloquial construction to refer only to works of literature. Rather, courts construe it broadly to refer to any written creative work. *See* 17 U.S.C. § 101 ("Literary works") (" 'Literary works' are works, other than audiovisual works, expressed in words, numbers, or other verbal or numerical symbols or indicia.").

          Answer (B) is incorrect because Author explicitly asked Publisher not to publish the existing manuscript or new ending until after she had the opportunity for revision. There is no way this language could be construed as implied or explicit permission to publish the copyrighted material contained in the letter.

          Answer (D) is incorrect for much the same reasons given for answer (A). Remember, a work need not amount to "literature" to count as a literary work or a work of authorship within the meaning of the Copyright Act.

II-5.   Although, as the answer to II-4 makes clear, Author owns the copyrighted material contained in the letter, this does not mean that Author also owns the physical object in which that material is fixed. Thus the letter, which Author gave to Publisher, is owned by publisher; while the copyrighted material contained in that letter is owned by Author. Publisher is thus under no obligation to return the letter to Author. *See Salinger v. Random House, Inc.*, 811 F.2d 90, 94–95 (2d Cir. 1987) (author of the letter owns the copyright in its contents, while the recipient of the letter retains ownership of the physical document).

II-6.   **Answer (D) is correct.** Agent did not copy the particular expression contained in Author's email, but only the general plot outlines that Author had suggested. However, that plot outline was expressed at such a high level of generality that it did not amount to copyrightable subject matter. *See Shipman v. RKO Pictures*, 100 F.2d 533, 538 (2d Cir. 1938) (bare plots are not protected by copyright). The ideas suggested are familiar themes from world literature: young, star-crossed lovers whose desire for each other is thwarted by venal family ambitions. Such "scenes a faire" (stock events and characters) are not copyrightable. *See Nelson v. Grisham*, 942 F. Supp. 649, 653 (D.D.C. 1996), *aff'd*, 132 F.3d 1481 (D.C. Cir. 1997).

          Answer (A) is incorrect because it misstates the facts of the question. Agent did not copy the particular expression contained in the email. Rather, Agent merely relied on the general ideas contained in the email when creating her own subsequent work.

Answer (B) is incorrect because copyright law does not protect any material that is created from the "sweat of the brow." This theory was rejected by the Supreme Court in *Feist Publications, Inc. v. Rural Telephone Service Company, Inc.*, 499 U.S. 340, 359 (1991).

Answer (C) is incorrect because although verbatim copying is evidence of infringement, it is not required to show infringement. The traditional test of the infringement of the reproduction right is whether the defendant's work is substantially similar, not verbatim.

II-7.   **Answer (C) is correct.** All of the expression contained in the material taken by Employee amounts to copyrightable subject matter. While these materials may not be typical subjects of copyright, the fact that they were produced in a business context does not deprive them of protection. *See, e.g., Khandji v. Keystone Resorts Management, Inc.*, 140 F.R.D. 697, 23 U.S.P.Q.2d 1156 (D. Colo. 1992) (settlement brochure is copyrightable); *Rexnord, Inc. v. Modern Handling Systems, Inc.*, 379 F. Supp. 1190 (D. Del. 1974) (manufacturer's catalogue is copyrightable).

   Answers (A), (B), and (D) are incorrect because they state that some of the material at issue is not copyrightable.

II-8.   **Answer (D) is correct.** Student took only generally available facts, such as names, addresses, and phone numbers, from the University's directory. Facts are not copyrightable. *See Harper & Row Publishers, Inc. v. Nation Enters.*, 471 U.S. 539, 556 (1985) ("No author may copyright . . . the facts he narrates."). While the University may have had a claim if Student had copied any original selection or arrangement of these facts, that was not the case here, because Student used only the facts in the University's directory and infused them with his own selection and arrangement.

   Answer (A) is incorrect because while Student copied certain elements of the directory verbatim, those elements were uncopyrightable facts, not protectable expression.

   Answer (B) is incorrect because the University's copyright in the directory is actually very thin. *See Kregos v. Associated Press*, 937 F.2d 700 (2d Cir. 1991). It extends no farther than the selection and arrangement of facts, and certainly does not include "the idea of all student directories for their employees."

   Answer (C) is incorrect because some elements of directories, such as their selection and arrangement of facts, are copyrightable. 17 U.S.C. §§ 101, 103; *Feist Publications, Inc. v. Rural Telephone Service Company, Inc.*, 499 U.S. 340, 357 (1991).

II-9.   Student would likely prevail in his copyright infringement suit against Compatriot. This would be a case involving wholesale, verbatim copying of a compilation of data. While the facts in Student's compilation are not copyrightable, any originality reflected in Student's selection or arrangement of those facts likely would be. Here, it appears that Student made an effort to select names from the database according to his own subjective evaluation of which University students are most popular. This evinces originality in his selection and thus would likely be copyrightable. By contrast, Student's arrangement of those facts is merely in alphabetical order, and this natural and predictable ordering does not merit copyright protection. Still, because Compatriot copied Student's directory without permission, and because the directory's selection of facts reflects a minimal quantum of creativity, Compatriot's copying likely amounts to infringement.

II-10.   **Answer (A) is correct.** While courts generally do not consider conversations to be copyrightable, they have, by contrast, held that prepared speeches are copyrightable literary works. *See, e.g., Jackson v. MPI Home Video*, 694 F. Supp. 483, 490 (N.D. Ill. 1988) (Jesse Jackson's speech at the 1988 Democratic Party Convention found protectable as a literary work). Because Professor's speech was composed in written form beforehand, and because his delivery cleaved closely to the written text, it is a copyrightable work, and Student's unauthorized reproduction and display of it would amount to infringement.

       Answer (B) is incorrect because no court has ever held that memorization amounts to fixation in a tangible medium of expression.

       Answer (C) is incorrect because lectures based on a written text are treated differently than extemporaneous spoken word performances, which typically are not protected by federal copyright because they are not fixed in a tangible medium of expression.

       Answer (D) is incorrect because courts do not treat prepared lectures as a form of conversation. Independently, some courts have implied that conversation may be copyrightable under certain circumstances, so the broad statement "conversation . . . is never copyrightable" inaccurately states the law. *See Estate of Hemingway v. Random House, Inc.*, 23 N.Y.2d 341, 296 N.Y.S.2d 771, 244 N.E.2d 250 (1969); *Falwell v. Penthouse International, Ltd.*, 521 F. Supp. 1204 (W.D. Va. 1981).

II-11.   Student's unauthorized reproduction of Professor's casual cocktail party banter would be very unlikely to incur copyright liability. Courts generally have a narrow view regarding the copyright protection of conversations. *See Falwell v. Penthouse International, Ltd.*, 521 F. Supp. 1204, 1207–08 (W.D. Va. 1981). In *Estate of Hemingway v. Random House, Inc.*, 23 N.Y.2d 341, 296 N.Y.S.2d 771, 244 N.E.2d 250 (1969), the New York Court of Appeals held that a conversation was presumed to be unprotected by copyright. The court noted that this presumption could be rebutted under the following conditions: First, the speaker must indicate that he or she intended to mark off the utterance from the ordinary stream of speech. Second, the speaker must indicate that he or she meant to adopt the utterance as a unique statement. Third, the speaker must indicate that he or she wished to exercise the control over the statement's publication. *Estate of Hemingway v. Random House, Inc.*, 23 N.Y.2d at 349, 296 N.Y.S.2d at 779, 244 N.E.2d at 256 (1969). There is nothing in the fact pattern that suggests Professor meets any of these conditions.

II-12.   **Answer (D) is correct.** Neither Amateur nor Nemesis copied copyrightable subject matter. Where Archaeologist's dig took place and what was discovered are scientific and historical facts, which are not copyrightable, so there is no infringement claim against Amateur's reporting these facts on his website. *See Rosemont Enterprises, Inc. v. Random House, Inc.*, 366 F.2d 303 (2d Cir. 1966). Similarly, the interpretation of those historical and scientific facts is also not copyrightable, *Hoehling v. Universal City Studios, Inc.*, 618 F.2d 972 (2d Cir. 1980), so the element of Nemesis' article that recounts Archaeologist's interpretation of his discoveries also does not amount to an infringement.

       Answers (A), (B), and (C) are incorrect because they wrongly assume that Nemesis, Amateur, or both, took copyrighted material.

II-13.   **Answer (B) is correct.** Courts have consistently held that characters are copyrightable as long as they are represented with sufficient distinctness, and are not represented in a generic or commonplace manner. *See Nichols v. Universal Pictures Corp.*, 45 F.2d 119, 121 (2d Cir. 1930) ("[T]he less developed the characters the less they can be copyrighted, that is the penalty an author must bear for marking them too indistinctly."). Characters depicted graphically (i.e., visually rather than in literature) are particularly likely to merit copyright protection. *See Walt Disney Productions v. Air Pirates*, 581 F.2d 751 (9th Cir. 1978). Here, the SuperCop character has a clearly recognizable image that has been appropriated without permission, so Cartoonist's infringement suit against Publisher will likely prevail.

Answer (A) is incorrect because it describes the scope of Cartoonist's rights in SuperCop too broadly. Cartoonist enjoys statutorily enumerated exclusive rights in the character, but does not have a broad right to control every subsequent graphic depiction of a heroic policeman.

Answer (C) is incorrect because placing a copyrighted literary character in a different context does not obviate a plaintiff's claim for infringement. The copyright in the character persists as long as the character is reproduced without permission, regardless of the context in which it is featured. *See Walt Disney Prods. v. Air Pirates*, 581 F.2d 751 (9th Cir. 1978); *Walt Disney Prods. v. Filmation Associates*, 628 F. Supp. 871 (C.D. Cal. 1986).

Answer (D) is incorrect because courts have consistently held that graphic characters are copyrightable. *See Metro-Goldwyn-Mayer v. American Honda Motor*, 900 F. Supp. 1287 (C.D. Cal. 1995).

II-14.   Cartoonist will likely fail in his infringement suit against Republisher. While there are some similarities between the two series, they all operate on the level of general, stock qualities or ideas, rather than distinct features that may be copyrighted. *See Nichols v. Universal Pictures Corp.*, 45 F.2d 119, 121 (2d Cir. 1930) ("[T]he less developed the characters the less they can be copyrighted, that is the penalty an author must bear for marking them too indistinctly."). Indeed, the notion of the bumbling cop has a long pedigree (e.g., the Keystone Cops and *Car 54, Where are You?*), and cannot be said to be original to Cartoonist's work. It is not relevant that Republisher may have been inspired to create PooperCop in part by the SuperCop series. As long as Republisher has not taken any copyrightable expression from the SuperCop series, Cartoonist has no infringement claim.

II-15.   **Answer (B) is correct.** All circuits, except the Ninth Circuit, have clearly held that literary characters depicted in novels are copyrightable as long as they are sufficiently distinctive. That is, they must be sufficiently fleshed out with recognizable physical traits, back story or personality traits in order to be copyrightable. *Filmvideo Releasing Corp. v. Hastings*, 509 F. Supp. 60 (S.D.N.Y.), *aff'd*, 668 F.2d 91 (2d Cir. 1981); *Silverman v. CBS, Inc.*, 870 F.2d 40, 50 (2d Cir. 1989). Here, the Judy McGee character is clearly distinctive in terms of her appearance and behavior, so she is copyrightable, and Studio's use of the character without seeking a license from Author amounts to infringement.

Answer (A) is incorrect because literary characters are not always copyrightable. Rather, they must be sufficiently well developed to be distinctive and recognizable in order to merit copyright protection. *See Nichols v. Universal Pictures Corp.*, 45 F.2d 119, 121 (2d Cir. 1930).

Answer (C) is incorrect because it refers to the minority view, the Ninth Circuit test for protectability of literary characters. This test sets a higher bar. It looks to whether the character at issue represents the actual story being told or is merely a plot device used to move the story along. Only if the character is sufficiently central to the narrative does it merit protection under this test. *See Warner Bros. Pictures, Inc. v. Columbia Broadcasting System, Inc.*, 216 F.2d 945, 950 (9th Cir. 1954) (literary character Sam Spade held not protected by copyright); *Rice v. Fox Broadcasting Co.*, 330 F.3d 1170, 1176 (9th Cir. 2003) ("Mystery Magician" held to be merely a chess piece in the game of telling the story of how magic tricks are performed). Even courts in the Ninth Circuit have moved away from exclusively applying the "Sam Spade" test. *See Shaw v. Lindheim*, 908 F.2d 531 (9th Cir. 1990); *Metro-Goldwyn-Mayer, Inc. v. American Honda Motor Co., Inc.*, 900 F. Supp. 1287 (C.D. Cal. 1995).

Answer (D) is incorrect because literary characters are copyrightable if they meet the standards described in the discussion of answer (B) above.

II-16.   **Answer (A) is correct.** Copyright protection is extended to a component part of a character that significantly aids in identifying the character. *See, e.g., New Line Cinema Corp. v. Easter Unlimited, Inc.*, 17 U.S.P.Q.2d 1631, 1633 (E.D.N.Y. 1989) (glove with razor fingers significantly aided in identifying Freddy Krueger character). Because Judy McGee is distinctively recognized by the oversized, pink-handled magnifying glass that she uses in all the novels, that magnifying glass is protected as part of the copyright in the character.

Answer (B) is incorrect because it overstates the scope of the law. Copyright in literary characters extends to distinctive, identifying features of those characters, but does not extend to everything that could possibly be associated with them.

Answer (C) is incorrect. Although it is true that claiming copyright in the idea of using a magnifying glass would be untenable, that is not what Author claims here. Rather, she claims copyright protection only for a particular, very distinctive magnifying glass, and only because it is uniquely associated with a character she has created.

Answer (D) is incorrect. Although the statement is correct as a general matter, a useful article can be used to flesh out a character, e.g. Indiana Jones' bullwhip and fedora hat. The useful article can be protected as part of the copyright in the character if it significantly aids in identifying the character.

II-17.   Ninth Circuit law creates a higher bar for the protectability of literary characters. That circuit looks to whether the character at issue represents the actual story being told or is merely a plot device used to move the story along. Only if the character is sufficiently central to the narrative does it merit protection under this test. *Warner Bros. Pictures, Inc. v. Columbia Broadcasting System, Inc.*, 216 F.2d 945, 950 (9th Cir. 1954). Under this test, a court would look to see whether the story in Author's novels was primarily the character Judy McGee herself, or whether Judy was merely a "chess piece" used to advance the plot along. If the former, a court would conclude that the character were copyrightable. If the latter, a court would conclude that the character were not copyrightable. *See Metro-Goldwyn-Mayer, Inc. v. American Honda Motor Co., Inc.*, 900 F. Supp. 1287, 1296 (C.D. Cal. 1995) (James Bond character protected under the "story being told" test because "audiences do not watch Tarzan, Superman, Sherlock Holmes, or James Bond for the story, they watch these films to see their heroes at work. A James

Bond film without James Bond is not a James Bond film."). Courts within the Ninth Circuit have applied both the story being told and fleshing out tests. *See, e.g., Metro-Goldwyn-Mayer v. American Honda Motor*, 900 F. Supp. 1287, 1296 (C.D. Cal. 1995). The Ninth Circuit itself has indicated an acceptance of the majority rule of literary character protection. *See Shaw v. Lindheim*, 908 F.2d 531 (9th Cir. 1990).

II-18. **Answer (C) is correct.** Characters, including graphic characters, fall into the public domain as soon as any work in which they are depicted falls into the public domain. A character will enter the public domain when the work in which the character was initially sufficiently delineated enters the public domain. *See Silverman v. CBS, Inc.*, 870 F.2d 40, 50 (2d Cir. 1989). Mikey the Mouse thus became public domain material when the first *Mice-a-Roni* comic became part of the public domain. Mikey the Mouse is no longer protected, so Publisher is free to use it without a license. That other elements of the series, such as new stories, characters, images, and dialogue, remain protected by copyright does not matter.

Answer (A) is incorrect. It gets the law exactly backwards: if any one literary work in which a character is sufficiently well delineated becomes part of the public domain, then the character becomes part of the public domain as well. It does not matter if there are other works depicting the public domain character that contain other copyrighted material.

Answer (B) is incorrect because it misstates the law. The period of protection for characters depicted in any works of authorship is no longer than it is for those works of authorship.

Answer (D) is incorrect. The reason that Mikey the Mouse is not protected is that Animator failed to preserve his copyright in the character, not because a court would look askance at his failure to follow those formalities on some equitable theory. Publisher will not have to rely on an affirmative defense, such as laches, when the subject matter at issue, the character of Mikey the Mouse, is no longer protected by copyright.

II-19. **Answer (B) is correct.** The source code that comprises computer programs is copyrightable, *Apple Computer, Inc. v. Franklin Computer Corp.*, 714 F.2d 1240, 1248–49 (3d Cir. 1983), but the functionality of computer programs is not, because it amounts to an unprotectable idea. *See Computer Associates International, Inc. v. Altai, Inc.*, 982 F.2d 693 (2d Cir. 1992). Programmer can successfully sue Pirate for infringing the source code, which Pirate copied verbatim, but the idea of a program that catalogs bird sightings operates at too high a level of generality to be protectable. The cataloging function may be protectable by patent law, if it is sufficiently novel, nonobvious, and useful, but not by copyright law.

Answers (A), (C), and (D) are incorrect because they falsely assume either that source code is not protectable or that ideas are.

II-20. **Answer (A) is correct.** The structure of computer chips has been given *sui generis* protection by the Semiconductor Chip Protection Act of 1984, 17 U.S.C. §§ 901–14. The duration of such protection is ten years, 17 U.S.C. § 904, therefore the federal protection of the chip will expire in 2000, because Techie created his chip in 1990. The structure of the computer chip is protected separately from the computer program embodied in the chip. The computer program is protected for the duration of works protected by copyright.

Answer (B) is incorrect because it incorrectly assumes the protection offered by the Semiconductor Chip Protection Act of 1984 lasts twenty years, which is the period of protection for patents.

Answer (C) is incorrect because it incorrectly assumes the protection offered by the Semiconductor Chip Protection Act of 1984 lasts for the life of the author plus seventy years, which is the period of protection for copyrights.

Answer (D) is incorrect because computer chips are protectable under federal law for the reasons discussed in explaining answer (A).

II-21.   **Answer (C) is correct.** The 1976 Copyright Act provides for the unauthorized copying of a computer program by the owner of the computer program when it is an essential step in the utilization of the program in conjunction with the computer or when the copy is used for archival purposes. 17 U.S.C. § 117. *See Allen-Myland, Inc. v. Int'l Business Machines Corp.*, 746 F. Supp. 520, 536 (E.D. Pa. 1990).

    Answer (A) is incorrect because, although object code is a copyrightable literary work, this answer fails to take into account the section 117 exception.

    Answer (B) is incorrect because object code is copyrightable. *See Apple Computer, Inc. v. Franklin Computer Corp.*, 714 F.2d 1240, 1248–49 (3d Cir. 1983) (computer programs are copyrightable subject matter regardless of whether they are expressed in human-readable source code or machine-readable object code); *Apple Computer, Inc. v. Formula Int'l, Inc.*, 725 F.2d 521, 523 (9th Cir. 1984).

    Answer (D) is incorrect because User's intent is irrelevant; copyright infringement is a strict liability tort.

II-22.   **Answer (D) is correct.** The owner of a computer program is permitted to make an adaptation of the computer program, without authorization from the copyright owner, as an essential step in the utilization of the computer program. 17 U.S.C. § 117. *See Aymes v. Bonelli*, 47 F.3d 23, 26–27 (2d Cir. 1995) (adaptation permitted where changes necessary to keep program current and to maintain its viability with an upgraded computer system).

    Answer (A) is incorrect. While User's alteration of the source code that comprises *DethKlok 2000* does create an unauthorized derivative work, this particular conduct falls within a narrow statutory exemption from liability.

    Answer (B) is incorrect. Even if User made a copy of the *DethKlok 2000* source code in revising it, that reproduction would also fall within the section 117 statutory exemption.

    Answer (C) is incorrect. User's ownership of an authorized copy of *DethKlok 2000* does not obviate the adaptation right enjoyed by the owner of the copyright in the source code that comprises the program. It merely permits a limited exception to the copyright owner's adaptation right.

II-23.   **Answer (D) is correct.** Though some typefaces may have sufficient originality to be copyrightable, Congress, as a matter of public policy, has determined that the design of typefaces will not be protected by copyright, though they may be protected by the law of unfair competition. *See Monotype Corp. PLC v. Int'l Typeface Corp.*, 43 F.3d 443 (9th Cir. 1994); *Eltra Corp. v. Ringer*, 579 F.2d 294 (4th Cir. 1978).

Answers (A) and (B) are incorrect. Whether pictorial, graphical, or literary works, fonts are not protectable by federal copyright.

Answer (C) is incorrect. Fonts could certainly possess the requisite degree of originality to merit copyright protection. Although the letters of the alphabet themselves are in the public domain, they could be altered with enough creativity that the result easily crosses the low bar of originality.

II-24.   **Answer (B) is correct.** Though the Copyright Act does not define "musical works," *see* 17 U.S.C. § 102(a)(2), courts have construed this term to include the harmony, melody, and accompanying words that comprise a musical composition. *See Mills Music, Inc. v. Arizona*, 187 U.S.P.Q. 22 (D. Ariz. 1975), *aff'd per curiam*, 591 F.2d 1278 (9th Cir. 1979). By contrast, the recording of a performance of a musical work constitutes a sound recording. *See* 17 U.S.C. § 101 (definition of "Sound recordings"). Thus Polly Math owns a copyright in both elements of the musical work, melody and lyrics, that comprise *Only Me*, while her recorded performance of *Only Me* constitutes a sound recording in which she owns the copyright.

Answer (A) is incorrect because it fails to recognize that Polly Math also owns the copyright in the sound recording of *Only Me*.

Answer (C) is incorrect because it wrongly states that Polly Math owns the copyright in the melody of *Only Me* as a sound recording, not a musical work.

Answer (D) is incorrect because it wrongly states that Polly Math owns the copyright in the recorded performance of *Only Me* as a musical work. Further, the recording of a performance of *Only Me* would constitute a sound recording, not a musical work. The performance of a work is not copyrightable subject matter. The work being performed and the recording of that performance are copyrightable subject matter.

II-25.   **Answer (A) is correct.** Choreographic works are copyrightable. 17 U.S.C. § 102(a)(4). Although Dancer's performance of her choreographic works was spontaneous and unplanned, the choreographic works can be fixed in a tangible medium of expression if they are recorded by the author or under her authority. *See Martha Graham School and Dance Foundation, Inc. v. Martha Graham Center of Contemporary Dance, Inc.*, 380 F.3d 624, 632 (2d Cir. 2004). Dancer's choreographic works that were performed in Carnegie Hall were recorded with her authorization. As a result, they were sufficiently fixed to meet the requirement for federal copyright protection.

Answer (B) is incorrect for two reasons: first, unless the audiovisual work contained in the original DVD was a work made for hire, Dancer does not own the copyright in the audiovisual work; and second, the copyright in the audiovisual work contained in the original DVD cannot prevent the creation of an independent recording of the same performance. There is no indication that the second unauthorized DVD contained any of the creative elements that made the first audiovisual work protected by copyright.

Answer (C) is incorrect because Dancer's performance was fixed in a tangible medium of expression: the authorized recording that served as the basis for the first DVD. If Dancer had not authorized any of the recordings of her Carnegie Hall performance, her choreographic works would not have been protected by federal copyright law and she would have to rely on state common-law copyright.

Answer (D) is incorrect because choreographic works are clearly copyrightable, as noted in the explanation to answer (A) above, whether they communicate a story or not. Under the 1909 Act, a choreographic work could only be protected as a dramatic work, and only if it communicated a story. Under the 1976 Act, there is no such limitation.

II-26.   **Answer (B) is correct.** Photog retains rights to his original photograph, which is a copyrightable work of authorship. However, the infringement claim applies to the photograph only; Photog does not have any copyright interest in the shirt, which is an uncopyrightable useful object. *See Poe v. Missing Persons*, 745 F.2d 1238 (9th Cir. 1984) (clothing not protectable by copyright). Knockoff's reproduction of the image on a shirt, as opposed to selling copies of it as a photograph, does not negate Photog's argument that his exclusive right of reproduction was infringed. Although courts consider clothing an uncopyrightable useful object, aesthetic features of utilitarian objects that are physically or conceptually separable from the objects on which they appear, such as, here, the kitten photograph on the shirts, are considered copyrightable. *See Mazer v. Stein*, 347 U.S. 201 (1954); *Esquire, Inc. v. Ringer*, 591 F.2d 796, 804 (D.C. Cir. 1978).

Answer (A) is incorrect because Photog's copyright is limited to his original photograph and does not extend to the utilitarian object on which it is depicted.

Answer (C) is incorrect. Although clothing is indeed not copyrightable, where, as here, a separate image or design is depicted on clothing, that image is copyrightable.

Answer (D) is incorrect because the copyrightable status of protectable images that have been appended to utilitarian objects is preserved by the separability doctrine.

II-27.   **Answer (C) is correct.** Video game screen displays are registrable as an audiovisual work. *Atari Games Corp. v. Oman*, 979 F.2d 242 (D.C. Cir. 1992). This illustrates that the term "audiovisual work" does not encompass only motion pictures or television programs, and is construed broadly by courts to allow copyright protection for new forms of technology. *See Midway Manufacturing Co. v. Artic International, Inc.*, 704 F.2d 1009, 1011 (7th Cir. 1982) (term "audiovisual work" should be broadly construed "to refer to any set of images displayed as some kind of unit").

Answers (A) and (B) are incorrect because they misstate the work of authorship at issue.

Answer (D) is incorrect because courts consistently have held that computer screens, including video game screen displays, are copyrightable. The elements appearing on the screen have been created and fixed by the author, even though each individual player may manipulate the elements differently. Although the musical work may be separately protected and registered, a sound recording created for an audiovisual work is deemed part of that audiovisual work, not a separate sound recording.

II-28.   **Answer (C) is correct.** The Copyright Act's definition of "sound recording" does not include the sounds accompanying a motion picture or other audiovisual work. A motion picture's music soundtrack is protected under the motion picture copyright. 17 U.S.C. § 101; *Maljack Productions, Inc. v. Goodtimes Home Video Corp.*, 81 F.3d 881, 888 (9th Cir. 1996).

Answers (A) and (B) are incorrect because they falsely presume that music soundtracks accompanying motion pictures must be separately registered.

Answer (D) is incorrect because the Copyright Act's registration provisions apply equally to all works of authorship.

II-29.   Answer (C) is correct. Pianoman's unauthorized recording and public distribution of his performance of the concerto infringes the copyright in the musical work that comprises the concerto. However, Pianoman did not infringe the copyright in the *Musician's Concerto Live* sound recording. The imitation or simulation of the sounds captured in the sound recording is permitted, so long as an actual duplication of the sound recording itself is not made. *Bridgeport Music, Inc. v. Dimension Films*, 410 F.3d 792, 800 (6th Cir. 2005).

Answers (A), (B), and (D) are incorrect because they state either that Pianoman infringed the sound recording or that he did not infringe the musical work.

II-30.   Answer (A) is correct. Donny Dank owns the federal copyright in the musical work, but Big Waves has no federal copyright ownership interest in the recording of that work. Sound recordings fixed prior to February 15, 1972, are not protected by federal copyright law. Because the sound recording that resulted from Big Waves' studio performance of *Sir Surfs-a-Lot* took place in 1969, that sound recording is unprotected by federal copyright law. Pre-1972 sound recordings may, however, be protected by state common-law copyright, property, unfair competition, or criminal law. *Capitol Records, Inc. v. Naxos of America, Inc.*, 372 F.3d 471, 477–78 (2d Cir. 2004).

Answers (B), (C), and (D) are incorrect because they wrongly state that it is possible to have a federal copyright in a sound recording prior to February 15, 1972.

II-31.   Answer (A) is correct. Prior to 1990, architectural structures generally were not copyrightable because they were deemed useful articles, though the blueprints on which they were based were copyrightable as pictorial works. *Robert R. Jones Associates, Inc. v. Nino Homes*, 858 F.2d 274, 278 (6th Cir. 1988). The Architectural Works Protection Act of 1990 created the new subject matter category of "architectural works," 17 U.S.C. § 102(a)(8), and structures can now be protected by copyright law. Protection is extended to individual original design elements and to the overall form of the building as well as the arrangement and composition of spaces, protected elements, and unprotectable elements in the design. 17 U.S.C. § 101. *See Shine v. Childs*, 382 F. Supp. 2d 602, 609 (S.D.N.Y. 2005). In addition to being protected as architectural works, architectural plans, drawings, and models continue to be protectable as pictorial, graphic, or sculptural works under § 102(a)(5). *See Hunt v. Pasternack*, 192 F.3d 877, 880 (9th Cir. 1999). Thus (A) correctly identifies that the blueprints are protectable as both pictorial and architectural works, and that the external design of the house as well as the interior staircase are protectable as an architectural work.

Answers (B), (C), and (D) are incorrect because they fail to correctly identify the kinds of works of authorship at issue as explained in the discussion of answer (A) above.

II-32.   Answer (C) is correct. A work prepared by an officer or employee of the United States government as part of that person's official duties can not be protected by copyright. 17 U.S.C. § 105. *See Matthew Bender & Co., Inc. v. West Publishing Co.*, 158 F.3d 674, 679 (2d Cir. 1998). However, the section 105 prohibition does not affect the copyrightability of works created by employees of state governments. Rather, for copyright purposes, state and local government entities are treated the same as non-governmental entities. *See, e.g.*,

McKenna v. Lee, 318 F. Supp. 2d 296, 301 (E.D.N.C. 2002) (State of North Carolina owned copyright in "First in Flight" license tag design), *aff'd*, 53 Fed. App'x 268 (4th Cir. 2002). In this case, the painting prepared by Fed in his official capacity as a federal employee would not be copyrightable, but the poem prepared by Statie in his official capacity as a state employee would be.

Answers (A), (B), and (D) are incorrect because they falsely state either that Fed's painting was protectable or that Statie's poem was not.

II-33.   **Answer (A) is correct.** Publisher has violated Novelist's exclusive rights by copying and publicly distributing an unauthorized derivative work based on Novelist's original copyrighted work of authorship. Although Critic created the derivative work, it was unauthorized, therefore no copyright interest in the work arose. The new elements of a derivative work that has been based on a copyrighted underlying work, without authorization, will be denied copyright protection. *See* 17 U.S.C. § 103(a); *Watkins v. Chesapeake Custom Homes, L.L.C.*, 330 F. Supp. 2d 563, 572 (D. Md. 2004) (a derivative copyright that is based on a copyrighted work requires the authorization of the copyright owner in order to be "lawful" and thus valid).

Answers (B), (C), and (D) are incorrect because they wrongly state either that Novelist will not prevail or that Critic will.

II-34.   **Answer (B) is correct.** Fan has clearly infringed the *PoundSigne* creator's copyright in the Le Mec character. Distinctive characters, especially graphic characters such as Le Mec, are copyrightable. *Walt Disney Productions v. Air Pirates*, 581 F.2d 751 (9th Cir. 1978). Publisher has created an authorized derivative work based on the original *PoundSigne* comics, but its copyright in this work extends only to the original contributions it made. The copyright in the derivative work extends only to the original new elements added by the author of the derivative work. 17 U.S.C. §§ 101, 103; *G. Ricordi & Co. v. Paramount Pictures, Inc.*, 189 F.2d 469 (2d Cir. 1951). Because the only original contribution added by Publisher was the new English text of the comics, Publisher has no copyright interest in the graphic character of Le Mec itself. Thus *PoundSigne*'s creator has a valid infringement suit against Fan, but Publisher does not.

Answers (A), (C), and (D) are incorrect because they wrongly state either that Publisher will prevail or that *PoundSigne*'s creator will not.

II-35.   **Answer (C) is correct.** If a freelance artist allows his copyrighted work of authorship to be used in a collective work, the section 201(c) privilege requires the collective work owner to get a new license if it seeks to release the collective work in a manner that is outside its original context. *See New York Times Co., Inc. v. Tasini*, 533 U.S. 483, 499–500 (2001) (inclusion of articles, written by freelance authors for newspapers and magazines, in electronic data bases and CD-ROM programs held not to be revisions of the collective works permitted by section 201(c)). However, where the original work is subsequently used in a revision of the collective work, or a later collective work in the same series, the section 201(c) privilege applies and collective work owners are free to engage in such reproduction and distribution without seeking an additional license from the owner of the work of authorship. *Greenberg v. Nat'l Geographic Soc'y*, 533 F.3d 1244, 1249 (11th Cir. 2008) (digital version of collective work constitutes a privileged revision if each page of the collective work appears as it did in the print version). In this case, because Photog's lion photograph was presented in the DVD in exactly the same context it was presented in the original print version of the magazine, the section 201(c) privilege applies and permits Adventure to release the DVD without seeking permission.

Answer (A) is incorrect because it falsely states that this use would not be covered by the section 201(c) privilege.

Answer (B) is incorrect because the Copyright Act imposes no such requirement.

Answer (D) is incorrect because licenses to use works of authorship in one manner or medium do not imply licenses to use those same works in a different manner or medium. On the contrary, licenses to use a work for a particular purpose or in a particular context suggest that the licensor did not grant a right to use the work for any other purpose or in any other context.

II-36. **Answer (B) is correct.** The transmission of a musical composition that is audible to a computer user is deemed a performance. When the transmission is audible to a number of computer users, it constitutes a public performance pursuant to the transmit clause of the definition of public performance in section 106(4).

Answer (A) is incorrect. Although the computer file containing the musical composition is divided into packets, transmitted through telephone lines, cables, and routers, and reassembled at the user's computer, this change in the computer file does not constitute a change in the musical composition that has resulted in the creation of any new elements. Therefore, a derivative work has not been created.

Answer (C) is incorrect. The musical composition has not appeared on the screen of the user's computer, so no display has been made of the musical composition. If the music and lyrics of the musical composition appeared on the computer screen, that would constitute a public display.

Answer (D) is incorrect. The digital transmission right of section 106(6) only applies to sound recordings, not musical compositions.

II-37. **Answer (D) is correct.** The digital transmission right of section 106(6) only applies to sound recordings. Here a sound recording has been transmitted, in digital form, to the public.

Answer (A) is incorrect. Although the computer file containing the sound recording is divided into packets, transmitted through telephone lines, cables, and routers, and reassembled at the user's computer, this change in the computer file does not constitute a change in the sound recording that has resulted in the creation of any new elements. Therefore, a derivative work has not been created.

Answer (B) is incorrect. Although the transmission of a work over the Internet is generally deemed to be a public performance under section 106(4), sound recordings do not have public performance rights.

Answer (C) is incorrect. The act of streaming does not create a display. In addition, sound recordings do not have public display rights.

III-1.   **Answer (C) is correct.** The "recently" created computer program falls within the 1976 Copyright Act that creates a presumption that the copyright in any work created by an independent contractor, such as Programmer in this case, is owned by the independent contractor. This presumption can be rebutted only if the parties have signed a written work made for hire agreement and the work to be created is included in one of the nine categories of works listed in section 101's definition of work made for hire. A computer program is not listed among those nine categories.

              Answer (A) is incorrect. Under the 1909 Act, any work created at the instance and expense of another would be considered a work for hire and the hiring party would be considered the author of the work and its initial copyright owner. The computer program in this case was not created under the 1909 Act. Even under the 1976 Act, Programmer is not an employee, therefore, Florist is not deemed the author as an employer. Programmer is an independent contractor who is presumed to be the copyright owner for the reason stated above.

              Answer (B) is incorrect. Even if the parties had signed a written work made for hire agreement, a computer program is not included in the nine categories of works that can be deemed a work made for hire when created by an independent contractor.

              Answer (D) is incorrect for the reasons stated above.

III-2.   **Answer (C) is correct.** While Frontera Bookstore is the rightful owner of the books themselves, those are only the objects in which the work of authorship, Author's novel, is fixed. The literary work that is the subject of copyright remains Author's intellectual property, regardless of who owns the physical copies in which that work is fixed. 17 U.S.C. § 202. *See Salinger v. Random House, Inc.*, 811 F.2d 90 (2d Cir. 1987) (explaining that the author owns the copyright in the content of a letter as a literary work, the recipient of the letter owns the paper on which the literary work is written, and the transfer of ownership of one does not transfer the ownership of the other). Therefore, the only party who can sue for copyright infringement is the owner of the copyright, Author. Frontera Bookstore may, of course, be able to sue Envy for replevin, to recover the actual books or damages, to compensate Frontera Bookstore for its loss, but not copyright infringement.

              Answers (A), (B), and (D) are incorrect because they wrongly state either that Author will not prevail in an action for copyright infringement or that Frontera Bookstore will.

III-3.   **Answer (D) is correct.** By virtue of the fact that Painter made the work himself, he is its creator. However, he may not be its author under the Copyright Act if the painting was a work made for hire. In that circumstance, the party that hired Painter to create the painting would be the author, not Painter. Finally, Painter may not be the owner of the work. Merely because he created the work does not mean that he retained an ownership interest in its copyright. For example, he could have assigned its copyright to another person.

Answers (A), (B), and (C) are incorrect because they falsely state that Painter is either the author or the owner of the work.

III-4.   Sculptor is the creator of the work because he is the one who conceived and executed it. Left Coast Studios is the author of the work, because the sculpture was a work made for hire. The work is deemed a work made for hire because it was created by an employee acting within the scope of his employment. The Copyright Act defines the hiring party as the "author" of any work made for hire. *See* 17 U.S.C. § 201(b). Finally, Museum is the owner of the sculpture because it purchased the object, but would not be able to exploit the sculpture through photographs or replicas without Left Coast Studios' permission. The ownership of the object is separate from the ownership of the copyright in the sculptural work. *See* 17 U.S.C. § 202. Left Coast Studios remains the owner of the copyright in the sculptural work after the Museum's purchase.

III-5.   **Answer (B) is correct.** First, it is important to note that this fact pattern is governed by the law regarding work for hire under the 1909 Copyright Act, not the work made for hire provisions of the 1976 Copyright Act. Authorship is determined at the time of its creation. Works created before January 1, 1978, are subject to the 1909 Copyright Act, and those created on or after January 1, 1978, are subject to the 1976 Copyright Act. *See Roth v. Pritikin*, 710 F.2d 934, 938–39 (2d Cir. 1983) (work made for hire rules of the 1976 Copyright Act are applied prospectively, not retroactively).

Under the 1909 Copyright Act, the party at whose "instance and expense" a work was created was presumed to be its legal "author" for copyright purposes because it was a work for hire. *Martha Graham School & Dance Foundation, Inc. v. Martha Graham Center of Contemporary Dance, Inc.*, 380 F.3d 624, 634–35 (2d Cir. 2004). That Fritzlinger directed Poet to create the poem means that it was created at Fritzlinger's "instance," *see Siegel v. National Periodical Publications, Inc.*, 508 F.2d 909, 914 (2d Cir. 1974). The fact that Fritzlinger paid Poet to write the poem means it was created at Fritzlinger's "expense," *see Playboy Enterprises, Inc. v. Dumas*, 53 F.3d 549, 555 (2d Cir. 1995). Under the 1909 Act "instance and expense" test, then, Fritzlinger is the poem's author.

Answers (A) and (D) are incorrect because a creator's status as an independent contractor is not relevant to the 1909 Act work made for hire standard. No distinction was made between an employer and an independent contractor by the "instance and expense" test.

Answer (C) is incorrect because, under the 1909 Act, the amount of creative control exercised over the project was not as important as who initiated the work and who paid for its creation.

III-6.   The work for hire status and authorship of the poem is the same, regardless of Poet's status as an independent contractor or Fritzlinger's employee. Under the 1909 Act, the standard for whether a work was a work for hire was whether it was made at the "instance and expense" of the hiring party, and this was true regardless of whether the creator was an employee or an independent contractor. *See Murray v. Gelderman*, 566 F.2d 1307 (5th Cir. 1978); *Easter Seal Society for Crippled Children and Adults of Louisiana, Inc. v. Playboy Enterprises*, 815 F.2d 323, 325–27 (5th Cir. 1987).

III-7. **Answer (A) is correct.** For a work created by an employee to be deemed a work made for hire, it must be created by the employee while she was acting within the scope of her employment. 17 U.S.C. §§ 101, 201(b). While Worker would be considered an employee of Manufacturer during her vacation, her work was clearly outside the scope of her employment. It was not performed at her employer's direction, had nothing to do with her job description or the subject matter of her employment, and was created away from her employer's place of business. The mere fact that the creator of a work happens to be an employee does not allow the employer to claim authorship of every work created by the employee. "[N]o one sells or mortgages all the products of his brain to his employer by the mere fact of employment." *Public Affairs Assocs. v. Rickover*, 177 F. Supp. 601, 604–05 (D.D.C. 1959), *rev'd on other grounds*, 284 F.2d 262 (1960), *vacated for insufficient record*, 369 U.S. 111 (1962), *on remand*, 268 F. Supp. 444 (D.D.C. 1967).

Answer (B) is incorrect because Worker would not be considered an independent contractor because the novel was not created at the instance and expense of the hiring party.

Answer (C) is incorrect because it is overly broad. A work made for hire created by an employee must be made not just by the employee, but by the employee acting within the scope of his employment.

Answer (D) is incorrect because it simply misstates the law. There is no such presumption about the ownership of works made for hire.

III-8. **Answer (C) is correct.** Polly clearly worked as an independent contractor: she used her own materials, acted with little or no influence from Big Press, created the work at her home, and was paid in a manner inconsistent with employee status. In the absence of an agreement, this would mean the English translation is not a work made for hire, and Polly would be its author. However, the agreement signed by both Polly and Big Press indicates that Big Press is to be considered the author of the translation. Although the phrase "work made for hire" was apparently not contained in the agreement, such language is not required if the agreement reflects the parties intent that the work to be created is to be a work made for hire. *See Armento v. Laser Image, Inc.*, 950 F. Supp. 719, 731 (W.D.N.C. 1996) (copyright statute does not demand that specific words "work made for hire" appear in the writing). In this case, the agreement did not state that Big Press is to be the "copyright owner," which would be consistent with an assignment of the copyright. Rather, the agreement stated that Big Press is to be the "author of the work," language with significance only to the issue of whether the work is to be a work made for hire. Therefore, the writing requirement has been met. Also, because this work is one of the nine categories of work for which such agreements are enforceable, a translation, the statutory category requirement has also been met. Therefore, the presumption that Polly, as an independent contractor, was the author of the English translation was overcome by the signed work made for hire agreement and the fact that the work fell within the statutory work made for hire categories, making the hiring party, Big Press, the author of the English translation. *See* 17 U.S.C. § 101; *Quintanilla v. Texas Television Inc.*, 139 F.3d 494, 497 (5th Cir. 1998).

Answer (A) is incorrect because the 1976 Copyright Act specifically provides for certain written agreements that determine authorship status in situations where the work is to be created by an independent contractor. An agreement to create a translation is such an agreement.

Answer (B) is incorrect because Polly's creation of the translation alone does not determine the answer to the question. The 1976 Copyright Act's work made for hire provisions mean that the creator of a work is not always its author. *See* 17 U.S.C. § 201(b); *Lulirama Ltd., Inc. v. Axcess Broadcast Services, Inc.*, 128 F.3d 872 (5th Cir. 1997).

Answer (D) is incorrect because Polly was clearly an independent contractor, not an employee acting in the scope of her employment.

III-9.   **Answer (B) is correct.** Works created by an officer of a corporation in the course and scope of her employment are considered to be works made for hire. *See Lulirama Ltd., Inc. v. Axcess Broadcast Services, Inc.*, 128 F.3d 872, 875 n.1 (5th Cir. 1997). The fact that the CEO made the memo at home rather than at the office does not change the fact that it was clearly within the scope of her employment, as she was acting on a direct order from the DynaCorp board of directors. Works created by employees at their homes, on their own time, are usually found to be works made for hire when the employee is a supervisor and the work is related to the supervisor's employment duties. *See Miller v. CP Chemicals, Inc.*, 808 F. Supp. 1238 (D.S.C. 1992) (computer program created by employee at home, on the employee's own computer, on the employee's own time and without extra pay deemed within the scope of employment).

Answer (A) is incorrect because it is overly broad. DynaCorp is not the owner of anything that CEO writes while she is employed, but only those copyrightable works of authorship that she creates in the course and scope of her employment. For example, if CEO wrote a love poem for her husband during the period of her employment, that would not be a work made for hire because it would be unrelated to her job.

Answer (C) is incorrect because CEOs are clearly salaried employees, not independent contractors.

Answer (D) is incorrect because memoranda, while not "literature" in a colloquial sense, are still potential subjects of copyright protection if they meet the low bar of originality. *See Salinger v. Random House, Inc.*, 811 F.2d 90 (2d Cir. 1987) (letters); *Grundberg v. Upjohn Company*, 137 F.R.D. 372, 19 U.S.P.Q.2d 1590 (D. Utah 1991) (litigation documents); *City Consumer Services, Inc. v. Horne*, 100 F.R.D. 740 (D. Utah 1983) (business records). Here the memo was long and detailed, meeting the originality requirement.

III-10.   ConsultCo will prevail. It is clearly an independent contractor because it was hired on a one-time basis, paid in a single lump sum, and was asked to do an independent report rather than one whose content was directed or determined by DynaCorp. *See Community for Creative Non-Violence v. Reid*, 490 U.S. 730, 751–52 (1989) (listing factors relevant to determination of independent contractor status). In the absence of a work made for hire agreement, ConsultCo is the author of the report and can do with it what it wants.

III-11.   **Answer (A) is correct.** Under the 1976 Act, in the absence of a signed work made for hire agreement, determining whether a work is made for hire depends on the creator's status as an employee. In order to determine that status, courts look to a multifactor test drawn from the law of agency. *See Community for Creative Non-Violence v. Reid*, 490 U.S. 730, 751–52 (1989). Here, because most of the factors: Fuchsia using her own design, GiantCo relinquishing creative control, lump sum payment, no ongoing relationship, weigh in the direction of Fuchsia's not being an employee, while only one factor, Fuchsia using GiantCo's materials, weighs in the direction of Fuchsia's being an employee, it is clear that Fuchsia is not an employee and that she is thus the author of the mural. Because the mural was created at the instance and expense of GiantCo, Fuchsia is an independent contractor who is deemed the author of the mural because there was no work made for hire agreement.

Answer (B) is incorrect because no single factor is dispositive in this analysis; rather, it is a context-sensitive, multifactor test.

Answer (C) is incorrect because the test does not require that all factors weigh in the same direction in order to determine whether a given creator is an independent contractor or an employee.

Answer (D) is incorrect because it is not necessary to know about the provision of health benefits, or about any other particular factor, in order to perform the *Reid* analysis.

III-12.   **Answer (C) is correct.** There are two ways a work can be regarded as a joint work under the Copyright Act. One way is for the work to be the product of a simultaneous collaboration, as was the case with *Spring*, where Writer and Author actively worked with one another as they wrote the piece. Another means by which a work can be regarded as a joint work, though, is for two creators to contribute with the intent that it be merged with the contribution of other authors as "inseparable, e.g. as in a novel or painting, or interdependent, e.g. as in words and music of a musical composition, parts of a unitary whole." 17 U.S.C. § 101 (definition of "joint work"). This is the means by which Writer and Musician created the final version of *Autumn*. Although there was no active collaboration, that is, meetings or mutual revisions, during the process of creating *Autumn*, the authors' mutual expectation that their work be merged into a unified whole makes it a joint work as well. In both cases, the material contributed by each of the putative joint authors was copyrightable.

Answers (A), (B), and (D) are incorrect because they assume either that *Spring* or *Autumn* is not a joint work.

III-13.   **Answer (D) is correct.** W.C. and E.C. each contributed to a collaborative work with the intent that it would be merged into a single, unified whole. In addition, each contributed copyrightable material to the project. This is enough to make it a joint work; it is not necessary that the authors know one another's identities. *Systems XIX, Inc. v. Parker*, 30 F. Supp. 2d 1225, 1229 (N.D. Cal. 1998) (as long as intent to create a joint work is present, the authors of that work need not know one another's identities).

Answers (A) and (B) are incorrect because it is irrelevant to a work's status as a joint work that a particular contributor began or completed the project.

Answer (C) is incorrect because in the absence of a written work made for hire, assignment, or exclusive license agreement securing the rights in the work, Producer owns nothing. Copyright vests initially in a work's creator, not in a work's producer, regardless of who is the "creative force" behind the project.

III-14.   **Answer (B) is correct.** Joint authorship requires that all joint authors mutually recognize one another's status as joint authors at the time of the collaboration. *Childress v. Taylor*,

945 F.2d 500 (2d Cir. 1991). Here, neither Haul nor Screenwriter considered Haul a co-author at the time of the collaboration. This is clear because Haul was paid up front in a single lump sum, rather than evincing any expectation of compensation resulting from the sale of the screenplay. Screenwriter offered to credit Haul as a "consultant," not a co-author, to which Haul did not object. Further, Haul described himself as merely "chip[ping] in" to the project. It is clear that neither party intended a full co-authorial relationship. Similar consultant work on motion pictures has been held by courts not to constitute joint authorship on the part of the consultant. *See Aalmuhammed v. Lee*, 202 F.3d 1227, 1233 (9th Cir. 1999).

Answer (A) is incorrect because it falsely assumes that there must be a written agreement in order for a work to be jointly authored. The Copyright Act contains no such requirement.

Answer (C) is incorrect because contributing substantially to a creative work is only one of the requirements for a determination of joint authorship and does not necessarily make one a joint author. The courts also look to the intent of the collaborators at the time of the collaboration as to the joint authorship status for all putative co-authors.

Answer (D) is incorrect because, although both Screenwriter and Haul intended their contributions to be merged into inseparable parts of a unitary whole, they did not share an intent to make Haul a joint author.

III-15.   On these facts, Haul has a very persuasive claim to joint authorship. Whether collaborators are joint authors is determined primarily by the parties' intent to contribute to a joint work and their actual contribution to the work. The rules regarding joint authorship that were codified by the 1976 Copyright Act required that joint authors must intend, at the time of the creation of the component materials, to create a joint work. Each author must intend his or her contribution to constitute a part of a total work to which another will make or has made a contribution. *See Weissmann v. Freeman*, 868 F.2d 1313 (2d Cir. 1989); *Systems XIX, Inc. v. Parker*, 30 F. Supp. 2d 1225, 1229 (N.D. Cal. 1998). In addition, each putative joint author was required to contribute material that was more than de minimis. *See M.G.B. Homes, Inc. v. Ameron Homes, Inc.*, 903 F.2d 1486, 1493 (11th Cir. 1990).

A majority of courts have since adopted more stringent requirements. The putative joint authors must mutually intend that each be a co-author at the time the work was created. *See Childress v. Taylor*, 945 F.2d 500 (2d Cir. 1991); *Thomson v. Larson*, 147 F.3d 195, 201–02 (2d Cir. 1998). In addition, the contribution of each joint author be copyrightable. *See Erickson v. Trinity Theatre, Inc.*, 13 F.3d 1061 (7th Cir. 1994) (actors participating in improvisational scenes did not provide independently copyrightable expression and were held not to be joint authors); *S.O.S., Inc. v. Payday, Inc.*, 886 F.2d 1081, 1087 (9th Cir. 1989); *Natkin v. Winfrey*, 111 F. Supp. 2d 1003, 1008–10 (N.D. Ill. 2000) (producer of television show did not provide copyrightable subject matter to photographs of the television set or individuals).

Factors to determine co-authorship status are "the contributor's decision making authority over what changes are made and what is included in a work, the way in which the parties bill or credit themselves with regard to the work, any written agreements with third parties, and any other additional evidence." *BTE v. Bonnecaze*, 43 F. Supp. 2d 619,

624–25 (E.D. La. 1999). Because Haul had complete control over the revisions, and because Screenwriter implicitly approved Haul's referring to himself as a co-author on the front page of the script, Haul can make a persuasive showing in light of this test.

III-16. **Answer (D) is correct.** The putative joint authors must intend, at the time of the creation of each of their component materials, to create a joint work. Moreover, the putative joint authors must mutually intend that each be a co-author at the time the work was created. *See Childress v. Taylor*, 945 F.2d 500 (2d Cir. 1991). Author never had any intent that Advisor would be a co-author, therefore, no joint authorship relationship ever arose.

Answer (A) is incorrect because the relative importance of a creative contribution to the completion of a work of authorship, without more, does not create a joint authorship relationship.

Answer (B) is incorrect because one party's unilateral subjective belief that he was a co-author is insufficient to create a joint authorship relationship. Rather, both parties must mutually intend that they are co-authors in order for such a relationship to arise.

Answer (C) is incorrect because the relative significance of various contributors' contributions to a work of authorship is not dispositive of joint authorship status.

III-17. **Answer (B) is correct.** The presence of a consensual, enforceable written agreement defining the contributors to a work of authorship as joint authors is, in the absence of any evidence to the contrary, determinative of their status as joint authors. *Cf. Childress v. Taylor*, 945 F.2d 500 (2d Cir. 1991) (listing written agreement between collaborators as factor in analysis for whether joint authorship relationship exists). As joint authors, the parties own the copyright in the work as tenants in common, and each has an equal, undivided share of the whole, unless expressly reapportioned in a written agreement signed by all the joint copyright owners. 17 U.S.C. § 201(a); *Glovaroma, Inc. v. Maljack Productions, Inc.*, 71 F. Supp. 2d 846, 853 (N.D. Ill. 1999); *Papa's-June Music, Inc. v. McLean*, 921 F. Supp. 1154, 1158 (S.D.N.Y. 1996) (writing requirement of section 204 applicable to transfers between joint authors).

Answer (A) is incorrect. Although it is presumed that all joint authors will share profits in equal amounts, judges will recognize any reapportionment authorized by the joint authors made in a signed written agreement. *See Papa's-June Music, Inc. v. McLean*, 921 F. Supp. 1154, 1158 (S.D.N.Y. 1996) (writing requirement of section 204 applicable to transfers between joint authors).

Answer (C) is incorrect. The amount of each author's contribution is not dispositive of joint authorship status, at least in light of an agreement clearly identifying the contributors as joint authors. In addition, once a person is acknowledged as a joint author, this person is presumed to share equally in all profits derived from the use or licensing of the jointly owned work, unless the joint authors decide otherwise in a signed written agreement.

Answer (D) is incorrect. Although courts are split on this issue, a majority hold that a co-author's contribution must be copyrightable in order to claim joint author status. *See Erickson v. Trinity Theatre, Inc.*, 13 F.3d 1061 (7th Cir. 1994); *Childress v. Taylor*, 945 F.2d 500 (2d Cir. 1991). *But see Gaiman v. McFarlane*, 360 F.3d 644, 658–59 (7th Cir. 2004). However, here it is clear that Slacker's contribution is copyrightable, even if much less substantial than Worker's, because it consists of three original pages and is thus sufficient to merit copyright protection.

III-18.   He would not. Each co-author need not contribute equal amounts of authorship, however, the contribution of each must be more than de minimis, and in the majority of jurisdictions must be copyrightable. Here, Neighbor's contribution would certainly not be copyrightable. Even in the minority of jurisdictions, where the contribution need not be copyrightable, but must be more than de minimis, Neighbor's contribution would not cross the de minimis threshold because it is such a minor addition to the musical composition. Even in *Gaiman v. McFarlane*, 360 F.3d 644, 658–59 (7th Cir. 2004), in which joint author status for the contribution of ideas for a comic book character was permitted, the ideas established the basis for the character and were not deemed to be de minimis.

III-19.   **Answer (D) is correct.** This question stresses that artistic collaboration, joint authorship, is not the only means by which co-ownership of a work may arise. Rather, creation of a joint work is only one method of creating co-ownership of the copyright in a work. The assignment of less than the entire interest in copyright, or the transfer of the copyright to a partnership also creates co-ownership of the copyright in a work. *See Oddo v. Ries*, 743 F.2d 630, 632 (9th Cir. 1984). Additional methods include willing the copyright to more than one person, or through state community property laws. *See In re Marriage of Worth*, 195 Cal. App. 3d 768, 241 Cal. Rptr. 135 (1987) (non-authoring spouse is joint owner of copyright in any work created by authoring spouse during the marriage). Thus, Author's transfer of part ownership to Wife, or his creation of a partnership with Wife with the copyright as an asset are both valid means of creating co-ownership status.

Answers (A) and (B) are incorrect because they are not the only means by which valid co-ownership may arise.

Answer (C) is incorrect because merely attributing abstract support to another person does not make her a joint author and the introductory note is not a sufficient transfer of copyright ownership.

III-20.   **Answer (B) is correct.** As joint authors of the musical work, Biggie and Smalls are tenants in common, which means that they each share equally in the ownership of the copyright in the work. *Glovaroma, Inc. v. Maljack Productions, Inc.*, 71 F. Supp. 2d 846, 853 (N.D. Ill. 1999); *Denker v. Twentieth Century-Fox Film Corp.*, 223 N.Y.S.2d 193, 195 (1961). However, because Smalls performed and recorded the track on his own, he owns the copyright in the sound recording outright. This does not mean that sales of the sound recording would not redound to Biggie's benefit as well. As a co-owner of the underlying musical work, Biggie would share in the mechanical license fees for the use of the musical work, but would have no claim to the profits generated by the sale of the sound recording.

Answer (A) is incorrect because it wrongly states that Biggie and Smalls co-own the copyright in the sound recording.

Answer (C) is incorrect because it wrongly states that Biggie alone owns the musical work.

Answer (D) is incorrect because it does not distinguish between the two works at issue, the musical work and the sound recording, the copyrights in which are owned by different individuals as indicated above.

III-21. **Answer (A) is correct.** Unless there is an agreement to the contrary, each co-owner has the independent right to use the work or to grant a nonexclusive license to non-owners to use the work. *See Oddo v. Ries*, 743 F.2d 630, 633 (9th Cir. 1984); *Cassidy v. Lourim*, 311 F. Supp. 2d 456, 459 (D. Md. 2004) (each band member who collaborated on album could license and promote the album). Thus, Guitarist was free to nonexclusively license Pianist to record and distribute her new arrangement of *Fighty Aphrodite.*

However, Guitarist must share the profits generated by the license with the other members of the Midnights. A joint owner must abide by the rule of mutual accountability. A joint owner is under a duty to account to other joint owners of the work for a prorateable share of profits realized from the use or licensing of the work. The right of accounting may be enforced only as against the joint owner-licensor, not against the licensee. *Oddo v. Ries*, 743 F.2d 630, 633 (9th Cir. 1984) (duty to account is derived from general principles of law governing the rights of co-owners).

Answer (B) is incorrect because it incorrectly states that co-owners do not owe one another a duty of accounting.

Answers (C) and (D) are incorrect because they wrongly state that a single owner cannot grant a nonexclusive license.

III-22. If the license granted by Guitarist to Pianist was exclusive rather than nonexclusive, Guitarist's unilateral grant would make the license unenforceable. An assignment of copyright or an exclusive license may be effected only by a grant in which all of the co-owners join. *See Glovaroma, Inc. v. Maljack Productions, Inc.*, 71 F. Supp. 2d 846, 853 (N.D. Ill. 1999); *Denker v. Twentieth Century-Fox Film Corp.*, 223 N.Y.S.2d 193, 195 (1961). Thus a single joint owner, such as Guitarist in this case, may not unilaterally grant an exclusive license. Such a unilateral grant of an exclusive license would be regarded by courts as invalid and thus unenforceable.

III-23. **Answer (B) is correct.** An agreement entered into by all of the co-owners cannot be rescinded by fewer than all of the co-owners. *Denker v. Twentieth Century-Fox Film Corp.*, 223 N.Y.S.2d 193, 195 (1961). Thus, here, because both co-authors agreed to exclusively license Singer to publicly perform and record *Temptations*, that license cannot be rescinded without their mutual consent. Composer's refusal to assent in the rescission means that the license remains valid.

Answer (A) is incorrect because it is an overly broad statement of the law. Exclusive licenses to exploit copyrighted works of authorship, like any other licenses, may be rescinded, so long as applicable legal requirements are met.

Answer (C) is incorrect because it wrongly states that a single co-owner's desire to rescind is sufficient to effect rescission of an exclusive license, when in fact all co-owners must agree to its rescission.

Answer (D) is incorrect because one co-owner's desire to rescind a license is not sufficient evidence to support an inference that all co-owners want to rescind the license. Such an inference would be plainly at odds with licensing norms. Indeed, here, Lyricist wanted to rescind, but Composer strongly disagreed.

III-24. **Answer (D) is correct.** When a musical composition has been licensed, by its copyright owner, for a recording and the distribution of the recording on phonorecords or digital phonorecord delivery to the public for its private use, section 115 of the Copyright Act permits a new recording and distribution of the musical composition without the permission of the owner of the copyright in the musical composition. In exchange for this compulsory mechanical license, the statutory rate set by the Copyright Office must be paid for each unit that is distributed. *See Leadsinger, Inc. v. BMG Music Publishing*, 512 F.3d 522 (9th Cir. 2008). Singer's licensed digital downloads of her recording constituted digital phonorecord deliveries of the musical composition that changed the status of *Temptations* to a distributed musical composition, making section 115's compulsory mechanical license available to Record Company.

Answer (A) is incorrect. It is true that the reproductions of the *Temptations* musical composition were unauthorized, but they did not constitute copyright infringement because they were permitted under section 115 of the Copyright Act.

Answer (B) is incorrect because Record Company did not rely on Singer's agreement because it could be licensed under section 115 of the Copyright Act.

Answer (C) is incorrect because section 115 of the Copyright Act becomes available when a musical composition is first distributed to the public on physical phonorecords or via digital phonorecord delivery, such as digital downloads.

III-25.   The first issue is whether any of the works under these facts have been infringed. The only work in which Michael has a copyright ownership is the novel. He did not supply any of the new elements that made up the screenplay or the two revisions to the screenplay, which are all derivative works. The Studio owns the copyright in the screenplay as a result of Clark's assignment of all right, title, and interest in the screenplay. Studio also owns the copyrights in the two revisions because Clark rendered those services as Studio's employee, making the revisions works made for hire and Studio the author and copyright owner of the revisions.

As for the claim that Studio has infringed the copyright in the novel, of which Michael, as joint author owns fifty percent, Clark assigned his copyright interest in the novel to Studio. As a result, the Studio stepped into the shoes of Clark and has all of the rights in the novel that were previously possessed by Clark. As a co-owner of the copyright in the novel, Studio cannot be sued for copyright infringement for any use it makes of the novel. One joint owner cannot be liable for copyright infringement to another joint owner of the work. *Richmond v. Weiner*, 353 F.2d 41 (9th Cir. 1965); *Donna v. Dodd, Mead & Co., Inc.*, 374 F. Supp. 429 (S.D.N.Y. 1974). *See Gaiman v. McFarlane*, 360 F.3d 644, 652 (7th Cir. 2004). Therefore, Michael's copyright infringement claims will not be successful.

Michael will likely have limited success with his accounting claims. For such claims, Michael must identify the profits in which he believes he is entitled to share. A joint owner must abide by the rule of mutual accountability. A joint owner is under a duty to account to other joint owners of the work for a prorateable share of profits realized from the use or licensing of the work. The right of accounting may be enforced only as against the joint owner-licensor, not against the licensee. *See Davis v. Blige*, 505 F.3d 90, 100 (2d Cir. 2007) (licensee need not pay any royalties or other consideration to co-owners not parties to license agreement); *Oddo v. Ries*, 743 F.2d 630, 633 (9th Cir. 1984) (duty to account is derived from general principles of law governing the rights of co-owners).

Michael's first claim will likely be for a share of the money received by Clark from Studio. Clark had received $100,000 for his copyright interest in the novel. Michael has no right to share in this payment because it did not flow from the use or licensing of the novel. One co-owner of a copyright is permitted to transfer his or her share of that copyright to a third party without the permission of the other co-owners and with no obligation to share the proceeds of that transfer. *See Glovaroma, Inc. v. Maljack Productions, Inc.*, 71 F. Supp. 2d 846, 853 (N.D. Ill. 1999); *Maurel v. Smith*, 271 F. 211, 214 (2d Cir. 1921).

The same is true for the $50,000 Clark received for revising the script. This payment was for the personal services rendered by Clark as an employee. Michael has no interest in the new material prepared by Clark as part of that employment.

The use of the novel in the screenplay and the motion picture, however, does require the application of the rule of mutual accountability. If Michael had a co-ownership interest in the copyright of the screenplay, then he would have a valid claim for $125,000 (fifty percent of the $250,000 sale price of the screenplay) from Clark. However, because Michael only has a copyright interest in the novel, not the screenplay, his accounting claim is relevant only to the portion of the sale price attributable to the elements in the novel that appeared in the original script.

Similarly, Studio must account to Michael for fifty percent of the profits from the motion picture that are attributable to the use of the novel. Michael is not entitled to half of the $10 million profit made by the motion picture. The elements of the novel that were included in the motion picture are one of the numerous components that went into the creation of a commercially successful motion picture, including the performances of the actors, the skill of the director, the production values, and the marketing campaign. The difficulty with such an apportionment is a major reason why motion picture studios will rarely, if ever, enter into unilateral agreements with a co-owner of a screenplay or its underlying work. Although copyright law may permit such agreements, business realities counsel against it.

III-26. **Answer (D) is correct.** Under the 1976 Copyright Act, a copyright is fully divisible. A copyright is now viewed as a bundle of exclusive rights. Any of the section 106 exclusive rights that make up a copyright and any subdivision of them can be transferred and owned separately, whether or not the transfer is limited in time, media, or geographic area. 17 U.S.C. § 201(d). *See Gamma Audio & Video, Inc. v. Ean-Chea*, 11 F.3d 1106 (1st Cir. 1993). Thus the various limitations placed by Studio on Distributor's exploitation of *Tiger Woman* are all valid and enforceable.

Answers (A), (B), and (C) are incorrect because they wrongly state that certain kinds of limitations on copyright licensing terms are invalid. While there is some debate that certain licensing terms, such as those included in shrink wrap and click wrap licenses that restrict fair use or first sale privileges, may be invalid, the limitations at issue in the Studio-Distributor license are undeniably valid.

III-27. **Answer (B) is correct.** Any transfer of statutory copyright ownership other than by operation of law, such as by assignment or exclusive license, must be in writing and signed by the owner of the rights conveyed or by the owner's authorized agent. 17 U.S.C. § 204; *Glovaroma, Inc. v. Maljack Productions, Inc.*, 71 F. Supp. 2d 846, 853 (N.D. Ill. 1999); *Billy-Bob Teeth, Inc. v. Novelty, Inc.*, 329 F.3d 586, 592 (7th Cir. 2003). Thus the oral transfer of rights in the novel from Writer to Speculator was never enforceable. Therefore, Writer can continue to act as the owner of the copyright, though Speculator can recover his $500 on a contract theory.

Answer (A) is incorrect because it wrongly states that creators that transfer their copyrights retain licensing rights; unless there is some agreement specifying an express reservation of such rights, no such reservation takes place.

Answer (C) is incorrect because the transfer in this case was invalid and never effectively shifted rights in the novel from Writer to Speculator.

Answer (D) is incorrect because there is no evidence here to suggest bad faith, and that issue is not dispositive anyway.

III-28.   This would not change the outcome, because the law requires that a transfer of statutory copyright ownership must be in writing and signed by the owner of the rights conveyed or by the owner's authorized agent. 17 U.S.C. § 204. Here, while there is a written agreement memorializing the transfer, and while it is signed, it is still unenforceable because it is signed by the transferee, Speculator, rather than the owner of the copyright, Writer. If Writer had signed the agreement, the transfer would have been enforceable, though the use of the term "transfer" in the agreement is ambiguous. The term "transfer" could mean an assignment or an exclusive license. In either case, the rights conveyed would likely be sufficient to meet the needs of Speculator, though the scope of his rights could be questioned.

III-29.   **Answer (B) is correct.** The Copyright Act does not dictate specific language or form needed to satisfy the writing requirement of section 204. Rather, the writing need only demonstrate an intent to transfer the copyright. *See Radio Television Espanola S.A. v. New World Entertainment, Ltd.*, 183 F.3d 922, 927 (9th Cir. 1999) ("No magic words must be included in a document to satisfy § 204(a)."); *Effects Associates, Inc. v. Cohen*, 908 F.2d 555, 557 (9th Cir. 1990) ("It doesn't have to be the Magna Carta; a one-line pro forma statement will do."); *Natkin v. Winfrey*, 111 F. Supp. 2d 1003, 1011 (N.D. Ill. 2000) (written invoice with "buy out" notation may be sufficient writing for exclusive license). *But see Playboy Enterprises, Inc. v. Dumas*, 53 F.3d 549, 564 (2d Cir. 1995) (writing that did not expressly mention copyright failed to meet requirements of section 204(a)); *Saxon v. Blann*, 968 F.2d 676, 680 (8th Cir. 1992) ("[T]he conveyance of 'ownership rights' to a book will not convey the copyright of the book. To transfer ownership of a copyright, the parties must state in writing that they intend to transfer a copyright.").

In light of this, it is clear that the check in this case suffices as the kind of "written memorandum" of transfer required by section 204(a). It is in writing, clearly indicates what is being transferred, for what consideration, and is signed by the owner of the rights. Any ambiguity as to whether Artist's endorsement on the back of the check counts as a valid endorsement of the terms of the transfer is eliminated by Artist's inclusion of her initials next to the written memorandum on the front of the check.

Answer (A) is incorrect because it incorrectly states that the reason the written memorandum is valid and enforceable is that it was signed by the transferee, Publisher. In fact, the criterion for validity is that the written memorandum be signed by the transferor copyright owner, in this case, Artist.

Answer (C) is incorrect because a minimal degree of formality is not required to satisfy the "written memorandum" requirement of section 204(a). Courts have consistently held that as long as the memorandum clearly memorializes the transfer and is signed by the owner, it is enforceable. *See Effects Associates, Inc. v. Cohen*, 908 F.2d 555, 557 (9th Cir.

1990).

Answer (D) is incorrect because section 204(a) does not require that the transferor copyright owner write the memorandum, but only that the copyright owner sign it.

III-30.   **Answer (A) is correct.** Prior to 1978, the transfer of common-law copyright in unpublished and unregistered works could be oral or inferred from conduct. *See Magnuson v. Video Yesteryear*, 85 F.3d 1424, 1428–29 (9th Cir. 1996); *Houghton Mifflin Co. v. Stackpole Sons*, 104 F.2d 306 (2d Cir. 1939) (mere delivery of manuscript by Adolf Hitler to publisher was sufficient to show transfer of the copyright in the manuscript). In this case, both the oral agreement between Executive and Screenwriter as well as the course of conduct between the two amply evidence their mutual understanding that a complete transfer of rights in the script should take place. Because the work of authorship at issue was both unpublished and unregistered, and because the situation occurred prior to 1978, this is sufficient to effect a complete transfer of copyright in the script.

Answer (B) is incorrect because it misstates the rule under the 1909 Copyright Act. For any work that was invested with federal copyright under the 1909 Act, any transfer of copyright in the work was required to be in writing. In this case, the script was not invested with federal copyright protection, so the statutory writing requirement was not applicable. The script was protected by state common-law copyright that permitted oral transfers of copyright.

Answer (C) is incorrect because it wrongly assumes that prior to 1978, agreements to transfer ownership of common-law copyrights had to be signed by transferor copyright owners.

Answer (D) is incorrect because the term "copyright" need not be mentioned where the conduct of the parties so clearly implies the transfer of copyright. *See Urantia Foundation v. Maaherra*, 114 F.3d 955 (9th Cir. 1997) (delivery of printing plates implied transfer of copyright in literary work).

III-31.   **Answer (C) is the best option.** Once the copyright owner has granted an assignment of a copyright or an exclusive right, the copyright or the right belongs to the assignee, not the assignor. *See Walker v. University Books, Inc.*, 602 F.2d 859, 862 (9th Cir. 1979). An assignee therefore has the right to transfer its rights to a third party without the consent of the assignor. *See Gardner v. Nike, Inc.*, 279 F.3d 774, 780 (9th Cir. 2002). In light of this, ShoeCo is free to assign the copyright, validly transferred from Designer, to whatever third party it chooses. Designer's distaste for BigCorp is immaterial in light of Designer's complete cession of his rights.

Answer (A) is incorrect because it wrongly states that a complete assignment of copyright does not include the right to subsequently assign the copyright to third parties.

Answer (B) is incorrect because assignees retain no such right of first refusal unless specifically provided for in the assignment agreement.

Answer (D) is incorrect because nothing suggests that the assignment from ShoeCo to BigCorp was invalid. Even if it were invalid, this would not mean that Designer would prevail, because he would still have validly assigned away his rights to ShoeCo and could not affect their subsequent disposition by ShoeCo.

III-32.   The case would come out differently if Designer had granted an exclusive license to ShoeCo rather than assigning the copyright. An exclusive license does not permit the licensee to sub-license the copyright without the consent of the original licensor. This is the key difference between an assignment and an exclusive license under the 1976 Copyright Act. *See Gardner v. Nike, Inc.*, 279 F.3d 774, 780 (9th Cir. 2002). Thus, if Designer had granted ShoeCo an exclusive license to use the copyrighted logo with no sub-licensing provision, ShoeCo's attempt to sub-license rights in the logo to BigCorp would be invalid because ShoeCo lacked the consent of the original licensor, Designer.

III-33.   **Answer (B) is correct.** When created by an independent contract, a work made for hire is a work that is created pursuant to a written work made for hire agreement, not a work that had already been created. *See* 17 U.S.C. § 201(b) (work made for hire is deemed authored by "the employer or other person for whom the work was prepared"). In such cases, the copyright in the created work would be obtained through an assignment or exclusive license. *Cf. Teevee Toons, Inc. v. MP3.com, Inc.*, 134 F. Supp. 2d 546, 549 (S.D.N.Y. 2001). Further, there was no written agreement signed by both parties in this case. As a result, the musical composition could not be deemed a work made for hire.

Answer (A) is incorrect because the agreement entered into by the parties was never reduced to a signed writing.

Answer (C) is incorrect because mere payment does not make a work a work made for hire. Payment may also be made for an assignment or license of copyright. Here the statutory requirements for a work made for hire were not met. In addition, the statement that Musician was paid to create the musical composition is false.

Answer (D) is incorrect because the focus of the work made for hire statutory categories is the type of work created pursuant to the work made for hire agreement. Here, the musical composition was created by Musician before AdAgency requested the compositions. Regardless, even if the musical composition had been created pursuant to AdAgency's request, that request for use in a television commercial, an audiovisual work that is one of the statutory categories, not a radio commercial which does not fall within any of those categories.

III-34.   **Answer (C) is correct.** Although the parties intended that the copyright in the musical composition be assigned to AdAgency, the attempted assignment failed to meet the writing requirement of section 204(a) of the Copyright Act. No exclusive license exists for the same reason. However, the writing requirement does not apply to nonexclusive licenses. A nonexclusive license can be oral or implied from conduct. *See John G. Danielson, Inc. v. Winchester-Conant Properties, Inc.*, 322 F.3d 26, 40 (1st Cir. 2003) (nonexclusive license may be implied from conduct that indicates owner's intent to allow a licensee to use the work); *Nelson-Salabes, Inc. v. Morningside Development, LLC*, 284 F.3d 505, 514 (4th Cir. 2002). Factors indicating the presence of a nonexclusive license include: the putative licensee asking the creator to provide the work; the creator delivering the work to the putative licensee; and the creator intending that the putative licensee use and/or distribute the work. *See Effects Associates, Inc. v. Cohen*, 908 F.2d 555, 558–59 (9th Cir. 1990).

In this case, AdAgency requested that Musician provide the musical composition, along with eleven other compositions, which Musician delivered. It was intended by the parties that the musical composition would be used in the television commercial for AdAgency's storage company client. By entering into an intended, albeit invalid, assignment of all rights to the musical composition, the intent of the parties was to give AdAgency the ability to use the composition in as many commercials as it wanted on behalf of any number of clients. Therefore, the scope of the implied nonexclusive license that was created by the conduct of the parties included the use in a radio commercial for a bank as well as a television commercial for a storage company.

Answer (A) is incorrect. The absence of a written memorandum memorializing an assignment of the copyright in the musical composition means that the attempted assignment was invalid. *See* 17 U.S.C. § 204(a).

Answer (B) is incorrect. As stated above, although the agreement between Musician and AdAgency did constitute an assignment or exclusive license, the conduct of the parties created an implied nonexclusive license that gave AdAgency the lawful right to use the musical composition in both commercials.

Answer (D) is incorrect. Although AdAgency's request to Musician was for a musical composition to be used in a television commercial for a storage company, the fact that the request envisioned the possibility of AdAgency selecting all twelve compositions, not all of which would be used in the storage company commercial. Therefore, it was foreseeable that the delivered musical compositions would be used for more than one commercial and for more than one AdAgency client. Furthermore, the hand-shake agreement establishes the intent of the parties that AdAgency would own the copyright in the musical composition, thereby giving AdAgency the ability to use the composition in as many commercials as it wanted on behalf of any number of clients. The fact that the Copyright Act does not permit the transfer of copyright under these circumstances does not change the intent of the parties which shapes the scope of the implied nonexclusive license that was created by the conduct of the parties.

III-35. **Answer (D) is correct.** In the case of conflicting transfers, the first good faith recorded transfer of a registered copyright is given priority unless an earlier transfer is recorded within one month after the earlier transfer's execution in the United States or two months after its execution outside the United States. 17 U.S.C. § 205(d). Thus, while Collector recorded her transfer agreement and Publisher did not, Collector's knowledge of a prior transfer of the copyright in *FireBash* means that she is not a good faith transferee, and the recordation cannot give her superior rights to Publisher.

Answer (A) is incorrect because recordation is not a precondition to validity of transfers of copyright ownership. Rather, it is a permissive, if advisable, means by which priority can be secured in the event of multiple conflicting transfers.

Answer (B) is incorrect because the first party to record a transfer does not have rights superior to all other purported transferees. Here, for example, Collector's status as a bad faith transferee means that recordation cannot give her superior rights to Publisher.

Answer (C) is incorrect because earlier transfers do not necessarily create rights superior to subsequent transfers.

III-36. **Answer (B) is correct.** In the absence of evidence of the specific intent of the parties, a court will attempt to identify any indicia of a mutual general intent to apportion rights to "new uses." These indicia may be discerned from the language of the license, the surrounding circumstances, and trade usage. *Rey v. Lafferty*, 990 F.2d 1379 (1st Cir. 1993).

Here, because the contractual clause is narrowly limited to "printed form," and because digital media did not exist at the time the agreement was executed, a court would almost certainly construe this agreement not to include the right to publish *Holidaze* in digital media. This interpretation of the agreement is strongly bolstered by the presence of the reservation of rights clause.

Answer (A) is incorrect because it overstates the scope of the law. There are circumstances under which a licensing agreement executed in the context of analog media will be construed to grant rights to use the work at issue in the context of digital media as well. This is particularly true where the granting clause uses particularly broad language, such as a new technology clause. *See, e.g., Rooney v. Columbia Pictures Industries, Inc.*, 538 F. Supp. 211 (S.D.N.Y.), *aff'd*, 714 F.2d 117 (2d Cir. 1982) (license to exhibit films "by any present or future methods or means"); *Platinum Record Co. v. Lucasfilm, Ltd.*, 566 F. Supp. 226, 227 (D.N.J. 1983) (synchronization license to perform a musical composition "perpetually throughout the world by any means or methods now or hereafter known").

Answer (C) is incorrect because it is by no means always true that an agreement to publish a work in analog format implies a license to publish the same work in digital format. *See, e.g., Tele-Pac, Inc. v. Grainger*, 570 N.Y.S.2d 521, *appeal dismissed*, 580 N.Y.S.2d 201, 588 N.E.2d 99 (1991) (broadcast rights do not encompass videocassette film rights).

Answer (D) is incorrect because a failure to explicitly exclude a reference to digital media does not imply an intent to include new media. This would be a particularly perverse approach where, as here, digital media did not exist at the time of the agreement's execution.

III-37. **Answer (C) is correct.** The date of creation of *Sunrise Over Shatto* is important to this analysis as it determines the rules to be applied to the issue of copyright ownership. The 1970 date indicates that the law to be applied is that of the 1909 Act and the corresponding common-law rules regarding the status of copyright authorship and ownership. *Sunrise Over Shatto* was not created at the instance and expense of Collector, therefore the painting was not a work for hire. *Sunrise Over Shatto* was created by Avant, for himself, though he likely created it for subsequent sale. This means that Avant was the creator and author of the work. Collector's subsequent purchase of *Sunrise Over Shatto* gave her the ownership of the canvas containing the copyrighted image, not the ownership of the copyright. *See* 17 U.S.C. § 202 (ownership of copyright is distinct from the ownership of the material object in which the copyrighted work is embodied). Avant retained the ownership of the copyright in the painting.

Answer (A) is incorrect. For the reasons stated above, the painting was purchased by Collector, not the copyright in the painting.

Answer (B) is incorrect. For the reasons stated above, the painting was not a work for hire, therefore, Collector could not be deemed its author. In addition, the painting was purchased by Collector, not the copyright in the painting.

Answer (D) is incorrect. *Sunrise Over Shatto* was painted by Avant, who is the creator of the work, not Collector.

III-38. **Answer (B) is correct.** The date of creation of *Sunset Over Palms* is important to this analysis as it determines the rules to be applied to the issue of copyright ownership. The

1970 date indicates that the law to be applied is that of the 1909 Act and the corresponding common-law rules regarding the status of copyright authorship and ownership. *Sunset Over Palms* was a commissioned work created at the instance and expense of Collector, therefore the painting was a work for hire. This means that the hiring party, Collector, is deemed the author of the work and the initial copyright owner of the work. *See Martha Graham School and Dance Foundation, Inc. v. Martha Graham Center of Contemporary Dance, Inc.*, 380 F.3d 624, 634–35 (2d Cir. 2004) ("[W]ith respect to works for hire, the employer is legally regarded as the 'author,' as distinguished from the creator of the work").

Answer (A) is incorrect. Because *Sunset Over Palms* is a work for hire, the hiring party, Collector, is deemed the author of the work.

Answer (C) is incorrect. Because *Sunset Over Palms* is a work for hire, the hiring party, Collector, is deemed the author of the work and the initial copyright owner of the work.

Answer (D) is incorrect. *Sunset Over Palms* was painted by Avant, who is the creator of the work, not Collector.

III-39.   **Answer (C) is correct.** The date of creation of *Sunrise Over Moon Bay* is important to this analysis as it determines the rules to be applied to the issue of copyright ownership. The recent date indicates that the law to be applied is that of the 1976 Copyright Act rules regarding the status of copyright authorship and ownership. Avant, Jr. was not an employee of Collector, therefore, *Sunrise Over Moon Bay* was not a work made for hire created by an employee within the scope of his employment. Also, *Sunrise Over Moon Bay* was not created at the instance and expense of Collector; therefore the painting was not a work for hire because Avant, Jr. was not acting as an independent contractor when he created the painting. *Sunrise Over Moon Bay* was created by Avant, Jr. for himself, though he likely created it for subsequent sale. This means that Avant was the creator and author of the work. Collector's subsequent purchase of *Sunrise Over Moon Bay* gave her the ownership of the canvas containing the copyrighted image, not the ownership of the copyright. *See* 17 U.S.C. § 202 (ownership of copyright is distinct from the ownership of the material object in which the copyrighted work is embodied). Avant, Jr. retained the ownership of the copyright in the painting.

Answer (A) is incorrect. For the reasons stated above, the painting was purchased by Collector, not the copyright in the painting.

Answer (B) is incorrect. For the reasons stated above, the painting was not a work made for hire, therefore, Collector could not be deemed its author. In addition, the painting was purchased by Collector, not the copyright in the painting.

Answer (D) is incorrect. *Sunrise Over Moon Bay* was painted by Avant, who is the creator of the work, not Collector.

III-40.   **Answer (C) is correct.** The date of creation of *Sunset Over Calm* is important to this analysis as it determines the rules to be applied to the issue of copyright ownership. The recent date indicates that the law to be applied is that of the 1976 Copyright Act rules regarding the status of copyright authorship and ownership. Avant, Jr. was not an employee of Collector, therefore, *Sunset Over Calm* was not a work made for hire created by an employee within the scope of his employment. However, *Sunset Over Calm* is a commissioned work created at the instance and expense of Collector, therefore, Avant, Jr.

was acting as an independent contractor when he created the painting. Unlike the law under the 1909 Copyright Act where a commissioned work was presumed to be a work for hire, under the 1976 Copyright Act, a commissioned work created by an independent contractor is presumed not to be a work made for hire. The independent contractor is presumed to be the author and initial owner of the copyright in the work created. This presumption can be overcome only if there is a work made for hire agreement signed by both the creator and the hiring party, and the work to be created falls within one of the nine statutory work made for hire categories set forth in the definition of work made for hire in section 101 of the 1976 Copyright Act. Here there was no writing and the painting does not fall with one of the statutory categories. Therefore, *Sunset Over Calm* is not a work made for hire. Avant, Jr. is deemed the author and copyright owner of the painting.

Answer (A) is incorrect. For the reasons stated above, the painting was purchased by Collector, not the copyright in the painting.

Answer (B) is incorrect. For the reasons stated above, the painting was not a work made for hire, therefore, Collector could not be deemed its author. In addition, the painting was purchased by Collector, not the copyright in the painting.

Answer (D) is incorrect. *Sunset Over Calm* was painted by Avant, who is the creator of the work, not Collector.

IV-1. **Answer (A) is correct.** The exclusive right of reproduction is defined as the right to produce a material object in which the work is duplicated, transcribed, or simulated in a fixed form. It is irrelevant whether the duplication is of only a portion of the protected work or that the reproduction is never released to the public. In either case, the right of reproduction is violated so long as a substantial amount of the plaintiff's work has been taken. *See, e.g., Walt Disney Productions v. Filmation Assocs.*, 628 F. Supp. 871 (C.D. Cal. 1986) (copying of Disney animation as part of an intermediate step in Filmation's development of a motion picture was held to constitute an infringement).

In this case, Animator's mere act of reproducing some elements of the animation cels he created for Studio violates its exclusive right of reproduction, regardless of the fact that Animator never publicly released the short film or that he reproduced only segments of the background images from Studio's original cels.

Answer (B) is incorrect because the right of public display is not at issue here. Animator never displayed his short film to the public.

Answer (C) is incorrect because it is not a prerequisite for copyright protection that the images Animator created for Studio appeared in the animated feature film on which he was working at that time. As long as the images were fixed in a tangible medium of expression, they merited copyright protection.

Answer (D) is incorrect because the right of reproduction applies to all protected elements of a work. It is not a defense that only subsets of the original work were copied.

IV-2. **Answer (C) is correct.** The copying of a computer program into the RAM of a computer has been found to constitute an infringing reproduction. *See MAI Systems Corp. v. Peak Computer, Inc.*, 991 F.2d 511 (9th Cir. 1993); *Advanced Computer Services of Michigan v. MAI Systems, Corp.*, 845 F. Supp. 356 (E.D. Va. 1994). Here, by effecting the creation of a copy of the Bonestorm object code in the RAM of his computer, Bo violated SoftCo's reproduction right in that object code.

Answer (A) is incorrect because courts have consistently rejected arguments that RAM copies of object code are too evanescent to count as copyrightable fixations.

Answer (B) is incorrect because while the Digital Millennium Copyright Act held that unauthorized RAM copies of object code for the purpose of repair or maintenance do not violate the reproduction right, 17 U.S.C. § 117(c), Bo's use was not for one of these purposes, and thus does not fall within the DMCA safe harbor. The DMCA abrogated the application of the *MAI* cases to computer repair, but the legal principle enunciated in those cases remain in force.

Answer (D) is incorrect because in order to violate SoftCo's adaptation right, Bo would have to make a derivative work based on the object code, but Bo made an exact copy of the object code.

IV-3.   Under these facts, there would be no liability. While courts initially held that any RAM copies of a computer program's object code infringed the reproduction right, *MAI Systems Corp. v. Peak Computer, Inc.*, 991 F.2d 511 (9th Cir. 1993), this holding was abrogated by the Digital Millennium Copyright Act. The DMCA held that RAM copies of computer programs' source code made for the purposes of repair or maintenance are not infringing. 17 U.S.C. § 117(c). Here, because Bo made the copy of the Bonestorm object code solely to diagnose and repair a problem with his personal computer, the reproduction of that object code would fall within the DMCA safe harbor and thus would not infringe SoftCo's reproduction right in the object code.

IV-4.   **Answer (C) is correct.** The ability to use a work, generally a musical composition or sound recording, in the soundtrack of an audiovisual work, in synchronization with the images in the audiovisual work, has been deemed part of the reproduction right. *See Agee v. Paramount Communications, Inc.*, 59 F.3d 317 (2d Cir. 1995); *Angel Music, Inc. v. ABC Sports, Inc.*, 631 F. Supp. 429, 433 n.4 (S.D.N.Y. 1986). In practice, when a musical composition is synchronized in an audiovisual work, a "synch" license is required. A "master use" license is necessary when a sound recording is synchronized in an audiovisual work.

Answers **(A), (B), and (D) are incorrect** because they incorrectly state the exclusive right that is at issue prior to the exhibition of the motion picture. The distribution of copies of the motion picture containing the musical composition and sound recording to theater owners would be considered a public distribution. The performance of the musical composition in theaters would be considered a public performance. Sound recordings have no public performance rights. *See* 17 U.S.C. § 114.

IV-5.   **Answer (B) is correct.** Although Band's live performance was unfixed and thus not copyrightable, Congress has amended federal law to prevent the unauthorized fixation of musical performances. One who fixes the sounds or images of a live musical performance, without the consent of the performer, is subject to the same remedies as an infringer of copyright. 17 U.S.C. § 1101. Groupie's unauthorized recording of Band's performance runs afoul of the federal anti-bootlegging statute and would incur liability for this reason.

Answer (A) is incorrect because Band's live performance is unfixed, and thus cannot merit copyright protection. The musical composition that was performed was in the public domain, with no copyright protection, and cannot be infringed.

Answer (C) is incorrect because while Band's live performance is not copyrightable and the musical works performed were in the public domain, Groupie's recording of the performance can incur liability due to federal anti-bootlegging provisions that operate separately from standard copyright analysis.

Answer (D) is incorrect because liability on an anti-bootlegging theory does not require that the copy was sold or distributed.

IV-6.   **Answer (D) is correct.** None of these acts will expose SBPL to copyright liability. Libraries and archives are specially privileged to make reproductions under certain circumstances. *See* 17 U.S.C. § 108. Public libraries may make copies of protected works for patrons so long as the copy is not made for commercial advantage and the copy clearly indicates that the work is protected by copyright. *Id.* § 108(a). Thus Librarian's making of the single copy of the news article for Adam's personal use does not amount to infringement. A library or archive will also not be held liable for any copyright infringement resulting from the unsupervised use of reproducing equipment located on its premises, provided that such equipment displays a notice that the making of a copy may be subject to copyright law. *Id.* § 108(f). Thus Bob's surreptitiously using SBPL's photocopier to make an unauthorized reproduction of *Novel* does not expose SBPL to infringement liability, though it will almost certainly expose Bob to infringement liability. Finally, libraries may make unauthorized reproductions of copyrighted works for other libraries or archives so long as (1) the copy will become the property of the requesting institution; (2) the library making the copy has no reason to think that it will be used for other than archival and/or borrowing purposes; (3) it has been determined that a copy or phonorecord of the copyrighted work cannot be obtained at a fair price; and (4) the library displays prominently on its order form a warning concerning copyright restrictions. Because Librarian's copy for Archivist meets all four of these criteria, it also does not expose SBPL to copyright liability. *Id.* § 108(d).

Answers (A), (B), and (C) are incorrect because they wrongly state that any of the acts described in the question IV-6 will expose SBPL to copyright infringement liability.

IV-7.   **Answer (C) is correct.** The owner of copyright in a collective work has the right to reproduce and publicly distribute an individual contribution as part of that particular collective work, has a statutory privilege to reproduce and distribute the individual contribution in any revision of that collective work and any later collective work in the same series. 17 U.S.C. § 201(c). Because *Bi-Coastal Magazine* published Journalist's article in its West Coast edition in substantially the same form as it appeared in the East Coast edition of the magazine, its use falls within the privilege, and Journalist's copyright infringement suit must fail.

Answer (A) is incorrect because it does not take into account the section 201(c) privilege that is available to *Bi-Coastal Magazine*.

Answer (B) is incorrect because the section 201(c) privilege permits the public distribution of an individual contribution in another edition of the collective work.

Answer (D) is incorrect because the privilege provided by section 201(c) is a limited privilege and does not create a license to use the individual contribution in all print mediums.

IV-8.   Under these facts, Journalist would likely succeed in a copyright infringement suit against *Bi-Coastal Magazine.* The collective work revision privilege, 17 U.S.C. § 201(c), applies only to the reproduction and public distribution of works in their original context, while works that are denuded of that context do not fall within the privilege. *See New York Times Co. v. Tasini,* 533 U.S. 483, 496–97 (2001) (use of individual newspaper articles in electronic database, retrievable separately from newspaper, deemed not to constitute a revision under section 201(c)). Here, because the online database presents users with articles separated from their original context, divorced from accompanying articles, photographs, and advertisements, the unauthorized use of Journalist's article would not fall within the privilege, and a copyright infringement suit by Journalist against Magazine would likely succeed. *See Faulkner v. National Geographic Enters. Inc.,* 409 F.3d 26, 38 (2d Cir. 2005) (searchable electronic replica of magazines held to be a permissible revision where new elements did not substantially alter the original context of the magazines).

IV-9.   **Answer (B) is correct.** While Dilettante is free to make a new sound recording of the *Winter* musical work, so long as she does not duplicate the original sound recording, Dilettante's unauthorized and uncompensated reproduction of the *Winter* musical work constitutes an infringement of Composer's copyright in the musical work. Dilettante did not need to acquire Composer's permission to reproduce the *Winter* musical work so long as she paid the statutory compulsory mechanical license. 17 U.S.C. § 115. However, Dilettante's failure to do this means that her reproduction and public distribution of the musical work amounts to infringement.

Answer (A) is incorrect because it wrongly states that Dilettante's conduct violates Composer's copyrights in the sound recording and the musical work, when in fact it only violates Composer's *Winter* musical work copyright.

Answer (C) is incorrect because the fact that the *Winter* musical work is subject to a compulsory mechanical license by statute, does not mean that Dilettante is simply entitled to reproduce Composer's musical work without compensation. It merely means that Dilettante need not seek Composer's permission to reproduce the musical work so long as she pays the statutorily fixed licensing fee.

Answer (D) is incorrect because a "master use" license is only necessary when a sound recording is duplicated in whole or in part. Here, Dilettante did not duplicate Composer's sound recording of *Winter.*

IV-10.   Attorney should advise Dilettante that a mechanical license is needed to record and distribute the *Winter* musical work. One option is to negotiate a consensual license with Composer. Because Composer has recorded and distributed the *Winter* musical work to the general public, on phonorecords, for the their private use, it is not necessary to seek Composer's permission to reproduce the *Winter* musical work on *Dilettante Performs Winter.* However, Attorney should emphasize that this is only true if Dilettante remits to Composer the statutory compulsory mechanical licensing fee for Dilettante's use of the *Winter* musical work.

This is because a nondramatic musical composition that has been reproduced and distributed with the authorization of the copyright owner thereafter may be reproduced and distributed without the consent of the copyright owner pursuant to a compulsory mechanical license. 17 U.S.C. § 115. Under this compulsory license, the composition can be recorded, manufactured in phonorecords, and sold to the public for its private use, as long as the statutory royalty of 9.1 cents per unit is paid to the copyright owner. Stylistic changes to the composition are permitted, as long as the composition is not perverted or distorted, nor the fundamental character of the work changed. *See ABKCO Music, Inc. v. Stellar Records, Inc.*, 96 F.3d 60 (2d Cir. 1996) (karaoke CD-ROM did not fall within section 115's compulsory mechanical license); *Rodgers and Hammerstein Organization v. UMG Recordings Inc.*, 60 U.S.P.Q. 2d 1354, 1360 (S.D.N.Y. 2001) (compulsory mechanical license does not permit reproduction onto servers or streaming of composition over the Internet).

IV-11.   **Answer (C) is correct.** Techie clearly owes a mechanical license fee to Composer for the reproduction and distribution of Composer's copyrighted musical work via an electronic phonorecord, known as a digital phonorecord delivery ("DPD"). 17 U.S.C. § 115. Such licenses may be consensual or may be obtained as a compulsory mechanical license under section 115. Until 1995, there was ambiguity as to whether the digital delivery of music, for example, via MP3 files, would trigger the compulsory mechanical license provisions of section 115. However, in that year, Congress settled the question when it passed the Digital Performance Right in Sound Recordings Act of 1995, which expanded the compulsory mechanical license to include "digital phonorecord delivery." Currently, the statutory fee set for DPDs is the same as the statutory fee set for traditional physical phonorecords. 17 U.S.C. § 115(c)(3)(A).

In addition, the streaming of the *Songbird* musical work on Techie's website constitutes a public performance that must be licensed to avoid a copyright infringement claim.

Answer (A) is incorrect because it does not recognize the need to obtain a public performance license.

Answer (B) is incorrect because it does not recognize the need to obtain a mechanical license.

Answer (D) is incorrect because, as explained above, a mechanical license is required for a digital download and the streaming of the musical work constitutes a public performance, whether or not the musical work at issue has been released in a physical copy.

IV-12.   **Answer (D) is correct.** Reproducing a sound recording and making it available as a digital download requires the authorization of Composer, the owner of the copyright in the sound recording. *See* 17 U.S.C. § 106(1). This authorization generally takes the form of a master use license, pursuant to which the licensee is given the right to make phonorecords of the sound recording. In addition, Techie is streaming the sound recording of *Songbird*. This constitutes a digital transmission of the sound recording to the general public, an exclusive right owned by Composer. *See* 17 U.S.C. § 106(6). To avoid a claim of copyright infringement regarding the sound recording of *Songbird*, Techie must obtain either a statutory license pursuant to section 114 of the Copyright Act, or obtain a consensual license from Composer.

Answer (A) is incorrect because it overlooks the digital transmission right of the sound recording of *Songbird*.

Answer (B) is incorrect on two grounds. First, a master use license is necessary to offer downloads of the sound recording of *Songbird*. Second, sound recordings have no public performance rights under section 106(4).

Answer (C) is incorrect because sound recordings have no public performance rights under section 106(4) and it does not address the need for a digital transmission license to stream the sound recording.

IV-13.   **Answer (A) is correct.** This conduct violates the reproduction rights of the copyright owners of all the musical works and sound recordings included on the CD Pal created for Friend. Pal's conduct does not fall within the home taping provisions of the Audio Home Recording Act ("AHRA"), 17 U.S.C. § 1008, because the reproduction of the copyrighted material onto the CD was done with a computer, which does not constitute a "digital audio recording device" under AHRA. *See Recording Indus. Ass'n of Am. v. Diamond Multimedia Sys., Inc.*, 180 F.3d 1072, 1078 (9th Cir. 1999) (computers do not constitute "digital audio recording devices" under AHRA); *A & M Records, Inc. v. Napster, Inc.*, 239 F.3d 1004, 1024–25 (9th Cir. 2001) (AHRA immunity for noncommercial taping held not applicable to MP3 music file sharing program that does not involve a digital audio recording device).

Answer (B) is incorrect because it does not address the reproduction of the sound recordings by Pal.

Answer (C) is incorrect because it does not address the reproduction of the musical works by Pal.

Answer (D) is incorrect. Although the Audio Home Recording Act of 1992 permits unauthorized audio recording for noncommercial use, 17 U.S.C. § 1008, it does so only when done so with a digital audio recording device. Computers are not deemed digital audio recording devices, therefore Pal's use of his computer makes section 1008 inapplicable, even though his use was clearly noncommercial because the mix tape was merely an interpersonal gift.

IV-14. **Answer (B) is correct.** The copyright owner has the exclusive right to prepare a derivative work that recasts, transforms, or adapts the underlying original work of authorship. 17 U.S.C. § 106(2); *see, e.g., Grove Press, Inc. v. Greenleaf Publishing Co.*, 247 F. Supp. 518 (E.D.N.Y. 1965). By modifying Artist's painting through the addition of substantial original creative material, Pomo violated Artist's adaptation right. *See Peker v. Masters Collection*, 96 F. Supp. 2d 216 (E.D.N.Y. 2000) (painting over a poster of an oil painting deemed an infringement).

Answer (A) is incorrect because the public display right is not at issue here due to the statutory exception that permits owners of lawfully made copies of copyrighted works of authorship to display them publicly without the owner's consent. *See* 17 U.S.C. § 109(c).

Answer (C) is incorrect because it is immaterial whether Pomo altered the original version or a copy of Artist's work because the alteration was of the copyrighted image. In either case, there would be substantial recasting of the work of authorship sufficient to violate the adaptation right.

Answer (D) is incorrect because copyright infringement does not depend on whether a work is offered for sale.

IV-15. Most courts would hold that Pomo would not be subject to liability because his frame mildly resituated the work without adding anything original to it. A majority of jurisdictions require that the defendant must have created a work with sufficient originality to be deemed a derivative work to violate the adaptation right. *See Lee v. A.R.T. Co.*, 125 F.3d 580 (7th Cir. 1997); *C.M. Paula Co. v. Logan*, 355 F. Supp. 189 (N.D. Tex. 1973) (placing the work in a new context must be sufficiently original to be protectable as a derivative work for such action to be found an infringement of the adaptation right).

Some courts, however, would hold that even a slight recasting of a work, without the addition of any original material, would amount to infringement of the adaptation right. The Ninth Circuit, for example, has held that placing a work in a new context in which the work is "recast, transformed or adapted" is sufficient to infringe the adaptation right without a showing that the change contained sufficient originality. *See Mirage Editions,*

Inc. v. Albuquerque A.R.T. Co., 856 F.2d 1341 (9th Cir. 1988) (removing prints from a book, pasting them on tile, and framing the print constitutes an infringement). In such a jurisdiction, Pomo's conduct would amount to copyright infringement.

IV-16. **Answer (C) is correct.** Linguo clearly violated the reproduction right in *Novel* by photocopying it without permission. *See* 17 U.S.C. § 106(1). Linguo also violated the adaptation right by creating an unauthorized translation of *Novel*. 17 U.S.C. § 106(2). *See, e.g., Grove Press, Inc. v. Greenleaf Publ'g Co.*, 247 F. Supp. 518 (E.D.N.Y. 1965).

Answer (A) is incorrect because it fails to state that Linguo's conduct violated the adaptation right.

Answers (B) and (D) are incorrect because they falsely state that Linguo's conduct violated the public distribution right in *Novel*. What Linguo did was likely not a public distribution because it was not public, but was distributed only to a small circle of known friends. *See Bagdadi v. Nazar*, 84 F.3d 1194, 1198–99 (9th Cir. 1996) (public distribution requires distribution of copies to the public, or the offering to distribute copies to a group of persons for purposes of further distribution, public performance, or public display).

IV-17. **Answer (A) is correct.** Although the Copyright Act provides no definition of "distribution," the term is viewed as essentially synonymous with "publication" and requires the dissemination of a material object. *See Hotaling v. Church of Jesus Christ of Latter-Day Saints*, 118 F.3d 199 (4th Cir. 1997) (listing work in library's catalog system, adding it to library's collection, and making it available to the public constituted "distribution" of the work). Here, Associate's conduct clearly amounts to public distribution because he disseminated numerous copies of Biglaw's employee handbook to the public.

Answer (B) is incorrect because it contains an incorrect statement of law. Pursuant to the first sale doctrine, a copyright owner only has an exclusive right to transfer the ownership, rent, lease, or lend an authorized copy without any right to the further distribution of that copy.

Answer (C) is incorrect because Associate was not the owner of the copies he distributed. Therefore, he cannot take advantage of the first sale doctrine. 17 U.S.C. § 109(a).

Answer (D) is incorrect because an infringer need not know the particular members of the public to whom an unauthorized dissemination is made in order to violate the public distribution right; a general dissemination is sufficient.

IV-18. On these facts, Biglaw's success would depend on the definition of "public" in connection with the exclusive right of public distribution. The term "public" is not defined in the Copyright Act. Its meaning, however, can be determined by looking at two analogous terms: "To perform or display a work 'publicly'" and "publication." The phrase "[t]o perform or display a work 'publicly'" is used in connection with the public performance [§ 106(4)], public display [§ 106(5)], and public digital audio transmission [§ 106(6)] exclusive rights. In those situations, the exclusive right is violated if the performance or display occurs in a place open to the public, or at any place "where a substantial number of persons outside of a normal circle of a family and its social acquaintances." 17 U.S.C. § 101. If the latter part of this definition is deemed analogous to the definition of "public" distribution, it would exclude any distribution to members of one's family or social acquaintances. Under this view, the distribution of copies of the employee handbook to close friends would not constitute a distribution to the public. *See Bagdadi v. Nazar*, 84 F.3d 1194, 1198–99 (9th Cir. 1996).

Another defined term that may be relevant is "publication." Under the common law, a publication occurred when a possessory interest in tangible copies of the work is made available to the general public with the consent of the copyright owner. *See Shoptalk, Ltd. v. Concorde-New Horizons Corp.*, 168 F.3d 586, 590 (2d Cir. 1999); *Burke v. National Broadcasting Co.*, 598 F.2d 688, 691 (1st Cir. 1979). The definition of "publication" in section 101 of the Copyright Act expands the common-law definition to include "offering to distribute copies or phonorecords to a group of persons for purposes of further distribution, public performance, or public display." Under this view, the distribution of the three copies of the employee handbook to close friends would not have made the tangible copies available to the general public. This is particularly true where the copies were to be used for a specific purpose, to establish the viability of a proposed lawsuit. While it is true that under this definition a publication can be found where only one copy reaches a member of the general public, *see Ford Motor Co. v. Summit Motor Prods., Inc.*, 930 F.2d 277, 299 (3d Cir. 1991), a distribution to three close friends likely would not be deemed a distribution to members of the general public.

IV-19.   **Answer (D) is correct.** Computo's conduct clearly amounts to public distribution because he facilitated the public library's dissemination of Techie's protected computer code to the public. However, pursuant to the "first sale doctrine," the copyright owner's distribution right ceases with respect to a particular authorized copy once the copyright owner has parted with ownership of that particular copy. 17 U.S.C. §§ 109(a), 109(b) (emphasizing that first sale doctrine applies to computer programs, except for rental, lease, or lending). *See Mirage Editions, Inc. v. Albuquerque A.R.T. Co.*, 856 F.2d 1341 (9th Cir. 1988). Therefore, the owner of a lawfully made copy of the work may sell or transfer the possession of that copy. Here, Techie parted with the CD-ROM on which his program was embodied when he gave it to Computo. This means that Computo was free to sell or transfer the CD-ROM, so long as it did not constitute disposing of the copy by rental, lease, or lending for commercial advantage. As a result, Computo's gift to the library is not actionable.

Answer (A) is incorrect because the first sale doctrine applies to any circumstance under which an owner of the physical instantiation of a copyrighted work of authorship gives it to another. By giving the CD-ROM to Computo, Techie parted ownership with it, triggering the application of the first sale doctrine.

Answer (B) is incorrect because it fails to note that while Computo's conduct may in itself amount to a violation of Techie's public distribution right, that conduct is immunized from liability pursuant to the first sale doctrine.

Answer (C) is incorrect because Computo's conduct clearly amounts to a public distribution of the Tech-Neeks computer program for the reasons explained above.

IV-20.   **Answer (A) is correct.** While the first sale doctrine generally allows purchasers of the physical objects in which copyrighted works of authorship are embodied to sell, rent, or give away those objects, the first sale doctrine no longer applies to the rental, lease, or lending of a sound recording of a musical composition embodied in a phonorecord. 17 U.S.C. § 109(b)(1)(A); *see A & M Records, Inc. v. A.L.W., Ltd.*, 855 F.2d 368, 370 n.6 (7th

Cir. 1988) (buy-back program pursuant to which customers purchased a record for two dollars, plus a five dollar deposit, which was returned at the customer's choice within a specified time limit, held to constitute a disguised rental). Because Entrepreneur's enterprise falls squarely within this exception to the first sale doctrine, the doctrine does not apply and the record companies have a valid cause of action against Entrepreneur for violating their exclusive right of public distribution in the sound recordings embodied in the CDs.

Answer (B) is incorrect because the first sale doctrine does allow purchasers of music CDs to sell or give them away without running afoul of the copyright owner's exclusive right of public distribution. In addition, nonprofit libraries and educational institutions may also rent, lease, or lend sound recordings. 17 U.S.C. § 109(b)(1)(A).

Answer (C) is incorrect because it wrongly states that the first sale doctrine immunizes Entrepreneur's conduct of renting sound recordings, which it does not for the reasons explained above.

Answer (D) is incorrect because Entrepreneur's attempts to insulate the record companies from piracy are unrelated to the question of whether he has infringed any exclusive rights in copyrighted works of authorship.

IV-21. **Answer (D) is correct.** To "perform" a work within the meaning of the Copyright Act means to recite, render, play, dance, or act it. 17 U.S.C. § 101 (defining "perform"). This means that Orchestra's presentation of the modern classical music piece is a "performance" within the meaning of the Copyright Act. However, a transmission and even a "secondary transmission," the simultaneous retransmission of a primary transmission, is a performance. *See Sailor Music v. Gap Stores, Inc.*, 668 F.2d 84 (2d Cir. 1981); *Broadcast Music, Inc. v. Claire's Boutiques, Inc.*, 949 F.2d 1482 (7th Cir. 1991). This means that Radio Station's primary transmission of the concert and Fan's retransmission of that broadcast in Hartford both amount to "performances" as well.

Answer (A) is incorrect because it does not include Radio Station's primary transmission and Fan's secondary transmission.

Answer (B) is incorrect because it does not include Fan's secondary transmission.

Answer (C) is incorrect because it does not include Orchestra's concert.

IV-22. **Answer (C) is correct.** A performance is "public" if it occurs at a place open to the public or at any place where a substantial number of persons outside of a normal circle of a family and its social acquaintances is gathered. *Sailor Music v. Gap Stores, Inc.*, 668 F.2d 84 (7th Cir. 1981). Under this standard, the outdoor concert clearly counts as a public performance. The poetry reading, while a less clear case, also counts as a public performance because it takes place at a public place. The performance would be deemed to be public even if no one attended the reading because the focus is on the public nature of the venue. *See* 17 U.S.C. § 101 (defining "[t]o perform or display a work 'publicly'") ("place open to the public"); *Video Views, Inc. v. Studio 21, Ltd.*, 925 F.2d 1010, 1020 (7th Cir. 1991) ("proper inquiry is directed to the nature of the place . . . and whether it is a place where the public is openly invited"). The comedy routine seems like a harder call still because a private club seems hard to define as public. Yet performances at "semipublic" places such as clubs, lodges, and schools are now found to be public performances. *See Bourne Co. v. Hunter Country Club, Inc.*, 990 F.2d 934 (7th Cir. 1993).

The presentation is thus the only one of these performances that is not public, because routine meetings of businesses and governmental personnel do not represent the gathering of a "substantial number of persons." *See* H.R. Rep. No. 94-1476, 94th Cong., 2d Sess. 64 (1976).

Answers (A), (B), and (D) are incorrect for the reasons explained above.

IV-23. **Answer (B) is correct.** Pursuant to the transmit clause in the Copyright Act's definition of "to perform . . . a work publicly," a performance is "public" if it is transmitted to a place specified by the public place clause; or to a place or separate places where the public is capable of receiving the transmission at the same time or at different times. 17 U.S.C. § 101. The transmit clause applies only when images or sounds are transmitted from one place to another place, but this is the case here because HG's transmission begins at its central server and terminates in numerous individual guest rooms. *See Columbia Pictures Indus., Inc. v. Aveco, Inc.*, 800 F.2d 59 (3d Cir. 1986) (holding that site-to-site transmissions are public performances within the meaning of the Copyright Act).

Answer (A) is incorrect because the Copyright Act does not define every performance of a motion picture as a public performance. For example, many times motion pictures are performed in private homes and are not deemed to be "public" performances. *See Columbia Pictures Indus., Inc. v. Redd Horne Inc.*, 749 F.2d 154, 157 (3d Cir. 1984).

Answer (C) is incorrect because courts have held that electronically transmitting a motion picture from a central device to individual hotel rooms constitutes a public performance. *See On Command Video Corp. v. Columbia Pictures Indus.*, 777 F. Supp. 787, 789–90 (N.D. Cal. 1991).

Answer (D) is incorrect because the transmit clause explicitly states that transmission of a work of authorship from one site to certain types of other sites is a public performance of that work.

IV-24. No. As we saw in question IV-23, the transmit clause in the Copyright Act's definition of "to perform . . . a work publicly" states that a performance is "public" if it is transmitted to a place specified by the public place clause, or to a place or separate places where the public is capable of receiving the transmission at the same time or at different times. 17 U.S.C. § 101 (defining "to perform . . . a work 'publicly"). Under these facts, HG is merely providing a conduit to the Internet. *See* 17 U.S.C. § 512(a). None of the copyrighted material at issue resides on HG's server. Any website that offered the streaming of copyrighted motion pictures without a public performance license would be liable for copyright infringement. *See Playboy Enters., Inc. v. Frena*, 839 F. Supp. 1552 (M.D. Fla. 1993) (transmission of an image from a computer bulletin board, an on-line service, or the Internet constitutes a public performance). HG, which did not copy, select, or request the delivery of the motion pictures would not suffer liability for the unauthorized public performance of the motion pictures. *See Perfect 10, Inc. v. Amazon.com, Inc.*, 487 F.3d 701, 715–19 (9th Cir. 2007).

IV-25. **Answer (A) is correct.** The fact that the restaurant's size is greater than 3,750 gross square feet requires Restaurateur to license its public performances of the musical compositions broadcast by the radio station unless the establishment has a total of not more than six loudspeakers, with no more than four loudspeakers located in any one room or adjoining outdoor space. The restaurant's size places a limitation of six speakers for the section 110(5)(B) exception. The existence of ten speakers means Restaurateur has to stop using the receiver or obtain licenses from ASCAP and BMI, and perhaps SESAC.

Answer (B) is incorrect. The sophistication of an establishment's sound system and the cost of its installation are not factors under section 110(5)(B). They are factors for the *Aiken* exception of section 110(5)(A) that offers an exemption to the public performance right where the reception of television and radio broadcasts is by way of home-style receivers which may be seen or heard by the public, so long as no direct charge is made. Many of the cases involving the *Aiken* exemption limit it to an establishment with four or fewer speakers.

Answer (C) is incorrect because section 110(5)(B) distinguishes between non-food service or drinking establishments and food service or drinking establishments regarding requirements for an exception from the public performance right. The section does not distinguish between food service and drinking establishments.

Answer (D) is incorrect because section 110(5)(B) does not apply to the performance of live music. The fact that the restaurant does not provide live music helps make it eligible for an exception to the public performance right.

IV-26.   **Answer (B) is correct.** The *Aiken* exception applies only to television and radio broadcasts. It does not apply to live performances. Playing music fixed in a CD via an amplifier and speakers is a live performance. Therefore, section 110(5)(A) does not apply to this situation.

Answer (A) is incorrect. Every musical composition protected by copyright enjoys the exclusive right of public performance, regardless of whether it has been distributed to the public. Whether a musical composition is a distributed composition is relevant to whether the compulsory mechanical license provisions of section 115 apply, not to whether the limitations on the public performance right provided by section 110 apply.

Answer (C) is incorrect. The fact that sound recordings do not have a public performance right has no impact on the public performance right enjoyed by musical compositions.

Answer (D) is incorrect. Even though the selection of musical composition is made by the children, it is still the employees of the Children's Play Center who actually cause the performance of the musical composition. As a result, the employees are engaged in direct infringement of the copyrights in the musical compositions.

IV-27.   **Answer (D) is correct.** The NHPD's failure to return Karma's drawings, however wrongful, does not violate her copyright-based exclusive rights in those works. Copyright law does not provide the copyright owner with a right of access to her work. *See Shell v. City of Radford*, 351 F. Supp. 2d 510, 511 (W.D. Va. 2005) (Copyright Act did not provide photographer with means to force police department to return photographs). Karma may, of course, have other, non-copyright-based causes of action against the NHPD, such as the tort of conversion.

Answer (A) is incorrect because the Copyright Act does not give owners a broad right of control over their work, only the six enumerated exclusive rights over those works set forth in section 106.

Answer (B) is incorrect because the Copyright Act does not give owners an exclusive right to profit from their works.

Answer (C) is incorrect because the creator of a work may well have some rights in the physical embodiment of that work. It is not the case, as this answer falsely states, that the creator never has an interest in the physical instantiation of the work.

IV-28.   **Answer (A) is correct.** Even if one assumes that Superfan's reading to her students and to the fan club are public performances within the meaning of the Copyright Act, they are each subject to section 110 exemptions. Specifically, face-to-face classroom teaching activities, such as Superfan's using *Ultraworld* to educate her sixth graders, are exempted from the public performance provision. 17 U.S.C. § 110(1). Also, certain nonprofit performances, such as Superfan's reading to her small group of fellow fans for no profit, are exempted from the public performance provision. 17 U.S.C. § 110(4). However, Superfan's reading at the open-mic night clearly violates Novelist's public performance right in the novel because it is an unauthorized reading of sections of *Ultraworld* for a paying audience of the general public, and is not subject to a section 110 exemption. Thus, that is Superfan's only act that may be actionable.

Answers (B), (C), and (D) are incorrect because they falsely assume either that Superfan's reading to her students or the fan club (or both) is actionable.

IV-29.   **Answer (A) is correct.** Pirate has clearly violated Musician's right of reproduction in the *Delight* sound recording by copying the MP3 file containing the sound recording from her website to his hard drive without authorization. And while there is no public performance right in sound recordings, 17 U.S.C. § 114(a), sound recordings are provided with a digital transmission right. 17 U.S.C. § 106(6). Because Pirate's unauthorized transmission of the *Delight* sound recording took place over a digital medium, that transmission did violate her section 106(6) digital transmission right, and Pirate can be held liable for infringement on that theory as well.

Answers (B), (C), and (D) are incorrect because they wrongly state that there is no violation of either the reproduction or the digital transmission right.

IV-30.   Under these facts, Musician would still be able to successfully argue that Pirate violated her exclusive right of reproduction in the *Delight* sound recording, for the straightforward reasons explained in the answer to question IV-29. However, Musician would not be able to sue Pirate for infringement on the theory that Pirate violated her digital transmission right in the *Delight* sound recording, because there is no general right of public performance in sound recordings. 17 U.S.C. § 114(a). *See Agee v. Paramount Commc'ns, Inc.*, 59 F.3d 317, 320 (2d Cir. 1995). The narrow digital transmission right for sound recordings, 17 U.S.C. § 106(6), does not apply here because the broadcast took place over an analog medium.

IV-31.   **Answer (C) is correct.** The exclusive right to publicly display a work extends to literary works; musical works; dramatic and choreographic works; as well as pictorial, graphic, or sculptural works, including the individual images of a motion picture or other audiovisual work. 17 U.S.C. § 106(5). Bookseller's unauthorized physical display of *Finality* clearly constitutes a public display. The internet display does as well. Courts have held that placing the digitized version of a work on a website to which the public has access via the Internet constitutes a public display of the work. *See Playboy Enters., Inc. v. Webbworld, Inc.*, 991 F. Supp. 543, 552–53 (N.D. Tex. 1997). However, there would be no liability in this case for the physical display because Bookseller, as the owner of the displayed lawful copy of *Finality*, is entitled to display it publicly pursuant to the limitation on the display right presented by section 109(c) of the Copyright Act.

This limitation does not apply to the online display, however. Section 109(c) permits the owner of a lawfully made copy of the work to display that copy by projection of no more than one image at a time, to viewers present at the place where the physical copy is located. 17 U.S.C. § 109(c). This limitation does not apply to the online display in this case for two reasons. First, to be placed on Bookseller's website, the page of *Finality* had to be scanned. Bookseller's scanning created an unauthorized copy, making the copy that was actually displayed on the website one that was not "lawfully made," therefore placing it outside the provisions of section 109(c). In addition, material that is displayed on the Internet does not come within section 109(c) because viewers are not present at the place where the copy is located, usually the server used to operate the website. *See Bryant v. Gordon*, 483 F. Supp. 2d 605, 613 (N.D. Ill. 2007) (section 109(c) does not entitle the owner of copy to publicly display copyrighted images to the world via the Internet); *Ringgold v. Black Entertainment Television, Inc.*, 126 F.3d 70 (2d Cir. 1997) (unauthorized use of copyrighted pictorial work on set of cable show transmitted to public did not fall within section 109(c)).

Answer (A) is incorrect because there is a public display right in literary works. 17 U.S.C. § 106(5).

Answer (B) is incorrect because the Copyright Act does not require that an entire work be displayed in order to violate the exclusive right to public display.

Answer (D) is incorrect because the physical display of *Finality* is not actionable pursuant to section 109(c).

IV-32.   **Answer (D) is correct.** The Digital Performance Right in Sound Recordings Act of 1995 provides protected sound recordings with a digital transmission right that gives the copyright owner of a sound recording the exclusive right to perform the copyrighted work publicly by means of a digital audio transmission. This right only applies to sound recordings that are transmitted digitally to the public. This right operates differently with respect to different forms of digital transmission. Some digital transmissions of sound recordings have been exempted, such as radio broadcasts within the service area of the radio station's FCC license. 17 U.S.C. § 114(d)(1). *See Bonneville Int'l Corp. v. Peters*, 347 F.3d 485, 495 (3d Cir. 2003) (media exemption has been limited to the geographic area set forth in the broadcaster's FCC license and does not exempt broadcast signals transmitted over the Internet). Thus BigMedia needs no license from the owners of the copyright in sound recordings to transmit their works over BigMedia's digital radio station.

Public performances of sound recordings by a noninteractive digital transmission may qualify for a "statutory license" (compulsory license). 17 U.S.C. § 114(d)(2). To qualify for the "statutory license," the transmission must meet several conditions, including a limitation on the number of recordings from a single album or artist transmitted during a specified time period and a prohibition of advance announcements of playlists. If the numerous requirements for the statutory license are not met, a negotiated consensual license from the owner of the copyright in the sound recording must be obtained. Thus BigMedia needs to pay either a statutory (compulsory) license or obtain a consensual license from sound recording owners in order to stream the sound recordings over

BigMedia.com.

Finally, the streaming of sound recordings by an interactive digital transmission requires a negotiated consensual license from the owner of the copyright in the sound recording. Thus BigMedia will need to negotiate licenses with sound recording owners for any works it wants to make available via its on-demand "BigMedia Plus" service.

Answer (A) is incorrect because, although the public performance right set forth in section 106(4) does not apply to sound recordings, the digital transmission right set forth in section 106(6) applies to BigMedia's planned use of sound recordings.

Answers (B) and (C) are incorrect because they wrongly characterize BigMedia's licensing obligations as explained above.

IV-33. **Answer (D) is correct.** Writer's objection in this case is that Publisher violated his right of attribution, but this is not a basis for copyright infringement under federal copyright law. As a general rule, United States copyright law does not recognize a right of attribution. *See Graham v. James*, 144 F.3d 229, 236 (2d Cir. 1998) (author who sells or licenses her work does not have an inherent right to be credited as its author). Although section 106A does provide for a right of attribution, it only applies to works of visual art, not literary works. Writer may have other causes of action against Publisher, such as common-law fraud, breach of contract, or false advertising, but copyright infringement is not among them.

Answer (A) is incorrect because merely changing the name of the author does not create a derivative work.

Answer (B) is incorrect because a violation of the right of attribution is not a basis for a copyright infringement claim, for the reasons explained above.

Answer (C) is incorrect because it misstates the scope of the law. Federal law does recognize some moral rights, including an attribution right, through the Visual Artists Rights Act (VARA), codified in section 106A of the Copyright Act.

IV-34. **Answer (B) is correct.** Moral rights have been specifically accorded only to a limited category of "works of visual art" pursuant to the Visual Artists Rights Act of 1990 ("VARA"), but Painter's painting is clearly among them. 17 U.S.C. §§ 101 (definition of "work of visual art"), 106A. An author of a qualifying work has the right to claim authorship in her work, to prevent the use of her name as the author of any work she did not create and to prevent the use of her name as the author of a work she did originally create, but which has been mutilated. 17 U.S.C. § 106A(a)(1-2); *see Berrios Nogueras v. Home Depot*, 330 F. Supp. 2d 48, 50 (D. Puerto Rico 2004). Thus Painter can successfully sue Buyer for his attempt to pass himself off as the author of the painting.

An author also has the right to prevent the intentional distortion, mutilation, or other modification of her work that would be prejudicial to her honor or reputation. 17 U.S.C. § 106A(a)(3)(A). However, modification of a work of visual art that is a result of conservation or the public presentation of the work, including lighting and placement, is not actionable unless the modification is caused by gross negligence. 17 U.S.C. § 106A(c)(2). Here, the reason that the painting degraded was due both to the inherent fragility of the paint used and to non-negligent environmental factors, so Painter cannot successfully sue Buyer for violating Painter's right of integrity in the painting.

Answers (A), (C), and (D) are incorrect because they incorrectly state either that Painter cannot successfully sue Buyer on a right of attribution theory, or that Painter can successfully sue Buyer on a right of integrity theory.

IV-35. On these facts, Painter would have no moral rights cause of action under VARA. The Visual Artists Rights Act applies only to certain qualifying works. Although photographs may be protected by VARA as works for visual art, VARA applies only to photographs where the initial rendering of a still photographic image was produced for exhibition purposes only and signed by the author. Any copy in a limited edition of 200 copies or fewer is also protected if the copies are signed and consecutively numbered by the author. Here, the photograph taken by Painter meets all of these standards except one: the limited series numbered 250 rather than 200. As a result, the prints at issue here do not qualify for protection under VARA, therefore, Painter cannot successfully sue Buyer for a violation of section 106A.

IV-36. **Answer (C) is correct.** For works of visual art created on or after June 1, 1991, the duration of rights under section 106A is life of the author. 17 U.S.C. § 106A(d)(1). Artist's rights under VARA died with him and can no longer be enforced.

Answers (A) and (B) are incorrect because no court has interpreted the rights of attribution or integrity to include a right of removal.

Answer (D) is incorrect because it wrongly states that Artist's rights under VARA remain enforceable. It is worth noting, however, that the second half of the statement is correct: VARA does not confer on artists a right to remove their work from circulation should they decide they no longer agree with it. This is in contrast to most continental European moral rights regimes, where artists do have a right of removal.

V-1.   **Answer (B) is correct.** The date of publication determines whether there is a need for a copyright notice. Different rules apply depending on whether the work was published under the 1909 Act (1909–1977), during the decennial period (1-1-78 to 2-28-89), or on or after March 1, 1989.

Answers (A), (C), and (D) are incorrect because the factors they identify are unrelated to the need for notice.

V-2.   **Answer (C) is correct.** In the case of conflicting transfers of copyright ownership, the first good faith recorded transfer of a registered copyright will be given priority. Section 205(d) of the Copyright Act gives priority to the transfer of copyright executed first if that transfer is recorded prior to the recordation of any conflicting transfer, or if the recordation is made within one month after its execution in the United States or within two months after its execution outside the United States, even if another transfer has been recorded during that time. Outside of that one- to two-month grace period, a later transfer prevails if it is recorded first, taken in good faith, and without notice of the earlier transfer.

Answer (A) is incorrect for the reason stated above. It is not relevant that Publisher A had acted on its contractual rights. When there is a recordation of assignment of a copyright, section 205(d) of the Copyright Act provides a resolution of the conflict.

Answer (B) is incorrect for the reason stated above. The rule is not the first to be assigned, but the first to record the assignment or other transfer of copyright.

Answer (D) is incorrect for the reason stated above. Publication with proper copyright notice no longer vests federal copyright in a work, as it did prior to 1978.

V-3.   **Answer (C) is correct.** The drawing was protected by state common-law copyright until it was published, registered with the Copyright Office, or state protection was preempted by federal copyright law. The 1960 distribution of the drawing constituted a limited publication that did not require a copyright notice, and did not divest the work of its state common-law protection. Because the drawing was a fixed work, its common-law protection was preempted by federal copyright law on January 1, 1978, when the 1976 Copyright Act took effect.

Answer (A) is incorrect. In 1910, a work was invested with federal copyright protection when it was either published with proper copyright notice or was registered with the Copyright Office. The creation of a work did not invest the work with federal copyright protection. State common-law copyright protected the work at the time of its creation.

Answer (B) is incorrect. The distribution of the work to three individuals as a gift with limitations placed on its further distribution was not a publication to the general public. It was a distribution to a limited number of individuals for a specific purpose. As such it was a limited publication that permitted state common-law protection of the drawing to continue. *See Academy of Motion Picture Arts and Sciences v. Creative House Promotions, Inc.*, 944 F.2d 1446, 1451–52 (9th Cir. 1991) ("Oscar" statuette underwent only limited publication and is not in the public domain); *White v. Kimmell*, 193 F.2d 744, 746–47 (9th Cir. 1952). Furthermore, the copies distributed did not contain a copyright notice. Therefore, even if the distribution constituted a publication, the absence of a copyright notice would have foreclosed the vesting of federal protection while, at the same time, divesting the work of its common-law protection. *See Letter Edged in Black Press, Inc. v. Public Bldg. Comm'n of Chicago*, 320 F. Supp. 1303 (N.D. Ill. 1970); *J.A. Richards, Inc. v. New York Post, Inc.*, 23 F. Supp. 619 (S.D.N.Y. 1938).

Answer (D) is incorrect. By the time the work was published with proper copyright notice, it had been invested with federal copyright on January 1, 1978, as a fixed original work. *See* 17 U.S.C. § 303(a); *Martha Graham School and Dance Foundation, Inc. v. Martha Graham Center of Contemporary Dance, Inc.*, 380 F.3d 624, 632–33 (2d Cir. 2004).

V-4.   **Answer (D) is correct.** In response to a split between the Ninth and Second Circuits as to whether the distribution of phonorecords containing a musical composition to the public is a general publication that required the use of a proper copyright notice to protect the copyright in the musical composition, *see La Cienega Music Co. v. ZZ Top*, 53 F.3d 950 (9th Cir. 1995) (general publication); *Rosette v. Rainbo Record Mfg. Corp.*, 354 F. Supp. 1183 (S.D.N.Y. 1973), *aff'd per curiam*, 546 F.2d 461 (2d Cir. 1976) (phonorecord held not to be a copy of musical composition), Congress decided that any distribution of a phonorecord before January 1, 1978, did not constitute a publication of a musical composition embodied within it. 17 U.S.C. § 303(b). *See ABKCO Music, Inc. v. LaVere*, 217 F.3d 684 (9th Cir. 2000) (section 303(b) has retroactive effect).

Answer (A) is incorrect. Under the 1909 Act, a performance did not constitute a publication. *See Estate of Martin Luther King, Jr., Inc. v. CBS, Inc.*, 194 F.3d 1211, 1215–16 (2d Cir. 1999).

Answers (B) and (C) are incorrect because, under section 303(b) of the 1976 Copyright Act, the release of a phonorecord containing a musical work prior to January 1, 1978, does not constitute a publication of the musical work embodied in it.

V-5.   Under this analysis, publication would have occurred with the limited-edition release of *Executive Sweet*. Under the 1976 Copyright Act, a general publication occurs when copies or phonorecords are distributed "for purposes of further distribution, public performance, or public display." 17 U.S.C. § 101 (definition of "Publication"). Thus the post-1977 release of a thousand phonorecords of *Executive Sw* eet would amount to a general publication of the musical works fixed in the phonorecords, even though it was not prior to 1978.

V-6.   **Answer (B) is correct.** You may have overlooked this answer believing that the distribution of a work in 1961 to merely five individuals for the purpose of deciding whether to bid on a novel's motion picture rights constituted a limited publication and did not constitute a general publication. If the manuscript of the novel had not contained a copyright notice, a limited publication that saved the novel's copyright from divestment would likely be found. Here, however, the issue is whether there was sufficient publication, with proper copyright notice, to invest the work with federal copyright protection. The answer is likely to be "yes," due to the case law under the 1909 Act that it takes "more" publication to destroy a common-law copyright, thereby divesting the work of copyright protection, than it takes to invest a work with federal statutory copyright, assuming a proper copyright notice is present. *See Dolman v. Agee*, 157 F.3d 708, 713–14 (9th Cir. 1998) ("[I]t takes 'more' publication to destroy a common-law copyright than to perfect a statutory copyright."); *American Visuals Corp. v. Holland*, 239 F.2d 740, 744 (2d Cir. 1956) ("The doctrine of limited publication . . . has generally been invoked by courts to protect the common law remedy where the statutory remedy is unavailable.").

Answer (A) is incorrect because this answer states the requirement for federal copyright protection under the 1976 Copyright Act, which is not applicable under these facts. Under the 1909 Copyright Act, merely embodying creative work in a tangible medium of expression was insufficient to effect publication.

Answer (C) is likely to be incorrect. The distribution of copies of the novel to book club members in 1962 certainly would constitute a general publication, but the 1961 distribution of the manuscript of the novel to potential buyers would likely be viewed as a sufficient publication to invest the novel with federal copyright protection.

Answer (D) is incorrect because the release of the film effected a general publication of the motion picture and, under the majority view, all of the copyrightable elements contained in it. However, only one character from the novel was published with the release of the motion picture, not the novel itself.

V-7.   **Answer (A) is correct.** The 1909 Act required that a proper copyright notice be placed on any work that underwent a general publication. Failure to meet the notice requirement led to harsh results. General publication of a work without proper copyright notice immediately and irreversibly divested the work of copyright protection, placing it into the public domain. *See Letter Edged in Black Press, Inc. v. Public Bldg. Comm'n of Chicago*, 320 F. Supp. 1303 (N.D. Ill. 1970); *J.A. Richards, Inc. v. New York Post, Inc.*, 23 F. Supp. 619 (S.D.N.Y. 1938). Here, there is clearly a general publication because Zealot released physical copies of his work broadly and not for any narrow purpose. *See Shoptalk, Ltd. v. Concorde-New Horizons Corp.*, 168 F.3d 586, 590 (2d Cir. 1999); *Burke v. National Broadcasting Co.*, 598 F.2d 688, 691 (1st Cir. 1979). Thus, Zealot's failure to include notice on the vast majority of his pamphlets forfeits his copyright in those pamphlets to the public domain.

Answer (B) is incorrect because there was no curing provision under the 1909 Copyright Act.

Answer (C) is incorrect because under the 1909 Act, notice must be included on all, or nearly all, copies of a work in order to preserve an author's copyright.

Answer (D) is incorrect because failure to include proper notice effects forfeiture regardless of the copyright owner's intent. Inadvertent failure to provide notice was actually a very common way to forfeit copyright. *See Sanga Music, Inc. v. EMI Blackwood Music, Inc.*, 55 F.3d 756, 759–61 (2d Cir. 1995); *Twin Books Corp. v. Walt Disney Co.*, 83 F.3d 1162, 1165–66 (9th Cir. 1996).

V-8.   On these facts, the contents of Zealot's pamphlet likely would not be forfeited to the public domain. Though the notice requirement of the 1909 Act was strict, it was excused where the notice was omitted from no more than a relatively small number of copies. Here, because the notice was left off ten copies, constituting only one percent of the pamphlets, it would be unlikely that this small omission would result in the total forfeiture of Zealot's copyright.

V-9. **Answer (D) is correct.** Under the 1976 Copyright Act, a general publication is the "distribution of copies or phonorecords of a work to the public by sale or other transfer of ownership, or by rental, lease, or lending." 17 U.S.C. § 101 (definition of "Publication"). However, the dissemination must be with the consent of the copyright owner. *See John G. Danielson, Inc. v. Winchester-Conant Properties, Inc.*, 322 F.3d 26, 38 (1st Cir. 2003). Here, because the dissemination of Writer's work was without her consent, that act does not amount to publication of the short story.

Answer (A) is incorrect because a general release of a physical instantiation of a work of authorship is not always a publication, including where, as here, that release was without the owner's consent.

Answer (B) is incorrect because the work was placed on the Internet without Writer's consent.

Answer (C) is incorrect because courts interpret the 1976 Copyright Act flexibly to adapt to new technologies, and the fact that the Internet did not exist when that legislation was passed does not mean that publication was limited to existing media.

V-10. **Answer (A) is correct.** During the decennial period, which is the period during which *American She* was published, a proper notice of copyright was required on all publicly distributed copies of a work which had undergone a general publication in the United States or elsewhere by authority of the copyright owner. 17 U.S.C. § 401(a). However, the omission of proper copyright notice could be cured under certain circumstances, saving the work from the public domain. 17 U.S.C. § 405. *See Hasbro Bradley, Inc. v. Sparkle Toys, Inc.*, 780 F.2d 189 (2d Cir. 1985). Where notice of copyright was omitted from a large number of copies, that omission could be cured if an author registered her work with the Copyright Office within five years of publication, and made a reasonable effort within a reasonable period of time to attach copyright notice to all domestically distributed copies from which it was missing. 17 U.S.C. § 405(a)(2). Here, Novelist published *American She* in 1980 and did not register it within five years. Therefore, the curing provision of section 405(a)(2) is not available to Novelist.

Answer (B) is incorrect for the reasons stated above.

Answer (C) is incorrect because Novelist is a United States author, therefore the restoration provisions of section 104A do not apply to her.

Answer (D) is incorrect for the reasons stated above.

V-11. The answer is different in this case because the decennial period ended on February 28, 1989. Copyright notice is no longer required on any work published after that date. *Martha Graham School and Dance Foundation, Inc. v. Martha Graham Center of Contemporary Dance, Inc.*, 380 F.3d 624, 633 n.14 (2d Cir. 2004). It is strongly suggested, however, that copyright owners continue to use copyright notice, in part because use of copyright notice precludes the ability of a defendant to mitigate damages pursuant to an innocent infringement defense. 17 U.S.C. §§ 401(d), 402(d).

V-12. **Answer (C) is correct.** The Copyright Act has a mandatory deposit provision that requires the copyright owner to deposit one copy of a published work with the Library of Congress. 17 U.S.C. § 407.

Answers (A), (B), and (D) are incorrect because they fail to accurately describe the obligations of copyright owners under the 1976 Copyright Act. Registration and deposit are not required to acquire a federal copyright in a work. *See Raquel v. Education Management Corp.*, 196 F.3d 171, 176 (3d Cir. 1999). Such protection automatically exists at the time of creation/fixation. *See Kodadek v. MTV Networks, Inc.*, 152 F.3d 1209, 1211 (9th Cir. 1998).

V-13. **Answer (B) is correct.** Although it is true that registration is a jurisdictional prerequisite for filing a copyright infringement suit, this refers to attempted registration, not actual registration. An unsuccessful applicant is entitled to file an action for copyright infringement so long as the Copyright Office is notified of the lawsuit and provided with a copy of the complaint. 17 U.S.C. § 411(a). *See Iconbazaar, L.L.C. v. America Online, Inc.*, 308 F. Supp. 2d 630, 632 n.2 (M.D. N.C. 2004). The Copyright Office has the statutory authority to join in such a lawsuit for the purpose of contesting registrability of the work for which registration was denied. *See Norris Industries, Inc. v. Int'l Telephone and Telegraph Corp.*, 696 F.2d 918, 920 (11th Cir. 1983).

Answer (A) is plainly incorrect. Registration, at least attempted registration, is a prerequisite for filing a copyright infringement suit.

Answer (C) is incorrect because copyright vests upon fixation in a tangible medium of expression, not upon registration with the Copyright Office.

Answer (D) is incorrect because it fails to take into account the possibility that a failed applicant can file suit in federal court pursuant to section 411.

V-14. You should advise Author to register the copyright for several reasons. First, registration, or, at least, attempted registration, is a prerequisite to filing a suit for copyright infringement. So if Author ever wants or needs to protect his copyright via lawsuit, registration will be a necessity. 17 U.S.C. § 411. *See Xoom, Inc. v. Imageline, Inc.*, 323 F.3d 279, 283 (4th Cir. 2003). Second, registration prior to the infringement of a work or within three months from a work's initial publication is a prerequisite for seeking statutory damages and attorneys fees. 17 U.S.C. § 412. *See Bouchat v. Baltimore Ravens Football Club, Inc.*, 346 F.3d 514, 517 n.2 (4th Cir. 2003). Statutory damages not only may be higher than actual damages in a particular case, but seeking statutory damages also carries with it the advantage of not having to prove the specific amount of actual damages, which can be a very time-consuming and expensive burden. Third, timely registrants enjoy the evidentiary advantage of several presumptions: copyright validity, facts stated in the certificate of registration are true, and the registrant is the copyright owner. 17 U.S.C. § 410(c); *Evans and Assocs. Inc. v. Continental Homes, Inc.*, 785 F.2d 897, 903 (11th Cir. 1986). *See Boisson v. Banian, Ltd.*, 273 F.3d 262, 268 (2d Cir. 2001) (registration certificates established statutory presumption that works are original); *Smith v. Jackson*, 84 F.3d 1213, 1219 (9th Cir. 1996).

V-15. **Answer (B) is correct.** This certificate constitutes prima facie evidence of the validity of the copyright and of the facts stated in the certificate if registration was made before or within five years after the first publication of the work. 17 U.S.C. § 410(c); *Evans and*

Assocs. Inc. v. Continental Homes, Inc., 785 F.2d 897, 903 (11th Cir. 1986). *See Boisson v. Banian, Ltd.*, 273 F.3d 262, 268 (2d Cir. 2001) (registration certificates established statutory presumption that works are original). The presumptive validity of the certificate of registration may be rebutted and defeated. *See Aalmuhammed v. Lee*, 202 F.3d 1227, 1236 (9th Cir. 1999) (validity of film consultant's certificate of registration containing claim that he was co-creator, co-writer, and co-director of *Malcolm X* rebutted on summary judgment).

Answer (A) is incorrect because the presumption of validity raised by a registration certificate certainly may be overcome by a sufficient contrary showing. *Fonar Corp. v. Domenick*, 105 F.3d 99, 104 (2d Cir. 1997) (evidence that work is copied from work in the public domain or is noncopyrightable may be sufficient to rebut presumption of validity).

Answer (C) is incorrect because the certificate does not shift all burdens of proof onto the defendant, but only creates a presumption of validity. The plaintiff retains the burden of proving the defendant infringed the plaintiff's copyright.

Answer (D) is incorrect because the trial judge has such discretion only when the registration is made five years after the initial publication of the work.

V-16. These facts raise the issue of whether the distribution of a motion picture constitutes a publication of its underlying screenplay. Although the issue remained unresolved for some time, the majority of courts analyzing this issue have reached a consensus. Most courts have found that any copyrightable elements that are contained in a motion picture are published when the motion picture is released. The result of this determination is that any elements of a screenplay that are contained in a motion picture that is published with a proper copyright notice prior to 1978 invested those screenplay elements with federal statutory protection that is separate from the copyright in the motion picture itself. Elements of the screenplay that were not included in the motion picture, and not independently published, remained protected by common-law copyright until January 1, 1978, when they received federal copyright protection. *See Shoptalk, Ltd. v. Concorde-New Horizons Corp.*, 168 F.3d 586, 591–92 (2d Cir. 1999); *Batjac Prods. Inc. v. GoodTimes Home Video Corp.*, 160 F.3d 1223, 1233–35 (9th Cir. 1998); *Classic Film Museum, Inc. v. Warner Bros., Inc.*, 597 F.2d 13, 14–15 (1st Cir. 1979).

Under this approach and the facts stated above, all of the elements of the *Fast Track* screenplay were included in the *Clashing Clouds* motion picture which was distributed with a proper copyright notice, investing the entire screenplay with federal statutory copyright protection. This provided the screenplay with twenty-eight years of copyright protection during the initial term of copyright. However, Screenwriter expectancy interest in the screenplay's renewal term of copyright did not materialize because Screenwriter did not affirmatively renew the copyright in *Fast Track*. The renewal of the *Clashing Clouds* copyright only applied to the motion picture, not the underlying screenplay. Moreover, the 1992 Automatic Renewal Amendment to the 1976 Copyright Act was not in effect at the time the initial term of copyright in *Fast Track* was in its twenty-eighth year. As a result, the copyright in *Fast Track* entered the public domain on December 31, 1989.

In *Richlin v. Metro-Goldwyn-Mayer Pictures, Inc.*, 531 F.3d 962 (9th Cir. 2008), the Ninth Circuit took the position that the inclusion of elements of an underlying work in a published motion picture did not secure a federal statutory copyright for the underlying work as an independent work. *Id.* at 975–77. Under this view, the underlying work could be invested with federal copyright protection only if it was separately registered or published as an independent work.

The facts at issue state that Screenwriter has never authorized a use of the *Fast Track* screenplay other than in connection with *Clashing Clouds*. Under the Ninth Circuit view as expressed in *Richlin*, this means that *Fast Track* remains protected by state common-law copyright and was not invested with federal copyright protection until January 1, 1978, when that common-law protection was preempted by federal law. That federal protection will end seventy years after Screenwriter's death. Therefore, Screenwriter continues to have a copyright in *Fast Track* and its unauthorized use by Cinemasters Publishing would constitute an actionable infringement.

VI-1. **Answer (B) is correct.** Because the work was created after 1977, its copyright was vested in the author at the time of creation. Once ownership of a copyright has vested, the owner of the copyright is free to devise the copyright via will to any person or institution the copyright owner desires.

Answer (A) is incorrect. Although the probate of a will follows state law, a federal court has jurisdiction to hear cases that require the court to interpret the Copyright Act. *See Bell v. Combined Registry Co.*, 397 F. Supp. 1241, 1246 (D. Ill. 1975) (federal courts have exclusive jurisdiction to determine questions of title to a copyright, even when the issue arises out of a bequest in a will).

Answer (C) is incorrect because the statutory successor provisions of the Copyright Act pertain to ownership of renewal terms of copyright in works created before 1978 that had not yet vested or the ownership of termination rights after the death of the author. Neither of these issues arises from this fact pattern.

Answer (D) is incorrect for reasons stated earlier.

VI-2. **Answer (C) is correct.** The work received an initial term of copyright protection of twenty-eight years. On its renewal, the copyright received an additional twenty-eight years of protection. On January 1, 1978, that renewal term was extended by nineteen years. Because the copyright in the novel was no longer in effect in 1998, the twenty-year extension offered by the Copyright Term Extension Act of 1998 did not apply to the copyright in the novel.

Answer (A) is incorrect because the duration of the copyright in the novel was not based on the life of the Author, but on the bifurcated copyright rules of duration that was applied to works invested with federal copyright protection prior to January 1, 1978.

Answer (B) is incorrect because the twenty-year extension offered by the Copyright Term Extension Act of 1998 did not apply to the copyright in the novel for the reasons stated above.

Answer (D) is incorrect because the copyright in the novel was in its renewal term on January 1, 1978. As a result, the renewal term was automatically extended by nineteen years.

VI-3. **Answer (D) is correct.** Because the work had been protected by state common-law copyright on January 1, 1978, the appropriate durational rule for the copyright in the poem is life of the author plus seventy years. Seventy years after 1970 is 2040. All terms of copyright extend until the end of the year. The second statutory minimum provided by the Copyright Act that provides for protection at least through 2047 does not apply because the poem was not published between January 1, 1978, and December 31, 2002. 17 U.S.C. § 303(a).

Answer (A) is incorrect for the reason stated above.

Answer (B) is incorrect because the proper durational analysis stated earlier provided protection for a longer period of time than the first statutory minimum protection to the end of 2002 offered to all works that had been protected by state common-law copyright on January 1, 1978.

Answer (C) is incorrect because works that had been protected by state common-law copyright on January 1, 1978, did not enter the public domain immediately once the 1976 Copyright took effect. A durational scheme of life plus seventy for works of individual authors went into effect on that date.

VI-4. Upon publication with proper copyright notice, the novel was vested with statutory copyright protection the initial term of which was owned by Novelist. The remaining two years of the initial term of copyright protection are owned by Neighbor who was devised the vested copyright interest owned by Novelist in the will. Novelist's intent to also give Neighbor the renewal term of copyright protection is not relevant under federal copyright law because Novelist did not own the renewal copyright at the time of Novelist's death. The Copyright Act determines the ownership and time of a vested copyright. Where the author dies before the renewal of a copyright, the renewal right is dictated by the Copyright Act which sets the priority of statutory succession in such cases as surviving spouse and children, if no children then the surviving spouse, if no surviving spouse then children, if no surviving spouse or children then the executor of the will to disperse the property pursuant to the will, if no will then the next of kin. Here there is no surviving spouse, but there is a surviving Son who has the right to renew the copyright, which he did. The Son owns the renewal term of copyright until the end of 2053 (twenty-eight-year initial term, twenty-eight-year renewal term, nineteen-year extension, and an additional twenty years provided by the Copyright Term Extension Act of 1998).

VI-5. **Answer (A) is correct.** The work was given an initial term of copyright of twenty-eight years. When the copyright was renewed, it received an additional twenty-eight years of protection. The copyright would have expired at the end of the fifty-sixth year of protection, 1964, but for the interim renewal term extension that, in effect, applied the nineteen-year extension of the renewal term to any work whose renewal term ended between 1962 and 1977. After the nineteen-year extension was applied to the renewal term, the work was protected by copyright through 1983.

Answer (B) is incorrect because the work fell with the interim renewal term extension as explained above.

Answer (C) is incorrect because the twenty-year extension provided by the Copyright Term Extension Act of 1998 did not apply to this work that entered the public domain before 1998.

Answer (D) is incorrect because the interim renewal term extension brought this work into the 1976 Copyright Act, but applied the nineteen-year renewal extension from 1964, not 1978.

VI-6. **Answer (B) is correct.** Because the novel had not been published or registered with the Copyright Office as of January 1, 1978, the applicable durational rule is life of the author plus seventy years, which may be extended, if necessary, by the minimum protections provided by the Copyright Act. Here, the durational rule would result in the copyright protection ending in 1975 (death of author in 1905 plus seventy years). As a result, the minimum protection available to all works in this category ensures the copyright protection for this work until December 31, 2002. Because the novel was published between January 1, 1978, and December 31, 2002, the second statutory minimum of December 31, 2047, applies here.

Answer (A) is incorrect because the novel, which had not been published or registered prior to January 1, 1978, was protected by state common-law copyright until January 1, 1978.

Answer (C) is incorrect because although state common-law copyright for the novel ended on January 1, 1978, the work was invested with federal copyright on that date.

Answer (D) is incorrect because the second statutory minimum applies here for the reasons explained above.

VI-7. **Answer (C) is correct.** Because this is a grant that was executed prior to January 1, 1978, termination is available only under section 304(c) of the Copyright Act. Pursuant to section 304(c), the grant of a copyright in a work made for hire is not subject to termination.

Answer (A) is incorrect because the exemption of grants of copyright in works made for hire from termination is not limited to work made for hire agreements. It applies to any grant of a copyright in a work made for hire.

Answer (B) is incorrect because the status of authorship of a work is determined at the time of the creation of the work and cannot be subsequently altered.

Answer (D) is incorrect because the right to terminate applies to any eligible grant of copyright and is not limited to the initial grant, nor is the right limited to transfers of copyright. Grants of nonexclusive licenses may also be terminated.

VI-8. **Answer (C) is correct.** The duration of copyright for a work, created as a work made for hire, that had been created prior to 1978, but had not been published or registered prior to 1978, is 120 years from the date of creation, or ninety-five years from the date of first publication, whichever computed date is earlier. In this case, the earlier computed date is 2025 (120 years from creation in 1905), not 2099 (ninety-five years from the first publication in 2004).

Answer (A) is incorrect because the applicable rule of duration is not fifty-six years from the date of creation. The photograph was not invested with federal copyright protection until January 1, 1978. It had been protected by state common-law copyright until that date.

Answer (B) is incorrect because the photograph was created as a work made for hire. Therefore, Employer was the author and initial owner of the copyright in the photograph, not Photographer who was the creator of the photograph, but not its author. As a result, the appropriate rule of duration is not life of the author plus seventy years.

Answer (D) is incorrect because the date of 2099, computed by adding ninety-five years to the date of first publication, is later than the date of 2025, which is computed by adding 120 years to the date of creation.

VI-9.   **Answer (C) is correct.** The term of protection for the screenplay is seventy years after the death of the author. 17 U.S.C. § 302(a). In the case of joint works, the term is measured from the date of the last surviving author's death. 17 U.S.C. § 302(b). Because Collaborator lived longer than Author, the term is measured from the end of her life: seventy years after 1990, or 2060.

   Answer (A) is incorrect; the term of copyright protection is not measured from the date of creation, but from the date of the author's death, or the last author's death in the case of joint works.

   Answer (B) is incorrect. The term of copyright protection in the case of joint authors is measured from the death of the last surviving co-author, not the first one to decease.

   Answer (D) is incorrect. The author's life determines the length of the copyright, regardless of who, or what, subsequently owns that copyright.

VI-10.   **Answer (C) is correct.** For pseudonymous works, the term of copyright protection is ninety-five years after the work's first publication or 120 years after its creation, whichever computed date is earlier. 17 U.S.C. § 302(c). Here, ninety-five years from publication would be 2095, while 120 years after creation would be 2115. Because the earlier computed date is 2095 (ninety-five years from the date of the initial publication, 2000), not 2115 (120 years from its creation in 1995), the copyright in *Stubbed Life* will expire in 2095.

   Answer (A) is incorrect; there is no reason to think the operative term would be the date of creation plus seventy years.

   Answer (B) is incorrect. Although normally the term of copyright is life of the author plus seventy years, in the case of pseudonymous works, this term is not applicable.

   Answer (D) is incorrect for the reasons explained above.

VI-11.   By changing the name on the copyright registration from a pseudonym to his own name, Author has converted the term to the standard, life plus seventy-year term. The Copyright Act states that such changes in registration, if made before the otherwise applicable term expires, change the term from that which governs pseudonymous works to that which governs standard works written by a known author. 17 U.S.C. § 302(c). This means that in light of the revised facts, copyright in *Stubbed Life* will expire in 2075.

VI-12.   **Answer (D) is correct.** The term of copyright runs to the end of the calendar year in which it would otherwise expire. 17 U.S.C. § 305. This means that the life plus seventy-year term that *Nocturne in Blue* enjoys does not expire on the seventy-year anniversary of Artist's death, but extends to the end of that calendar year. Thus the work was still protected when Joe Public tried to make use of it, and the heirs can bring a viable copyright infringement suit against him.

   Answer (A) is incorrect for the reason set forth above.

   Answer (B) is incorrect because it falsely presumes that the term of protection is dated from registration. It is in fact dated from the author's death.

   Answer (C) is incorrect because only common-law copyright had perpetual protection. However, common-law copyright is not available to a work fixed after January 1, 1978.

VI-13. **Answer (D) is correct.** The unpublished and unregistered poem was initially protected by common-law copyright. Works protected by state common-law copyright when the 1976 Copyright Act took effect on January 1, 1978, lost their perpetual common-law protection and received the same duration of protection as those works created on or after January 1, 1978, and were provided certain statutory minimum protections not applicable under these facts. 17 U.S.C. § 303; *Martha Graham School & Dance Foundation, Inc. v. Martha Graham Center of Contemporary Dance, Inc.*, 380 F.3d 624, 632–33 (2d Cir. 2004). The term is life of the author plus seventy years, so the term of protection for this work, whose author died in 1935, continues through 2005.

Answer (A) is incorrect because it assumes that the federal term of protection under the 1909 Act applies to the poem. It does not because this poem was not published or registered, and was thus protected by common-law copyright.

Answer (B) is incorrect for the reasons explained above.

Answer (C) is incorrect because the automatic statutory minimum of December 31, 2002, applies only to works that were due to expire before December 31, 2002, when converted to the life-based term of the 1976 Copyright Act. Works that would get protection that lasted longer than 2002 under this new regime enjoy that longer term of protection instead.

VI-14. **Answer (C) is correct.** Because Writer never registered the work nor published his work with valid copyright notice, it never took on the federal term of protection available under the 1909 Act, but was protected by state common-law copyright. Works protected by state common-law copyright when the 1976 Copyright Act took effect on January 1, 1978, have now lost their perpetual common-law protection and receive the same duration of protection as those works created on or after January 1, 1978. *See Martha Graham School & Dance Foundation, Inc. v. Martha Graham Center of Contemporary Dance, Inc.*, 380 F.3d 624, 632–33 (2d Cir. 2004). In no case, however, did the protection of any of these works expire prior to December 31, 2002. 17 U.S.C. § 303(a). Because the life plus seventy-year term would result in the copyright in Writer's play ending in 1990, the work instead is protected through 2002. In any event, though, this means that by the time Writer's heir discovered the play, its protection had expired.

Answers (A), (B), and (D) are incorrect for the reasons explained above.

VI-15. Writer's heir's publishing the play in 2001 changes the duration of protection. The copyright in the play will now expire at the end of 2047. Works protected by state common-law copyright as of the effective date of the 1976 Copyright Act were converted to a federal copyright by that Act, and given a term of copyright protection lasting either seventy years after the death of the author, or until December 31, 2002, whichever computed length of protection is greater. However, where the previously unpublished and unregistered work is published between January 1, 1978, and December 31, 2002, the minimum term of copyright protection is extended through December 31, 2047. 17 U.S.C. § 303(a). The publication of the play by Writer's heirs in 2001 meets this last criterion and, by doing so, extends the play's protection until the end of 2047.

VI-16. **Answer (B) is correct.** Any renewal terms of federal copyright protection which would have expired between September 19, 1962, and December 31, 1977, were automatically continued through December 31, 1977, and brought into the new Act. These interim extensions of copyright protection were periodically passed by Congress in anticipation of the "new" Copyright Act that was expected to extend the renewal term. As of January 1, 1978, these works, which were previously protected by the 1909 Copyright Act, obtained the protection of the 1976 Act. Specific duration rules are then applied which provide copyright protection for seventy-five years from the date federal protection initially vested, unless the renewal occurred after 1950, in which case copyright protection is provided for ninety-five years from the date federal protection initially vested, due to the twenty-year increase provided by the Copyright Term Extension Act of 1998 to any copyright in existence in 1998. 17 U.S.C. § 304. Thus *Summer Rapture* enjoys a term of seventy-five years after its initial vesting in 1910, hence, copyright in the work expired at the end of 1985.

Answer (A) is incorrect because it fails to account for the fact that the renewal term was extended for copyrights due to expire between 1962 and 1977.

Answer (C) is incorrect for the reasons explained above. As a registered work, *Summer Rapture* was invested with a federal statutory copyright, not common-law copyright. Therefore, the statutory minimum protections do not apply here.

Answer (D) is incorrect because it wrongly assumes that the life plus seventy-year term applies to the work at issue.

VI-17.   **Answer (A) is correct.** If the author was deceased prior to renewal, the author's statutory successor could renew the copyright. The statutory successor is the spouse and any children. If none are alive, then the author's executor is deemed the statutory successor. If the author left no will, then the statutory successor is the author's next of kin. 17 U.S.C. § 304(a)(1)(C); *Music Sales Corp. v. Morris*, 73 F. Supp. 2d 364, 373 (S.D.N.Y. 1999). *See generally* Jeffrey M. Lowy, *When Does the Renewal Term Vest: Before and After the Copyright Renewal Act of 1992*, 13 LOY. L.A. ENT. L.J. 437 (1993). In light of this statutory scheme, Artist's son would prevail. Artist's ex-wife does not have a place in this scheme because she is not a widow.

Answers (B), (C), and (D) are incorrect because they identify individuals other than the ones identified in the statutory scheme. Answer (C), in particular, makes no sense, because Artist died intestate, so there was no will in which to name an executor.

VI-18.   In terms of the right to apply for a renewal with the Copyright Office, the Artist's widow, his son, or his daughter may do so. Any one of these individuals may apply for the renewal. That renewal application will be deemed to include all of the owners of the renewal term of copyright. In terms of who owns what share of the renewal term, as statutory successors, the surviving spouse holds a fifty percent share in the renewal copyright and the surviving children hold equal divided shares in the remaining fifty percent. *See Broadcast Music, Inc. v. Roger Miller Music, Inc.*, 396 F.3d 762, 782 (6th Cir. 2005). *But see Venegas-Hernandez v. Peer*, 283 F. Supp. 2d 491 (D.P.R. 2003) (surviving spouse and children share in renewal copyright equally). In this case, Artist's widow owns a fifty percent interest in the renewal term, and his son and daughter each own equal shares of the other half-interest in the renewal term, twenty-five percent each.

VI-19.   **Answer (D) is correct.** In the case of a work made for hire, the proprietor of the copyright in the original term, that is, the employer or its assignee, is entitled to the renewal term. 17 U.S.C. § 304(a)(1)(B). *See Estate of Hogarth v. Edgar Rice Burroughs,*

Inc., 342 F.3d 149, 157 (2d Cir. 2003). Heir is the proprietor of the rights in this literary work, because he acquired them by devise after a valid transfer from BizCorp to Magazine Publisher.

Answer (A) is incorrect. BizCorp is no longer the proprietor, having assigned away the rights in the literary work.

Answer (B) is incorrect. This was a work for hire, and Writer thus had no interest in the copyright.

Answer (C) is incorrect. Magazine Publisher's demise and devise to Heir means he is no longer the proprietor of rights in the work.

VI-20.   For works in the first term of copyright protection as of the effective date of the 1976 Act, and whose twenty-eighth year of protection will occur prior to 1992, failure to affirmatively renew the copyright resulted in the work entering the public domain. *See Martha Graham School and Dance Foundation, Inc. v. Martha Graham Center of Contemporary Dance, Inc.*, 380 F.3d 624, 633 (2d Cir. 2004). A work that has entered the public domain may be freely used by the public. *See Frederick Warne & Co., Inc. v. Book Sales Inc.*, 481 F. Supp. 1191, 1197 (S.D.N.Y. 1979). Thus the proprietor's failure to renew the copyright term in 1983 placed the literary work in the public domain and resulted in the work being available for anyone to use.

VI-21.   **Answer (D) is correct.** In 1992, the Copyright Act was amended to make renewal automatic. The automatic renewal applies to any work which was initially invested with federal protection from 1964 through 1977. *Martha Graham School and Dance Foundation, Inc. v. Martha Graham Center of Contemporary Dance, Inc.*, 380 F.3d 624, 633 & n.15 (2d Cir. 2004); *Dimensional Music Publishing v. Kersey*, 435 F. Supp. 2d 452, 458 (E.D. Pa. 2006). Sculptor's failure to affirmatively renew the copyright in *Elk at Rest*, while it may have other negative implications, did not result in the work entering the public domain at the end of the initial term of copyright protection. The copyright in *Elk at Rest* is thus protected for the full ninety-five-year term established by the 1976 Copyright Act and its amendments (i.e., a twenty-eight-year initial term, twenty-eight-year renewal term, nineteen-year renewal term extension, and an additional twenty years for works protected by copyright in 1998).

Answer (A) is incorrect because it assumes that the work will fall into the public domain unless a renewal application is filed. The 1992 Amendment to the 1976 Copyright Act obviated this requirement.

Answer (B) is incorrect because it assumes that the 1909 Copyright Act's fifty-six-year term (twenty-eight-year initial term and twenty-eight-year renewal term) still prevails.

Answer (C) is incorrect because it assumes that the original seventy-five-year term for preexisting works established in the 1976 Copyright Act (twenty-eight-year initial term, twenty-eight-year renewal term, and nineteen-year renewal term extension) still applies. This ignores the term's twenty-year extension in 1998 that was established by the Copyright Term Extension Act of 1998.

VI-22.   **Answer (A) is correct.** In the event of the death of the author prior to the renewal of the copyright, the ownership of the renewal term of copyright is determined by the statutory successor provision of the Copyright Act, not the testamentary intent or the contractual obligations of the author. *See Miller Music Corp. v. Charles N. Daniels, Inc.*, 362 U.S. 373, 375 (1960); *Broadcast Music, Inc. v. Roger Miller Music, Inc.*, 396 F.3d 762, 774 (6th Cir. 2005) ("A renewal copyright will automatically vest as of the last day of the original copyright in any person entitled to the renewal copyright even absent an affirmative act by any such person."). Thus Writer's assignment of the initial term to Shyster is enforceable because Writer had a vested interest in the initial term of copyright at the time he contracted with Shyster. However, the assignment of the right of renewal and the renewal term itself is not enforceable because it has been obviated by Writer's death before the vesting of his interest in the renewal term.

Answers (B), (C), and (D) are incorrect for the reasons explained above.

VI-23.   Under these facts, if a renewal application was filed by Writer or on his behalf, Shyster would own the right of renewal, the renewal term, and the initial term, while Writer's statutory successors would own nothing. The author may, during the first term of copyright, assign her expectancy interest in the renewal rights to a third party by contract. If, as here, the author survives until the renewal copyright vests, the assignment to the third party is binding. *Music Sales Corp. v. Morris*, 73 F. Supp. 2d 364, 371 (S.D.N.Y. 1999). *See Fisher Music Co. v. W. Witmark & Sons*, 318 U.S. 643, 658–59 (1943). If Writer, or Shyster on his behalf, failed to affirmatively renew the copyright in the screenplay, it entered the public domain at the end of the initial term of copyright protection.

VI-24.   **Answer (C) is correct.** The Supreme Court held in *Stewart v. Abend*, 495 U.S. 207 (1990), that the creator of a derivative work could not continue to utilize its derivative work after the copyright in the underlying work was renewed by a statutory successor, unless it was licensed by that statutory successor. The *Abend* rule was modified by Congress in 1992 when it required that a statutory successor must affirmatively renew the copyright in the twenty-eighth year of the copyright term in order to take full advantage of the *Abend* decision. 17 U.S.C. § 304(a)(4)(A). So here, Daughter's failure to file for renewal means that she cannot take full advantage of *Abend*, and cannot require De Marco Studios to negotiate a new license to exploit the preexisting derivative works based on Author's novel. De Marco Studios may continue to exploit its derivative works created during the initial term of copyright, but it is precluded from making any new uses of them.

Answer (A) is incorrect because it is overly broad. Author's statutory successor could only gain the ability to control preexisting derivative works if she had affirmatively filed for renewal in the twenty-eighth year of the initial term.

Answer (B) is incorrect because an author's death in the initial term of protection does not automatically terminate licenses, though it may affect those agreements.

Answer (D) is incorrect because, although Daughter cannot take full advantage of *Abend*, she has control over any new uses of preexisting derivative works, as well as the creation of all future derivative works.

VI-25.   In light of these facts, Daughter would be able to force De Marco Studios to negotiate new licenses for its continued exploitation of preexisting derivative works based on *Empire*. The Supreme Court held in *Stewart v. Abend*, 495 U.S. 207 (1990), that the creator of a derivative work could not continue to utilize its derivative work after the copyright in the underlying work was renewed by a statutory successor, unless it was licensed by that statutory successor. However, as of 1992, statutory successors must file for renewal in the twenty-eighth year of the copyright term in order to take advantage of the *Abend* decision. 17 U.S.C. § 304(a)(4)(A). So here, because Daughter has fulfilled this latter condition, she can take advantage of the *Abend* decision and require De Marco Studios to enter into new license agreements if it wants to continue exploiting the film version of *Empire*. As a result, even if De Marco Studio had released the motion picture on DVD and permitted its broadcast on television during the initial term of copyright protection of the *Empire* novel, this continued exploitation would constitute copyright infringement without a license from Daughter.

VI-26.   **Answer (B) is correct.** The author or the author's statutory successor is permitted to terminate the grant of rights beginning thirty-five years from the date of the initial grant. The grant may be terminated any time during the five-year period beginning at the end of the thirty-five years from the day of execution of the grant. 17 U.S.C. § 203(a)(3). Here, the assignment took place in 1985, so the termination period begins thirty-five years later, in 2020.

Answer (A) is incorrect because the termination window for grants entered into after 1977 begins thirty-five years from the date of the grant, not thirty-five years from the date of the creation of the work.

Answer (C) is incorrect because, for grants entered into after 1977, the termination window does not begin fifty-six years from the date the work was invested with federal copyright protection. For such works, the termination window begins thirty-five years from the date of the executed grant.

Answer (D) is incorrect because in the event of an author's death, termination can be effected by his statutory successors.

VI-27.   **Answer (C) is correct.** Where the author is dead, the author's termination interest is owned and may be exercised by the widow, widower, children, grandchildren, executor, administrator, personal representative, or trustee as set forth in 17 U.S.C. § 203(a)(2). The termination interest may be exercised only with the support of a majority of the termination interest shares. 17 U.S.C. § 203(a)(1). Where the termination right is owned by the surviving spouse and children, a fifty percent share of the termination interest vests in the surviving spouse and the surviving children divide the remaining fifty percent in equal divided shares. *See Broadcast Music, Inc. v. Roger Miller Music, Inc.*, 396 F.3d 762, 771 (6th Cir. 2005).

Here, Musician's widow owns fifty percent of the termination right, and his sons each own twenty-five percent. In order to exceed the fifty percent minimum, the widow can exercise the termination right only if she has the support of at least one of the sons. *See Penguin Group (USA) Inc. v. Steinbeck*, 537 F.3d 193, 202–03 (2d Cir. 2008).

Answers (A) and (B) are incorrect because Musician's widow acting alone amounts to only fifty percent of the termination interest which is insufficient because it is not a majority interest. Musician's sons acting alone similarly fail to constitute a majority because together they reach, but do not exceed, fifty percent of the termination interest.

Answer (D) is incorrect because termination is clearly possible via the combination described above.

VI-28.   It would not affect the termination date at all. For purposes of section 203, only the date of execution of the conveyance, not the date on which the original copyright was subsisting, has significance. *See Broadcast Music, Inc. v. Roger Miller Music, Inc.*, 396 F.3d 762, 772 (6th Cir. 2005). Thus, while the revised facts would mean that the work would be governed differently in terms of its length of protection, this distinction is irrelevant to the date on which termination could begin, which continues to be in the year 2020.

VI-29.   **Answer (D) is correct.** For grants made after January 1, 1978, transfers effected by authors can be terminated beginning thirty-five years after the date of the transfer. However, grants conveyed by statutory successors cannot be terminated. 17 U.S.C. § 203(a). *See Broadcast Music, Inc. v. Roger Miller Music, Inc.*, 396 F.3d 762, 771 n.9 (6th Cir. 2005). Because the exclusive license to base a screenplay in *Molto Maria* was executed not by Author himself, but by his statutory successor, Son, it cannot be terminated.

Answers (A), (B), and (C) are incorrect because they assume the grant by Son can be terminated, when for the reasons explained above, it cannot.

VI-30.   Unlike the facts in question VI-29, this termination scenario is governed by section 304(c), not section 203 because the grant was executed prior to 1978. Unlike section 203 terminations, section 304 terminations do apply to grants made by statutory successors. 17 U.S.C. § 304(c). Thus, pursuant to the terms of section 304(c), the termination window begins fifty-six years after the copyright's original vesting. Because the copyright in *Molto Maria* in the revised scenario vested in 1960, the earliest possible termination date would be January 1, 2017. Because under the 1976 Copyright Act the term of copyright runs to the end of the calendar year in which it would otherwise expire, 17 U.S.C. § 305, the earliest date of termination would be the first day of the fifty-seventh year of copyright protection.

VI-31.   **Answer (C) is correct.** "A derivative work prepared under authority of the grant before its termination may continue to be utilized under the terms of the grant after its termination." 17 U.S.C. § 304(c)(6)(A). Because Publisher created the derivative work *Greater Plains* before the termination of the transfer of the copyright in the underlying work *Great Plains*, Publisher remains entitled to exploit the latter in the same manner. Publisher is precluded from making any new uses of the existing derivative works and from creating and exploiting any new derivative works without permission from Heir.

Answers (A) and (B) are incorrect because they plainly misstate the law. Terminating a transfer neither entitles the terminating party to all profits derived from the derivative work nor transfers ownership of that work to the terminating party.

Answer (D) is incorrect because the derivative works privilege "does not extend to the preparation after the termination of other derivative works based upon the copyrighted work covered by the terminated grant." 17 U.S.C. § 304(c)(6)(A). If Publisher wants to create new derivative works based on *Great Plains*, it must obtain the right to do so from Heir.

VI-32.   **Answer (B) is correct.** A music publisher may continue to receive its share of royalties derived from the sale of pre-termination licensed recordings of a musical composition after the termination of the grant to the music publisher of the copyright in the musical composition. *Mills Music, Inc. v. Snyder*, 469 U.S. 153 (1985). Therefore, Music Publisher may continue to collect mechanical royalties from the post-termination sales of the recording of *Andalucia* made pre-termination.

Answer (A) is incorrect because the Supreme Court held just the opposite in *Mills Music*. The Court determined that when a music publisher facilitates the creation of a derivative work by permitting the use of a musical composition, the music publisher is allowed to take advantage of the derivative work continuing use exception.

Answer (C) is incorrect both because it is inconsistent with *Mills Music* and because transferees never have to disgorge past profits earned from works for which transfers have been terminated.

Answer (D) is incorrect because termination of the 1939 transfer certainly does entitle Heir or his assigns to profit from new uses of the 1940 *Andalucia* recording by RecordCo or any new post-termination recording.

VI-33.   **Answer (D) is correct.** The Copyright Act unambiguously states that termination of copyright assignments may be effected notwithstanding any agreement to the contrary. 17 U.S.C. § 304(c)(5). As such, an agreement not to terminate is invalid. *See Stewart v. Abend*, 495 U.S. 207, 230 (1990) ("The 1976 Copyright Act provides . . . an inalienable termination right."); *Music Sales Corp. v. Morris*, 73 F. Supp. 2d 364, 372 (S.D.N.Y. 1999) ("[A]ny contract provision that purports to assign [the termination] right is void."). Thus, the provision of the 1935 assignment in which Composer is purported to have alienated his termination rights to MusicCo is invalid and MusicCo cannot rely on it to oppose Composer's termination of the 1935 assignment of the copyright in *Dancing Shoes*.

Answer (A) is incorrect because it is directly contrary to the plain language of the Copyright Act, which makes terminations of transfers inalienable.

Answer (B) is incorrect because the termination right is never alienable, regardless of the transferring party.

Answer (C) is incorrect because termination cannot be assigned to any party, individual or corporate.

VI-34.   **Answer (A) is correct.** The termination notice must be recorded in the United States Copyright Office prior to the date of termination. 37 C.F.R. § 201.10. Because this notice was served after the date of termination, it is not valid.

Answer (B) is incorrect because it is not merely the intent to terminate that must be communicated to the grantee. The party attempting to terminate must meet the requirements set forth in the regulations of the Copyright Office.

Answer (C) is incorrect because a termination notice must be issued at least two, but not more than ten years, prior to the effective date of the termination. 37 C.F.R. § 201.10. The notice sent by Composer fell within the required time span.

Answer (D) is incorrect because the notice was invalid for the reasons explained above.

VI-35.   Not necessarily. Typically, an unlimited grant of rights that is not terminated will continue in effect for the duration of the term of copyright. 17 U.S.C. § 304(c)(6)(F). In this case, however, Composer would have sufficient time to give another termination notice to

MusicCo within the five-year termination window that began on January 1, 1990. Composer would have until December 30, 1992, to give a termination notice that is two years in advance of the termination date, the minimum period of notice required for termination. In addition, in the case of pre-1978 assignments such as this one, there is an additional opportunity to terminate the final twenty years of the copyright's ninety-five-year term even if the owner of the termination right does not take advantage of the initial opportunity to terminate the transfer. In 1998, Congress created a second termination opportunity for pre-1978 grants that had not been terminated after the fifty-sixth year of copyright protection, but now benefit from a twenty-year extension of the renewal term. 17 U.S.C. § 304(d). *See Music Sales Corp. v. Morris*, 73 F. Supp. 2d 364, 372, 380 (S.D.N.Y. 1999). Under this provision, Composer could also effect termination of the final twenty years of the copyright in *Dancing Shoes* for a five-year period beginning on January 1, 2009.

VII-1. **Answer (D) is correct.** By continuing to distribute the motion picture on DVD after the expiration of the license, Distributor is doing so without the consent of the copyright owner. This constitutes infringement of the public distribution right owned by Motion Picture Studio. *See Jarvis v. K2 Inc.*, 486 F.3d 526, 530 (9th Cir. 2007) (use of photographer's images after expiration of contractual usage term constituted infringement); *Powell v. Green Hill Publishers, Inc.*, 719 F. Supp. 743 (N.D. Ill. 1989) (continued publication of book following termination of license found to be copyright infringement).

Answer (A) is incorrect because ownership of the distribution right to the motion picture reverted to Motion Picture Studio at the end of the five-year agreement, pursuant to the agreement's contractual provision.

Answer (B) is incorrect because a contractual termination provision of an agreement that is of shorter duration than the statutory termination provided by the Copyright Act is enforceable and makes the statutory termination inapplicable. *See Walthal v. Rusk*, 172 F.3d 481, 485 (7th Cir. 1999).

Answer (C) is incorrect because copyright infringement is not the only remedy available to Motion Picture Studio. Under these facts, Distributor could be sued for breach of contract. *See Effects Associates, Inc. v. Cohen*, 817 F.2d 72, 73 (9th Cir. 1987) ("plaintiff is master of his claim and in some cases will have the choice of framing his action either as one for infringement or for breach of contract").

VII-2. **Answer (B) is correct.** An owner of an exclusive right obtained via an exclusive license has standing to sue for infringement of that right. 17 U.S.C. § 501(b). *See Gamma Audio & Video, Inc. v. Ean-Chea*, 11 F.3d 1106 (1st Cir. 1993). Thus, Production Company, as the exclusive licensee, would have standing to sue Whanna Bee for infringement.

Answer (A) is incorrect because Author has assigned away the exclusive right to make or authorize the making of a derivative of the novel in the form of a screenplay. Having been paid a flat fee for the exclusive license, Author no longer has an interest in such an exploitation of the novel.

Answers (C) and (D) are incorrect for the reasons explained above.

VII-3. Author does have the right to grant an exclusive license to Book Publisher to translate the novel into Spanish and then publish the Spanish version of the novel. An exclusive right, such as the adaptation right, can be divided into different types of derivative works as well as different types of media. Any of the section 106 exclusive rights that make up a copyright and any subdivision of them can be transferred and owned separately, whether or not the transfer is limited in time, media, or geographic area. 17 U.S.C. § 201(d). *See Gamma Audio & Video, Inc. v. Ean-Chea*, 11 F.3d 1106 (1st Cir. 1993). In this case,

Author has relinquished the right to authorize the creation of a screenplay based on the novel, but has retained the right to other types of derivative works based on the novel, such as the Spanish translation right for use in a published novel.

VII-4. In light of these changed facts, only Author would have standing to sue Whanna Bee. Although an owner of the copyright, or subsequent assignee, or an exclusive licensee of an exclusive right has standing to sue for copyright infringement of that right, a nonexclusive licensee does not have standing to sue. 17 U.S.C. § 501(b). *See Gamma Audio & Video, Inc. v. Ean-Chea*, 11 F.3d 1106 (1st Cir. 1993). As the copyright's owner, Author would have standing to sue, but as the nonexclusive licensee, Production Company would not.

VII-5. **Answer (D) is correct.** Composer can sue Lil Flasher and Flasher Music for copyright infringement, because although Composer is no longer a legal owner of the copyright in *Red Rhapsody*, she is a beneficial owner of that copyright. A beneficial owner is one who, like Composer, has relinquished legal ownership in exchange for an economic interest in the exploitation of the copyright. *See Cortner v. Israel*, 732 F.2d 267 (2d Cir. 1984). And a "beneficial owner" of an exclusive right under a copyright is entitled to sue for infringement. 17 U.S.C. § 501(b).

Answer (A) is incorrect because the views of private parties regarding the similarity between two works do not determine the outcome of a copyright infringement action. The finder of fact will make that determination as part of the litigation. Further, Lyrical Publishing may be protecting its affiliated record company by using the lack of similarity as an excuse not to file an infringement action.

Answer (B) is incorrect because it does not take into account Composer's status as a beneficial owner.

Answer (C) is incorrect. Composer assigned all of her copyright interest in *Red Rhapsody* to Lyrical Publishing, making the music publisher the legal owner of the copyright in the musical work, not merely its administrator.

VII-6. **Answer (A) is correct.** Federal district courts have exclusive original jurisdiction over actions that arise under the Copyright Act. 28 U.S.C. § 1338(a). An action "arises under" the Copyright Act if: (1) the complaint is for a remedy expressly granted by the Act; (2) the claim requires a construction of the Act; or (3) a distinctive policy of the Act requires that federal principles control the disposition of the claim. *T.B. Harms Co. v. Eliscu*, 339 F.2d 823, 828 (2d Cir. 1964). Here, Wise's claim that she is a joint author clearly belongs before a federal court because it requires a construction of the Copyright Act.

It is true that state law governs both construction of the assignment of royalty interests, *see Yount v. Acuff Rose-Opryland*, 103 F.3d 830, 835 (9th Cir. 1996), and the validity of ownership transfers themselves, *see T.B. Harms Co. v. Eliscu*, 339 F.2d at 827. However, federal courts have the authority to hear state as well as federal causes of action pursuant to their supplemental jurisdictional authority. 28 U.S.C. § 1367. The test for whether supplemental jurisdiction is appropriate is whether the state and federal claims arise out of the same case or controversy. 28 U.S.C. § 1367(a). Here, it is clear that they do. Both claims concern Wise's entitlements to the royalties generated by *In tha Biz*. Additionally, the state and federal claims each require interpretation of the same instrument. For these reasons, adjudication in state and federal courts would be inefficient, and an exercise of supplemental jurisdiction by the federal court is appropriate.

Answers (B) and (C) are incorrect because they wrongly assume that supplemental jurisdiction in this matter is not appropriate, and that the matter would be better adjudicated separately by state and federal courts

Answer (D) is incorrect because the construction of the Copyright Act is clearly a matter a federal court is jurisdictionally competent to hear.

VII-7.   Answer (D) is correct. Although a party has no right to a jury trial when the relief sought is solely equitable, i.e., when only an injunction is being sought, when the relief sought is both equitable and legal, i.e., when both an injunction and money damages are being sought, then the entire matter must be tried to a jury if either party so requests. There had been some questions as to whether statutory damages are deemed a legal or equitable remedy, because the statute creating the right to statutory damages does not define them as either. *See* 17 U.S.C. § 504(c). However, the Supreme Court considered this issue and held unequivocally that "if a party so demands, a jury must determine the actual amount of statutory damages under § 504(c) in order to preserve the substance of the common law right of trial by jury." *Feltner v. Columbia Pictures Television, Inc.*, 523 U.S. 340, 355 (1988).

Answers (A), (B), and (C) are incorrect for the reasons explained above.

VII-8.   Answer (C) is correct. United States copyright law has no application to infringements that occur wholly outside the United States. *Subafilms, Ltd. v. MGM-Pathe Communications Co.*, 24 F.3d 1088 (9th Cir. 1994); *Armstrong v. Virgin Records, Inc.*, 91 F. Supp. 2d 628, 634 (S.D.N.Y. 2000). Because DistroCo's conduct was entirely extraterritorial, it is not actionable in federal court.

Answer (A) is incorrect because, while the conduct alleged would normally amount to a clear violation of the right of public distribution, that does not resolve this question because of the extraterritoriality issue.

Answer (B) is incorrect because there is no such exception for international subsidiaries with domestic parents.

Answer (D) is incorrect because EuroDistro's conduct clearly amounts to a "public distribution" within the meaning of the Copyright Act. Here, the distribution occurs outside the United States where the Copyright Act does not apply.

VII-9.   Studio still cannot sue DistroCo in United States federal court for violations of United States copyright law, even though it authorized its subsidiary, EuroDistro, to engage in unlicensed distribution of *Action Man*. Because the conduct alleged is not actionable under the Copyright Act due to its extraterritoriality, there can be no liability for authorizing that conduct. *See* 17 U.S.C. § 106. Thus, the mere authorization of extraterritorial acts of infringement does not state a claim under the Copyright Act. *Subafilms, Ltd. v. MGM-Pathe Communications Co.*, 24 F.3d 1088, 1090–95 (9th Cir. 1994).

VII-10.   Answer (A) is correct. Ownership of copyright issues is determined by the law of the country with the most significant relationship to the work and the parties. *See Itar-Tass Russian News Agency v. Russian Kurier, Inc.*, 153 F.3d 82, 90 (2d Cir. 1998) (Russian law deemed appropriate source of law to determine issues of ownership of rights in works created by Russian nationals and first published in Russia). Whether the copyright in a work has been infringed is determined by the law of the place, the situs, where the alleged violation occurred. *See id.* at 91.

Here, the country with the most significant relationship to the work and the parties is clearly Canada. The original article was published in a Canadian newspaper, and its author was Canadian as well. Thus, the ownership issue must be determined by Canadian law. However, the alleged violation of the work took place in the United States when Smith published an unauthorized translation of Anglais' article. As a result, the infringement issue must be governed by United States copyright law.

Answers (B), (C), and (D) are incorrect for the reasons explained above.

VII-11.   **Answer (D) is correct.** Copyright infringement is a strict liability tort. A defendant need not have intended the infringement in order to be held liable. *See Shapiro, Bernstein & Co. v. H.L. Green Co.*, 316 F.2d 304, 308 (2d Cir. 1963). Brown's lack of awareness that his conduct amounted to infringement does not provide a defense to that infringement.

Answer (A) is incorrect. Personal use of copyrighted works may be permitted under some circumstances, but is certainly not always a full defense to infringement.

Answer (B) is incorrect. Copyright infringement is a strict liability offense, as explained above, so Brown's innocent state of mind cannot negate his liability. Here, the actionable conduct lies in violating Hot Ten's exclusive right of reproduction, whether or not a commercial use is subsequently make of the works.

Answer (C) is incorrect. The user agreement may create a contract cause of action, but it does not create an infringement cause of action.

VII-12.   No. Direct copyright infringement requires volitional conduct that directly results in the violation of an exclusive right. *See Cartoon Network LP, LLP v. CSC Holdings, Inc.*, 536 F.3d 121, 131–33 (2d Cir. 2008) (volitional conduct of cable customer makes copy of protected material on cable operator's digital video recorder system that reproduces the material on central hard drives housed and maintained by cable operator at a remote location, resulting in no direct infringement by cable operator). An Internet service provider has been found not to be a direct infringer of copyrighted works posted on the Internet as it did not take any affirmative action that directly resulted in copying. *See Costar Group, Inc. v. Loopnet, Inc.*, 373 F.3d 544, 549–52 (4th Cir. 2004) (Copyright Act requires conduct by a person who causes an infringement); *Religious Technology Center v. Netcom On-Line Communication Services, Inc.*, 907 F. Supp. 1361, 1368 (N.D. Cal. 1995); *Hendrickson v. Amazon.com, Inc.*, 298 F. Supp. 2d 914, 915 (C.D. Cal. 2003) (online retailer that facilitated sale of infringing motion picture by independent third-party seller held not to be a direct infringer). *See also Bernstein v. J.C. Penney*, 50 U.S.P.Q.2d 1063 (C.D. Cal. 1998) (website owner not liable for linking to a second website that in turn linked to an infringing third website). *But see Kelly v. Arriba Soft Corp.*, 280 F.3d 934, 947 (9th Cir. 2002) (owner of Internet visual search engine acted as more than a passive conduit of images by trolling the web, finding the images, and having its program inline link and frame those images within its own website).

VII-13.   **Answer (B) is correct.** A co-owner of a copyright cannot be liable to another co-owner for infringement of the copyright. *Oddo v. Ries*, 743 F.2d 630, 632–33 (9th Cir. 1984). However, while this means that Lyricist would not be able to sue Musician on a copyright infringement theory, under the rule of mutual accountability of joint copyright owners, Lyricist would still be able to sue Musician on a state property-law theory because co-owners of property are obligated to share the profits generated by that property with the other joint owners. *See Harrington v. Mure*, 186 F. Supp. 655, 657–58 (S.D.N.Y.1960) (superseded by 1976 Copyright Act on other grounds). This would not entitle Lyricist to all of the proceeds from Musician's shows. The rule of mutual accountability requires Musician to account to Lyricist for any profits she earns from the use of the copyrighted work. *See Shapiro, Bernstein & Co. v. Jerry Vogel Music Co.*, 221 F.2d 569, *modified*, 223 F.2d 252 (2d Cir. 1955). Lyricist has a right to share in the proceeds attributable to the public performance of the musical work, but not in the proceeds attributable to Musician's personal services, which include the performance of additional musical works not owned by Lyricist. As a practical matter, this would require the determination of a reasonable public performance license fee, of which Lyricist would receive half.

Answer (A) is incorrect because as a joint owner of *The View From My Window*, Musician is entitled to publicly perform it without running afoul of Lyricist's exclusive rights. Musician and Lyricist, as joint owners, each has ownership of the entirety of the copyright, including all of the exclusive rights protected by the copyright.

Answer (C) is incorrect because Musician has not violated any of Lyricist's exclusive rights.

Answer (D) is incorrect because Lyricist does have a valid cause of action against Musician based on a state-law theory of mutual accountability.

VII-14. **Answer (A) is correct.** CEO is liable to Author for violations of both the right of reproduction (as a direct infringer because he made unauthorized photocopies of the novel embodying the literary work) and the right of adaptation (as a contributory infringer because he authorized adaptations of the literary work without permission and facilitated that adaptation).

Answer (B) is incorrect. The first sale doctrine does not apply here, because it entitles users only to further distribute the original authorized copy of the work they purchased, not to make unauthorized reproductions of that work. 17 U.S.C. § 109(a).

Answer (C) is incorrect because a corporate officer who personally participates in infringing activity may be personally liable for the infringement. *See Southern Bell Tel. & Tel. v. Associated Tel. Directory Publishers*, 756 F.2d 801, 811 (11th Cir. 1985); *Columbia Pictures Industries, Inc. v. Redd Horne, Inc.*, 749 F.2d 154, 160 (3d Cir. 1984) ("An officer or director of a corporation who knowingly participates in the infringement can be held personally liable, jointly and severally, with the corporate defendant.").

Answer (D) is incorrect because a copyright owner is free to choose which infringer to sue and is not required to sue all infringers. *Bassett v. Mashantucket Pequot Tribe*, 204 F.3d 343, 360 (2d Cir. 2000).

VII-15. **Answer (D) is correct.** Production of a copyright registration certificate is prima facie proof of the ownership of a valid copyright if the owner of the copyright filed the registration before or within five years of the date of first publication. 17 U.S.C. § 410(c); *Evans and Assocs. Inc. v. Continental Homes, Inc.*, 785 F.2d 897, 903 (11th Cir. 1986). However, the presumptive validity of the certificate of registration may be rebutted and defeated. *See Aalmuhammed v. Lee*, 202 F.3d 1227, 1236 (9th Cir. 1999) (validity of film consultant's certificate of registration containing claim that he was co-creator, co-writer, and co-director of *Malcolm X* rebutted on summary judgment); *Glovaroma, Inc. v. Maljack Productions, Inc.*, 71 F. Supp. 2d 846, 854 (N.D. Ill. 1999). Here, the submission of a valid agreement assigning copyright ownership of the work in suit from Author to User clearly suffices to overcome that presumption.

Answer (A) is incorrect because proof of valid ownership need not be produced or contested only at trial.

Answer (B) is incorrect because timely registration gives rise only to a presumption of validity, and is not incontrovertible proof of validity.

Answer (C) is incorrect because a registration certificate need only be filed within five years of publication in order to amount to prima facie proof of validity.

VII-16. **Answer (C) is correct.** Access can be proven by evidence that the defendant had actually read or heard plaintiff's work, or had a reasonable opportunity to view or hear the plaintiff's work. *See Peel & Co. v. The Rug Market*, 238 F.3d 391, 394 (5th Cir. 2001) ("reasonable opportunity to view the copyright work").

Answer (A) is incorrect because it is not necessary to show actual access, only a reasonable opportunity for access.

Answer (B) is incorrect because the standard of proof regarding access is not extraordinarily high, merely a reasonable opportunity for the defendant to view or hear the plaintiff's work. *See Jason v. Fonda*, 698 F.2d 966 (9th Cir. 1983) ("bare possibility" that the producers and broadcasters of the motion picture had access to the author's book was insufficient to prove access).

Answer (D) is incorrect because access is invariably an important consideration in copyright infringement suits regarding unauthorized reproduction; in fact, it is often the most important consideration.

VII-17. Although access considerations are always fact-specific, there is a good chance that a court would regard these facts as establishing a sufficient degree of access to support a finding of infringement. The reasonable opportunity for defendant to view or hear the plaintiff's work may be established by showing a particular chain of events by which the alleged infringer might have gained access through an intermediary. *See Swirsky v. Carey*, 376 F.3d 841, 844 n.3 (9th Cir. 2004) (fact that a number of individuals involved in the recording of plaintiff's musical work also were involved in recording of defendant's work found sufficient to prove access); *Bouchat v. Baltimore Ravens, Inc.*, 241 F.3d 350 (4th Cir. 2001); *Towler v. Sayles*, 76 F.3d 579, 583 (4th Cir. 1996) (court may infer that alleged infringer had a reasonable possibility of access if the author sent the copyrighted work to a third-party intermediary who has a close relationship with the infringer, such as one who supervises or works in the same department as the infringer or who contributes creative ideas to the infringer); *Moore v. Columbia Pictures Indus., Inc.*, 972 F.2d 939, 942 (8th Cir. 1992); *Gaste v. Kaiserman*, 863 F.2d 1061, 1067 (2d Cir. 1988). *But see Shaw v. Lindheim*, 809 F. Supp. 1393 (C.D. Cal. 1992) (relationship between two "co-creators" of allegedly infringing television series held insufficient to prove access); *Weygand v. CBS, Inc.*, Copyright L. Rep. (CCH) ¶ 27,660 (C.D. Cal. 1997) (access by producer not imputed to co-producer).

The fact that Pirate was only a part-time employee in Sid's department at Creative House Publishing lessens the probability that Pirate had a reasonable opportunity to read *Lulubelle*. An investigation as to whether *Lulubelle* was reviewed at Creative House Publishing, and by whom, would be very important in making a determination of access. For example, if Sid Bishop testifies that he assigned the review of *Lulubelle* to a reviewer other than Pirate, and that reviewer testifies that no one else in the department had possession of *Lulubelle* or its review, access would be difficult for Writer to prove.

VII-18. Yes. Access may be presumed where the plaintiff's work has been widely distributed to the public. *Bright Tunes Music Corp. v. Harrisongs Music, Ltd.*, 420 F. Supp. 177 (S.D.N.Y. 1976), *aff'd sub nom. ABKCO Music, Inc. v. Harrisongs Music, Ltd.*, 722 F.2d 988 (2d Cir. 1983). *But see Three Boys Music Corp. v. Bolton*, 212 F.3d 477 (9th Cir. 2000) (limited record sales and regionally sporadic radio and television broadcasts sufficient evidence for jury to find access where defendant admitted to closely following band's career). The fact that *Lulubelle* had sold enough copies to appear on several bestseller lists increases the likelihood that Pirate read *Lulubelle* to create a rebuttable presumption that Pirate had a reasonable opportunity to do so.

VII-19. **Answer (B) is correct.** In a copyright infringement action, the court must distill the material in the plaintiff's work which is not protected by copyright, such as ideas, facts, scene a faire, elements dictated by efficiency, or non-original material, from the material in plaintiff's work which is protected by copyright. This latter material constitutes the only elements for which plaintiff may press her claim. *See Incredible Technologies, Inc. v. Virtual Technologies, Inc.*, 400 F.3d 1007, 1011 (7th Cir. 2005) ("copyright laws preclude appropriation of only those elements of the work that are protected by the copyright"); *Kohus v. Mariol*, 328 F.3d 848, 855 (6th Cir. 2003) (court is required to identify which aspects of the artist's work, if any, are protectable by copyright); *Fisher-Price, Inc. v. Well-Made Toy Mfg. Corp.*, 25 F.3d 119, 123 (2d Cir. 1994); *Landsberg v. Scrabble Crossword Game Players, Inc.*, 736 F.2d 485, 489 (9th Cir. 1984); *Jarvis v. A & M Records*, 827 F. Supp. 282, 291 (D.N.J. 1993) (because it is not unlawful to copy noncopyrightable portions of a plaintiff's work, noncopyrightable elements must be factored out in an inquiry into infringement).

Here, the setting, Niagara Falls, is clearly a public domain element and cannot be considered in a substantial similarity analysis. However, the distinctive image of the man in a rowboat, which is substantially similar because it is depicted with only trivial differences in Painter's version, is an original and protectable element, and Painter's appropriation of that significant original element of Artist's work renders the two substantially similar.

Answer (A) is incorrect because Painter is entitled to choose a setting that is in the public domain, even if Artist has already done so.

Answer (C) is incorrect because verbatim similarity is not a requirement in this type of copyright infringement action. Substantial similarity is what Artist must prove.

Answer (D) is incorrect because the mere presence of a public domain element alone does not preclude a finding of substantial similarity between plaintiff's protected elements and the defendant's work.

VII-20. **Answer (A) is correct.** Contributory infringement can be imposed when a party has knowledge of the infringing activity of another and induces, causes, or materially contributes to that infringing conduct. *Gershwin Publishing Corp. v. Columbia Artists Management, Inc.*, 443 F.2d 1159 (1971). Owner meets both elements of contributory infringement. He had knowledge that the performance of the motion pictures constituted an infringement, and provided the physical means for it to take place.

Vicarious liability can be imposed when a party has the right and ability to supervise the infringing activity and also has a direct financial interest in such activities. *Shapiro, Bernstein & Co., Inc. v. H.L. Green Co., Inc.*, 316 F.2d 304 (2d Cir. 1963). Owner also meets both elements of vicarious infringement. He profited financially from the showing of the motion pictures, while, as the proprietor of the theater, he also exercised control over the performance of the motion pictures.

Answers (B), (C), and (D) are incorrect for the reasons explained above.

VII-21. **Answer (A) is correct.** Stealio clearly meets the standard for secondary liability under the theory of inducement as articulated in *Grokster*. *See Metro-Goldwyn-Mayer Studios Inc. v. Grokster, Ltd.*, 545 U.S. 913, 940–41 (2005). Stealio was clearly aware of the illegality that its application, VidCap, enabled. It also actively encouraged the infringing uses.

Answer (B) is incorrect because the Supreme Court in *Grokster* rejected the argument that it is a full defense to secondary liability for copyright infringement via inducement merely to show that a device is capable of substantial noninfringing uses.

Answer (C) is incorrect because the Supreme Court in *Grokster* did not overrule its earlier decision in *Sony*. It merely held that the manufacturer of a device that is capable of substantial noninfringing uses may still be held liable on a secondary infringement theory where there is evidence that the manufacturer knew about and induced the direct infringer to engage in the substantial infringing uses to which its device was put.

Answer (D) is incorrect because a showing of financial gain is not required by the inducement theory of secondary liability.

VII-22. **Answer (B) is correct.** There is original expression in the selection and arrangement of the ten samples that Matt used to comprise *Three-Bar Loop*. Tiffany's unauthorized use of *Three-Bar Loop* infringes those protected elements of Matt's work. The fact that Tiffany acquired the copyrights in the works of authorship that Matt used in creating *Three-Bar Loop* does not entitle her to use, without permission, a legally created compilation based on those works.

Answer (A) is incorrect because purchasing a nonexclusive license to use a protected work of authorship does not confer an ownership interest in that copyrighted work or standing to sue for infringement of that work.

Answer (C) is incorrect because Matt's selection and arrangement of the samples constitutes sufficient originality for independent copyright protection, even though he did not create the underlying works of authorship himself.

Answer (D) is incorrect because, while it is true that Matt acquired only a limited use right in the samples, his creation of an original compilation gave rise to copyright in the compilation that exists independently of the copyrights in the underlying works.

VII-23. No. A sufficiently original compilation of unprotectable elements may be protected by copyright. *See Metcalf v. Bochco*, 294 F.3d 1069, 1074 (9th Cir. 2002) ("The particular sequence in which an author strings a significant number of unprotectable elements can itself be a protectable element. Each note in a scale, for example, is not protectable, but a pattern of notes in a tune may earn copyright protection."); *Three Boys Music Corp. v. Bolton*, 212 F.3d 477, 485 (9th Cir. 2000) (unique compilation of unprotectable musical elements held to be protected). A compilation such as Matt's that is comprised of unprotected elements is thus still protectable in its entirety. *See Yurman Design, Inc. v. Golden Treasure Imports*, 275 F. Supp. 2d 506, 517 (S.D.N.Y. 2003).

VII-24. **Answer (C) is correct.** There is substantial similarity between the defendant's infringing work and the plaintiff's protected work where "the ordinary observer, unless he set out to detect the disparities, would be disposed to overlook them, and regard their aesthetic appeal as the same." *Peter Pan Fabrics, Inc. v. Martin Weiner Corp.*, 274 F.2d 487, 489 (2d Cir. 1960). *See Atari, Inc. v. North American Philips Consumer Elecs. Corp.*, 672 F.2d 607, 614 (7th Cir. 1982) (ordinary observer test is "whether the accused work is so similar to the plaintiff's work that an ordinary reasonable person would conclude that the defendant unlawfully appropriated the plaintiff's protectable expression by taking material of substance and value"). Here, it is an undisputed fact that both works possess the same aesthetic appeal. That is enough to support a finding of substantial similarity.

Answer (A) is incorrect because survey evidence is not categorically prohibited as evidence in copyright infringement trials.

Answers (B) and (D) are incorrect because the focus of an infringement inquiry is on the similarities between the plaintiff's and defendant's works, and cannot be overcome simply by enumerating differences between the two. *See Sheldon v. Metro-Goldwyn Pictures Corp.*, 81 F.2d 49, 56 (2d Cir. 1936) ("[N]o plagiarist can excuse the wrong by showing how much of his work he did not pirate.").

VII-25. **Answer (C) is correct.** The names of characters are generally not protected by copyright. *See* 37 C.F.R. § 202.1(a) (identifying names as a subject matter that are typically not copyrightable). Even if what Writer copied was protected by copyright, not every instance of copying constitutes actionable infringement. The copying must be substantial and material, either quantitatively or qualitatively, to constitute an infringement. *See Arnstein v. Porter*, 154 F.2d 464, 468–69 (2d Cir. 1946); *Newton v. Diamond*, 388 F.3d 1189, 1195 (9th Cir. 2004) ("Substantiality is measured by considering the qualitative and quantitative significance of the copied portion in relation to the plaintiff's work as a whole."). Here, the taking of a two-word name consisting of only fourteen letters clearly falls below the de minimis threshold. Therefore, Writer's taking, however intentional, is not actionable on a copyright infringement theory.

Answer (A) is incorrect because copyright infringement does not depend on whether the alleged infringer intentionally copied the plaintiff's work. Thus, even where the fact of copying is conceded, the copying must be substantial to be actionable. *See Newton v. Diamond*, 388 F.3d 1189, 1193 (9th Cir. 2004).

Answer (B) is incorrect because, although literary characters are copyrightable where sufficiently detailed and distinctive, *Nichols v. Universal Pictures Corp.*, 45 F.2d 119 (2d Cir. 1930), this does not mean that every feature or trait associated with those characters is separately copyrightable. Here, Writer copied only a single feature associated with

Author's "Eva Destruction" character. This does not amount to actionable appropriation, even if "Eva Destruction" is sufficiently fleshed out to merit copyright protection.

Answer (D) is incorrect because literary characters are copyrightable, at least where they are sufficiently fleshed out.

VII-26.   **Answer (D) is correct.** Independent creation is a complete defense to copyright infringement. "[I]f by some magic a man who had never known it were to compose anew Keats's Ode on a Grecian Urn, he would be an 'author,' and, if he copyrighted it, others might not copy that poem, though they might of course copy Keats's." *Sheldon v. Metro-Goldwyn Pictures Corp.*, 81 F.2d 49, 54 (2d Cir. 1936). Here, there is no way that Zao could have copied Ray's work, even though the two are identical, because Zao had no contact whatsoever with western society, including Ray's *Only Just*, at the time he created and subsequently recorded *Number Three*.

Answer (A) is incorrect because independent creation is a complete defense to a claim of copyright infringement even where the defendant's work possesses verbatim similarity to the plaintiff's work.

Answer (B) is incorrect because copyright infringement is not determined by market share or financial impact, but by proof of access, substantial similarity, and substantial taking.

Answer (C) is incorrect because intent to infringe is not an element of copyright infringement.

VII-27.   No. That Zao was not conscious of Ray's work at the time he composed *Number Three* does not preclude the possibility that Zao may have subconsciously copied Ray's work. Copyright infringement is a strict liability tort, thus, the fact that a person has subconsciously copied a work protected by copyright does not preclude a finding of liability. *See Three Boys Music Corp. v. Bolton*, 212 F.3d 477 (9th Cir. 2000); *Bright Tunes Music Corp. v. Harrisongs Music, Ltd.*, 420 F. Supp. 177 (S.D.N.Y. 1976), *aff'd sub nom. ABKCO Music, Inc. v. Harrisongs Music, Ltd.*, 722 F.2d 988 (2d Cir. 1983); *Sheldon v. Metro-Goldwyn Pictures Corp.*, 81 F.2d 49, 54 (2d Cir. 1936); *Fred Fisher, Inc. v. Dillingham*, 298 F. 145, 147–48 (S.D.N.Y. 1924). Ray will still be required to prove that Zao had a reasonable opportunity to see or hear *Only Just*. The fact that Ray's recording of *Only Just* had only moderate success may not be sufficient, by itself, to prove access by Zao. *See Repp v. Webber*, 132 F.3d 882 (2d Cir. 1997).

VII-28.   **Answer (C) is correct.** The knowledge requirement may be met with proof of constructive knowledge. *See UMG Recordings, Inc. v. Sinnott*, 300 F. Supp. 2d 993, 999 (E.D. Cal. 2004). Here, the facts clearly indicate that Ben was aware of Joe's previous use of printing presses to engage in copyright infringement, which, along with Joe's reference to a "big score," clearly suggests that Joe is going to use the printing press to infringe again. Additionally, Ben's telling Joe that Ben did not want to hear about Joe's purposes further suggests that he was aware of the illegality of Joe's purposes. Willful blindness to the infringing actions of the direct infringer may be construed as evidence of actual knowledge. *See UMG Recordings, Inc. v. Sinnott*, 300 F. Supp. 2d 993, 1000 (E.D. Cal. 2004) (not reading cease-and-desist letter deemed evidence of knowledge).

Answer (A) is incorrect. Although it is true that Ben must have been aware of the illegality of Joe's conduct prior to the infringing conduct, *see UMG Recordings, Inc. v. Sinnott*, 300 F. Supp. 2d 993, 998 (E.D. Cal. 2004), Ben did have such knowledge, for the reasons explained above.

Answer (B) is incorrect because Ben clearly knew of the illegality of Joe's conduct in light of Joe's previous infringement, Joe's statement regarding a "quick score," and Ben's statement that he did not want to know any of the details of Joe's planned project.

Answer (D) is incorrect because knowledge of illegality cannot be imputed from primary to secondary infringers.

VII-29. **Answer (B) is correct.** Directing users to sites where infringing content may be found, with full knowledge of the illegality of the conduct, is sufficient to show secondary infringement. *Intellectual Reserve, Inc. v. Utah Lighthouse Ministry, Inc.*, 75 F. Supp. 2d 1290, 1294 (D. Utah 1999) (proprietor of website that listed website addresses where infringed work could be found and who posted emails to third parties suggesting they log onto the infringing website was deemed a sufficient contribution for a finding of contributory infringement).

Answer (A) is incorrect because financial profit from direct infringement is not an element of contributory infringement.

Answer (C) is incorrect because Barry has provided clear directions to the infringing websites even in the absence of actual links.

Answer (D) is incorrect because Barry cannot absolve himself of liability on a secondary liability theory simply by disclaiming it.

VII-30. **Answer (B) is correct.** Clean Channel directly profited from Barlow's conduct because its affiliate, WXTM, gained listener share due to Barlow's inflammatory feature, which increased the value of Clean Channel's advertising time. *Cf., e.g., Famous Music Corp. v. Bay State Harness Racing and Breeding Ass'n*, 554 F.2d 1213 (1st Cir. 1977) (racetrack owner found to financially benefit from unlicensed music performed by contractor between races); *Polygram Int'l Publishing v. Nevada/TIG, Inc.*, 855 F. Supp. 1314, 1333 (D. Mass. 1994) (trade show organizer found to have direct financial interest in infringing activity of exhibitors by attracting attention to infringer's booth). Clean Channel also had the ability to control Barlow's conduct because it had contractual approval rights over the content of WXTM's local programming. *See Hard Rock Café Licensing Corp. v. Concession Servs., Inc.*, 955 F.2d 1143, 1150 (7th Cir. 1992); *Jobete Music Co., Inc. v. Johnson Communications, Inc.*, 285 F. Supp. 2d 1077, 1083–84 (S.D. Ohio 2003).

Answer (A) is incorrect because it lists the elements of contributory, not vicarious, liability.

Answer (C) is incorrect because Clean Channel clearly possessed a significant degree of control over the conduct of their affiliates due to Clean Channel's contractual approval rights.

Answer (D) is incorrect because Clean Channel profited directly, not indirectly, from Barlow's performances. As the WXTM affiliate of Clean Channel gained market share and ratings due to Barlow's increasing popularity, Clean Channel's advertising time became more profitable.

VII-31. **Answer (C) is correct.** James clearly profited from Dan's infringement, because he earned a rental fee for letting Dan sell infringing CDs and DVDs on the vacant lot in Maine. However, James did not have supervisory control over Dan's conduct on the lot. James lived in another state, had no knowledge of Dan's infringing activities, nor any reason to know about them, had never supervised activity on the lot in any way, and did not place conditions on or create rules governing Dan's conduct on the lot. *Compare, e.g., Fonovisa, Inc. v. Cherry Auction, Inc.*, 76 F.3d 259 (9th Cir. 1996) (operator of swap meet that had the right to terminate vendors who rented space, promoted the swap meet, and controlled customer access was held to have sufficient ability to control the activities of the vendors who were selling counterfeit sound recordings at the swap meet); *Metro-Goldwyn-Mayer Studios v. Grokster*, 380 F.3d 1154, 1160 (9th Cir. 2004), *rev'd on other grounds*, 545 U.S. 913 (2005) (ability to exclude individual participants, a practice of policing aisles, ability to block individual users directly at the point of log-in, or ability to delete individual filenames from one's own computer is the sort of monitoring and supervisory relationship that supports a finding of vicarious liability); *UMG Recordings, Inc. v. Sinnott*, 300 F. Supp. 2d 993, 1001 (E.D. Cal. 2004) (rules of flea market owner prohibiting vendors from selling certain classes of goods constituted right and ability to supervise and control the vendors selling infringing recordings); *Polygram Int'l Publishing v. Nevada/TIG, Inc.*, 855 F. Supp. 1314 (D. Mass. 1994) (trade show organizer found to have the ability to supervise the infringing activity of exhibitors).

Answer (A) is incorrect because it states the elements of contributory, not vicarious infringement.

Answers (B) and (D) are incorrect for the reasons explained above.

VII-32. **Answer (D) is correct.** Criminal liability may attach where a person "infringes a copyright willfully and for purposes of commercial advantage or private financial gain . . . or by the reproduction or distribution . . . of 1 or more copies or phonorecords of 1 or more copyrighted works, which have a total retail value of more than $1,000." 17 U.S.C. § 506(a). While Bill's infringing acts did not total more than $1,000 in sales, those sales had an impact on the revenues obtained from authorized DVDs. In addition, Bill's conduct was willful because he was well aware that he was infringing multiple copyrights, and this subjects him to the full range of penalties available under the Copyright Act's criminal provisions. Penalties for criminal copyright infringement, which may be deemed a felony, include up to six years in prison and heavy monetary fines. *See* 18 U.S.C. § 2319.

Answers (A), (B), and (C) are incorrect for the reasons explained above.

VII-33. **Answer (B) is correct.** Internet service providers (ISPs) can take advantage of the statutory immunity for secondary liability based on their users' conduct if they adopt, reasonably implement, and inform subscribers of, a policy that provides for termination of repeat infringers, and do not interfere with content owners' standard technology protection measures. 17 U.S.C. § 512(i). When an ISP meets these qualifications, it cannot be held liable for monetary relief if it is acting as a mere conduit for infringing communications. 17 U.S.C. § 512(a). *See In re Charter Comm., Inc. Subpoena Enforcement Matter*, 393 F.3d 771, 775 (8th Cir. 2005). This is even true where, as here, the ISP also automatically stores those communications for a brief period of time due to technical processes. *See, e.g., Ellison v. Robertson*, 357 F.3d 1072, 1081 (9th Cir. 2004) (AOL found to have functioned as a conduit service provider even though it stored Usenet messages for fourteen days).

Answers (A), (C), and (D) are incorrect for the reasons explained above.

VII-34. Probably not. LOA has met several of the elements that immunize Internet service providers from liability for the infringing conduct of their users. LOA has implemented a notice-and-takedown regime; it has neither actual nor constructive knowledge of Alice's infringing conduct; and it has not received a takedown notice from any of the owners whose copyrights Alice has infringed. In order, however, to avoid secondary liability for users' storage of infringing material, an Internet service provider must also show that it has not received a financial benefit directly attributable to the infringing activity where the service provider has the right and ability to control such activity. 17 U.S.C. § 512(c)(1)(B). LOA clearly received a financial benefit from Alice's conduct, she paid them to store the infringing material, but it is less clear whether merely allowing users to store files amounts to the "right and ability to control [infringing] activity." Current authority suggests that the ability of a service provider to remove or block access to materials posted on its website or stored in its system does not mean that the service provider has the right and ability to control the infringing activity. *See Hendrickson v. eBay Inc.*, 165 F. Supp. 2d 1082, 1093 (C.D. Cal. 2001) (infringing activity of the sale and distribution of pirated copies of motion picture by sellers via auction website are consummated offline and are not controlled by service provider); *Costar Group Inc. v. Loopnet, Inc.*, 164 F. Supp. 2d 688, 704 (D. Md. 2001), *aff'd*, 373 F.3d 544 (4th Cir. 2004). In light of these cases, a court would likely hold that LOA did not have the "right and ability to control [Alice's infringing] activity." In that case, the safe harbor would apply, immunizing LOA from liability on a secondary infringement theory.

VII-35. **Answer (A) is correct.** Although this notice meets nearly all the requirements imposed by statute, 17 U.S.C. § 512(c)(3)(A), it is incomplete because it does not include an attestation that the owner believes Alice's conduct to be unauthorized. 17 U.S.C. § 512(c)(3)(A)(v). A notice that fails to substantially comply with any of these requirements is insufficient to give rise to a duty on behalf of the Internet service provider to remove the allegedly infringing material. 17 U.S.C. § 512(c)(3)(B). *See Hendrickson v. eBay Inc.*, 165 F. Supp. 2d 1082, 1089–90 (C.D. Cal. 2001) (failure to include statement that use of the materials is not authorized renders notification of claimed infringement deficient). Thus, in light of this omission, LOA would have no obligation to remove Alice's infringing material from its servers.

Answers (B) and (C) are incorrect because neither identify statutory requirements applicable to notice and takedown letters.

Answer (D) is incorrect for the reasons explained above.

VII-36. **Answer (C) is correct.** Although the safe harbor provisions of the Copyright Act require that LOA adopt, reasonably implement and inform subscribers of, a policy that provides for termination of repeat infringers, *see* 17 U.S.C. § 512(i)(1)(A); *Ellison v. Robertson*, 357 F.3d 1072, 1080 (9th Cir. 2004), LOA is under no obligation to terminate its services to Alice after only one claim of copyright infringement.

Answers (A), (B), and (D) are incorrect because they describe some of LOA's obligations that arise upon receipt of the takedown notice. Where a valid takedown notice is issued to an Internet service provider, the ISP must remove the identified material and notify the user that it has done so. Upon receipt of a counter notification, the ISP must promptly provide the copyright owner with a copy of the counter notification and inform the copyright owner that the ISP will replace the removed material or cease disabling access to it in ten business days. 17 U.S.C. § 512(g).

VIII-1. **Answer (B) is correct.** The four statutory fair use factors are not exhaustive. The statute states that a court "must consider" those four factors, but does not state that the court must consider *only* those factors. 17 U.S.C. § 107. Indeed, some courts have considered custom in analyzing fair use issues. *Cf., e.g., Harper & Row Publishers, Inc. v. Nation Enters.*, 471 U.S. 539, 550 (1985) (observing that the fair use doctrine was originally "predicated on the author's implied consent to 'reasonable and customary use' ").

Answer (A) is incorrect because customary use is not one of the four statutory fair use factors that courts must consider.

Answer (C) is incorrect because the four fair use factors are not exclusive, as explained above.

Answer (D) is incorrect because fair use does not relate exclusively to economic considerations.

VIII-2. **Answer (C) is correct.** The purpose and character of FreeBooks.com's unauthorized use of the literary works is not sufficiently transformative, *see* 17 U.S.C. § 107(1), because it merely transforms the medium in which those works are expressed, *see, e.g., Castle Rock Entertainment, Inc. v. Carol Publishing Group, Inc.*, 150 F.3d 132, 142–43 (2d Cir. 1998). The use is further unlikely to be fair because FreeBooks.com would likely harm present markets for sales of the owners' literary works. *See* 17 U.S.C. § 107(4).

Answer (A) is incorrect because transformation from one medium to another does not make a use transformative. *See A & M Records, Inc. v. Napster, Inc.*, 239 F.3d 1004, 1015 (9th Cir. 2001) (downloading MP3 files does not transform the copyrighted work); *Infinity Broad. Corp. v. Kirkwood*, 150 F.3d 104, 108 n.2 (2d Cir. 1998) (retransmitting radio transmissions over telephone lines deemed not transformative); *UMG Recordings, Inc. v. MP3.com, Inc.*, 92 F. Supp. 2d 349, 351 (S.D.N.Y. 2000) (defendant's claim that its service provided "space shifting" of sound recordings was deemed to merely be a repackaging of the recordings to facilitate their transmission through another medium that was not transformative); *Video Pipeline, Inc. v. Buena Vista Home Entertainment, Inc.*, 342 F.3d 191, 199 (3d Cir. 2003) (defendant's database of unauthorized film clips held not to improve access to authorized material on the Internet). *But see Kelly v. Arriba Soft Corp.*, 280 F.3d 934, 941 (9th Cir. 2002) (use of digital thumbnail images of photographs found to be transformative in that it made it easier to use the Internet); *Bill Graham Archives v. Dorling Kindersley Ltd.*, 448 F.3d 605, 611 (2d Cir. 2006) (reducing size of posters for use on a timeline in biographical book on the Grateful Dead permitted readers to recognize historical significance of posters, but inadequate to offer more than a glimpse of their expressive value); *Warner Bros. Entertainment Inc. v. RDR Books*, 575 F. Supp. 2d 513, 541 (S.D.N.Y. 2008) (use of more than 2,400 elements from *Harry Potter* book series, from which were extracted and synthesized fictional facts, presented information in format that allowed readers to access it quickly, thereby serving a reference purpose that was transformative).

Answer (B) is incorrect because placing literary works online at a discount is likely to undercut traditional markets for physical versions of those same works.

Answer (D) is incorrect because courts have never held that the fair use defense does not apply in online contexts. *See, e.g., Kelly v. Arriba Soft Corp.*, 280 F.3d 934, 941 (9th Cir. 2002) (use of plaintiff's image as a thumbnail image in an Internet visual search engine held to be a fair use because the thumbnails were much smaller, lower-resolution images that served an entirely different function, improving access to information on the Internet, than the plaintiff's original image).

VIII-3.   **Answer (D) is correct.** In *Campbell v. Acuff-Rose*, 510 U.S. 569 (1994), the Supreme Court held that the distinction between parody and satire has special significance in the fair use context. The Court viewed parody as an infringing work which targets the plaintiff's work, at least in part, as the object of the parody. *See, e.g., Leibovitz v. Paramount Pictures Corp.*, 137 F.3d 109 (2d Cir. 1998) (teaser ad for motion picture deemed a fair use as it targeted photograph of nude pregnant Demi Moore as an object of parody); *Dr. Seuss Enterprises, L.P. v. Penguin Books USA, Inc.*, 109 F.3d 1394 (9th Cir. 1997) (defendant's work, which mimicked Dr. Seuss' style, did not target it for comment or criticism, and therefore did not constitute a fair use).

By contrast, the *Campbell* Court viewed satire as a more generalized social commentary which uses the plaintiff's work merely as a vehicle for social criticism without commenting on the copyrighted work through which the criticism is expressed. Although a work of satire could possibly make a successful claim of fair use, it is not deemed deserving of the special consideration given to parody. *See MCA, Inc. v. Wilson*, 677 F.2d 180 (2d Cir. 1981); *Columbia Pictures Industries, Inc. v. Miramax Films Corp.*, 11 F. Supp. 2d 1179, 1188 (C.D. Cal. 1998) ("Miramax has merely used [Columbia's poster] as a vehicle to poke fun at another target — corporate America. It has not used its advertising to comment on or criticize the copyrighted work.").

Here, John's work is clearly satire, not parody, because he explains to Betty that he was not seeking to comment on her novel, but only to use it as a vehicle for criticizing Bill Clinton. As such, John's work is less likely to be considered a fair use.

Answer (A) is incorrect because John's work is a satire, not a parody, for reasons explained above.

Answer (B) is incorrect because political commentary is not categorically immune from copyright infringement via the fair use defense.

Answer (C) is incorrect because the Supreme Court did not hold in *Campbell* that satires are categorically not fair uses, merely that satires are less likely to be fair uses than are parodies.

VIII-4.   Yes. If John's work poked fun at Betty's novel as well as at Bill Clinton, then it would be a parody under the definition articulated in *Campbell v. Acuff-Rose Music, Inc.*, 510 U.S. 569, 579 (1994). Although parody is not categorically considered a form of fair use, courts have historically favored parodic uses as fair ones. *See id.; see also, e.g., Mattel Inc. v.*

Walking Mountain Prods., 353 F.3d 792, 802 (9th Cir. 2003) (by depicting Barbie as being harmed by kitchen appliances or in sexually suggestive contexts, defendant photographer was commenting on Barbie's influence on gender roles and the position of women in society).

VIII-5.   **Answer (C) is correct.** Although fair use was first codified in the 1976 Copyright Act, 17 U.S.C. § 107, it has long common-law roots pre-dating the passage of that statute. *See, e.g., Folsom v. Marsh*, 9 F. Cas. 342 (1841).

Answer (A) is incorrect because the common-law history of fair use pre-dates the passage of the Copyright Act of 1976.

Answer (B) is incorrect because the Constitution's Intellectual Property Clause, U.S. Const. art. I, § 8, cl. 8, does not explicitly mention fair use, and courts have never interpreted the clause to require the fair use defense. *See Universal City Studios, Inc. v. Corley*, 273 F.3d 429, 458 (2d Cir. 2001).

Answer (D) is incorrect because fair use is modernly a matter of judicial interpretation of *statutory* language. As explained above, it does not have an explicit constitutional source.

VIII-6.   **Answer (B) is correct.** Courts have held that merely recasting the facts that comprise a television show without adding any original content or commentary is not transformative. *See Castle Rock Entertainment, Inc. v. Carol Publishing Group, Inc.*, 150 F.3d 132, 143 (2d Cir. 1998) (book containing trivia questions about *Seinfeld* television series had "little, if any, transformative purpose"). *The Definitive Guide to "Eat at Joe's"* thus would not be considered transformative. By contrast, academic commentary about a television show would be much more likely to be considered transformative because it takes the material presented in the television show and recasts it in the context of original expression. The unauthorized takings of text and images would thus be viewed as a paradigmatic fair use in order to support the academic commentary; indeed "commentary" is one of the illustrative categories of fair use listed in the preamble to the statutory fair use factors. 17 U.S.C. § 107. *But cf. Campbell v. Acuff-Rose Music, Inc.*, 510 U.S. 569, 577 (1994) (warning that the preamble provides "only general guidance about the sorts of copying that courts and Congress most commonly had found to be fair uses"). Thus a court would be very likely to regard *Deconstructing "Eat at Joe's"* as transformative.

Answers (A), (C), and (D) are incorrect for the reasons explained above.

VIII-7.   **Answer (D) is correct.** Although courts have expressed some ambivalence about whether artists who appropriated and recast others' work had transformed it, *see Rogers v. Koons*, 960 F.2d 301, 310 (2d Cir. 1992), more recent decisions suggest that "appropriation art" is transformative, at least where it clearly expresses a different message than the original, *see Blanch v. Koons*, 467 F.3d 244 (2d Cir. 2006) (finding defendant's appropriation of fashion photographs into large canvas painting to be transformative because it had an "entirely different purpose and meaning" than the original). Here, Jody recasts Kara's work entirely by seeking to make a strongly negative political point about it; these two factors suggest that a court would regard Jody's work as transformative.

Answer (A) is incorrect because one artist's appropriating another's content does not categorically preclude a fair use defense. In addition, the content of Jody's paintings is not "exactly the same" as the content of Kara's photographs.

Answer (B) is incorrect because recasting work in a different medium, without more, is not transformative. *See Castle Rock Entertainment, Inc. v. Carol Publishing Group, Inc.*, 150 F.3d 132, 142–43 (2d Cir. 1998).

Answer (C) is incorrect because a defendant is not required to show that the use was necessary in order for it to be transformative.

VIII-8. **Answer (B) is correct.** SoundSearch.com's use is transformative in two ways. First, it has transformed the sound files from full-length versions into brief, low fidelity five-second versions. Second, and related, it has presented those versions for the purpose of information rather than entertainment, transforming the manner in which the Internet can be used. Although a mere change in format is not transformative, courts have held, in the context of search engines, that where unauthorized takings possess these two features, the use is transformative. *See, e.g., Kelly v. Arriba Soft Corp.*, 280 F.3d 934, 941 (9th Cir. 2002) (use of plaintiff's image as a thumbnail image in an Internet visual search engine held to be a fair use because the thumbnails were much smaller, lower-resolution images that served an entirely different function, improving access to information on the Internet, than the plaintiff's original image).

Answer (A) is incorrect because courts have never held that any use of copyrighted works of authorship by a search engine is categorically a fair use.

Answer (C) is incorrect because it is possible (though not likely) that a use can be transformative without the addition of critical commentary.

Answer (D) is incorrect because a use need not alter the content of the copyrighted work of authorship in order to be transformative. For example, in many instances of fair use, the defendant has only added material. *See, e.g., Mattel, Inc. v. Walking Mountain Prods.*, 353 F.3d 792, 800–03 (9th Cir. 2003) (placing Barbie dolls in unusual contexts held to constitute a fair use). Even so, SoundSearch.com does alter the sound files by automatically cutting each of them down to a five-second version.

VIII-9. **Answer (C) is correct.** The operation of a website that does not charge a fee has been found to be a commercial use. The fact that the website operator seeks to attract a sufficiently large subscription base to draw advertising and otherwise make a profit has been found to make its purpose commercial. *See UMG Recordings, Inc. v. MP3.com, Inc.*, 92 F. Supp. 2d 349, 351 (S.D.N.Y. 2000). That Cat Sludge could have charged a licensing fee, given his substantial income, but chose not to in order to save costs, further weighs in favor of a conclusion that this is a commercial use. *See A & M Records, Inc. v. Napster, Inc.*, 239 F.3d 1004, 1015 (9th Cir. 2001).

Answer (A) is incorrect because Cat's intent to profit is not determinative of the commercial character of his use.

Answer (B) is incorrect because the amount of Cat's profit is not determinative of the commercial character of his use.

Answer (D) is incorrect because sites that do not charge a fee but earn profits in other ways have been found to engage in commercial use.

VIII-10. No. Although the United States Supreme Court stated in *Sony Corp. of America v.*

Universal City Studios, Inc., 464 U.S. 417, 451 (1984), that "every commercial use of copyrighted material is presumptively an unfair exploitation of the monopoly privilege that belongs to the owner of the copyright," the Court subsequently retreated from this strongly stated position. The mere fact that a use is commercial does not bar a finding of fair use. *Campbell v. Acuff-Rose Music, Inc.,* 510 U.S. 569, 583–84 (1994) (holding that the only "presumption" of market harm supported by *Sony* would apply in a case involving mere duplication for commercial purposes). The mere fact that a copyright user is a commercial enterprise will not preclude the applicability of the fair use defense. *See Kelly v. Arriba Soft Corp.,* 280 F.3d 934, 940 (9th Cir. 2002); *Warner Bros., Inc. v. American Broadcasting Companies, Inc.,* 523 F. Supp. 611 (S.D.N.Y.), *aff'd,* 654 F.2d 204 (2d Cir. 1981).

VIII-11. Answer (C) is correct. The second fair use factor weighs against a finding of fair use where a work is close to the "core" of copyright protection. The scope of fair use is greater when the plaintiff's work constitutes an informational type work, as opposed to a more creative product. *Marcus v. Rowley,* 695 F.2d 1171 (9th Cir. 1983). *See Stewart v. Abend,* 495 U.S. 207, 237–38 (1990) ("fair use is more likely to be found in factual works than in fictional works"). Moreover, published works are more likely to qualify as fair use because the first appearance of the author's expression has already occurred. *See Kelly v. Arriba Soft Corp.,* 280 F.3d 934, 943 (9th Cir. 2002).

Here, both of these aspects of the second factor of the fair use analysis weigh in favor of Janie. Although her work has a historical setting, it is still predominantly a work of fiction, which lies very close to the core of copyright. *See Harper & Row, Publishers, Inc. v. Nation Enterprises,* 471 U.S. 539, 563 (1985) ("The law generally recognizes a greater need to disseminate factual works than works of fiction or fantasy."). And while Janie gave her manuscript to Alice, this single act of explicitly limited sharing is insufficient to undermine the work's status as unpublished. *See Academy of Motion Picture Arts and Sciences v. Creative House Promotions, Inc.,* 944 F.2d 1446, 1451–52 (9th Cir. 1991) (holding that a limited publication occurs when tangible copies of the work are distributed to a limited class of persons and for a limited purpose).

Answers (A), (B), and (D) are incorrect for the reasons explained above.

VIII-12. No. Fair use traditionally was not recognized as a defense to charges of copying from an author's as yet unpublished works. *Harper & Row, Publishers, Inc. v. Nation Enterprises,* 471 U.S. 539, 550–55 (1985). To clarify the rule that a fair use may be found even though the plaintiff's work is unpublished, section 107 was amended in 1992 to add: "The fact that a work is unpublished shall not itself bar a finding of fair use if such finding is made upon consideration of all the above factors." 17 U.S.C. § 107. *See Sundeman v. The Seajay Society, Inc.,* 142 F.3d 194, 204–05 (4th Cir. 1998). Thus the question whether Janie's work is published would not be dispositive of the fair use issue overall, though a finding that it is unpublished would strongly weigh against fair use.

VIII-13. Answer (B) is correct. The third fair use factor focuses on the amount and substantiality of the defendant's taking of the plaintiff's work. This factor requires an analysis of both the quantity and quality of the alleged infringement. *Marcus v. Rowley,* 695 F.2d 1171 (9th Cir. 1983); *Salinger v. Random House, Inc.,* 818 F.2d 252 (2d Cir. 1987). Use of the "heart" of the plaintiff's work reduces the likelihood that a fair use will be found. *See Harper & Row Publishers, Inc. v. Nation Enter.,* 471 U.S. 539, 565–66 (1985) (discussion of Nixon pardon was "heart" of Gerald Ford's memoir); *Elvis Presley Enterprises, Inc. v. Passport Video*, 349 F.3d 622, 630 (9th Cir. 2003) (using key portions of Elvis Presley's classic television appearances extracted the most valuable part of plaintiff's copyrighted television shows); *Los Angeles News Service v. Reuters Television Int'l, Limited*, 149 F.3d 987, 994 (9th Cir. 1998).

Max's taking one-page from each of Jayne Martel's novels may not be quantitatively large, but it is qualitatively significant because it appropriates the most salient part of each work, the mystery's end. Courts have held that giving away the ending of any literary work amounts to appropriation of the "heart" of that work. *Cf. Video Pipeline, Inc. v. Buena Vista Home Entertainment, Inc.*, 342 F.3d 191, 201 (3d Cir. 2003) (defendant's unauthorized two-minute clips taken only from first half of plaintiff's films, did not "give away" ending of films, and were used "to whet customer's appetite, not to sate it," held not designed to reveal the heart of the films).

Answer (A) is incorrect because even quantitatively small takings can be qualitatively significant, as this one clearly was.

Answer (C) is incorrect because good faith and market effect are not relevant to factor three of the fair use analysis, which focuses exclusively on the amount and substantiality of the taking.

Answer (D) is incorrect because the fact that a taking is verbatim is relevant to, but not dispositive of, its status under a factor three analysis. For example, Max would most likely not be liable if he had made a verbatim reproduction of a single sentence.

VIII-14. Answer (D) is correct. When analyzing fair use factor three, courts are sympathetic to takings that appropriate no more than necessary of the plaintiff's work. *See Bill Graham Archives v. Dorling Kindersley Limited*, 448 F.3d 605, 611 (2d Cir. 2006) (reducing size of posters for use on a timeline in biographical book on the Grateful Dead permitted readers to recognize historical significance of posters, but inadequate to offer more than a glimpse of their expressive value); *Kelly v. Arriba Soft Corp.*, 280 F.3d 934, 943 (9th Cir. 2002) (use of thumbnail image of plaintiff's photographs deemed a fair use because it was necessary to copy plaintiff's entire image to allow users of visual search engine to recognize the image). Also, a defendant may be permitted to take a greater amount of the copyrighted work where there is a special need for accuracy. *See Meeropol v. Nizer*, 560 F.2d 1061, 1071 (2d Cir. 1977).

Here, Lloyd appropriated only the three scenes from *Bloody Mary* necessary to support his academic thesis, as illustrated by the modest lengths of the clips and the fact that he continued to lecture through each of them rather than simply sitting back and observing while they were playing. In light of these facts, a court would be likely to conclude that factor three militates in favor of Lloyd.

Answer (A) is incorrect because the quantity of taking is not relevant to the qualitative question whether the heart of the defendant's work has been appropriated.

Answer (B) is incorrect because there are no absolute rules as to how much of a copyrighted work may be copied and still be considered a fair use. *See, e.g., Sony Corp. of America v. Universal City Studios, Inc.*, 464 U.S. 417, 449–50 (1984) (fact that entire work is reproduced by defendant does not have its ordinary effect of militating against a finding of fair use when the viewer has been invited to witness the work in its entirety free of charge); *Higgins v. Detroit Education Television Foundation*, 4 F. Supp. 2d 701, 707 (E.D. Mich. 1998) (use of thirty-five seconds of musical composition, without lyrics, as background music in an educational television program held to be a fair use).

Answer (C) is incorrect because the purpose of Lloyd's use is not relevant to the amount and substantiality of his taking.

VIII-15. Answer (D) is correct. Although Crawling Id Films is not exploiting Asian markets currently, and has not announced any plans to do so, this does not mean it may not exploit those markets in the future. The fourth factor does not require current exploitation or current plans to exploit a potential market, but includes markets that may reasonably or likely be developed. 17 U.S.C. § 107(4) (referring to "the effect of the use upon the *potential market* for or value of the copyrighted work") (emphasis added); *American Geophysical Union v. Texaco, Inc.*, 60 F.3d 913, 921 (2d Cir. 1995) ("Only an impact on potential licensing revenues for traditional, reasonable, or likely to be developed markets should be legally cognizable when evaluating a secondary use's 'effect upon the potential market for or value of the copyrighted work.'"). Because film companies are increasingly exploiting Asian markets, it is entirely reasonable that Crawling Id would eventually do so. The fourth factor would thus weigh in favor of Crawling Id, and against Mark.

Answers (A) and (B) are incorrect because the fourth factor does not require current exploitation or current plans to exploit a potential market, but includes markets that are reasonably or likely to be developed.

Answer (C) is incorrect because whether or not a defendant has attempted to negotiate a license is not conclusive with respect to the fourth factor of a fair use analysis.

VIII-16. No. Earlier decisions suggested that the fourth factor was particularly important, though none went so far as to state that it was dispositive of fair use analysis altogether. *See Harper & Row, Publishers, Inc. v. Nation Enters.*, 471 U.S. 539, 566 (1985) (calling the fourth factor "undoubtedly the single most important element of fair use"). Subsequent decisions have pulled back from the position that the fourth factor should be disproportionately important in a fair use analysis. *See Campbell v. Acuff-Rose Music, Inc.*, 510 U.S. 569, 590 n.21 (1994) ("Market harm is a matter of degree, and the importance of this factor will vary, not only with the amount of harm, but also with the relative strength of the showing on the other factors."). Thus if the fourth factor were to weigh against Mark, that would tend to indicate that the use was not fair, but would not be determinative of the fair use defense on its own.

VIII-17. Answer (B) is correct. Regardless of whether CBA originally expressed approval of or indifference to Gina's unauthorized creation of *The Very Ben Game*, it is entitled to raise an infringement claim at any time because copyright is a strict liability tort. In terms of the fourth factor of a fair use analysis, Gina's unauthorized creation of the board game may not interfere with the primary market for *Very Ben*, such as syndicated broadcasting, but it does undermine the creation of secondary markets that CBA might have exploited through licensing. *Campbell v. Acuff-Rose Music, Inc.*, 510 U.S. 569, 590 (1994) ("[T]he licensing of derivatives is an important economic incentive to the creation of originals.").

Answer (A) is incorrect because the availability of the fair use defense does not depend on the kind of relief sought.

Answer (C) is incorrect because an owner need not have current plans to exploit a market in order to prevail on the fourth factor.

Answer (D) is incorrect because an owner's initial acquiescence in an unauthorized use does not preclude that owner from making a successful claim on factor four of a fair use analysis at a later time. *See, e.g., Castle Rock Entertainment v. Carol Publishing Group, Inc.*, 150 F.3d 132, 145 (2d Cir. 1998).

VIII-18. Probably not. Most courts have held that the fact that the defendant's use may have a positive impact on copyright holder's market does not exonerate that use. *See Ringgold v. Black Entertainment Television*, 126 F.3d 70, 81 n.16 (2d Cir. 1997) (even if use in television program increased poster sales, plaintiff retained right to licensing fee); *UMG Recordings, Inc. v. MP3.com, Inc.*, 92 F. Supp. 2d 349, 352 (S.D.N.Y. 2000) ("Any allegedly positive impact of defendant's activities on plaintiffs' prior market in no way frees defendant to usurp a further market that directly derives from reproduction of the plaintiffs' copyrighted works."); *Los Angeles Times v. Free Republic*, 2000 U.S. Dist. LEXIS 5669, at * 73 (C.D. Cal. Mar. 31, 2000) ("Courts have routinely rejected the argument that a use is fair because it increases demand for the plaintiff's copyrighted work.").

However, recently some courts have begun to take more seriously the argument that the unauthorized but financially beneficial uses of a copyrighted work may help a defendant's fair use case. The Ninth Circuit has suggested, though by no means clearly held, that it is relevant in the context of the fourth factor to consider whether the purportedly fair use would increase demand for the owner's work. *See Kelly v. Arriba Soft Corp.*, 280 F.3d 934, 944 (9th Cir. 2002) (use of thumbnail images of plaintiff's photographs in visual search engine would guide users to plaintiff's website rather than away from it).

VIII-19. Answer (B) is correct. Although in theory, any possible use might be licensed, plaintiffs can only make arguments that a defendant's use creates market harm within the meaning of the fourth fair use factor where the market is actual or reasonably likely to develop. Parody and criticism comprise a special case where courts have consistently held that licensing markets are neither present nor reasonably likely to develop. *See Campbell v. Acuff-Rose Music, Inc.*, 510 U.S. 569, 592 (1994); *Mattel Inc. v. Walking Mountain Prods.*, 353 F.3d 792, 805 (9th Cir. 2003) (not likely that Mattel would license an artist to create a work that is critical of Barbie); *Sundeman v. The Seajay Society, Inc.*, 142 F.3d 194, 207 (4th Cir. 1998). Thus Dolly's argument that Wendy's parody infringed on her market to license parodies of her work will fail.

Answer (A) is incorrect because whether a work is fiction or nonfiction relates to the second fair use factor, nature of the plaintiff's work, and not to the fourth factor, market effects. And in any event, the non-fiction status of a work means that fair use would be more likely for the defendant, not the plaintiff. *See Kelly v. Arriba Soft Corp.*, 280 F.3d 934, 943 (9th Cir. 2002).

Answer (C) is incorrect because courts have consistently held that no such licensing markets exist or are reasonably likely to emerge.

Answer (D) is incorrect because a plaintiff need not produce evidence of pending negotiations to prove that a licensing market is reasonably likely to emerge.

VIII-20. Answer (C) is correct. Although the Supreme Court held in *Sony* that manufacturers of video recording devices were not liable for infringement on a secondary liability theory, this did not mean that the underlying act, unauthorized videotaping by users of the device, did not constitute primary infringement. The *Sony* Court held that while "time-shifting" (recording television programs for the purpose of watching them at a more convenient time) was fair use, it did not address whether the practice of recording television programs for the purpose of keeping a permanent videotape library of them constituted a fair use. *See Sony Corp. of America v. Universal City Studios, Inc.*, 464 U.S. 417, 423 n.3 (1984). Jack's conduct clearly falls into the category of library building because he records *Crime Dogs* solely for the purpose of keeping a permanent videotape library of the show. Therefore, his conduct does not fall within the holding of *Sony*.

Answer (A) is incorrect because it misstates the Court's holding in *Sony*.

Answer (B) is incorrect because courts have never held that a use is fair if it is made solely for personal purposes.

Answer (D) is incorrect because it misstates the relationship between *Sony* and *Grokster*; not only did *Grokster* not explicitly overrule *Sony*, it did not address the question whether videotaping television shows amounts to fair use.

VIII-21. Answer (D) is correct. Kendra's photocopying was minimally transformative because it represents a bare change in medium at best (codex version of a literary work to loose-leaf). Moreover, courts have held that the existence of the Copyright Clearance Center suggests that there is a present, plausible licensing market for individual photocopies. In a case similar to this one, the Second Circuit held that photocopying a journal article by an industrial scientist was not a fair use. *See American Geophysical Union v. Texaco, Inc.*, 60 F.3d 913, 918 (2d Cir. 1994).

Answers (A), (B), and (C) are incorrect for the reasons explained above.

VIII-22. Answer (C) is correct answer. There is a three-year statute of limitations for copyright infringement actions. 17 U.S.C. § 507(b). Because Greco was well aware of "Strange Mel's" unauthorized use in 2001, but waited a total of seven years to bring an infringement suit, "Strange Mel" would have a plausible statute of limitations defense.

The equitable defense of laches may apply in the copyright setting when there has been a sufficient passage of time between the plaintiff's knowledge of the injury and the date of bringing suit, as well as the presence of prejudice to the defendant. *See Broadcast Music, Inc. v. Roger Miller Music, Inc.*, 396 F.3d 762, 783 (6th Cir. 2005) (laches is an affirmative defense for claims asserted under the Copyright Act). "Strange Mel" can raise a laches defense because Greco waited seven years to bring an infringement suit, *compare Trust Company Bank v. Putnam Publishing Group, Inc.*, 5 U.S.P.Q.2d 1874 (C.D. Cal. 1988) (nineteen-month delay in bringing action against alleged infringing novel was deemed sufficient to constitute laches), and because "Strange Mel" relied to his detriment on Greco's delay in bringing a lawsuit by investing time and money in the music video, *see Trust Company Bank v. Putnam Publishing Group, Inc.*, 5 U.S.P.Q.2d 1874 (C.D. Cal. 1988) (subsequent to plaintiff's knowledge of the infringing nature of the novel, defendants acquired the soft-cover rights to the novel and expended substantial sums promoting and publishing the novel).

Abandonment of copyright may also be a valid affirmative defense to copyright infringement, but can be raised only if there is an intent by the copyright proprietor to surrender the rights in her work. *Dam Things From Denmark v. Russ Berrie & Co., Inc.*, 290 F.3d 548, 560 (3d Cir. 2002) ("there must be either an act, or a failure to act, from which we can readily infer an intent to abandon the right"). The failure to pursue third-party infringers is not an indication of abandonment. *See Capitol Records, Inc. v. Naxos of America, Inc.*, 372 F.3d 471, 484 (2d Cir. 2004). Here, Greco's general indication of indifference toward "Strange Mel" does not come close to the level of indicating a general relinquishment of all rights in the musical work and sound recording that comprise *Only Me.* An abandonment defense would thus not be available to "Strange Mel."

Answers (A), (B), and (D) are incorrect because they inaccurately state the affirmative defenses available to "Strange Mel."

VIII-23. Answer (D) is correct. A plaintiff's knowing failure to advise the Copyright Office of material facts is grounds for holding the registration invalid and incapable of supporting an infringement action. *See Masquerade Novelty, Inc. v. Unique Industries, Inc.*, 912 F.2d 663, 667 (3d Cir. 1990). Here, Jeff made an intentional misstatement on his registration by claiming that he, not Chuck, is the author of *Well Hey*. This is also clearly a material misrepresentation because it caused registration to issue in his name rather than the name of the true author. In light of these facts, Mike has a valid affirmative defense of fraud on the copyright office.

Answer (A) is incorrect because Jeff's status as the registered owner of the copyright in *Well Hey* does not give rise to standing since it is fraudulent.

Answer (B) is incorrect because non-registration does not constitute abandonment.

Answer (C) is incorrect because any valid owner of a copyright can sue for infringement, and the owner may well not be the author.

VIII-24. Answer (A) is correct. The Copyright Act explicitly preempts state laws where the subject matter of the law comes within the subject matter of copyright as defined by sections 102 and 103 of the 1976 Copyright Act and the right asserted under the state law must be equivalent to a right protected by federal copyright law. 17 U.S.C. § 301; *see Mayer v. Josiah Wedgwood & Sons, Ltd.*, 601 F. Supp. 1523 (S.D.N.Y. 1985); *Facenda v. N.F.L. Films, Inc.*, 542 F.3d 1007, 1027–28 (3d Cir. 2008) (person's voice is outside the subject matter of copyright); *Valente-Kritzer Video v. Pinckney*, 881 F.2d 772 (9th Cir. 1989) (state fraud claim requirement of misrepresentation constituted an extra element). Ideas have been held to come within the subject matter of copyright. 17 U.S.C. § 102(b). *See Katz, Dochtermann & Epstein, Inc. v. Home Box Office*, 1999 Copy. L. Dec. (CCH) ¶ 27,907 (S.D.N.Y. 1999) (uncopyrightable idea that underlies copyrightable expression falls within "subject matter of copyright" for preemption purposes). In addition, the rights provided by the hypothetical California statute, reproduction, adaptation, public distribution, and public performance, are among the same rights protected by the Copyright Act. *See* 17 U.S.C. § 106; *Daboub v. Gibbons*, 42 F.3d 285, 288, 289–90 (5th Cir. 1995). Therefore, the hypothetical California state law that seeks to protect ideas as an exclusive right incident to authorship would be deemed preempted and unenforceable.

Answer (B) is incorrect. It is true that where state and federal law conflict, federal law prevails pursuant to the U.S. Constitution's Supremacy Clause. U.S. Const. art. IV, cl. 2. *See Goldstein v. California*, 412 U.S. 546 (1973) (state penal law protection of pre-1972 sound recordings did not conflict with federal copyright law). However, in this case, one could comply with both laws at the same time even though they are otherwise in tension.

Answer (C) is incorrect because states are not generally permitted to provide more copyright protection to authors, especially where, as here, that protection conflicts with both the text and policy of federal law.

Answer (D) is incorrect because the hypothetical California law is unenforceable for the reasons explained above.

VIII-25. This is a difficult question for which there are at least two plausible answers. The Copyright Act provides for a three-year statute of limitations, though the statute of limitations begins to run only when the plaintiff's claim accrues. 17 U.S.C. § 507(b) ("No civil action shall be maintained under the provisions of this title unless it is commenced within three years after the claim accrued."). Amusement Development will argue that Hermit's claim accrued when Futureland's plans and blueprints that allegedly copied Hermit's *Promises of Tomorrow* painting were created. Amusement Development will argue that Hermit's claim would have accrued at the latest upon the opening of Futureland. Because both of these events occurred more than three years prior to Hermit filing his lawsuit, Amusement Development will claim that the District Court has no subject matter jurisdiction to hear the case. *See Broadcast Music, Inc. v. Roger Miller Music, Inc.*, 396 F.3d 762, 783 (6th Cir. 2005) (statute of limitations is an affirmative defense for claims asserted under the Copyright Act).

The vast majority of courts apply the discovery rule in copyright infringement actions, under which a claim accrues only when a plaintiff knows or has sufficient reason to know of the conduct on which the claim is grounded. *See Warren Freedenfeld Assocs., Inc. v. McTigue, D.V.M.*, 531 F.3d 38, 44 (1st Cir. 2008); *see also, e.g., Bridgeport Music, Inc. v. Diamond Time, Ltd.*, 371 F.3d 883, 889 (6th Cir. 2004). Under this rule, a claim accrues only when a reasonably prudent person in the plaintiff's shoes would have discovered, or acquired an awareness of, the putative infringement. *See Stone v. Williams*, 970 F.3d 1043, 1048 (2d Cir. 1992). The reasonable person standard incorporates a duty of due diligence, under which plaintiffs can be charged with inquiry notice sufficient to start the limitations clock, once they possess information fairly suggesting some reason to investigate whether they may have suffered an injury at the hands of a putative infringer. *Warren Freedenfeld Assocs., Inc. v. McTigue, D.V.M.*, 531 F.3d 38, 44–45 (1st Cir. 2008) ("Typically, inquiry notice must be triggered by some event or series of events that comes to the attention of the aggrieved party.").

Pursuant to the discovery rule, Hermit will argue that he has been preoccupied with his and his wife's health issues and that, because of his remote residence, his removal from media coverage, and his reclusive nature, the statute of limitations should be tolled until he discovered the photographs of Futureland shortly before filing suit. The opening of Futureland took place when Hermit was undergoing open heart surgery, at a time when he was clearly focused on staying alive. In addition, Hermit will note that the absence of children in his life made it unlikely that he would pay any attention to an amusement park directed at children.

Amusement Development will counter that a reasonably prudent person would have become aware of the massive publicity surrounding Futureland, as well as the pervasive advertising campaign that has continued since its opening. Even though Hermit did not have a television, he apparently had access to print media over the years when visiting his barber. As a result, the corporation will argue that the three-year statute of limitations should not be tolled and the lawsuit should be dismissed.

VIII-26. **Answer (D) is correct.** The majority of courts find that each act of infringement is a distinct harm giving rise to an independent claim for relief. Recovery is allowed only for those acts occurring within three years of the filing of the lawsuit, and is disallowed for earlier infringing acts. *See Roley v. New World Pictures, Ltd.*, 19 F.3d 479 (9th Cir. 1994); *Stone v. Williams*, 970 F.2d 1043 (2d Cir. 1992); *Hoste v. Radio Corp. of America*, 654 F.2d 11 (6th Cir. 1981). Therefore, only the $175,000 in damages from the most recent infringement is available to MusicCo. Although MusicCo has the ability to elect statutory damages under these facts, they would not do so because the maximum statutory damages available, $150,000, would be less than the non-statutory damages.

Answer (A) is incorrect because MusicCo could not obtain Ripp-Off's net profits from its infringing acts of five years ago.

Answer (B) is incorrect because MusicCo could not obtain Ripp-Off's net profits from its infringing acts of five years ago. In addition, MusicCo could not receive both statutory and non-statutory damages for the same infringement.

Answer (C) is incorrect because MusicCo would undoubtedly elect to receive the larger amount of $175,000 in non-statutory damages.

VIII-27. It is clear that Bleeding Ears Records has no basis for bringing a federal copyright infringement lawsuit because pre-1972 sound recordings have no federal copyright protection. *See* 17 U.S.C. § 301(c) ("no sound recording fixed before February 15, 1972, shall be subject to copyright under this title"). That means that the only recourse for Bleeding Ears Records is to bring an action under the state law of East Dakota. States offer various protections for pre-1972 sound recordings, including common-law copyright, unfair competition, and criminal laws against piracy and bootlegging. But for the recently enacted East Dakota legislation, it is likely that the record company would have a viable claim against DeadVinyl.com for the infringement of the common-law copyright in the sound recordings. *See, e.g., Capitol Records, Inc. v. Naxos of America, Inc.*, 372 F.3d 471, 477–78 (2d Cir. 2004).

The possibility of such an action for common-law copyright infringement has been removed by the East Dakota legislation. If Bleeding Ears Records can prove that the recent legislation is preempted by federal copyright law, East Dakota's common-law copyright would be available to the record company, because the United States Supreme Court has held that common-law copyright is not preempted by federal law. *See Goldstein v. California*, 412 U.S. 546 (1973).

Although the record company may have a viable claim of preemption under section 301(a), arguing that pre-1972 sound recordings may not be protected by federal copyright, but are within the subject matter of copyright, and the downloading or streaming involve the exclusive rights of reproduction, public performance, and public transmission of sound recordings, that claim is prohibited by section 301(c) of the Copyright Act. Under section 301(c), federal copyright law cannot preempt any state laws regarding pre-1972 sound recordings. *See* 17 U.S.C. § 301(c) ("With respect to sound recordings fixed before February 15, 1972, any rights or remedies under the common law or statutes of any State shall not be annulled or limited by this title until February 15, 2067."). This means that Bleeding Ears Records and other record companies must live with the East Dakota law that provides for a compulsory master license for pre-1972 sound recording downloads and the free streaming of such recordings.

IX-1. **Answer (C) is correct.** Injunctive relief is a traditional remedy for copyright infringement. *See, e.g., Cable/Home Comm. Corp. v. Network Productions, Inc.*, 902 F.2d 829, 849 (11th Cir. 1990); *United Feature Syndicate, Inc. v. Sunrise Mold Co., Inc.*, 569 F. Supp. 1475 (S.D. Fla. 1983). However, a court may not issue an injunction where a defendant has ceased its infringing actions and shows no inclination to infringe in the future. *See Harrison Music Corp. v. Tesfaye*, 293 F. Supp. 2d 80, 83 (D.D.C. 2003). Here, the request for injunctive relief is no longer appropriate because Pirate has ceased his infringing conduct and radically changed the course of his life so that there is no indication that the infringement will recur.

Answer (A) is incorrect for the reasons explained above.

Answer (B) is incorrect because injunctive relief does not follow automatically on a showing of copyright infringement, but rather only where the plaintiff convinces a court that it is appropriate under the circumstances. The elements a court will analyze when determining whether to grant an injunction include: (1) whether the plaintiff would suffer irreparable harm if a preliminary injunction does not issue; (2) whether the plaintiff can show a likelihood of success on the merits; (3) balancing competing claims of injury to the parties; and (4) consideration of the public interest. *See Warren Pub., Inc. v. Microdos Data Corp.*, 115 F.3d 1509, 1516 (11th Cir. 1997).

Answer (D) is incorrect because the federal courts have jurisdiction to enjoin the actions of parties regardless of their geographic location.

IX-2. No. Traditionally, courts have consistently held that the enjoining of copyright infringement does not violate the First Amendment. *See Elvis Presley Enters., Inc. v. Passport Video*, 349 F.3d 622, 626 (9th Cir. 2003) ("[I]f the use of the alleged infringer is not fair use, there are no First Amendment prohibitions against granting a preliminary injunction."); *Intellectual Reserve, Inc. v. Utah Lighthouse Ministry, Inc.*, 75 F. Supp. 2d 1290, 1295 (D. Utah 1999).

More modernly, concerns that the blunt force of the traditional rule may lead to the diminishment of speech have been voiced. One court has suggested that under some circumstances, injunctive relief in copyright infringement suits may raise First Amendment problems. *See Suntrust Bank v. Houghton Mifflin Co.*, 252 F.3d 1165, 1166 (11th Cir. 2001) (district court's granting of preliminary injunction, enjoining the publication of *Wind Done Gone*, a parody of *Gone With the Wind*, amounted to an unlawful prior restraint in violation of the First Amendment). *Suntrust* is likely distinguishable, though, because the purportedly fair use in that case — a parody of the novel *Gone With the Wind* — was highly expressive, while merely performing another author's work without authorization, the activity engaged in by Pirate, is not.

IX-3. **Answer (C) is correct.** Once the plaintiff in a copyright infringement action demonstrates a likelihood of success on the merits, courts have presumed that irreparable harm exists. *ABKCO Music, Inc. v. Stellar Records, Inc.*, 96 F.3d 60, 65 (2d Cir. 1996). *But see Salinger v. Colting*, 607 F.3d 68, 80 (2d Cir. 2010) (rejects general rule of presumption of irreparable harm). The availability of money damages does not rebut the presumption of irreparable harm. *Cadence Design Systems, Inc. v. Avanti! Corp.*, 125 F.3d 824, 827 (9th Cir. 1997). A handful of courts have disagreed, *see, e.g., Belushi v. Woodward*, 598 F. Supp. 36, 37 (D.D.C. 1984) ("If a legal remedy will adequately compensate for any infringement, then injury, if any, is not irreparable."), but they represent a vanishingly small minority of opinion.

Answer (A) is incorrect because courts typically hold just the opposite: that the availability of money damages is not inconsistent with irreparable harm.

Answer (B) is incorrect because irreparable harm is not limited solely to emotional or reputational harm.

Answer (D) is incorrect because past injuries may well be considered reparable, regardless of whether this one is.

IX-4.   Possibly, but not necessarily. Undue delay in seeking a preliminary injunction may rebut the presumption of irreparable harm. *See Richard Feiner and Co. v. Turner Ent. Co.*, 98 F.3d 33, 34 (2d Cir. 1996); *Metro-Media Broadcasting Corp. v. MGM/UA Entertainment Co.*, 611 F. Supp. 415, 427 (C.D. Cal. 1985) (four-month delay in seeking injunctive relief supported denial of plaintiff's motion for preliminary injunction).

Here, if Author could advance some convincing explanation that justified his waiting six months to request the injunction after learning of the infringement to file suit, a court might still find that the harm was irreparable. But absent some saving explanation, an otherwise unjustified six-month delay in filing suit may well cause a court to conclude that the harm inflicted by Seller on Author was not irreparable.

IX-5.   **Answer (A) is correct.** For a preliminary injunction, the movant must show a reasonable probability of eventual success in the litigation. *See Value Group, Inc. v. Mendham Lake Estates, L.P.*, 800 F. Supp. 1228, 1232 (D.N.J. 1992). Painter has done this, so he should prevail on this element of the test for a preliminary injunction.

Answers (B) and (C) are incorrect because they describe this element of the test for a preliminary injunction too loosely.

Answer (D) is incorrect because it describes that element too broadly.

IX-6.   Such a conclusion would likely lead a court to find that Painter had shown irreparable harm as well. A presumption of irreparable injury traditionally arises if the plaintiff is able to show a likelihood of success on the merits of its copyright infringement claim. *ABKCO Music, Inc. v. Stellar Records, Inc.*, 96 F.3d 60, 65 (2d Cir. 1996); *Apple Computer, Inc. v. Formula Int'l, Inc.*, 725 F.2d 521, 525–26 (9th Cir. 1984). There is some dissent from this general principle, particularly in the Fifth Circuit. *See Plains Cotton Coop. Ass'n v. Goodpasture Computer Serv., Inc.*, 807 F.2d 1256, 1261 (5th Cir. 1987) (Fifth Circuit does not presume irreparable harm on a showing of likelihood of success on the merits).

In the majority of federal circuits, however, a court would conclude that because Painter has been able to show a reasonable likelihood of success on the merits, a showing of irreparable harm necessarily follows. *But see Salinger v. Colting*, 607 F.3d 68, 80 (2d Cir. 2010) (rejects general rule of presumption of irreparable harm).

IX-7. This is a hard question. On one hand, Author can invoke the public interest by arguing that the public generally has a strong interest in seeing that the copyright laws are enforced and that infringement is limited. Courts have often expressed solicitude for this position. *See, e.g., Intellectual Reserve, Inc. v. Utah Lighthouse Ministry, Inc.*, 75 F. Supp. 2d 1290, 1295 (D. Utah 1999); *Value Group, Inc. v. Mendham Lake Estates, L.P.*, 800 F. Supp. 1228, 1234 (D.N.J. 1992) ("The public has no interest in permitting one company to copy another company's work.").

On the other hand, Satirist can argue that there is a strong public interest favoring the publication of books and novels. *Trust Company Bank v. Putnam Publishing Group, Inc.*, 5 U.S.P.Q.2d 1874 (C.D. Cal. 1988); *Belushi v. Woodward*, 598 F. Supp. 36, 37–38 (D.D.C. 1984) (promotion of free expression and robust debate is a competing public interest to the public interest that favors maintaining the integrity of the copyright laws). In particular, where the work at issue is not a verbatim copy, but possesses substantial original material, courts recently been inclined to find that preliminary relief is not in the public interest. *See, e.g., Suntrust Bank v. Houghton Mifflin Co.*, 252 F.3d 1165, 1166 (11th Cir. 2001).

IX-8. **Answer (D) is correct.** Although the Copyright Act clearly places impoundment within the discretion of courts, 17 U.S.C. § 503(a) ("the court *may* order impounding") (emphasis added), courts have been unwilling to issue ex parte impoundment orders due to concerns that such orders may unduly burden property rights without due process. *See Paramount Pictures Corp. v. Doe*, 821 F. Supp. 82, 87 (E.D.N.Y. 1993) ("[A] literal reading of the rules [regarding *ex parte* seizures] would result in procedures of dubious constitutional validity in light of Supreme Court decisions handed down since the time of the rules' adoption."). In light of this, a court would be likely not to order the studios' requested impoundment.

Answer (A) is incorrect because the plain language of the Copyright Act clearly makes impoundment discretionary, not mandatory.

Answer (B) is incorrect because, while the Rules of Practice in Copyright Cases promulgated under the 1909 Act appeared to make impoundment mandatory upon a plaintiff's motion, those rules have since been abrogated by the Supreme Court and are no longer in force. *See AdobeSystems, Inc. v. South Sun Prods., Inc.*, 187 F.R.D. 636, 640 (S.D. Cal. 1999).

Answer (C) is incorrect because the Copyright Act makes impoundment available "at any time while an [infringement] action . . . is pending." 17 U.S.C. § 503.

IX-9. **Answer (D) is correct.** The Copyright Act enables impoundment of infringing "copies or phonorecords," such as Al's infringing DVDs, 17 U.S.C. 503(a)(1)(A); "articles by means of which such copies . . . may be reproduced," *id.* § 503(a)(1)(B), such as Al's computer and DVD-making device; and "records documenting the manufacture, sale, or receipt of things involved in any such violation," *id.* § 503(a)(1)(C), such as the records contained in Al's file cabinet.

Answers (A), (B), and (C) are incorrect for the reasons explained above.

IX-10. **Answer (B) is correct.** A plaintiff in a copyright infringement action is entitled to recover actual damages suffered as a result of the infringement and any of the defendant's profits that are attributable to the infringement. *See Frank Music Corp. v. Metro-Goldwyn-Mayer, Inc.*, 772 F.2d 505 (9th Cir. 1985). Thus, here, Composer would be entitled to any profits that Xplicit generated attributable to its use of *Happy Springtime*, as well as any revenue composer lost due to the boycott of Composer's work.

Answer (A) is incorrect because it does not take Composer's actual damages into account.

Answer (C) is incorrect because it does not take Xplicit's profits into account.

Answer (D) is incorrect because any plaintiff who proves infringement is entitled to nonstatutory damages, including actual damages and defendant's profits, if proven.

IX-11. No. The overwhelming majority of courts have held that punitive damages are not available in federal copyright infringement actions. *Oboler v. Goldin*, 714 F.2d 211 (2d Cir. 1983). *See also Budget Cinema, Inc. v. Watertower Associates*, 81 F.3d 729, 733 (7th Cir. 1996); *Viacom Int'l, Inc. v. YouTube, Inc.*, 540 F. Supp. 2d 461, 464 (S.D.N.Y. 2008); *Calio v. Sofa Express, Inc.*, 368 F. Supp. 2d 1290, 1291 (M.D. Fla. 2005). *But see TVT Records v. Island Def Jam Music Group*, 262 F. Supp. 2d 185, 186 (S.D.N.Y. 2003), which has been described as a "rogue decision" that runs counter to a profusion of contrary cases.

IX-12. **Answer (B) is correct.** The appropriate measure of damages is Betty's profits (gross profits minus costs, or $50,000 − $10,000 = $40,000), though only to the extent that they are attributable to her infringement of Alice's work. 17 U.S.C. § 504(b) ("The copyright owner is entitled to recover the actual damages suffered by him or her as a result of the infringement, and any profits of the infringer *that are attributable to the infringement* and are not taken into account in computing the actual damages.") (emphasis added). Because half of the profits for Betty's wildlife guide were attributable to her unauthorized use of Alice's work, half of those profits, $20,000, is the best measure of Alice's nonstatutory damages. *See id.* ("In establishing the infringer's profits, the copyright owner is required to present proof only of the infringer's gross revenue, and the infringer is required to prove his or her deductible expenses and the elements of profit attributable to factors other than the copyrighted work.").

Answers (A), (C), and (D) are incorrect because they give the wrong measure of actual damages, for the reasons explained above.

IX-13. **Answer (D) is correct.** Alice is required to prove not only the gross revenues resulting from the sales of the wildlife guide, but also the gross revenues that are attributable to defendant's infringing activities. 17 U.S.C. § 504(b). *See Bouchat v. Baltimore Ravens Football Club, Inc.*, 346 F.3d 514, 524–26 (4th Cir. 2003) (plaintiff unable to recover any damages for infringing use of his logo design by professional football team because sales of tickets, sponsorships, broadcast rights, trading cards, video games, and merchandise are not responsive to logo design); *John G. Danielson, Inc. v. Winchester-Conant Properties, Inc.*, 322 F.3d 26, 47 (1st Cir. 2003).

Betty's failure to show how much she expended in making her wildlife guide means that she forfeits the opportunity to do so. *See Russell v. Price*, 612 F.2d 1123, 1130–01 (9th Cir. 1979) (holding that the gross revenue figure proven by the plaintiff stands as the profit factor if the defendant fails to prove deductible expenses). However, Alice's failure to provide evidence that any of the gross revenues earned by the sale of the wildlife guide were due to her photographs precludes any award of nonstatutory damages.

Answers (A), (B), and (C) are incorrect because they misstate the appropriate amount of actual damages.

IX-14.   This is a difficult question, the answer to which would depend on the jurisdiction in which the case was filed. On this variation of the question, Betty would be a willful infringer because she used Alice's photographs knowing of their protected status, yet without making any effort to secure a license. Some circuits do not allow willful infringers to deduct overhead from their costs. *See Saxon v. Blann*, 968 F.2d 676, 681 (8th Cir. 1992) (willful infringers cannot deduct overhead); *Frank Music Corp. v. Metro-Goldwyn-Mayer, Inc.*, 772 F.2d 505 (9th Cir. 1985) (not allowing deduction of overhead expenses). Other circuits, however, do allow willful infringers to deduct expenses in this calculation. *See Hamil Am., Inc. v. GFI*, 193 F.3d 92, 106–07 (2d Cir. 1999) (overhead expenses may be deducted after a heightened scrutiny of proof of sufficient nexus and allocation formula).

The question of whether Betty's status as a willful infringer would affect the damages calculation thus varies circuit-by-circuit. The Second Circuit would allow her to reduce the gross profits by the amount of her overhead, resulting in a relatively lower award; while the Eighth and Ninth Circuits would not permit this, resulting in a relatively higher award.

IX-15.   **Answer (C) is correct.** Multiple recoveries are permitted for the violation of two distinct rights resulting from the same conduct, but only to the extent that two different types of harm have been suffered. *See Nintendo v. Dragon Pacific Int'l*, 40 F.3d 1007 (9th Cir. 1994) (recovery for statutory damages under Copyright Act and additional award for trebled profits under Lanham Act permitted because the interests protected by copyright law are separate from the interests protected by trademark law); *Sparaco v. Lawler, Matusky, Skelly Engineers LLP*, 313 F. Supp. 2d 247, 250–51 (S.D.N.Y. 2004). By contrast, multiple damages are not permitted where the harm suffered as a result of each legal wrong is identical. *See Bowers v. Baystate Techs, Inc.*, 320 F.3d 1317, 1328 (Fed Cir. 2003) (no double recovery where breach of contract damages arose from same copying and lost sales that formed the basis for copyright damages); *Computer Associates Int'l v. Altai, Inc.*, 982 F.2d 693, 720 (2d Cir. 1992) (double recovery not permitted where damages for copyright infringement and trade secret misappropriation are coextensive).

Here, the injury that Ed claims to have suffered as a result of Vic's conduct, lost profits, is the same, even though there are two theories of legal wrongs: breach of contract and copyright infringement, that could frame this injury. As a result, Ed can only recover the actual damages he suffered — $50,000.

Answers (A), (B), and (D) are incorrect for the reasons stated above.

IX-16.   **Answer (B) is correct.** Typically, registration with the Copyright Office at the time of the infringement is a condition precedent to obtaining statutory damages. 17 U.S.C. § 412; *see Bouchat v. Baltimore Ravens Football Club, Inc.*, 346 F.3d 514, 517 n.2 (4th Cir. 2003). Registration within three months after the first publication of the work will satisfy the registration requirement even though the infringement commenced after the first publication, but before the registration. 17 U.S.C. § 412(2). Because Hy registered within three months of first publication, he can still seek statutory damages against Guy.

Answer (A) is incorrect because registration certainly is a prerequisite for seeking statutory damages.

Answer (C) is incorrect because the general rule that registration must precede infringement does not apply where, as here, registration is made within three months of publication.

Answer (D) is incorrect because it is possible to obtain statutory damages for published as well as unpublished works. In addition, the script was published when Hy placed it on his personal website prior to Guy's infringement.

IX-17.　**Answer (D) is correct.** If the plaintiff is entitled to statutory damages, it is the plaintiff's election to receive either statutory or actual damages, not both. 17 U.S.C. § 504(c)(1); *see Hamil America, Inc. v. GFI*, 193 F.3d 92, 103 (2d Cir. 1999); *Jordan v. Time, Inc.*, 111 F.3d 102 (11th Cir. 1997). This election can be made any time before final judgment, and so certainly does not need to be made in the initial complaint. 17 U.S.C. § 504(c)(1); *see Feltner v. Columbia Pictures Television, Inc.*, 523 U.S. 340, 347 n.5 (1998) ("election may occur even after a jury has returned a verdict on liability and an award of actual damages"); *Business Trends Analysts v. Freedonia Group, Inc.*, 887 F.2d 399, 403–04 (2d Cir. 1989) (election may be made at any time before final judgment).

Answers (A), (B), and (C) are incorrect for the reasons stated above.

IX-18.　**Answer (B) is correct.** Yancey's infringement was willful because he did it with actual knowledge that he was infringing a copyright. *See Peer Int'l Corp. v. Pausa Records, Inc.*, 909 F.2d 1332, 1335 n.3 (9th Cir. 1990) (infringement is "willful" if the actions of the defendant were taken "with knowledge that the defendant's conduct constitutes copyright infringement"). Courts have discretion to increase the maximum statutory damage to $150,000 in the case of willful infringement. 17 U.S.C. § 504(c)(2). However, Zed is only entitled to one iteration of damages because only one of his works was infringed; multiple acts of infringing the same work by the same defendant do not merit multiple damage awards. *See Venegas-Hernandez v. Sonolux Records*, 370 F.3d 183, 194 (1st Cir. 2004); *Walt Disney Co. v. Powell*, 897 F.2d 565, 569 (D.C. Cir. 1990).

Answer (A) is incorrect because statutory damages are calculated with respect to different works infringed, not by looking at different acts of infringement with respect to the same work.

Answer (C) is incorrect because statutory damages for willful infringement are increased to $150,000 per work infringed.

Answer (D) is incorrect because even matters that lie within judicial discretion may be overturned on appeal where they constitute clear error or abuse of discretion.

IX-19.　The precise amount of damages is not certain because it lies within the judge's discretion, but the ultimate award will certainly be lower than in question IX-18. Yancey's conduct in this instance amounts to innocent infringement, where the defendant "was not aware and had no reason to believe that [its] acts constituted an infringement of copyright." 17 U.S.C. § 504(c)(2); *Los Angeles News Service v. Reuters Television Int'l, Limited*, 149 F.3d 987, 995 (9th Cir. 1998). The court has the discretion to reduce the minimum statutory damage to $200 in the case of innocent infringement. 17 U.S.C. § 504(c)(2); *see Jobete Music Co., Inc. v. Johnson Communications, Inc.*, 285 F. Supp. 2d 1077, 1084 (S.D. Ohio 2003). But even if it chose not to do this, an award at the lower end of the statutory damage range ($750–$30,000) would be appropriate.

IX-20.   **Answer (D) is correct.** Statutory damages are to be calculated according to the number of works infringed, not the number of infringements. *See Walt Disney Co. v. Powell*, 897 F.2d 565, 569 (D.C. Cir. 1990). Each episode of a television series is a separate work for purposes of statutory damages, particularly if each episode can stand on its own by telling an individual story and is separately registered. *See Columbia Pictures Television v. Krypton Broadcasting of Birmingham, Inc.*, 106 F.3d 284, 295 (9th Cir. 1997), *rev'd and remanded on other grounds*, 523 U.S. 340 (1998); *MCA Television Ltd. v. Feltner*, 89 F.3d 766 (11th Cir. 1996). Each separately liable infringer involved in the suit acts as a multiplier. *See Columbia Pictures Television v. Krypton Broadcasting, Inc.*, 106 F.3d 284, 294 (9th Cir. 1997) (each television station broadcasting unlicensed television program held to be separate defendants for purposes of statutory damages), *rev'd and remanded on other grounds*, 523 U.S. 340 (1998).

In light of all this, there are three separate actors (each of the television stations) who have committed twelve separate acts of infringement (broadcasting each of the twelve episodes of the series), which means there are a total of thirty-six acts of infringement.

Answers (A), (B), and (C) are incorrect for the reasons stated above.

IX-21.   Possibly as high as $5.4 million. The standard range for statutory damages is from $750 to $30,000 per work infringed, per actor. 17 U.S.C. § 504(c)(1). However, here the television stations broadcast *Insurgents* during the summer, knowing full well that their actions constituted infringement of Wall of Reality's copyrights. This likely makes their conduct willful infringement. *See Peer Int'l Corp. v. Pausa Records, Inc.*, 909 F.2d 1332, 1335 n.3 (9th Cir. 1990) (infringement is "willful" if the actions of the defendant were taken "with knowledge that the defendant's conduct constitutes copyright infringement"). In light of that, a judge could award damages as high as $5.4 million ($150,000 times 36 acts of infringement).

IX-22.   **Answer (A) is correct.** Plaintiffs are entitled to multiple recoveries for the same conduct where that conduct inflicts different harms. Here, Mitch and Fred inflicted two separate kinds of harm on Tasty Cola. They violated Tasty Cola's exclusive right to reproduce the Tasty Swoop, and they also diminished the consumer goodwill associated with the Tasty Cola brand. This is not considered a double recovery because the interests protected by the copyright law are separate from the interests protected by trademark law. *See Nintendo v. Dragon Pacific Int'l*, 40 F.3d 1007 (9th Cir. 1994).

Answer (B) is incorrect because plaintiffs are not entitled to recovery on any number of theories, but only theories that articulate different kinds of harm.

Answer (C) is incorrect because the interests protected by copyright and trademark are quite different, for the reasons explained above.

Answer (D) is incorrect because plaintiffs are not limited to only one theory of recovery in intellectual property cases.

IX-23. $1 million. All defendants who engage in the same act of copyright infringement are jointly and severally liable for plaintiff's statutory damages. *See Fitzgerald Publ'g Co., Inc. v. Baylor Publ'g Co., Inc.*, 807 F.2d 1110, 1116 (2d Cir. 1986). Therefore, even though Fred is judgment-proof, Tasty Cola can still seek the full amount of the recovery from Mitch alone.

IX-24. **Answer (C) is correct.** The court has the discretion to allow the recovery of full costs by or against any party other than the United States or its officers. 17 U.S.C. § 505.

Answer (A) is incorrect because, in this case, Norm cannot recover the costs of suit. However, expert witness fees are typically recoverable. Recoverable expenses include court fees, printing, photocopying, expert fees, cost of interpreters, long distance telephone calls, and parking. *See Invessys, Inc. v. McGraw-Hill Cos., Ltd*, 369 F.3d 16, 22 (1st Cir. 2004); *Brewer-Giorgio v. Bergman*, 985 F. Supp. 1478, 1485 (N.D. Ga. 1997).

Answer (B) is incorrect because Norm cannot recover any of the fees associated with the suit.

Answer (D) is incorrect because prevailing parties in infringement actions are entitled to both expert witness fees and costs. 17 U.S.C. § 505.

IX-25. **Answer (B) is correct.** Registration with the Copyright Office at the time of the commencement of infringement is a condition precedent to obtaining attorneys fees. 17 U.S.C. § 412. *See M.G.B. Homes, Inc. v. Ameron Homes, Inc.*, 903 F.2d 1486, 1493 (11th Cir. 1990). Moreover, infringement is commenced as of the first act of infringement, even though a series of separate infringements of the work by the defendant may later take place. *See Mason v. Montgomery Data, Inc.*, 967 F.2d 135, 143 (5th Cir. 1992). Therefore, because *Norm's Diner* was not registered at the time of the initial infringement, Jane forfeited the opportunity to recover attorney's fees.

Answer (A) is incorrect because even though some acts of infringement took place after registration, the relevant measuring point is the *initial* infringement, and this took place prior to registration.

Answer (C) is incorrect because registration within three months of the initial infringement does not enable recovery of attorney's fees. However, registration within three months after the first publication of the work will satisfy the registration requirement even though the infringement commenced after the first publication, but before the registration. 17 U.S.C. § 412(2).

Answer (D) is incorrect because willful or malicious infringement is not a prerequisite for recovery of attorney's fees.

IX-26. **Answer (C) is correct.** The court in its discretion may award reasonable attorney's fees to the prevailing party. 17 U.S.C. § 505; *Harrison Music Corp. v. Tesfaye*, 293 F. Supp. 2d 80, 84 (D.D.C. 2003). When determining whether to grant attorney's fees, courts in the Ninth Circuit consider five *Fogerty* factors. *See Jackson v. Axton*, 25 F.3d 884, 890 (9th Cir. 1994). These include the degree of success obtained, frivolousness, motivation, objective unreasonableness, and considerations of deterrence and compensation. A court's consideration of attorney's fees is not limited to the five factors. *Smith v. Jackson*, 84 F.3d

1213, 1221 (9th Cir. 1996).

Here, four of the factors strongly weigh in favor of granting attorney's fees to Henderson. Jackson's suit was largely frivolous and lacked legal foundation, as the court explained when issuing its judgment. Henderson's success was complete because the award of summary judgment in his favor was not equivocal. Deterrence considerations weigh in favor of awarding attorney's fees to Henderson as well, because it will send a message to plaintiffs in Jackson's situation that they should not confuse copyright infringement with negative criticism.

Answer (A) is incorrect because while motivation is one of the *Fogerty* factors, an innocent state of mind does not categorically preclude an award of attorney's fees.

Answer (B) is incorrect because merely showing that there is a nonzero chance of prevailing in an infringement suit does not preclude a finding of attorney's fees.

Answer (D) is incorrect because in the Ninth Circuit, prevailing parties in copyright infringement suits are not entitled to attorney's fees as a matter of course. By contrast, courts in some other circuits have held that an award of attorneys fees in copyright cases is the rule, rather than the exception, and should be awarded routinely. *See, e.g., Eagle Services Corp. v. H2O Industrial Services, Inc.*, 532 F.3d 620, 625 (7th Cir. 2008) (defendants in copyright infringement cases have a very strong presumptive entitlement to an award of attorney's fees); *Compaq Computer Corp. v. Ergonome Inc.*, 387 F.3d 403, 411 (5th Cir. 2004) (affirming award of $2.7 million against corporation and one of its principals).

IX-27.   No. The Supreme Court has rejected any dual standard which treats prevailing plaintiffs differently than prevailing defendants under section 505. *See Fogerty v. Fantasy, Inc.*, 510 U.S. 517 (1994). Courts thus cannot treat prevailing defendants categorically differently than they treat prevailing plaintiffs when considering a fee award.

IX-28.   **Answer (A) is correct.** Courts have wide discretion to award attorney's fees, 17 U.S.C. § 505, but the award must be reasonable. *Moorish Vanguard Concert v. Brown*, 498 F. Supp. 830 (E.D. Pa. 1980). The "reasonable" fees are based on a lodestar figure represented by the reasonable hourly rate multiplied by the hours expended in the litigation, but the court retains discretion to adjust this figure. *See Crescent Publ'g Group, Inc. v. Playboy Enters., Inc.*, 246 F.3d 142, 150 (2d Cir. 2001).

When considering adjustment of the lodestar figure, excessive, redundant, or unnecessary hours should be excluded. *See Harrison Music Corp. v. Tesfaye*, 293 F. Supp. 2d 80, 85 (D.D.C. 2003) (number of requested attorney hours deemed excessive for straightforward case where plaintiffs admitted liability); *Queenie, Ltd. v. Nygard Int'l*, 204 F. Supp. 2d 601, 609 (S.D.N.Y. 2002) (court found it unreasonable to shift more than fifty percent of pre-trial attorneys fees to plaintiff in light of straightforward factual issues and absence of novel legal issues or case dispositive motions).

Here, the court was acting well within its discretion to reduce the fee amounts submitted by Bram & Gower, particularly because the hours the firm submitted were viewed as excessive.

Answer (B) is incorrect because a court's discretion to award fees is not absolute, but is constrained by reasonableness.

Answer (C) is incorrect because a court should use the lodestar amount as a starting point when considering a fee award, but is not absolutely constrained by that amount.

Answer (D) is incorrect because a court is free to exercise its discretion to reduce fee awards regardless of whether a motion has been filed by the non-prevailing party.

IX-29.   **Answer (D) is correct.** A prevailing plaintiff is entitled to recover its actual damages and the profits attributable to the infringement. *See* 17 U.S.C. § 501(b). Therefore, West Company is entitled to its actual damages of $25,000, which are not speculative because it has sold to this retailer for a long time. West Company is also entitled to the $60,000 in profits of East Company attributable to its infringing activity. Because the two companies market their goods in different retailers, the defendant's sales are not to be taken into account when establishing plaintiff's actual damages. West Company is entitled to $85,000, the sum of the $25,000 in actual damages and the $60,000 in profits.

Answer (A) is incorrect because it does not include the profits of the defendant attributable to its infringement.

Answer (B) is incorrect because the lost sales of West Company and the profits from sales made by East Company are not the same sales made to the same retailer.

Answer (C) is incorrect because it does not include the lost sales suffered by West Company.

IX-30.   West Company is entitled to its actual damages, which consist of its lost profits of $25,000. West Company is also entitled to the $60,000 in profits attributable to the infringing activities of East Company. These profits were derived from the sale of dresses on the east coast and have no effect on the actual damages of West Company. As for the $20,000 profit from East Company's sale to Phasion Phrenzi, that profit was derived from the same sale that West Company had lost. Therefore, East Company's profit from that sale cannot be taken into account. To do so would count the profit from the Phasion Phrenzi twice. Such double-counting is not permitted. As a result, the amount of damages to which West Company is entitled is $85,000.

X-1. **Answer (B) is correct** because it most accurately describes the relevant features of the DMCA. *See generally* 17 U.S.C. §§ 1201–1203.

Answer (A) is incorrect because it fails to note that the DMCA protects the use of copyright management information.

Answer (C) is incorrect because it fails to note that the DMCA prohibits certain efforts to circumvent technology protection measures.

Answer (D) is incorrect because the DMCA does not protect any and all efforts to circumvent technology protection, but only some of them.

X-2. **Answer (A) is correct.** The DMCA prohibits the act of circumvention of a technological measure, such as scrambling, encryption, or password protection, put in place by a copyright owner to effectively control access to a copyrighted work, without the authority of the copyright owner. 17 U.S.C. § 1201(a)(1); *see Chamberlain Group, Inc. v. Skylink Technologies, Inc.*, 381 F.3d 1178, 1203 (Fed. Cir. 2004). Thus Jane would be liable to the extent that she used the program to circumvent the access-control measures (i.e., the password protections) that George put in place.

The DMCA also prohibits the manufacture and distribution of products and services used to defeat a technological measure that effectively controls access to a work protected by copyright. 17 U.S.C. § 1201(a)(2); *see Universal City Studios, Inc. v. Corley*, 273 F.3d 429 (2d Cir. 2001) (posting of decryption software on website and linking to other sites posting decryption software is actionable). Thus, although Harriet herself did not use the program to circumvent the access-control measures protecting funfish.com, she can be held liable for distributing the program to others and enabling them to do so. Jane would also be found liable for her creation and distribution of the software program.

Answers (B), (C), and (D) are incorrect because they wrongly state the parties who can be held liable under the DMCA.

X-3. No. It is true that the DMCA applies only to technology protection measures that "effectively control access" to digital material, *see* 17 U.S.C. § 1201(a), and some defendants have argued that if an access-control device is weak or rudimentary, it does not "effectively" control access to the protected digital material. *See, e.g., RealNetworks, Inc. v. Streambox, Inc.*, 2000 U.S. Dist. LEXIS 1889 (W.D. Wash. 2000). However, courts have rejected this argument and in so doing, have developed a broad definition of what it means to "effectively control access" to digital material. A technological measure effectively controls access to a work if the measure, in the ordinary course of its operation, requires the application of information, or a process or a treatment, with the authority of the copyright owner, to gain access to the work. *Id.* § 1201(a)(3)(B); *see 321 Studios v.*

Metro Goldwyn Mayer Studios, Inc., 307 F. Supp. 2d 1085, 1094 (N.D. Cal. 2004).

In light of this broad definition, a court would regard it as immaterial that programmers would regard George's access control efforts as poor. The password-protection would ordinarily have required entry of information provided by George in order to permit access, and this is all courts require in order to find that a technology protection measure "effectively" controls access to the underlying material.

X-4.   **Answer (C) is correct.** The DMCA prohibits the manufacture and distribution of products and services used to defeat technological measures that impose limitations on the use of a copyrighted work. 17 U.S.C. § 1201(b); *see 321 Studios v. Metro Goldwyn Mayer Studios, Inc.*, 307 F. Supp. 2d 1085, 1094 (N.D. Cal. 2004) (DVD content encryption is a copy control system to which section 1201(b)(1) applies); *United States v. Elcom Ltd.*, 203 F. Supp. 2d 1111, 1120 (N.D. Cal. 2002) (developer and marketer of software program that allowed users to remove use restrictions on ebook files, thereby making the ebook file copyable, printable, and easily distributed electronically without the permission of the copyright owner violated section 1201(b)).

Congress did not, however, ban the act of circumventing use restrictions, only the trafficking in and marketing of devices used to circumvent use restrictions. *See United States v. Elcom Ltd.*, 203 F. Supp. 2d 1111, 1120–21 (N.D. Cal. 2002) ("circumventing use restrictions is not unlawful").

Warren cannot be held liable because the law does not create liability for the use of the device. By contrast, Lloyd can be held liable for his conduct, because even though he did not create or use dePSS, he did make it available to others, which amounts to the kind of trafficking rendered unlawful by the DMCA.

Answers (A), (C), and (D) are incorrect because they wrongly state the parties who can be held liable under the DMCA.

X-5.   No. The legal use of copyrighted material accessed through a circumvention of technological measure is not a defense to a violation of the anti-trafficking provisions of section 1201(b). *See 321 Studios v. Metro Goldwyn Mayer Studios, Inc.*, 307 F. Supp. 2d 1085, 1097–98 (N.D. Cal. 2004). And while the statutory text does say that remedies, limitations, or defenses to copyright infringement, including fair use, are not to be affected by the DMCA, 17 U.S.C. § 1201(c)(1), this means merely that Lloyd would still have a fair use defense to *copyright* theories of liability that Greta might bring. It does not get Lloyd off the hook for *DMCA* theories of liability.

X-6.   **Answer (D) is correct.** The DMCA permits the circumvention of a technological measure in furtherance of good-faith encryption research. *See* 17 U.S.C. § 1201(g). Here, Vanna's work was clearly in bad faith because she decrypted ContentKey in order to get back at DynaCorp, one of many corporations she dislikes. Moreover, Vanna took no steps to notify DynaCorp about the results of her research, *see Universal City Studios, Inc. v. Reimerdes*, 111 F. Supp. 2d 294, 321 (S.D.N.Y. 2000), *aff'd sub nom. Universal City Studios, Inc. v. Corley*, 273 F.3d 429 (2d Cir. 2001) (Internet posting of software used to decrypt DVD encryption technology deemed evidence of absence of good-faith encryption research), and did not disseminate it in a manner likely to result in advancing the state of encryption research generally (i.e., in a research journal or a credible website as opposed to her personal website).

Answer (A) is incorrect because encryption research can be in good faith regardless of whether it is undertaken for profit.

Answer (B) is incorrect because, while the DMCA protects encryption research, it does so only for good-faith encryption research, and Vanna's work does not fall into that category for the reasons explained above.

Answer (C) is incorrect because there are various research safe harbors under the DMCA, including, but not limited to, the encryption safe harbor discussed above.

X-7. **Answer (A) is correct.** The DMCA prohibits the providing or distribution of false copyright management information ("CMI"), 17 U.S.C. § 1202(a), and the removal or alteration of CMI, *id.* § 1202(b). "Copyright Management Information" includes information that identifies a copyrighted work, its author, its copyright owner, its creator, as well as terms and conditions for use of the work. *Id.* § 1202(c).

Here, the notice that Sculptor placed on "Step" is clearly CMI because it identifies terms and conditions for the use of the work, and Collector has violated the DMCA's CMI regulations by removing the label.

Answer (B) is incorrect because violating the licensing agreement may give rise to a cause of action on a breach of contract or copyright infringement theory, but does not implicate the CMI regulations of the DMCA.

Answer (C) is incorrect because nothing in the DMCA's CMI provisions indicates that they are limited to digital material only.

Answer (D) is incorrect because CMI need not identify the author, but can include information about the author of the work, the owner of the work, the creator of the work, or terms and conditions of its use. *Id.* CMI need only list one of these features, not all of them.

X-8. No. The DMCA's provisions protecting the integrity of CMI require that in order to be actionable, any removal or alteration of CMI must be intentional. 17 U.S.C. § 1202. Because Collector's eradication of the label in this question was a mere inadvertent by-product of cleaning the statue, Sculptor cannot recover against Collector on a DMCA theory. This does not mean that Sculptor is entirely out of luck, of course. Collector's conduct was still wrongful because it violated the terms of the license, and so Sculptor may have a valid breach of contract cause of action, as well as a copyright infringement claim for the unauthorized public distribution of "Step."

X-9. **Answer (C) is correct.** Courts have broad discretion to impose a variety of penalties when a defendant is found to have violated sections 1201 or 1202 of the DMCA. These include injunctive relief, 17 U.S.C. § 1203(b); actual or statutory damages, *id.* § 1203(c); court costs and attorney's fees, *id.* § 1203(b); and criminal fines and imprisonment, *id.* § 1204(a).

Answer (A) is incorrect because it fails to include any of the criminal penalties available for violations of sections 1201 and 1202.

Answer (B) is incorrect because it includes punitive damages, which are not available for violations of sections 1201 and 1202.

Answer (D) is incorrect because it does not include imprisonment, which is available for violations of sections 1201 and 1202.

X-10.   **Answer (D) is correct.** In cases of repeated violations of sections 1201 or 1202 of the DMCA, courts have the discretion, but are not required, to increase the damages award up to three times. 17 U.S.C. § 1203(c)(3). In cases of innocent violations of those sections, courts may, but are not required to, reduce or remit the total award of damages. *Id.* § 1203(c)(5).

   Answers (A), (B), and (C) are incorrect for the reasons stated above.

X-11.   **Answer (A) is correct.** Fair use is a defense to copyright infringement, but not DMCA liability. 17 U.S.C. § 107. Here, Christa's claim against Eber is based only on the DMCA, alleging that Eber's accessing her film constitutes an unlawful circumvention of a technological measure put in place by a copyright owner to effectively control access to a copyrighted work. Eber's invocation of fair use is thus irrelevant. *See Universal City Studios, Inc. v. Corley*, 273 F.3d 429, 459 (2d Cir. 2001) (rejecting applicability of fair use defense to DMCA actions).

   Answer (B) is incorrect because while bad-faith behavior like hacking might make a court less disposed to find that a use is fair, it does not categorically preclude a finding of fair use.

   Answer (C) is incorrect because fair use is actually less available where authors have not yet published their works of authorship. *See* 17 U.S.C. § 107(3); *Harper & Row, Publishers, Inc. v. Nation Enterprises*, 471 U.S. 539, 554 (1985) ("The unpublished nature of a work is a key, though not necessarily determinative, factor tending to negate a defense of fair use.").

   Answer (D) is incorrect because courts have never held that fair use gives users an unlimited right of access, for the reasons explained above.

X-12.   Your client can rest easy tonight. Lexi has not manufactured or distributed the *Free Gutenberg* program, nor has she used the program to gain access to eBook files, because she has paid the rental fee for each. Therefore, Lexi has not violated 17 U.S.C. § 1201(a). Lexi has used the *Free Gutenberg* program to manipulate the use limitations set in place by the technological measures installed by eBooksOnline.com. Because Lexi has not manufactured or distributed the *Free Gutenberg* program, she has not violated 17 U.S.C. § 1201(b). Lexi's use of the *Free Gutenberg* program to gain greater use of a file to which she already has access, is not unlawful.

X-13.   **Answer (D) is correct.** Circumvention of a technological measure that effectively controls access is prohibited only when access to a work protected by copyright is controlled. 17 U.S.C. § 1201(a). All of the works that are protected by Maxwell's encryption are no longer protected by copyright. Therefore, the anti-circumvention protections of section 1201 do not apply.

   Answer (A) is incorrect because the owner of a copy of a work that has entered the public domain has the right not to license the use of that work.

   Answer (B) is incorrect because the owner of a copy of a work that has entered the public domain has the right not to grant access to that work.

   Answer (C) is incorrect because, unless it is expressly permitted by the exceptions listed in section 1201, an ultimate use of an accessed work that is beneficial to the public does not excuse the circumvention of a technological measure that made the access possible.

PRACTICE FINAL EXAM: ANSWERS

PRACTICE FINAL EXAM
MULTIPLE-CHOICE & SHORT-ANSWER ANSWERS

XI-1.   **Answer (C) is correct.** *Gorgon's Delight* is a pictorial work that was fixed in a tangible medium of expression: the skin on Carlos' back. That this "copy" is unusual does not mean that it is not a copy. Copies are "material objects, other than phonorecords, in which a work is fixed and from which the work can be perceived, reproduced, or otherwise communicated, either directly or with the aid of a machine." 17 U.S.C. § 101. Carlos' back meets all of these criteria.

The fixation requirement demands only that the work persist in the medium for more than a transitory duration, and most tattoos last for the duration of their recipient's life. Hence the adage: "Love lasts forever, but a tattoo lasts six months longer." In this case, of course, that did not happen; rather, Carlos (and his body) ceased to exist shortly after the fixation of *Gorgon's Delight*. That this particular medium of expression happened to disintegrate quickly, though, does not mean that at the time of fixation it was not tangible. A poem written in ink on paper is clearly sufficiently fixed in order for copyright to vest, even if its author burns the paper seconds after completing the poem. *See Peter Pan Fabrics, Inc. v. Rosstex Fabrics, Inc.*, 733 F. Supp. 174, 177 (S.D.N.Y. 1990) ("Once a work is fixed, its subsequent destruction does not vitiate its copyright.").

Answer (A) is incorrect because *Gorgon's Delight* was fixed, and in a tangible medium of expression: Carlos' back.

Answer (B) is incorrect because the length of fixation in a tangible medium of expression is not relevant to whether the initial fixation was in a tangible medium of expression.

Answer (D) is incorrect because courts have not held that tattoos are objectionable as a matter of public policy.

XI-2.   **Answer (D) is correct.** Gene's plot treatment is likely an uncopyrightable *scene a faire*, because it is nothing more than a collection of familiar plot clichés. *See, e.g., Nelson v. Grisham*, 942 F. Supp. 649, 653 (D.D.C. 1996) (presence in the novel, *The Chamber*, of media, politicians, and jail house personnel, as well as the frenzy with which last minute appeals are made, "are all stock events and scenes that are expected in any book about the representation of a death row inmate"). In addition, the Jack character in *Seeing the Light* is insufficiently developed in the plot treatment to merit copyright protection. The drunk, abusive husband is a stock character that appears in numerous literary works, and Gene has done nothing to make Jack more than just a stereotype. That the characters share the same name is some evidence that Bill may have been affected by Gene's plot treatment in writing *The Last Runaway*, but this is irrelevant because Gene's character did not possess enough originality to merit copyright protection. *See Nichols v. Universal Pictures Corp.*, 45 F.2d 119 (2d Cir. 1930) (characters must be "sufficiently fleshed out" to merit copyright protection).

Answer (A) is incorrect. While the rule governing the copyrightability of literary characters in the Second Circuit — and indeed, the majority of federal circuits — is broader than the minority rule (which may require that, in order to gain copyright protection, literary characters constitute the story being told rather than a mere plot device, *see Rice v. Fox Broadcasting Co.*, 330 F.3d 1170, 1176 (9th Cir. 2003) ("Mystery Magician" held to be merely a chessman in the game of telling the story of how tricks are performed)), the prevailing test for copyrightability of literary characters is not nearly broad enough to encompass the Jack character in *Seeing the Light*.

Answer (B) is incorrect because Jack is not nearly sufficiently original to merit copyright protection, even when all of the character's features are taken into account. That Bill used the name "Jack" in his screenplay does not change matters. Names are typically not copyrightable. U.S. Copyright Office Circular No. 34 (Nov. 2009) ("Copyright law does not protect names[.]").

Answer (C) is incorrect because the unauthorized use of a copyrighted work of authorship in any tangible medium of expression amounts to infringement, regardless of the medium in which the author fixed the initial work.

XI-3.   **Answer (A) is correct.** Mal copied Cal's object code for *Iterate* without permission. The literal elements of computer operating programs and application programs — such as object code — are copyrightable subject matter, protectable as literary works. *Apple Computer, Inc. v. Formula Int'l, Inc.*, 725 F.2d 521, 523 (9th Cir. 1984) (object code held to be copyrightable). Mal's unauthorized copying thus amounts to infringement.

Answer (B) is incorrect because Cal's argument is a breach of contract claim, and (regardless of its validity) it cannot give rise to a copyright infringement cause of action.

Answer (C) is incorrect because both object and source code amount to copyrightable literary works. *Apple Computer, Inc. v. Franklin Computer Corp.*, 714 F.2d 1240, 1248–49 (3d Cir. 1983) (computer programs are copyrightable subject matter regardless of whether they are expressed in human-readable source code or machine-readable object code).

Answer (D) is incorrect because Mal reproduced Cal's computer code and sold it as *ReIterate*.

XI-4.   **Answer (B) is correct.** Chris can reproduce and distribute Betty's musical work if he is licensed to do so. Chris must either obtain a consensual mechanical license from Betty, or he can reproduce and distribute *Summer Fugue* without her permission so long as he pays her the applicable mechanical license fee required by the Copyright Act. 17 U.S.C. § 115 (creating limitation on exclusive rights of owners of musical works whereby via compulsory license the composition can be recorded, manufactured in phonorecords, and sold to the public for its private use, as long as the statutory royalty per unit is paid to the copyright owner). KHIT must also pay royalties to Betty for publicly performing her musical work, though it need not pay royalties to Chris for publicly performing his sound recording. Sound recording owners do not have a right of public performance via analog media. *See* 17 U.S.C. § 106(4) (excluding sound recordings from public performance right); *but cf. id.* § 106(6) (creating digital public transmission right for sound recording owners).

Answers (A), (C), and (D) are incorrect because they inaccurately describe the owners' rights and users' obligations described above.

XI-5. **Answer (C) is correct.** The "ZoomMeister" model is not a useful article, but an aesthetic object. *See* 17 U.S.C. § 101 (definition of "useful article"); *Pivot Point Int'l, Inc. v. Charlene Products, Inc.*, 372 F.3d 913, 919 (7th Cir. 2004) ("A work that merely portrays a useful article or conveys information is not deemed a useful article and may be protected by copyright."). It was not built as a serious design prototype, but simply as a fanciful aspiration for what an imaginary futuristic vehicle might look like. Nor do the models have any utilitarian functions (except as a mere paperweight), and it is clear that they are valued primarily for their aesthetic, not utilitarian functions (hence the executives' saying that the models "[l]ook so cool"). In light of this, the model is simply an aesthetic object, similar to a sculpture or painting, and falls well within the ambit of copyright protection. This means that FunCo's unauthorized reproduction of the model is actionable, and MWB can bring a successful infringement suit.

Answer (A) is incorrect because it gets the law exactly backward. It is where objects are *not* useful articles that they are clearly protected by copyright law.

Answers (B) and (D) are incorrect because separability analysis is unnecessary where an object is not a useful article.

XI-6. **Answer (B) is correct.** Assuming that Len has not transferred ownership in the musical work *Green Acres*, he still owns the copyright in it as of 1980, because the work will still be in the initial twenty-eight-year term of protection. Janine, by contrast, is out of luck. Her rendition of *Green Acres* did not vest any federal copyright in the sound recording. Sound recordings fixed prior to February 15, 1972, are not protected by federal copyright law. Such works may be protected, if at all, by state common-law copyright, property, unfair competition, or criminal law. *See Capitol Records, Inc. v. Naxos of America, Inc.*, 372 F.3d 471, 477–78 (2d Cir. 2004).

Answers (A), (C), and (D) are incorrect because they inaccurately describe the rights of the respective federal ownership interests at issue.

XI-7. **Answer (D) is correct.** A derivative work that has been based upon an underlying work which is protected by copyright, without authorization, may be denied copyright protection. *See* 17 U.S.C. § 103(a); *Pickett v. Prince*, 207 F.3d 402, 406 (7th Cir. 2000) (creator of an unauthorized guitar shaped like a copyrighted symbol has no claim to copyright); *Watkins v. Chesapeake Custom Homes, L.L.C.*, 330 F. Supp. 2d 563, 572 (D. Md. 2004) (a derivative copyright that is based on a copyrighted work requires the authorization of the copyright owner in order to be "lawful" and thus valid). Because KaraokeCo did not acquire the permission of the musical work owners before it made its karaoke arrangements of those works, KaraokeCo forfeits any copyright protection in its works, and does not have any rights to enforce against Krooner Ken, though the owners of the musical works may well be able to sue Ken for infringement.

Answer (A) is incorrect because while copyright infringement is a strict liability offense, KaraokeCo has no enforceable copyrights because it used the initial musical works unlawfully.

Answer (B) is incorrect because Krooner Ken need not invoke the fair use privilege in light of KaraokeCo's having no enforceable copyrights in its arrangements. That said, Krooner Ken's obvious profit motivation in releasing his DVD and the existence of licensing procedures would cast doubt on any fair use claims.

Answer (C) is incorrect because the section 115 compulsory mechanical license does not apply where, as here, the lyrics are separately provided, making the CD a copy, rather than a phonorecord, that falls outside the ambit of section 115. *See ABKCO Music, Inc. v. Stellar Records, Inc.,* 96 F.3d 60 (2d Cir. 1996) (karaoke CD-ROM did not fall within section 115's compulsory mechanical license). Moreover, section 115 does not give users carte blanche to reproduce and distribute musical works without limit. Rather, it allows them to do so only where they remit a statutory mechanical license fee to the musical work owners, which KaraokeCo did not do here.

XI-8.   **Answer (D) is correct.** Lola's personal, descriptive reviews of restaurants are fixed literary works that easily exceed the minimum requirements for originality. Moreover, her selection of particular restaurants is separately copyrightable as a compilation because it evinces originality insofar as Lola personally chose restaurants to feature (and not feature) in her guide. 17 U.S.C. § 103; *Feist Publications, Inc. v. Rural Telephone Service Company, Inc.,* 499 U.S. 340, 357 (1991) (copyright in factual compilations is limited to selection or arrangement of material).

Answer (A) is incorrect because while facts and research are not copyrightable on their own, *Hoehling v. Universal City Studios, Inc.,* 618 F.2d 972 (2d Cir. 1980) (historical facts are not copyrightable), compilations of facts can be copyrightable to the extent that the author contributes original expression about, or selection or arrangement of, those facts, *Feist Publications, Inc. v. Rural Telephone Service Company, Inc.,* 499 U.S. 340, 357 (1991), as Lola did here.

Answers (B) and (C) are incorrect because the arrangement of the information in Lola's guide did not evince sufficient originality to be copyrightable. Lola merely placed the reviews in alphabetical order, which is a commonplace organizational scheme that does not reflect any original input. *Feist Publications, Inc. v. Rural Telephone Service Company, Inc.,* 499 U.S. 340, 357 (1991) (organizing a compilation alphabetically does not reflect any original input by the author).

XI-9.   **Answer (C) is correct.** Regardless of Melissa's status relative to the U.S. Government (i.e., whether she is an employee or independent contractor), *Against the Current* cannot be a work made for hire because it was clearly created outside the scope of her employment. 17 U.S.C. § 101 ("A 'work made for hire' is . . . a work prepared by an employee within the scope of his or her employment.").

Factors used in determining the scope of employment include whether the creation of the work is within the employee's job description; whether the work is of a type traditionally created by a person in the employee's position; whether it was created during official hours; on the employer's premises; using the employer's equipment; with the aid of the employer's support personnel; or using information available to the employee as part of the employee's employment and whether the work was related to the employer's projects. *See Scherr v. Universal Match Corp.,* 417 F.2d 497, 500–01 (2d Cir. 1969); *Shaul v. Cherry Valley-Springfield Central School Dist.,* 363 F.3d 177, 186 (2d Cir. 2004) (educational materials produced in furtherance of employment duties of teacher deemed work made for hire). Here, Melissa created *Against the Current* during her free time, in her own studio, using her own art supplies. In light of all this, the painting was not within the scope of her part-time employment for the U.S. Government, and the author of the copyright is Melissa.

Answer (A) is incorrect because while Melissa may be an employee of the federal government, she was not acting in the scope of her employment when she created *Against the Current*, so that the painting cannot be a work made for hire.

Answer (B) is incorrect because Melissa is, at least to some extent, an employee of the federal government, though this does not dispose of the work made for hire status of *Against the Current*, for reasons explained above.

Answer (D) is incorrect because while works of the U.S. Government are not subject to copyright protection, *see* 17 U.S.C. § 105, works created for the U.S. Government by independent contractors, *United States v. Washington Mint, LLC*, 115 F. Supp. 2d 1089 (D. Minn. 2000) (design of Sacajawea coin created by independent contractor authored by the independent contractor, not U.S. Government), or by U.S. Government employees outside the scope of their employment, *see* 17 U.S.C. § 101 ("A 'work of the United States Government' is a work prepared by an officer or employee of the United States Government as part of that person's official duties."), can be copyrighted.

XI-10.   **Answer (D) is correct.** The copyright in *South Atlantic* vested in 1921, upon publication with proper copyright notice, and its renewal in the twenty-eighth year of its initial term initially entitled the copyright owner to fifty-six years of copyright protection, which would have meant that the work entered the public domain in 1977. However, the Interim Copyright Term Renewal Act specified that renewal terms of federal copyright protection which would have expired between September 19, 1962, and December 31, 1977, were automatically continued through December 31, 1977, and brought into the 1976 Act. These interim extensions of copyright protection were periodically passed by Congress in anticipation of the "new" Copyright Act extending the renewal terms still further. As of January 1, 1978, these works, which were previously protected by the 1909 Copyright Act, obtained the protection of the 1976 Act. Specific duration rules are then applied which provide copyright protection for seventy-five years from the date federal protection initially vested, unless the renewal occurred after 1950, in which case copyright protection is provided for ninety-five years from the date federal protection initially vested. 17 U.S.C. § 304. Thus, the total coverage for *South Atlantic* is seventy-five years from its date of vesting, so that it will enter the public domain at the end of 1996.

Answer (A) is incorrect because it wrongly assumes a vesting date of 1919, when *South Atlantic* was fixed in a tangible medium of expression. Under the 1909 Act, copyright did not vest until publication with proper notice or registration with the Copyright Office.

Answer (B) is incorrect because it fails to take into account the term extensions effected by the Interim Copyright Term Renewal Act, as explained above.

Answer (C) is incorrect because while it does take into account the term extensions effected by the Interim Copyright Term Renewal Act, it wrongly assumes a vesting date of 1919, rather than the actual vesting date of 1921.

XI-11.   **Answer (C) is correct.** Federal copyright vested in *Prohibition Blues* in 1928, when the authors registered the unpublished work with the Copyright Office. The renewal term of the copyright was due to expire in 1984, but was extended by the 1976 Act and 1998 Copyright Term Renewal Act, so that the total copyright term for *Prohibition Blues* will be ninety-five years, set to expire at the end of 2023.

Answer (A) is incorrect because it fails to take into account the two extensions of the renewal term effected by the 1976 Act and 1998 Copyright Term Extension Act.

Answer (B) is incorrect because it fails to take into account the twenty-year extension to the renewal term effected by the 1998 Copyright Term Extension Act.

Answer (D) is incorrect because it wrongly assumes that a life-based 1976 Act copyright term applies, measuring seventy years from the death of the latest surviving joint author. For reasons explained above, this is not the case.

XI-12.   **Answer (C) is correct.** Because Sam's self-portrait was unpublished and unregistered, it was initially unprotected by federal copyright, but was protected by perpetual state common-law copyright. Works, such as the self-portrait, were protected by state common-law copyright when the 1976 Copyright Act took effect on January 1, 1978. At that time they lost their perpetual common-law protection and received the same duration of protection as those works created on or after January 1, 1978. *See Martha Graham School and Dance Foundation, Inc. v. Martha Graham Center of Contemporary Dance, Inc.*, 380 F.3d 624, 632–33 (2d Cir. 2004). In no case, however, did the protection of these works expire prior to December 31, 2002. If the work was published between January 1, 1978, and December 31, 2002, copyright protection will not expire before December 31, 2047. 17 U.S.C. § 303(a).

On January 1, 1978, the copyright term of Sam's self-portrait was converted into a term of the author's life plus seventy years, or 2010. The display of the self-portrait at the gallery by Tracy did not constitute a publication; therefore, the second statutory minimum period of protection does not apply.

Answer (A) is incorrect because it assumes that a standard 1909 Act bifurcated term applies to the self-portrait. It does not, because federal copyright never vested in the work prior to 1978.

Answer (B) is incorrect because the first statutory minimum period of protection for common law works does not apply where, as here, the standard 1976 Act term would be longer.

Answer (D) is incorrect because Tracy's display of the self-portrait in 1992 did not extend the copyright term through 2047, as explained above.

XI-13.   **Answer (A) is correct.** In order for a work to be a joint work, the authors must intend, at the time of the creation of each of their component materials, to create a joint work. Each author must intend his or her contribution to constitute a part of a total work to which another will make or has made a contribution. As long as this intent is present, the authors need not even know one another. *Edward B. Marks Music Corp. v. Jerry Vogel Music Co.*, 140 F.2d 266 (2d Cir. 1944). *See Weissmann v. Freeman*, 868 F.2d 1313 (2d Cir. 1989); *Systems XIX, Inc. v. Parker*, 30 F. Supp. 2d 1225, 1229 (N.D. Cal. 1998). Here, Sal did not intend to create a joint work with Ed; indeed, Sal did not even consider Ed to be a meaningful contributor to the work. Because there was no mutual intent to create a joint work, Ed's claim to joint authorship must fail.

Answer (B) is incorrect because mere financial contributions do not suffice to make the contributor a joint author. Rather, the contribution of each joint author must be copyrightable material. *E.g., Natkin v. Winfrey*, 111 F. Supp. 2d 1003, 1008–10 (N.D. Ill. 2000) (producer of television show did not provide copyrightable subject matter to photographs of the television set or individuals).

Answer (C) is incorrect because Ed's self-perception as a joint author is insufficient, on its own, to give rise to joint authorship status. Courts require that both authors think of themselves as joint authors. *Childress v. Taylor*, 945 F.2d 500 (2d Cir. 1991) (stressing the centrality of mutual intent to create a joint work).

Answer (D) is incorrect because the jointly authored status of a work turns on the intent of the respective authors, not on the substantiality of the relative contributions. Even a significant contribution to the work by the alleged co-author does not automatically suffice to confer co-authorship status on that contributor. *See Aalmuhammed v. Lee*, 202 F.3d 1227, 1233 (9th Cir. 1999). Even if the dialogue contributed by Ed were copyrightable (and it may not be if it was not fixed), this would not suffice to make Ed a co-author.

XI-14.   **Answer (D) is correct.** These are all valid ways of creating joint ownership in a work of authorship. Note that the question dealt with joint ownership, not joint authorship. Creation of a jointly authored work is the most familiar way to give rise to joint ownership, but it is only one way of doing so. Other methods include transferring or willing the copyright to more than one person, or through state community property laws. *See In re Marriage of Worth*, 195 Cal. App. 3d 768, 241 Cal. Rptr. 135 (1987) (non-authoring spouse is joint owner of copyright in any work created by authoring spouse during the marriage). *But cf. Rodrigue v. Rodrigue*, 218 F.3d 432 (5th Cir. 2000) (under state community property law, the authoring-spouse retains copyright ownership and management, while non-authoring spouse retains right to enjoy one-half interest in the economic benefits of the copyrighted works). When the copyright is owned by a partnership, each partner is a co-owner of the copyright. *See Oddo v. Ries*, 743 F.2d 630, 632 (9th Cir. 1984).

Answers (A), (B), and (C) are incorrect because they do not take into account all the ways that a joint ownership can be created.

XI-15.   **Answer (C) is correct.** While Kelly clearly transferred to Rosalind ownership over the copy of *Good Friends* that she gave to her as a present, this gift did not effect transfer of the copyright in the poem. Therefore, the copyright in the poem was part of Kelly's estate when she died and became James' by devise. Any transfer of statutory copyright ownership (assignment or exclusive license), other than by operation of law, must be in writing and signed by the owner of the rights conveyed or her authorized agent. 17 U.S.C. § 204.

Answer (A) is incorrect. While the copy of the poem Kelly gave Rosalind was signed, the signature did not attest to a statement of copyright ownership transfer, but was only a way of authenticating the work, much like an artist may sign a portrait.

Answer (B) is incorrect. Transfers of copyright ownership must be written and signed; verbal transfers are insufficient. *Effects Associates, Inc. v. Cohen*, 908 F.2d 555 (9th Cir. 1990) (producer's argument that moviemakers do lunch, not contracts, was insufficient to make an oral agreement an exclusive license); *Weinstein Co. v. Smokewood Entertainment Group LLC*, 664 F. Supp. 2d 332, 339 (S.D.N.Y. 2009). Moreover, Kelly's statement to Rosalind does not clearly seek to transfer ownership over the poem's copyright, and may more sensibly be thought to refer to Rosalind being the owner of that copy of *Good Friends*.

Answer (D) is incorrect because there was no 2007 transfer of the copyright in *Good Friends*. Had there been such a transfer, though, the devise would not have extinguished it.

XI-16.   **Answer (B) is correct.** A transmitting organization that has the right to transmit any work may make an "ephemeral recording," a single copy of a particular program that must be subsequently destroyed if not preserved for archival purposes. 17 U.S.C. § 112; *Agee v. Paramount Communications, Inc.*, 59 F.3d 317 (2d Cir. 1995).

Answer (A) is incorrect because, while copyright is indeed a strict liability offense, this does not take into account the limitations on owners' rights imposed by section 112.

Answer (C) is incorrect because no courts have so held; public performance licenses are construed to extend only to public performance rights.

Answer (D) is incorrect because copying a part of any protected work amounts to a violation of the reproduction right, as long as the copying is more than de minimis. *See Walt Disney Productions v. Filmation Associates*, 628 F. Supp. 871 (C.D. Cal. 1986).

XI-17.   **Answer (A) is correct.** One who distributes or offers to distribute copies or phonorecords containing the sounds or images of a live musical performance, made without the consent of the performer, is subject to the same remedies as an infringer of copyright. 17 U.S.C. § 1101. By distributing copies of the unauthorized Smack bootlegs, then, Paramecium becomes liable under these provisions of federal law, even though its conduct does not violate any copyrights. Criminal liability exists for such conduct pursuant to 18 U.S.C. § 2319A.

Answer (B) is incorrect. The first sale defense applies only to copyright infringement, which is not the basis for Paramecium's federal liability.

Answer (C) is incorrect because while lack of fixation makes the concerts unavailable as a basis for liability on a copyright infringement theory, this does not obviate the possibility that Paramecium could be liable under the federal anti-bootlegging provisions. In addition, many concerts are fixed by the band and are sold at the end of the concert or subsequently streamed on a band's website.

Answer (D) is incorrect because selling is a form of distribution, and distribution of unauthorized bootlegs is a basis for liability under the federal anti-bootlegging provisions.

XI-18.   **Answer (D) is correct.** Zed is clearly liable to Deke because he reproduced copies of many of the poems to which Deke owned the copyright without authorization. Zed is also liable to B.P. McGee, because he copied the original selection and arrangement of poems that the publisher added to *Finding Grace* when McGee created the collective work. B.P. McGee is not, however, liable to Deke, because the owner of copyright in a collective work has the right to distribute to the public individual contributions as part of that particular collective work, any revision of that collective work, and any later collective work in the same series. 17 U.S.C. § 201(c). This privilege entitled B.P. McGee to create the second edition of *Finding Grace* without fear of an infringement suit from Deke.

Answers (A), (B), and (C) are incorrect because they misstate the correct liability of the respective parties, as explained above.

XI-19.   **Answer (C) is correct.** Sound recording owners do not have a right of public performance via analog means, such as radio stations, so Ray will not have to pay any royalties for publicly performing sound recordings via KRAY. Under the Digital Performance Right in Sound Recordings Act of 1995, copyright owners of sound recordings have a limited exclusive right to transmit their works to the public by means of digital audio transmissions. 17 U.S.C. § 106(6). Transmissions of sound recordings to the public by a noninteractive digital transmission may qualify for a "statutory license" (compulsory license). 17 U.S.C. § 114(d)(2). Courts have held that Internet transmissions fall into this category, even when originated by a local radio station exempted from section 106(6). *Bonneville Int'l Corp. v. Peters*, 347 F.3d 485, 495 (3d Cir. 2003). Ray will thus have to pay sound recording copyright owners a compulsory license or a negotiated license fee for digitally transmitting their works via www.kray.com and via the satellite radio service. Finally, transmissions of sound recordings to the public by an interactive digital transmission require a negotiated license from the owner of the copyright in the sound recording, so Ray will have to negotiate with sound recording copyright owners in order to transmit their works to the public via the on-demand streaming service.

Answers (A), (B), and (D) are incorrect because they misstate Ray's obligations to sound recording copyright owners as described above.

XI-20.   **Answer (B) is correct.** Only certain still photographs are protected by VARA, depending on their intended use. *See Pollara v. Seymour*, 344 F.3d 265, 269–70 (2d Cir. 2003) ("Congress explicitly limited VARA's protection to works 'intended for exhibition only,' as opposed to works intended for use in a publication or the photographer's photo album."). Photographs are protected only where the initial rendering of a still photographic image was produced for exhibition purposes only and signed by the author. Any copy in a limited edition of 200 copies or fewer is also protected if the copies are signed and consecutively numbered by the author. 17 U.S.C. § 101 (defining the kind of "work of visual art" that is protected by VARA). Bill's casual cellphone picture of Denise clearly does not qualify, because it was not meant for exhibition and was not signed.

Answer (A) is incorrect because the photograph was not produced for exhibition purposes. In addition, the protection of a "limited edition" applies only where there is a series of reproductions that number 200 or fewer, and they are signed and numbered by the author. 17 U.S.C. § 101.

Answer (C) is incorrect because VARA does vest a right of integrity in authors of works of visual art. An author has the right to prevent the intentional distortion, mutilation, or other modification of her work that would be prejudicial to her honor or reputation. 17 U.S.C. § 106A(a)(3)(A); *see Berrios Nogueras v. Home Depot*, 330 F. Supp. 2d 48, 50 (D. Puerto Rico 2004).

Answer (D) is incorrect because there is no such affirmative defense.

XI-21.   **Answer (C) is correct.** During the decennial period (1/1/1978–2/28/1989), federal copyright vested in original works fixed in tangible mediums of expression, but could be forfeited to the public domain through general publication without inclusion of proper copyright notice, though owners had an opportunity to cure the lack of notice by registering the work before or within five years of publication without notice and making a reasonable effort to add notice to all copies publicly distributed in the United States after the omission has been discovered. 17 U.S.C. §§ 401(a), 405(a)(2). Here, Iris' copyright vested upon fixation in a tangible medium of expression in 1980, but was ceded to the public domain for failure of notice, and a corresponding failure to cure that notice, by the time Queen Burger published its brochure in 1986.

Answer (A) is incorrect because it fails to take into account the copyright notice requirement that prevailed during the decennial period.

Answer (B) is incorrect because Iris' publication of the work without proper copyright notice divested (not invested) federal copyright in the work.

Answer (D) is incorrect because, unlike the situation under the 1909 Act, Iris' omission of copyright notice from a published work in 1981 was curable, not irrevocable.

XI-22.   **Answer (D) is correct.** A general publication occurred when a possessory interest in tangible copies of the work is made available to the general public with the consent of the copyright owner. *See Shoptalk, Ltd. v. Concorde-New Horizons Corp.*, 168 F.3d 586, 590 (2d Cir. 1999). Posting the work in her break room did not effect publication because it constituted a display and did not make tangible copies of the speech available to her co-workers who, in addition, constituted a limited group of twenty people, rather than to the general public. Reading the speech during a broadcast did not effect publication because it did not cause copies of the work to be available to the public. A performance does not constitute a publication. *See Estate of Martin Luther King, Jr., Inc. v. CBS, Inc.*, 194 F.3d 1211, 1215–16 (2d Cir. 1999). Jean's distribution of individual copies did not effect a general publication, because the distribution was carefully limited to personal acquaintances, rather than to the public at large and for a limited purpose, thus constituting a limited publication. *See White v. Kimmell*, 193 F.2d 744, 746–47 (9th Cir. 1952). Schriver & Co.'s offering the book to the public for sale did constitute a general publication, though, because it met all the applicable criteria for publication that prevailed under the 1909 Act.

Answers (A), (B), and (C) are incorrect for the reasons explained above.

XI-23.   Ken's screenplay was initially an unpublished work, which means that it was protected by state common-law copyright under the 1909 Act. However, in most jurisdictions, an unpublished screenplay protected by common law is published by a motion picture to the extent the screenplay is incorporated into the motion picture. *See Shoptalk, Ltd. v. Concorde-New Horizons Corp.*, 168 F.3d 586, 590 (2d Cir. 1999); *Classic Film Museum, Inc. v. Warner Bros., Inc.*, 453 F. Supp. 852 (D. Me. 1978), *aff'd*, 597 F.2d 13 (1st Cir. 1979). As a result, where the motion picture contains a copyright notice, as in this case, the screenplay is invested with federal copyright protection with an initial term of twenty-eight years. If the copyright in the screenplay is not renewed, the screenplay falls into the public domain. That means the copyright in the *Blood Feud* screenplay entered the public domain at the end of 1984. The copyright in the *Blood Feud* motion picture will enter the public domain at the end of 2051. However, the Ninth Circuit has ruled that where the entirety of a script or treatment is not incorporated into the motion picture, the underlying work was not published by the motion picture and remained protected by common-law copyright until it was published independent of the motion picture, at which time it was invested with federal copyright law if it was published with copyright notice. If no such independent publication occurred prior to January 1, 1978, the underlying work became invested with federal copyright protection. *See Richlin v. Metro-Goldwyn-Mayer Pictures, Inc.*, 531 F.3d 962, 975–77 (9th Cir. 2008) (inclusion of elements of underlying work in motion picture published with proper copyright notice did not secure a federal statutory copyright for the underlying work as an independent work, which is available only if it was separately registered or published as an independent work). Assuming no independent publication of the *Blood Feud* screenplay occurred prior to January 1, 1978, it will be protected by federal copyright for seventy years after Ken's death.

XI-24.   **Answer (A) is correct.** The filing of a registration is a prerequisite to the filing of a copyright infringement action. 17 U.S.C. § 411. Most courts require that a copyright owner formally register a derivative work with the Copyright Office as a prerequisite to filing a suit for infringement of that derivative work. *See, e.g., Murray Hill Publications, Inc. v. ABC Communications, Inc.*, 264 F.3d 622, 630–32 (6th Cir. 2001); *Creations Unlimited, Inc. v. McCain*, 112 F.3d 814, 816 (5th Cir. 1997).

Answer (B) is incorrect because amending the registration for the screenplay would not have enabled the court to exercise jurisdiction over the motion picture.

Answer (C) is incorrect because registration of an individual work does not give courts jurisdiction over derivative works without a separate registration of the latter.

Answer (D) is incorrect because federal subject-matter jurisdiction cannot be waived.

XI-25.   **Answer (C) is correct.** This is a work made for hire because it was created by Vince Virtual, an Initech employee acting within the scope of his employment. 17 U.S.C. § 101 (defining "work made for hire"). The term of copyright protection for such works is ninety-five years after the work's first publication or 120 years after its creation, whichever is earlier. 17 U.S.C. § 302(c). The work was created in 1980, but generally published in 1995. The brochure will enter the public domain in the earlier of (1980 +120) or (1995+95), which is 2090.

Answers (A), (B), and (D) are incorrect because they specify the wrong date at which the work will enter the public domain.

XI-26.   **Answer (B) is correct.** Access can be proven by evidence that the defendant had actually read or heard plaintiff's work, or had a reasonable opportunity to view or hear the plaintiff's work. *See Peel & Co. v. The Rug Market*, 238 F.3d 391, 394 (5th Cir. 2001) ("reasonable opportunity to view the copyright work"). Here, the Acme employee who became a consultant at Zenith shortly after leaving Acme had heard about Harriet's script in detail during the pitch meeting. This is sufficient evidence to enable an inference of access, since that employee easily could have discussed the script with Zenith.

Answer (A) is incorrect because substantial similarity is not sufficient to enable an inference of access. Such a rule would fail to take account of the possibility that two works are similar because of independent creation.

Answer (C) is incorrect because the corporate receipt doctrine applies only to employees, *Moore v. Columbia Pictures Industries, Inc.*, 972 F.2d 939, 942–43 (8th Cir. 1992), while the source of access at Zenith was an independent consultant. A reasonable possibility of access can be established where a supervisory employee or an employee within the work unit from which the corporate defendant's work was developed had the opportunity to view or hear the plaintiff's work.

Answer (D) is incorrect because copying is typically proven by circumstantial evidence, because direct evidence of copying is characteristically difficult to find. *Swirsky v. Carey,*

376 F.3d 841, 844 (9th Cir. 2004) ("element of copying is rarely the subject of direct evidence").

XI-27.   **Answer (D) is correct.** That Jamie's copying was inadvertent or unconscious does not amount to a defense to infringement. *See Three Boys Music Corp. v. Bolton*, 212 F.3d 477 (9th Cir. 2000) (holding that subconscious copying amounts to infringement). Nor is Jamie's taking de minimis. A taking is de minimis if it is so meager and fragmentary that the average audience would not recognize the misappropriation. *Fisher v. Dees*, 794 F.2d 432, 435 n.2 (9th Cir. 1986). Here, by contrast, Jamie took six full paragraphs of original expression from Ken's treatise. It also diminishes Jamie's de minimis argument that Ken immediately recognized the taking. *See Jobete Music Co., Inc. v. Johnson Communications, Inc.*, 285 F. Supp. 2d 1077, 1088–89 (S.D. Ohio 2003) (de minimis defense not available where anyone familiar with the musical work would recognize it instantly). Finally, it is not relevant that the portion of Ken's treatise that Jamie took was small in relation to the whole. The focus is on the similarities between the plaintiff's and defendant's works. *Sheldon v. Metro-Goldwyn Pictures Corp.*, 81 F.2d 49, 56 (2d Cir. 1936) ("[N]o plagiarist can excuse the wrong by showing how much of his work he did not pirate."). Because she does not have a defense, Jamie's unauthorized taking of Ken's protected literary work amounts to infringement.

Answers (A), (B), and (C) are incorrect for the reasons explained above.

XI-28.   **Answer (A) is correct.** Vicarious liability can be imposed when a party has the right and ability to supervise the infringing activity and also has a direct financial interest in such activities. *Shapiro, Bernstein & Co., Inc. v. H.L. Green Co., Inc.*, 316 F.2d 304 (2d Cir. 1963). Here, First Waltz clearly has vicariously infringed because it has the right and ability to stop New Biz from selling the infringing CDs at the flea market. In addition, First Waltz has a financial interest in those sales because it profits from the entrance fees of those who purchase the CDs, from the rental fee paid by New Biz, and its sales of food and beverages at the flea market. *See Metro-Goldwyn-Mayer Studios Inc. v. Grokster, Ltd.*, 125 S. Ct. 2764, 2776 (2005) ("One . . . infringes vicariously by profiting from direct infringement while declining to exercise a right to stop or limit it."). Contributory infringement can be imposed when a party has knowledge of the infringing activity of another and induces, causes, or materially contributes to that infringing conduct. *Gershwin Publishing Corp. v. Columbia Artists Management, Inc.*, 443 F.2d 1159 (1971). Here, First Waltz has also contributorily infringed. First Waltz did have actual knowledge of the distributor's illegal activity because the wholesale prices of the CDs were suspiciously low, and because First Waltz engaged in willful ignorance by preventing New Biz from discussing his illegal acquisition of the sound recordings. Willful blindness to the infringing actions of the direct infringer may constitute actual knowledge. *See UMG Recordings, Inc. v. Sinnott*, 300 F. Supp. 2d 993, 999–1000 (E.D. Cal. 2004). First Waltz contributed to the infringing activity by providing a site for the sale of the infringing CDs.

Answers (B), (C), and (D) are incorrect for the reasons explained above.

XI-29.   **Answer (C) is correct.** Criminal liability may attach either where a person "infringes a copyright willfully and for purposes of commercial advantage or private financial gain," or "by the reproduction or distribution . . . of 1 or more copies or phonorecords of 1 or more copyrighted works, which have a total retail value of more than $1,000." 17 U.S.C. § 506(a). Here, while Quentin's infringement was willful, it was not done for the purpose of commercial advantage or private financial gain. Nor was Tina's photograph worth more than $1,000; rather, as Tina conceded, it was not worth anything financially.

Answer (A) is incorrect because willful infringement alone is not a sufficient basis for criminal copyright infringement.

Answer (B) is incorrect because bad faith is not the statutory standard for criminal copyright infringement.

Answer (D) is incorrect because Quentin infringed Tina's copyright in the picture as soon as he made an unauthorized digital copy of it; whether he actually printed the photograph is not relevant to whether he can be held criminally liable.

XI-30. **Answer (B) is correct.** Edgar's use clearly meets the four fair use factors codified by Congress in the 1976 Act. 17 U.S.C. § 107. His use is transformative because it recasts a political tract in the context of an expository article. The tract written by Felice is not creative. The amount of the tract Edgar took is reasonable in relation to the purpose and scale of his article. Finally, there does not seem to be any market for the tract, so his use of unauthorized quotations cannot damage any economic interests that Felice may have in it.

Answer (A) is incorrect because while reporting is one of the examples of fair uses featured in the preamble to section 107, no court has held that these categories are entitled to a per se fair use defense. The preamble provides "only general guidance about the sorts of copying that courts and Congress most commonly had found to be fair uses." *Campbell v. Acuff-Rose Music, Inc.*, 510 U.S. 569, 577 (1994).

Answer (C) is incorrect because Edgar's receiving a financial award for his article does not make that article wholly commercial. The mere fact that the use takes place in the context of a nominally commercial enterprise will not preclude the applicability of the fair use defense. *See Kelly v. Arriba Soft Corp.*, 280 F.3d 934, 940 (9th Cir. 2002).

Answer (D) is incorrect because seeking permission before use is not a prerequisite to claiming the fair use defense. *See, e.g., Campbell v. Acuff-Rose Music, Inc.*, 510 U.S. 569 (1994).

XI-31. **Answer (C) is correct.** The fair use defense has long common-law roots, *see, e.g., Folsom v. Marsh*, 9 F. Cas. 342 (1841), and was finally codified in the 1976 Act at 17 U.S.C. § 107. The Copyright Act requires judges to consider all four enumerated factors when evaluating a fair use defense, but the factors are nonexclusive. *See id.* ("In determining whether the use made of a work in any particular case is a fair use the factors to be considered *shall include*.") (emphasis added). In other words, judges must consider at least all four listed factors, but can include other factors in their analysis (though they rarely do so).

Answers (A) and (B) are incorrect because courts have never held that fair use is a constitutional right. *See Universal City Studios, Inc. v. Corley*, 273 F.3d 429, 458 (2d Cir. 2001).

Answer (D) is incorrect because courts *must* (not may) consider all four fair use factors when evaluating such a defense, for the reasons explained above.

XI-32. **Answer (D) is correct.** Dennis' use was essentially commercial, even if he did not formally sell the book, because he sought to have users give him money in exchange for downloading the text from his website. Nor was Dennis' use meaningfully transformative, because it was a mere change in medium, rather than a change in purpose or content. A mere change of format has been held not to be transformative. *See A & M Records, Inc. v. Napster, Inc.*, 239 F.3d 1004, 1015 (9th Cir. 2001) (downloading MP3 files does not transform the copyrighted work); *Infinity Broadcast Corp. v. Kirkwood*, 150 F.3d 104, 108 n.2 (2d Cir. 1998) (retransmitting radio transmissions over telephone lines deemed not transformative). Finally, it is not a defense that Dennis' use ultimately increased demand for Genevieve's work. The fact that the defendant's use may have a positive impact on copyright holder's market does not exonerate that use. *See Ringgold v. Black Entertainment Television*, 126 F.3d 70, 81 n.16 (2d Cir. 1997) (even if use in television program increased poster sales, plaintiff retained right to licensing fee).

Answer (A), (B), and (C) are incorrect for the reasons explained above.

XI-33. There is a three-year statute of limitations for copyright infringement actions. 17 U.S.C. § 507(b). The limitations period had more than lapsed by the time Fran brought her infringement suit in 2005, with all arguably infringing acts taking place decades before. As a result, Fran will not be able to bring an infringement action until D Films once again exploits the *One Man Down* motion picture.

The equitable defense of laches applies when there has been a sufficient passage of time between the plaintiff's knowledge of the injury and the date of bringing suit, and the presence of prejudice to the defendant. *Kling v. Hallmark Cards*, 225 F.3d 1030, 1036–37 (9th Cir. 2000). There is considerable debate, however, as to whether the defense of laches is applicable in a situation where the legislative act that creates a cause of action, such as the Copyright Act, expressly provides a statute of limitation. To allow a defense of laches during the three years that the Copyright Act permits an infringement action to be brought would undermine congressional power. To consider a laches defense outside of the three-year statute of limitations is unnecessary because the Copyright Act expressly prohibits such a copyright infringement action. That said, the Ninth Circuit has produced several decisions, though strongly criticized, that do recognize a defense of laches in copyright infringement actions. Under those cases, D Films may have a successful laches defense. While the time period to assert a laches defense varies, the very long delay by Fran in bringing her infringement suit against Zelda and D Films — with no real justification for the wait — likely supports such a defense, especially because D Films was prejudiced by Fran's long wait before filing an infringement suit. *Cf., e.g., Jackson v. Axton*, 25 F.3d 884 (9th Cir. 1994) (musician's claim of co-authorship was barred by laches after waiting twenty-two years to assert claim); *Trust Company Bank v. Putnam Publishing Group, Inc.*, 5 U.S.P.Q.2d 1874 (C.D. Cal. 1988) (nineteen-month delay in bringing action against alleged infringing novel was deemed sufficient to constitute laches).

Abandonment of copyright occurs only if there is an intent by the copyright proprietor to surrender the rights in her work. *Dam Things from Denmark v. Russ Berrie & Co., Inc.*, 290 F.3d 548, 560 (3d Cir. 2002) ("there must be either an act, or a failure to act, from which we can readily infer an intent to abandon the right"). Here, there is no overt act on Fran's part evidencing abandonment. D Films may argue that Fran abandoned her copyright when she gave a copy of the script to Zelda, but this argument will certainly fail. Fran gave Zelda the copy for comments only, and that copy had a clear indication of

Fran's reservation of copyright ownership in the underlying literary work.

XI-34. **Answer (A) is correct.** None of these purported affirmative defenses are availing. First, obscenity is not a defense to copyright infringement. The general rule is that copyright protection is to be accorded a work that has met the statutory prerequisites, even if it is obscene. *See Mitchell Brothers Film Group v. Cinema Adult Theater*, 604 F.2d 852 (5th Cir. 1979). Second, fraud on the Copyright Office arises only where a plaintiff knowingly fails to advise the Copyright Office of material facts related to the copyrightability of the work. *See Masquerade Novelty, Inc. v. Unique Industries, Inc.*, 912 F.2d 663, 667 (3d Cir. 1990). In light of the fact that the work's obscenity did not compromise its copyrightability, Joe had no obligation to disclose it, and his failure to do so cannot be construed as fraudulent. Finally, Joe's failure to police his work does not, without more, deprive him of the ability to bring suit for infringement. The failure to pursue third-party infringers is not a defense to copyright infringement. *See Capitol Records, Inc. v. Naxos of America, Inc.*, 372 F.3d 471, 484 (2d Cir. 2004).

Answers (B), (C), and (D) are incorrect for the reasons explained above.

XI-35. **Answer (B) is correct.** Most courts have found that the Copyright Act preempts state law claims of conversion. *See, e.g., United States ex rel. Berge v. Board of Trustees of Univ. of Alabama*, 104 F.3d 1453 (4th Cir. 1997). Unfair competition claims based on the unauthorized reproduction of the plaintiff's copyrightable work are generally held to be preempted. *See, e.g., Kodadek v. MTV Networks, Inc.*, 152 F.3d 1209, 1212–13 (9th Cir. 1998). By contrast, however, an action for the violation of the right of publicity is generally deemed not to be preempted. *See Facenda v. N.F.L. Films, Inc.*, 542 F.3d 1007, 1026–28 (3d Cir. 2008) (right of publicity statute's requirement of proof of commercial value provides an additional element beyond what copyright infringement claim requires); *Waits v. Frito-Lay, Inc.*, 978 F.2d 1093 (9th Cir. 1992) (tort of appropriation of voice is not preempted); *Landham v. Lewis Galoob Toys, Inc.*, 227 F.3d 619, 623 (6th Cir. 2000) (actor's right of publicity suit against toy manufacturer for marketing an action figure based on actor's screen persona was held to evoke the actor's personal identity, an inchoate idea not amendable to copyright protection).

Answers (A), (C), and (D) are incorrect for the reasons explained above.

XI-36. **Answer (A) is correct.** When considering a motion for a preliminary injunction in a copyright infringement case, most courts — including those in the Eleventh Circuit — traditionally analyze four elements. Those elements are the movant's likelihood of success on the merits, the irreparable harm that the movant would suffer in the absence of an injunction, balancing of these harms to the movant against the harm that the injunction would inflict on the nonmoving party, and public policy. *See Warren Pub., Inc. v. Microdos Data Corp.*, 115 F.3d 1509, 1516 (11th Cir.1997).

Here, all four elements weigh in favor of entering preliminary injunctive relief in favor of Hank. First, Hank has an extremely high likelihood of success on the merits because Welter unambiguously violated Hank's exclusive rights in *Trains and Levees* by making thousands of unauthorized copies of the literary work. Second, the injury is irreparable because Hank has shown that the actions of Welter Publishing causes Hank to lose control over his work, the time and manner in which it is to be presented to the public, as well as the effectiveness of Gladman's marketing campaign. Third, the balance of harms weighs in Hank's favor because an injunction would only delay Welter's releasing *Trains and Levees*, while the release of the book before its authorized publication date with Gladman would cost Hank much more in terms of lost revenue and decreased publicity. Fourth, courts typically find that it is in the public's interest to protect the copyright laws and the interests of copyright holders. *See, e.g., Intellectual Reserve, Inc. v. Utah Lighthouse Ministry, Inc.*, 75 F. Supp. 2d 1290, 1295 (D. Utah 1999).

Answer (B) is incorrect because there is no presumptive right to a preliminary injunction. On the contrary, Hank, as the nonmoving party, bears the burden of proof on this issue (though he has carried that burden, as explained above). The Supreme Court's decision in *eBay, Inc. v. MercExchange, L.L.C.*, 547 U.S. 388, 391 (2006), that disallowed a presumption of irreparable harm on a showing of likelihood of success on the merits, has been applied to copyright infringement actions. *See Metro-Goldwyn-Mayer Studios, Inc. v. Grokster, Ltd.*, 518 F. Supp. 2d 1197, 1211 (C.D. Cal. 2007) (plaintiff seeking injunctive relief in copyright infringement action has the burden of proving the four traditional factors).

Answer (C) is incorrect because loss of control of a copyrighted work and its release to the public likely constitutes an irreparable harm.

Answer (D) is incorrect because an injunction would only delay Welter's publishing *Trains and Levees*, while the release of the book before its authorized publication date with Gladman would cost Hank much more in terms of lost revenue and decreased publicity.

XI-37. **Answer (B) is correct.** A prevailing plaintiff in a copyright infringement action is entitled to recover actual damages suffered as a result of the infringement and any of the defendant's profits that are attributable to the infringement. *See Frank Music Corp. v. Metro-Goldwyn-Mayer, Inc.*, 772 F.2d 505 (9th Cir. 1985). Where, however, giving a prevailing plaintiff both actual damages *and* infringer's profits would amount to double-counting; the prevailing plaintiff is entitled only to the greater of the two figures. *See Abeshouse v. Ultragraphics, Inc.*, 754 F.2d 467 (2d Cir. 1985) (improper double-counting arises "when an infringing seller has to disgorge profits on sales that a copyright holder might have made and for which he may therefore claim damages in the form of lost profits.").

Here, Madelyn's actual damages attributable to TekCo's infringement are $10,000. TekCo's profits attributable to that infringement are $4,000 ($5,000 in gross profit less $1,000 in manufacturing expenses). Here, though, Madelyn's actual damages *are* TekCo's profits, and giving Madelyn both would amount to double-counting. She is thus entitled to the greater of the two figures, or $10,000.

Answers (A), (C), and (D) are incorrect because they state the wrong amount of damages.

XI-38. **Answer (A) is correct.** Statutory damages are to be calculated according to the number of works infringed, not the number of infringements. *See Venegas-Hernandez v. Sonolux Records*, 370 F.3d 183, 194 (1st Cir. 2004); *Walt Disney Co. v. Powell*, 897 F.2d 565, 569 (D.C. Cir. 1990). So here, the existence of two separate infringing works (screenplay and motion picture) does not increase statutory damages. Moreover, while multiple defendants may multiply statutory damages where they act separately, *Columbia Pictures Television* *v. Krypton Broadcasting, Inc.*, 106 F.3d 284, 294 (9th Cir. 1997), joint acts of infringement do not multiply statutory damages, so the presence of three individuals who contributed to the infringements (Amy, Mike, and Jane) also does not increase statutory damages. Finally, all the parts of a compilation or derivative work constitute one work for purposes of statutory damage calculations. 17 U.S.C. § 504(c)(1); *see UMG Recordings, Inc. v. MP3.Com, Inc.*, 109 F. Supp. 2d 223 (S.D.N.Y. 2000) (statutory damages computed on the basis of number of audio CDs, not individual recordings). So here, the existence of separate short stories within Vic's book (a collective work) does not multiply the statutory damages.

Ultimately, we have multiple infringements by joint infringers of a single work. This amounts to a single infringement as defined by the Copyright Act, so the total amount of statutory damages is (only) $1,000.

Answer (B), (C), and (D) are incorrect for the reasons stated above.

XI-39. **Answer (D) is correct.** The DMCA prohibits the providing or distribution of false copyright management information (CMI), 17 U.S.C. § 1202(a), and the removal or alteration of CMI, *id.* § 1202(b). "Copyright Management Information" includes information that identifies a copyrighted work, its author, its copyright owner, its creator, as well as terms and conditions for use of the work, *id.* § 1202(c). Because this definition clearly includes Jane's digital watermark, and because Redwood Town removed the watermark without permission, its conduct is liable under the DMCA.

Answer (A) is incorrect because there is no exemption under the DMCA for owners of copies.

Answer (B) is incorrect because there is no exemption under the DMCA for state actors, though there is one for "lawfully authorized investigative, protective, information security, or intelligence activity of federal, state or local law enforcement or intelligence agencies." 17 U.S.C. § 1202(d).

Answer (C) is incorrect because, while the imposition of misleading copyright management information (CMI) is actionable, it is not the only cause of action created by the DMCA. Removal or alteration of CMI is also actionable on its own. 17 U.S.C. § 1202(b).

XI-40. **Answer (B) is correct.** The DMCA prohibits the act of circumvention of a technological measure, such as scrambling or encryption, put in place by a copyright owner to effectively control access to a copyrighted work, without the authority of the copyright owner. 17 U.S.C. § 1201(a)(1). Brad will be liable on that basis, because he circumvented the password-protection that MacroHard used to restrict access to YouFace.

The DMCA also prohibits the manufacture and distribution of products and services used to defeat technological measures that impose limitations on the use of a copyrighted work. 17 U.S.C. § 1201(b). Brad did not violate this provision. Brad did create a hack that allowed YouFace to operate on a non-MacroHard operating system, but this provision of the DMCA only regulates *trafficking* in such circumventions of use limitations, not the use or creation of such measures. Brad is thus only liable for circumventing MacroHard's access control measures, not its use-limitation measures.

Answers (A), (C), and (D) are incorrect for the reasons explained above.

XI-41. I have been asked to advise three of my clients concerning issues with Left Coast Pictures:

Grace Hopper

If Ms. Hopper is to bring a copyright infringement action against Left Coast Pictures, she must prove that her father's novel, *An Inventor in Paradise* continues to be protected by copyright, that she is the current owner of that copyright, and that Left Coast Pictures has infringed one or more of her exclusive rights set forth in section 106 of the Copyright Act.

The novel was invested with federal copyright protection in 1940 when it was published with a proper copyright notice, as well as registered with the Copyright Office. The facts indicate that the work was renewed by the author in 1968. On January 1, 1978, the renewal term of the novel's copyright was extended by nineteen years to 2015. The renewal term was further extended in 1998 by twenty years pursuant to the Sonny Bono Copyright Term Extension Act. As a result, the copyright in the novel will enter the public domain in the United States at the end of 2035.

Harry Hopper died in 1985, without a surviving spouse. As his only child, Grace Hopper is his statutory successor for purposes of exercising the termination right for the copyright in the novel. The author had granted an exclusive motion picture license, for both the initial and renewal terms of the copyright in the novel, to Left Coast Pictures on September 2, 1942. Because the grant was executed prior to 1978, section 304(c) of the Copyright Act dictates the termination right that Grace is entitled to exercise. Under section 304(c), the five-year termination window began in 1996 and extended through 2001. Grace selected a termination date within that window, January 5, 1999, and sent a proper termination notice on January 10, 1989, which was more than the required two years' notice prior to termination and less than the ten-year maximum period of notice allowed. Therefore, Grace's termination of the September 2, 1942 agreement was valid. Grace now owns the exclusive right to make and exploit a motion picture based on the novel.

Pursuant to the continued use of a derivative work provision of section 304(c), Left Coast Pictures is permitted to continue to exploit its derivative motion picture, *Mr. Diffie's Soul*, in the same manner that it had before Grace Hopper's termination on January 5, 1999. Left Coast is not permitted to create a sequel, prequel, or remake of *Mr. Diffie's Soul* post-termination, nor can the studio make any other new uses of its existing motion picture. *See Fred Ahlert Music Corp. v. Warner/Chappell Music, Inc.*, 155 F.3d 17 (2d Cir. 1998).

Grace Hopper has raised concerns about three post-termination uses of *Mr. Diffie's Soul*: the selling of the motion picture on videocassette copies; the release of *Mr. Diffie's Soul* on DVD; and the use of a three minute film clip of the purgatory scene from *Mr. Diffie's Soul* on Left Coast's website.

Sale of videocassette copies of the film

Grace Hopper will have a difficult time with this argument. *Mr. Diffie's Soul* was created pre-termination pursuant to a grant to Left Coast Pictures from the author of the underlying work, Harry Hopper, which included the renewal term of the novel. The motion picture constitutes a derivative that was released on videocassette prior to Grace Hopper's termination. Pursuant to the derivative work exclusion of section 304(c), Left Coast may continue to release the motion picture on videocassette, thereby helping to insure that Left Coast recoups its investment in the film. Left Coast is obligated to continue to pay Grace Hopper the royalty that was paid prior to her termination. *See Mills Music, Inc. v. Snyder*, 469 U.S. 153 (1985).

DVD release

The release of *Mr. Diffie's Soul* on DVD is a somewhat closer issue than the continued sales of the motion picture on videocassettes. To stop the DVD release of *Mr. Diffie's Soul*, Grace Hopper must prove that the DVD release constitutes a new use of her father's novel. The facts surrounding the release indicate that the analog motion picture has been digitized, without changing the substance of the motion picture, and is being released with no additional information or features. This allows Left Coast to argue that its DVD release does not contain any new elements, is not a new derivative work, and does not constitute a new use. In addition, changes in media, particularly mechanical translations into digital media, are generally viewed as lacking the originality necessary to create a new work. As such Left Coast would be permitted to release the DVD of the motion picture post-termination. To bolster its argument, Left Coast will point to the cases where new performances of pre-termination works have been found not to constitute new uses. *See Woods v. Bourne Co.*, 60 F.3d 978 (2d Cir. 1995).

Grace Hopper will want to investigate the DVD and its packaging to determine whether they contain a copyright notice with the current date by which Left Coast is claiming a derivative work copyright in the DVD version of the motion picture. If such a new copyright notice is used, Left Coast will be hard pressed to deny that the DVD release constitutes a new use. However, even if the DVD release does not contain a new copyright notice, Grace Hopper will argue that for purposes of section 304(c), there is a difference between adding new elements to a post-termination version of the motion picture and making a new use of the motion picture. New types of exploitation of a work, post-termination, should be deemed new uses, regardless of whether the new uses are found to be new derivative works, because such new exploitations provide new sources of revenue that the termination provisions of the Copyright Act are meant to ensure are given to the author or the author's statutory successors. *See Broadcast Music, Inc. v. Roger Miller Music, Inc.*, 396 F.3d 762 (6th Cir. 2005). Grace will point to the cases where the use of a musical composition in a motion picture or soundtrack CD created post-termination have been found to be new uses. *See, e.g., Fred Ahlert Music Corp. v. Warner/Chappell Music, Inc.*, 155 F.3d 17 (2d Cir. 1998). The release of *Mr. Diffie's Soul* on DVD likely constitutes a new use and an infringement of the copyright in the novel.

The fact that the 1942 agreement between Harry Hopper and Left Coast Pictures contained a new technology clause merely granted Left Coast the right to use the novel in new medias while the grant was still in effect. That right ceased to exist once the grant was terminated by Grace Hopper. Therefore, the existence of the new technology clause does not provide Left Coast with an argument that the DVD release is not a new use.

Use of clip on website

Many of the same arguments raised in connection with the DVD release would also apply to the use of the novel on the website. It is clear from the facts that the portion of the motion picture included on the website constitutes a use of the novel as well. In addition to the fact that this constitutes a new method of exploitation, post-termination, which is likely to be deemed a new use, only a portion of the novel is being used. Apparently this is the first time the novel has been used in a clip. This fact adds to Grace Hopper's argument that the website use constitutes a new use.

Left Coast Pictures may argue that its agreement with Harry Hopper gave it the right to use any version of the novel "for the purpose of advertising, publicizing or exploiting the motion picture." It is unclear whether that right survives post-termination. Grace Hopper argues that her termination has ended the existence of the 1942 agreement and that any right of Left Coast to continue to use its derivative motion picture is derived from the termination provisions of the Copyright Act, which does not permit any new uses of the derivative motion picture post-termination. Left Coast can argue that its right to advertise its motion picture through use of the novel should survive termination. It makes little sense to have the continuing right to sell its motion picture in videocassettes if it is not permitted to advertise the motion picture, which contains elements of the novel.

Grace Hopper may answer that, while it makes sense for the owner of a derivative work to be able to advertise its exploitation post-termination, that right should be limited only to pre-termination uses, not new uses such as the website. In addition, Left Coast's website does not use the classic purgatory scene from *Mr. Diffie's Soul* to sell only videocassette copies of the motion picture, but DVD copies also, as well as other motion pictures in Left Coast's film library that are also offered for sale on the website and are linked to the viewing of the purgatory scene. The use of the clip from *Mr. Diffie's Soul* on the website constitutes a new use and an infringement of the copyright in the novel.

Alan Cadabra

Mr. Cadabra has no right to terminate his 1944 composer agreement with Left Coast Pictures. The work created pursuant to that agreement, the musical work titled *Optical Rectosis*, was a work made for hire. It was created prior to 1978 at the instance and expense of Left Coast Pictures. *See Martha Graham School and Dance Foundation, Inc. v. Martha Graham Center of Contemporary Dance, Inc.*, 380 F.3d 624 (2d Cir. 2004). In addition, the composer agreement expressly stated that *Optical Rectosis* would be created as a work made for hire. Grants involving works made for hire are not subject to statutory termination. *Marvel Characters, Inc. v. Simon*, 310 F.3d 280 (2d Cir. 2002).

Bert Schreck

The musical work *Piety and Iron* is still protected by copyright. Therefore, the only way Mr. Schreck could record and distribute the musical work without negotiating directly with its copyright owner, Left Coast Pictures, would be to take advantage of the compulsory mechanical license provided by section 115 of the Copyright Act. Section 115 permits the recording and distribution via phonorecord or digital phonorecord delivery, to the public for its private use, without the permission of the copyright owner, of any nondramatic musical work that had previously been recorded and distributed via phonorecord or digital phonorecord delivery, to the public for its private use. In return, the party taking advantage of the compulsory mechanical license is required to pay a license fee at the current statutory rate set by the Copyright Office. Although Mr. Schreck's planned recording and distribution would meet the requirements of section 115, that section is not applicable to the musical work *Piety and Iron*. The musical work has only been distributed to the public as part of the *American Outback* motion picture, which has been released on copies, not phonorecords. Nondramatic musical works that have only been released on copies do not fall within the ambit of section 115. Therefore, no compulsory mechanical license is available to Mr. Schreck. *See Leadsinger, Inc. v. BMG Music Publishing*, 512 F.3d 522 (9th Cir. 2008).

XI-42.

Flusterated Records v. Anne Droid

Flusterated Records owns two versions of the sound recording of *Bail Before They Bite*: the 1966 analog recording and the 1990 digital release. The 1966 analog recording by Rick Rail and the Bailettes was made at the instance and expense of Flusterated Records prior to 1978; therefore, it is deemed a work for hire. However, the recording was initially fixed prior to February 15, 1972. Therefore, it was not protected by federal copyright, which attaches only to sound recordings first fixed on or after that date. *Capitol Records, Inc. v. Naxos of America, Inc.*, 372 F.3d 471 (2d Cir. 2004). The call of the question asks for a discussion of federal copyright issues only. As a result, any state common-law copyright protection for the 1966 analog recording is not relevant to this exam.

The federal copyright infringement claim raised by Flusterated Records must be based on the 1990 digital recording. The digital recording was first fixed after February 15, 1972, but it must contain sufficient originality to meet the statutory requirements for federal copyright protection. To prove originality, Flusterated Records must prove that the digital recording contains elements that were independently created by Flusterated Records and that the elements were sufficiently creative to be deserving of copyright protection. The vast majority of the elements contained in the 1990 digital recording were copied from the 1966 analog recording of *Bail*. Flusterated Records will have to prove that it added or changed elements to the analog recording and that those additional elements are sufficiently original to protect the 1990 digital recording as a derivative work. *See Maljack Productions, Inc. v. UAV Corp.*, 964 F. Supp. 1416 (C.D. Cal. 1997), *aff'd*, 160 F.3d 1223 (9th Cir. 1998).

There is no evidence that Flusterated Records has obtained a copyright registration for the 1990 digital recording, therefore, if Flusterated Records wanted to sue Anne Droid for copyright infringement, it would have to apply for a registration. Flusterated Records would have to show that its digital reissue of *Bail Before They Bite* is fixed. It must show that the sound recording was fixed in a tangible medium of expression that is sufficiently permanent to permit it to be reproduced for a period of more than transitory duration. The reproduction of the sounds from the sound recording in a digital computer file is sufficiently fixed to meet the statutory fixation requirement because the sound can be replayed each time the file is accessed. *See Midway Manufacturing Co. v. Artic International, Inc.*, 547 F. Supp. 999 (N.D. Ill.), *aff'd*, 704 F.2d 1009 (7th Cir. 1982).

Flusterated Records will claim that its employee, Bobby Banger, did not merely make a mechanical recording of the 1966 analog *Bail* recording, but made several creative decisions to augment the digital recording that resulted from the transfer of the analog sounds via the DigiCom computer program. These decisions involved whether the volume, tones, and acoustics of the sounds contained in the digital recording should be adjusted. In addition to these decisions, Banger actually made adjustments at the sound board by raising the level of the bass guitar and lowering the level of the snare drum. These decisions and actual adjustments resulted in variations between the analog sounds of the 1966 analog recording and the 1990 digital recording. To be protected as a derivative work, Flusterated Records must prove that these variations were more than merely trivial variations. *See Alfred Bell & Co. v. Catalda Fine Arts, Inc.*, 191 F.2d 99, 102–03 (2d Cir. 1951). These variations were deemed necessary by a music professional and were variations that can be heard throughout the 1990 digital recording. As such they are not merely trivial. All that is required is proof of a modicum of creativity and this was clearly evidenced by the changes that resulted from Banger's actions.

Anne Droid will counter that Flusterated Records is attempting to protect a pre-1972 sound recording with federal copyright protection by merely copying the sound recording in a new digital medium, thereby ensuring copyright protection of the recording to the end of 2085. Courts have found that the act of merely mechanically reproducing a work in another media is insufficiently creative to meet the statutory originality requirement. *See Entertainment Research Group, Inc. v. Genesis Creative Group, Inc.*, 122 F.3d 1211 (9th Cir. 1997). Although Droid would likely concede that an analog sound recording that is fully digitally remastered is worthy of federal copyright protection as a derivative work, the bare tweaking of the volume of a bass guitar and a snare drum is merely a trivial variation that does not meet the level of creativity required by the originality requirement.

If the digital recording satisfied the statutory requirements for copyright protection, Flusterated Records will be the author and initial copyright owner of the derivative work. The facts indicate that Bobby Banger was an employee acting within the scope of his employment when he created the digital sound recording. Therefore, the sound recording constituted a work made for hire. *See Community for Creative Non-Violence v. Reid*, 490 U.S. 730 (1989). Flusterated Records would likely be able to prove that Droid has infringed its copyright in the digital sound recording when she reproduced and publicly distributed the digital sound recording in her CD-ROM program *Before California Fell Into the Ocean*.

Ambigua Peace v. Anne Droid

To succeed in her threatened copyright infringement action against Anne Droid, Ambigua Peace will have to prove that she owns a valid copyright in the musical composition *Bail Before They Bite* and that Droid has infringed one or more of the exclusive rights of section 106 protected by that copyright.

The copyright validity of the *Bail* musical work is really not at issue. The work was first invested with federal copyright protection in 1965 at the time of its registration with the

Copyright Office. This gave the work twenty-eight years of initial copyright protection. The first issue is whether the copyright in the composition was renewed. The facts state that Peace never filed a document with the Copyright Office, which means that she never filed an application to renew the copyright. However, because the twenty-eighth year of the initial term was 1993, such an affirmative act of renewal was no longer required. The automatic renewal amendment to the Copyright Act went into effect in 1992. Under this amendment, affirmative renewal of the copyright in the twenty-eighth year by the owner of the renewal right is no longer required. Whoever owns the renewal right at the end of the twenty-eighth year is automatically vested with the renewal copyright. In this case, Rick Rail died in 1975, before he was able to renew the copyright. He had never married, therefore there is no spouse who would be recognized as a valid statutory successor to the renewal right. The next statutory successor category is children. Ambigua Peace is the only child of Rick Rail. Under the 1976 Copyright Act, children born out of wedlock are included in the statutory successor category of children. Therefore, she was automatically vested with the renewal term at the end of 1993. This renewal term is for a period of sixty-seven years: the twenty-eight-year traditional term of the renewal copyright, the nineteen-year extension to the renewal term that was added by the 1976 Copyright Act, and the additional twenty years added by the Sonny Bono Copyright Term Extension Act to any work still protected in 1998, which includes the *Bail* musical work.

The facts of this case present a problem similar to that in *Stewart v. Abend*, 495 U.S. 207 (1990). In that case, the United States Supreme Court held that when the author of an underlying work had licensed its use as the basis for a derivative work for both the initial and renewal terms of the copyright in the underlying work and the author died before renewing the copyright, the statutory successor who owns the renewal copyright is not in privity of contract with the creator of the derivative work and is not bound by the earlier license. In this case, the author, Rick Rail, had entered into a license agreement in 1975 with Anne Droid to use the *Bail* musical work during the initial and renewal terms and any extensions. At the time he entered into the license, however, Rick Rail owned only an expectancy interest in the renewal term for the *Bail* musical work. His expectancy interest was not realized because Rail died before he was able to renew the copyright, thus it never vested in him. As stated earlier, the renewal term did vest in Ambigua Peace. Because she was not a party to the 1975 license, Peace owns the renewal term without any obligations under the agreement. Under the *Abend* case, this ownership would have given Peace the right to sue Droid for copyright infringement, because Peace is not bound by the 1975 license agreement. However, the 1992 automatic renewal amendment to the Copyright Act modified the application of the *Abend* decision. Pursuant to that amendment, a statutory successor can take advantage of the *Abend* decision only if the statutory successor affirmatively filed a renewal application with the Copyright Office in the twenty-eighth year of copyright protection. For those statutory successors who did not affirmatively renew the copyright in the twenty-eighth year, but own the renewal copyright because of automatic renewal, the creator of a derivative work, created pursuant to a grant that included the renewal term, is permitted to continue using the derivative work during the renewal term, under the provisions of the original grant.

In this case, Peace cannot take advantage of the *Abend* decision because she did not affirmatively renewal the copyright in *Bail* in its twenty-eighth year. That means that Droid is permitted to continue to exploit her CD-ROM program if that use of *Bail* falls within the parameters of the 1975 license agreement. Anne Droid has the statutory right to use the *Bail* musical composition in her CD-ROM program if the 1975 license gives her that right.

Whether the CD-ROM program meets the requirement of "in connection with a documentary"

Droid argues that the 1975 grant gives her a nonexclusive right to use the *Bail* musical composition "in connection with a documentary" and that her CD-ROM program, *Before California Fell Into the Ocean* is a documentary because it presents a history of California surfing music. It utilizes biographical material, photographs, and music to inform viewers and listeners of that history. The 1975 license used the term "documentary" in its general sense and did not use it as a defined term, the use of which would have been capitalized. Therefore, her use falls within the parameters of the 1975 license.

Peace responds that the intent of the parties to the 1975 license was to permit the use of *Bail* in a documentary on the life of Rick Rail, not a general work on California surfing music. This intent is evidenced by the fact that Rick Rail also permitted the use of his life story and agreed to cooperate in the making of the motion picture. If a court finds that the term "documentary" in the license is not ambiguous, it is likely that the court will interpret the license to permit the use of the *Bail* composition in any documentary created by Droid. This would allow Droid to continue to exploit the *Before California Fell Into the Ocean* derivative work.

New technology issue

Ambigua Peace will likely argue that the 1975 license does not extend to the use of the *Bail* composition in a CD-ROM, because the parties did not know of that technology at the time they entered into the license. Droid will successfully argue, however, that the 1975 license contained the language "by any means or methods now or hereafter known," which is a new technology clause that permits the use of the *Bail* composition in connection with technology that was not known at the time. A court will be faced with the issue of whether the reservation of rights clause (paragraph 9), by which Rail reserved all rights and uses to *Bail* "except those herein granted to Anne Droid," would be sufficient to counter the new technology clause. Because the use of the composition in unknown technology was granted to Droid in paragraph 6, it is likely that a court would find that the new technology clause would control, though that is not certain.

Application of the compulsory mechanical license of section 115

If the 1975 license were found to be inapplicable to Droid's CD-ROM program, the compulsory mechanical license provision of section 115 of the Copyright Act would not be available to her. First, she is using the *Bail* musical work in an audiovisual work that is distributed in a copy. Section 115 only applies to musical works that are distributed in phonorecords. *See ABKCO Music, Inc. v. Stellar Records, Inc.*, 96 F.3d 60, 65 (2d Cir. 1996). Second, even if she were distributing the *Bail* composition in a phonorecord, she is distributing it in connection with a preexisting sound recording. Section 115 will not permit a compulsory mechanical license for such a use unless a license to use the preexisting sound recording has been obtained. In this case, Droid has not obtained a license to the sound recording from Flusterated Records.

XI-43. Fiona Photog (FP) is the creator of *Ranch Heroes*, a copyrighted work of authorship that falls into the category of pictorial, graphical, or sculptural work. Her claim is that PubliCo's (PC) use of *Ranch Heroes* on its Pulitzer website without FP's explicit authorization amounts to a violation of her exclusive rights as the owner of the copyright in the photograph. If FP's claim is accurate, PC's actions would violate her exclusive rights of reproduction, public display, and, possibly, adaptation. The reproduction right is at issue because this is a near-verbatim copy of the original *Ranch Heroes*. By placing a version of *Ranch Heroes* on its website, PC has displayed the work to the public. It is a harder question whether the adaptation right is at issue because there may not be enough originality in the online version of *Ranch Heroes* to make that version a derivative work. *See L. Batlin & Son, Inc. v. Snyder*, 536 F.2d 486 (2d Cir. 1976). PC can advance three arguments to resist FP's allegations of infringement.

<u>PC is the author and owner of *Ranch Heroes* because the photograph was a work made for hire</u>

Although FP is clearly the creator of *Ranch Heroes*, that does not mean she is necessarily the author or the owner of the copyright in that work. If *Ranch Heroes* is a work made for hire, then the Copyright Act defines the commissioning party, not the creator, as the author. 17 U.S.C. § 201(b). So if *Ranch Heroes* is a work made for hire, that means that PC (not FP) is the author, and also copyright owner (in the absence of a transfer), and FP cannot object to its use without her consent.

A work made for hire is one prepared by an employee in the scope of his or her employment. 17 U.S.C. § 101. Here, if FP is not an employee, but rather an independent contractor, then *Ranch Heroes* cannot be a work made for hire unless both FP and PC signed a work made for hire agreement and *Ranch Heroes* falls within one of the nine statutory work made for hire categories. The fact that FP has not signed a work made for hire agreement precludes *Ranch Heroes* from being deemed a work made for hire if FP is found to be an independent contractor.

Numerous factors suggest that FP is an independent contractor rather than an employee. FP works out of her own studio as an independent contractor would, not the *Tempo* offices as an employee would. FP also covers events on her own schedule and at her own instance as an independent contractor would, rather than taking assignments from *Tempo* as an employee would. Finally, FP's financial relationship with *Tempo* is not an employee-like regular paycheck arrangement, but a series of one-off, individually negotiated contracts.

PC can point to several factors that may suggest instead that FP is its employee. FP consistently refers to herself as a "*Tempo* photographer," which suggests identification with a particular publication rather than freelance status. FP's equipment comes to a large extent from *Tempo* as well — three of her six cameras are holiday gifts from *Tempo* — and this could be taken to indicate that *Tempo* supplies FP with equipment as it would any other employee. Moreover, the fact that *Tempo* regularly gives FP a gift during the holidays suggests the presence of an ongoing relationship with her. Finally, *Tempo* sometimes gives Fiona a tip about events and even a ride to sites in their company helicopter, which is the kind of service that employers typically provide to employees.

Examined more closely, though, none of these factual assertions resisting independent contractor status bear scrutiny. FP referred to herself as a "Tempo photographer" not because it reflected her actual status, but just to gain professional cachet or to get access to tightly controlled news areas. And even if FP uses the cameras she got from *Tempo*, they are still hers (given as gifts), so she is not using *Tempo* equipment when she takes pictures with them. Nor does the fact of gift-giving necessarily mean that FP is a PC employee; the cameras likely reflect PC's appreciation of her good work and represent an incentive to keep up an otherwise informal relationship. Finally, the occasional tip or ride does not mean that FP is in PC's employ, but merely that PC has provided marginal assistance that is overwhelmed by the independence FP maintains in all other respects.

So, although there is no nearly dispositive factor here, for example, we do not know whether PubliCo takes taxes out of the checks they issue to FP, these facts strongly indicate that FP is an independent contractor for two reasons. First, the factors suggesting her independent contractor status — payment arrangements and professional relationship — are core matters that go to the heart of the work relationship between FP and *Tempo*, while the ones that militate in the other direction — a holiday gift or ride to an event site here or there — are far more marginal in their significance. Also, the factors arguably militating in favor of employee status are far weaker when examined closely. In light of all this, *Ranch Heroes* is very likely not a work made for hire, so FP, not PC, would be its author.

PC's use of *Ranch Heroes* was not improper because FP authorized it

Even though FP, not PC, is likely the author and owner of *Ranch Heroes*, PC's use of the photograph on its website will not amount to infringement if it can mount an argument that FP permitted that use. There are two possible arguments that FP permitted this use.

PC's use of *Ranch Heroes* falls within the original license pursuant to the section 201(c) collective work privilege

FP's license clearly allowed PC to use *Ranch Heroes* only in that single edition of *Tempo*. The Copyright Act, however, permits owners of collective works to reproduce and distribute validly acquired works of authorship in future editions and revisions of the original collective work in which the licensed work of authorship was used. 17 U.S.C. § 201(c). *Tempo* is clearly a collective work because, like a newspaper, it consists of a variety of different separately copyrighted works of authorship such as FP's *Ranch Heroes*. E.g., *New York Times Co., Inc. v. Tasini*, 533 U.S. 483 (2001).

The difficult question, though, is whether PC's Pulitzer website counts as the kind of revision or new edition that falls within the section 201(c) privilege. FP will argue that the website is not a new revision or edition because it is a different medium. This argument will fail, however, because the Supreme Court held that mere reissuance in the context of a digital medium from an analog one does not automatically preclude application of the section 201(c) privilege. *See New York Times Co., Inc. v. Tasini*, 533 U.S. 483 (2001).

FP will also argue that the use of *Ranch Heroes* on the website is not within the section 201(c) privilege because the website takes the picture out of its original context. This argument has a stronger legal foundation because the Supreme Court has held that the standard for whether a new use falls within the section 201(c) privilege is whether it is presented in its original context. Here, *Ranch Heroes* is presented outside its original context for two reasons. First, the website does not merely post full-text versions of *Tempo* articles online, but only excerpts, and does not include the Blanco Valley fire article in the context of the other articles in that issue of *Tempo*. C.F. *Greenberg v. Nat'l*

Geographic Society, 533 F.3d 1244 (11th Cir. 2008). Second, *Ranch Heroes* itself is not presented in its original version, but is rather shrunken, cropped, and in black-and-white (as opposed to color). In light of all this, PC's argument that its website is a revision or new edition that falls within the section 201(c) privilege, and thus moots the need to ask FP for permission for the new use, would very likely fail.

FP granted PC a nonexclusive license to use *Ranch Heroes* on the Pulitzer website

In light of the above, there is no argument that FP's original license allowing PC to use *Ranch Heroes* in *Tempo* extends to PC's use on the Pulitzer website. There may, however, be an argument that FP subsequently licensed PC to do so.

PC will argue that FP granted a license to use *Ranch Heroes* on its website when she was approached by a PC executive at a party who mentioned the Pulitzer website and FP responded, "Sure, whatever you say."

An argument that this exchange amounts to a transfer (i.e., assignment or exclusive license) by FP to PC will certainly fail, because transfers of copyrights must be written. 17 U.S.C. § 204(a). However, nonexclusive licenses are not included in the Copyright Act's definition of transfer of copyright ownership, 17 U.S.C. § 101, so PC may be able to argue that the cocktail party exchange resulted in the grant of a nonexclusive license to PC. Courts have held that nonexclusive licenses can be granted in three ways: written, verbally, and implied through conduct. *Effects Associates, Inc. v. Cohen*, 908 F.2d 555 (1990).

PC will first attempt to argue that FP verbally granted a nonexclusive license to PC when she responded to the PC executive's suggestion that they put her photo online by saying "Sure, whatever you say." This argument will likely fail for several reasons. First, the language itself is very ambiguous. FP did not clearly indicate assent, as she would have if she had said "Yes, that sounds great, please post my picture online." Rather, her language was dismissive and sarcastic, and almost certainly not meant to be taken at face value. Second, the context — a brief, offhand encounter at a cocktail party — strongly suggests that neither party believed a serious negotiation was taking place. Third, at least the PC executive and possibly also FP were intoxicated, which cuts back against their ability to meaningfully grant legal rights. And finally, FP's response to the situation (and the fact that she did not even remember it had happened) indicates that she was merely trying to blow off a drunk, rather than give consent to the use of *Ranch Heroes* online.

PC may also try to argue that FP implied a nonexclusive license through her conduct. A nonexclusive license may be implied through conduct where there is a physical handover of the copyrighted work of authorship, and the circumstances surrounding the handover indicate a grant of use rights as well. *Oddo v. Ries*, 743 F.2d 630 (9th Cir. 1984). Here, there is physical handover because FP gave *Tempo* a copy of *Ranch Heroes*, but there is nothing about that handover that suggests she meant to allow the online use. On the contrary, FP explicitly limited that grant to one single use in *Tempo*, and made very clear that she preferred working with *Tempo* because she did not want to have her work go online, and *Tempo* did not have an online edition.

In light of all this, a court would be very unlikely to find that PC's use of *Ranch Heroes* was permitted either by FP's original license in combination with the section 201(c) privilege, or by a later nonexclusive license granted by FP.

PC's online use of *Ranch Heroes* is a fair use

Even if FP is the author and owner of *Ranch Heroes,* and even if there is no argument that she has sanctioned PC's online use of the photograph, PC still may prevail if it can successfully argue that the online version of *Ranch Heroes* amounts to a fair use.

Fair use is a statutory affirmative defense to copyright infringement. Whether a use is fair depends on four nonexclusive factors: the purpose and character of the defendant's use; the nature of the plaintiff's work; the amount and substantiality of the taking; and the effect of the defendant's use on present and future markets for the plaintiff's work. 17 U.S.C. § 107.

Factor one: the purpose and character of the use

This factor considers two separate issues: the extent to which the use is transformative, *Campbell v. Acuff-Rose Music, Inc.,* 510 U.S. 569, 577 (1994), and the extent to which it is commercial, *Harper & Row, Publishers, Inc. v. Nation Enterprises,* 471 U.S. 539 (1985).

Whether PC's use of *Ranch Heroes* on its website is transformative depends on a comparison of the original purpose of the use in *Tempo* as compared to the photograph's use on the Pulitzer site. The original purpose of the photograph was to dramatically and effectively document the fires at Blanco Valley, and to highlight the heroism of the workers who saved horses from those fires. Seen from this perspective, the purpose of PC's use was very transformative, because it was not for the purpose of news reporting (the fires happened long before the site went up, so there was no need to inform anyone), but rather to increase attention to the magazine from the Pulitzer search committee. Adding to this conclusion is that the photograph was transformed in a very physical sense — cropped, shrunk, changed to black-and-white. That PC's use is transformative weighs in its favor and makes it more likely that the online use of *Ranch Heroes* is a fair use.

PC may argue that the original purpose of the photos was not merely to report the news, but also to gain readership and impress possible prize committees, which would make the use on the Pulitzer site much less transformative. This may well have been a secondary or tertiary consideration, but was by no means a primary one, and so likely will not cause this factor to weigh in favor of FP.

PC may argue that its use of *Ranch Heroes* was transformative because it shifted the photograph from an analog to an online medium, but this argument will certainly fail because shifts in medium, without more, are not considered transformative. *UMG Recordings, Inc. v. MP3.com, Inc.,* 92 F. Supp. 2d 349 (S.D.N.Y. 2000).

It is clear that there is some commerciality inherent in PC's use. It has placed *Ranch Heroes* online in order to garner the Pulitzer Prize, journalism's highest honor. Winning this award would have both direct financial benefits (a $10,000 prize) and indirect ones (wider circulation). However, this possibility, and its nexus with FP's single photograph, is rather remote. Nor is PC's use entirely commercial; it has already extracted commercial value from *Ranch Heroes* by including it in the print version of the magazine, and the website is both free to the public and designed mostly to garner nonmonetary benefits such as fame and prestige. Moreover, courts have recently held that because almost any use can be regarded as commercial in some respect, this factor deserves relatively less weight. *See, e.g., Castle Rock Entertainment v. Carol Publishing Group, Inc.,* 150 F.3d

132 (2d Cir. 1998). The relatively remote commerciality of PC's use likely does not do much to weigh in favor of FP.

Factor two: the nature of the plaintiff's work

This factor looks at two considerations: whether the plaintiff's work is published, and whether it is creative or factual. *Ranch Heroes* was clearly published in *Tempo*, which works in favor of FP and against fair use. PC will argue that the photo was entirely factual, though, which militates in favor of fair use. Although *Ranch Heroes* was clearly a photo of factual events, this does not mean it lacked any creative elements. Photos can possess creativity by virtue of staging, choice of subject matter, and use of equipment to achieve certain effects, all of which would cause *Ranch Heroes* to seem closer to the core of copyright. In light of all this, the second factor weighs in favor of FP and against fair use, albeit very weakly.

Factor three: the amount and substantiality of the taking

This factor looks at the qualitative and quantitative amount taken from plaintiff's work, with an aim of determining the ratio of the taking in relation to plaintiff's work overall and whether that amount of taking was necessary.

PC took nearly all of *Ranch Heroes*, except for a section toward the top where the photo was cropped. However, the taking was limited in another sense because the photo was diminished in terms of its overall size (only a few inches square) and colors (the black-and-white format did not capture the richness of the original version). In light of these considerations, the taking was far from total. Moreover, in a qualitative sense, the taking failed to take the "heart" (or at least, all of the "heart") of FP's work because by cropping out the clouds, the effect of the smoke in the sky was lost, and FP had identified this as one of the main features distinguishing the photo.

Moreover, the amount taken was justified in light of the purpose of the taking. PC's reason for including *Ranch Heroes* on its website was to impress the Pulitzer committee. In order to do this, it had to include all, or nearly all, of the photo to give a sense of its quality. Courts have held that where a photo was used without permission, but in a smaller form to give some indication of its content, that taking was justified in light of the taking's purpose. *Kelly v. Arriba Soft Corp.*, 280 F.3d 934 (9th Cir. 2002). The modesty of the taking interacts with its purpose to further cause this factor to weigh in favor of PC and fair use.

Factor four: the effect of the defendant's use on present and future markets for the plaintiff's work

This factor considers the impact of the defendant's use on both present and future markets (both primary and secondary) for the plaintiff's work. The impact of PC's use on the primary market for FP's work is negligible. The primary market for a news photograph is immediate, and since the Blanco Valley fires have long since passed, there is virtually no chance that another news outlet will want to acquire the photo to run alongside its coverage.

This does not, however, mean that PC's use has not damaged FP's secondary market — that is, selling licensing rights — for *Ranch Heroes*. Because there is always a theoretical market for licensing copyrighted works, the only relevant secondary markets are ones that are present, customary, or likely to emerge. *American Geophysical Union v. Texaco, Inc.*, 60 F.3d 913 (2d Cir. 1994). Here, though, there is some evidence that there is a secondary market for prints that has been harmed: Eagle Prints, the company with which FP traditionally works to license prints of her work, has complained that the appearance of *Ranch Heroes* online makes it want to reconsider its relationship with FP.

On the other hand, this argument seems implausible because the kind of photos Eagle Prints sells are high-quality editions one would use for aesthetic enjoyment, hung in a house or an office. By contrast, the version that appeared online could not be used for this purpose since it was low-quality and in black-and-white. Even though it would be theoretically possible for a user to download *Ranch Heroes* from the Pulitzer website and blow it up into a large print, the result would likely be too pixilated to have the same aesthetic appeal as a professionally made print, and in any event would be missing its color as well as the cropped-out area (which, FP indicated, was a major part of the photo's aesthetic appeal). It is also worth considering that some courts would find that the photo's appearance online might have positive effects for FP's reputation, particularly if it earned her or *Tempo* a Pulitzer prize, and this may overwhelm any marginal negative impact on secondary markets. In light of all this, the effect of PC's online use of *Ranch Heroes* will likely have a negligible effect on FP's market for the work, and this factor weighs in favor of fair use.

Factor analysis

Factors one, three, and four — (one and four likely being the most important factors in this case) — weigh in favor of fair use, while factor two weighs slightly against. This indicates that a court would likely consider PC's use to be defensible as a fair one.

* * *

FP will likely be able to show both that she is the author and owner of *Ranch Heroes*, and that she did not license its use on PC's website. Despite this, however, PC will likely be able to mount a persuasive fair use defense, and so will likely prevail on this affirmative defense.

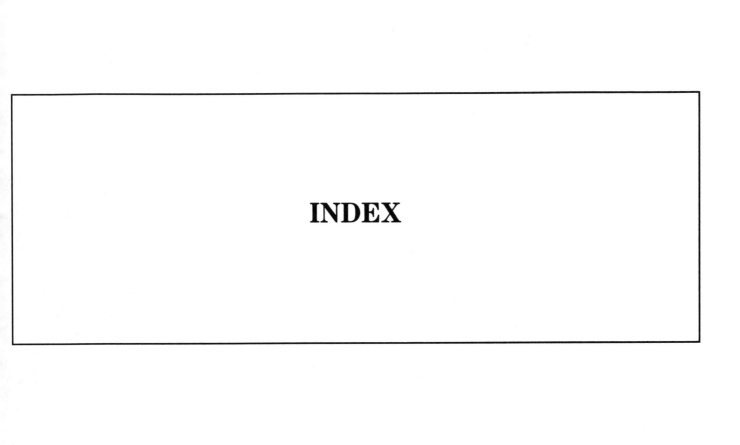

INDEX

INDEX